Families, Schools, and Communities

Together for Young Children

Second Edition

We dedicate this book to our families:

Clifford and Delores Stokum Couchenour
Bryan Maughan
Jay, Stacey, Chelsea, and Christopher Couchenour

James and Martha Douglas Chrisman
Cindy and Kate Chrisman

and to the many families, schools, and communities
that added to our nurturing.

D.C.
K.C.

Join us on the web at
EarlyChildEd.delmar.com

Families, Schools, and Communities

Together for Young Children

Second Edition

Donna Couchenour, Ph.D.
Kent Chrisman, Ed.D.

Shippensburg University

THOMSON

DELMAR LEARNING™

Australia • Canada • Mexico • Singapore • Spain • United Kingdom • United States

THOMSON

DELMAR LEARNING

Families, Schools, and Communities: Together for Young Children, second edition
Donna Couchenour and Kent Chrisman

Vice President, Career Education SBU:
Dawn Gerrain

Director of Editorial:
Sherry Gomoll

Acquisitions Editor:
Erin O'Connor

Developmental Editor:
Pat Gillivan

Editorial Assistant:
Ivy Ip

Director of Production:
Wendy A. Troeger

Production Editor:
J.P. Henkel

Technology Project Manager:
Joseph Saba

Director of Marketing:
Donna J. Lewis

Channel Manager:
Nigar Hale

Cover Design:
TDB

Composition:
Type Shoppe II.

NOTICE TO THE READER

Publisher does not warrant or guarantee any of the products described herein or perform any independent analysis in connection with any of the product information contained herein. Publisher does not assume, and expressly disclaims, any obligation to obtain and include information other than that provided to it by the manufacturer.

The reader is expressly warned to consider and adopt all safety precautions that might be indicated by the activities herein and to avoid all potential hazards. By following the instructions contained herein, the reader willingly assumes all risks in connection with such instructions.

The Publisher makes no representation or warranties of any kind, including but not limited to, the warranties of fitness for particular purpose or merchantability, nor are any such representations implied with respect to the material set forth herein, and the publisher takes no responsibility with respect to such material. The publisher shall not be liable for any special, consequential, or exemplary damages resulting, in whole or part, from the readers' use of, or reliance upon, this material.

CONTENTS

Since Bronfenbrenner's seminal work, *The Ecology of Human Development and Learning* (1979), the early childhood education profession has been "reconstructing" itself in relation to creating environments and strategies that empower children, families, communities, and the profession itself. This process of renewal and transformation has been stimulated by the most rapid and dramatic social, economic, and technological changes ever to occur in human history. Our conceptions of what families, schools, and communities are like or should be like are experiencing revolutionary paradigm shifts. Several changes are powerful in their impact on how children and families learn and function: new work and family structures require more parent time, but society has actually reduced its support and resources; new technology and related educational advancements require more education for people to function effectively, but society has not responded with increased educational quality for all people; our knowledge of parenting and child/family development has improved, but too many early childhood professionals and too many parents and citizens lack this new knowledge and skills; and a self-centered and individualistic society requires more parent/family skills and bonding time, yet our society has busied parents and families with mostly isolated activities that contribute to continued economic and environmental abuses. Certainly there are exceptions to the above stressors that are so real in all families, but one need only read the pages of Couchenour and Chrisman's book, *Families, Schools, and Communities: Together for Young Children,* to realize that the battle in the new millennium will be for a human competence that creates social decency and fosters spiritual and psychological relationships that empower everyone to be carers of each other.

Perhaps the most critical facet of Couchenour and Chrisman's work is their articulation of a theoretical construct that early childhood education professionals and concerned parents and citizens can use to develop strategies for having optimal conditions for everyone's learning and development. Their synthesis of the bioecological, contextualist, and family systems theory into a conceptual structure to use in addressing the many issues parents, children, families, schools, and communities experience is invaluable. The synthesis provides five important starting points for early childhood education professionals to use in crafting their "map" for being truly high-quality family helpers.

1. The human development and learning process is the result of everyone's effort; that is, it is an interactive and renewing process that is influenced by all parts of the human community.

2. An empowering approach to working with the diverse and ever-changing needs and contexts of children and families must replace a deficit-oriented way of relating to children and families.

3. The power of parents and families to nurture healthy and proactive ways of living in children can occur within various forms and structures. The key is for families to have strong and nurturing relationships with each other and their supportive helpers.

4. Early childhood educators must create diverse and adaptive ways to support families in a world of constant change and stress.

5. Early childhood educators must lead the way for "community transformation" to create family-embracing ways of functioning. Each of these "starting points" for crafting a new vision and new paradigm for helping create powerful families is addressed by Couchenour and Chrisman.

Children's school and life success is indeed embedded within the multiple bioecological systems of person and environment relationships. Couchenour and Chrisman point to several examples within the multiple life systems that impact families: individual bioecological dynamics, social interactions, economic involvement, and cultural and societal events and experiences.

Throughout history. families have needed nurturing and supportive relationships with the environment to thrive and contribute to the community. The need for a "systems" perspective of families is very critical in the complex and highly technological society in which parents and children now function. The prevailing belief that the individual can manage all of the factors that happen in life is myopic and distorted. As Couchenour and Chrisman so aptly describe, the challenges parents face in nurturing healthy and happy children are indeed great and require a total community structure to empower this critical child-nurturing function. Thus, the recognition that the human development and learning process is systemic requires us to approach parent, child, and family growth from an empowerment perspective. Engaging total families in the process of building on their strengths, identifying and addressing needs, and taking leadership in building strong communities are key strategies noted by Couchenour and Chrisman. This empowerment approach calls for the following:

- understanding that families are the caring people who commit themselves to the child's lifelong well-being

- nurturing children and adults in the family to reach their full potential and engaging them in activities in which they become the leaders in their communities

- creating a sense of "mutuality" in families and in our professional and community relationships with families

- validating parents and children—and their helpers—as the most important people in our communities

- advocating and structuring schools and communities to be places in which parents, children, and families can renew and enrich their lives, thus empowering them to be the tremendously capable people they can be

Diversity in family and parenting forms and styles must be used as means to enrich and further develop family, child, and school-community strengths. If early childhood educators approach cultural and familial differences

as sources of strength, so will parents, children, and other people in the community. As Couchenour and Chrisman suggest, the prevailing theme should be that of nurturing, caring relationships in all families by validating and valuing human differences as essential. This validating process can be achieved by early childhood professionals in several ways:

- highlighting parent achievements across the diversity of family and cultural groups in and beyond the community

- utilizing the diversity of parent and family talents as teaching resources for all children and teachers in the school

- helping parents see the strengths present in themselves and their children, and then engaging parents and children in developing their strengths and talents

- empowering everyone in the community to value and validate cultural diversity through needed social and economic changes

The only viable paradigm for developing successful family involvement in schools and communities is the partnership approach. This means crafting all facets of the family-school-community partnership together:

- learning about each other in relation to strengths, skills, and talents that can be used to empower everyone

- establishing equality in roles and relationships in family, school, and community, and in the transactions that occur between these groups

- seeing, treating, and affirming parents as the key leaders in families, and as powerful leaders in the family-school-community triad

- developing family-friendly strategies that invite parents and families to be actively engaged in school and community decisions

- using diverse strategies that account for the varying work and family schedules, and situations that today's parents and families experience

- valuing parents and family members as caring and capable people who are full members of the community team

Early childhood professionals can provide the needed "leadership" in stimulating community transformation toward becoming a family-centered place to live and grow. As the authors note, several important starting points provide the foundation for this transformational process:

- provide a "model" of family-centered functioning in the school and in relations with families and community members

- engage members of the community in the total school program in ways that empower them to take ownership of creating the very best schools for children and families

- educate the community on the key educational, social, and family needs that exist, and on strategies for addressing these needs

- advocate for policy changes that will strengthen families in the community

- participate in actions that help reshape the community toward being a positive force in the lives of families

Couchenour and Chrisman offer a wealth of ideas and information for building a new and stronger commitment to children and families. Most important, they provide a conceptual structure for crafting new strategies and approaches to engage families, schools, and communities in building healthy and positive places for children. Further, they connect this structure to the profession's standards of quality, to the urgent needs of families, and to our desire for a better future for all of our children. We owe the authors a big thanks for developing this powerful tool for reshaping our approach to supporting children and families. We can best thank them, however, by becoming active partners in our schools and communities in creating strong and nurturing environments and relationships for children and their families.

Kevin J. Swick
Professor of Education
University of South Carolina—Columbia

PREFACE

This book was written to meet a need for a textbook that included a theoretical and research foundation for early childhood educators' work with families, schools, and communities. As societal changes are mirrored in schools, the use of a contextualist model as a basis for family, school, and community partnerships makes sense. For early childhood educators, the current findings by neuroscientists about the importance of early stimulation for optimal brain development point to the importance of supporting families. Further, early childhood educators are in a position of having knowledge that should be used by communities to enhance the lives of children and families.

New scientific information and current societal concerns about children's safety have led to a change in the charge of early childhood professionals. Teachers of young children must effectively involve families and communities in educating all of our children. Neglecting to do this at this critical time in history demonstrates both a lack of knowledge and a lack of caring about providing the best possible education for all children.

The *Instructor's Guide to accompany Families, Schools, and Communities: Together for Young Children* provides philosophy, a research base, and resources for early childhood teacher–educators. Using the Harvard Family Research Project as a foundation, the authors provide a framework for both family involvement content and effective teaching strategies. This textbook addresses the Harvard framework for content in at least the following ways:

General family involvement: Chapters 1, 7, 8, 9, 10
General family knowledge: Chapters 2, 3, 4, 5, 6
Home–school communication: Chapters 7, 8, 9
Family involvement in learning activities:
    Chapters 7, 9
Families supporting schools: Chapter 1, 7
Schools supporting families: All chapters
Families as change agents: Chapter 1, 7, 10.

Use of this textbook along with assigned, focused field experiences will provide both breadth and depth of knowledge for early childhood educators, future and present. Further, for each chapter of the textbook, the *Instructor's Guide* delineates knowledge, attitudes, and skills; a variety of instructional strategies; and reading lists for additional information.

Resources include an updated list of suggested readings for further information about the content of each chapter. Videos related to each chapter are included with instructional strategies.

We are especially pleased with and proud of an important addition to our *Instructor's Manual.* Dr. Rose Casement from the University of Michigan-Flint has compiled an annotated bibliography of children's literature to accompany many of the topics in this textbook. Rose's knowledge of high quality children's literature and the significance of families in children's lives make this addtion especially relevant. We believe that early childhood educators will find this resource to be beneficial in their work to support families and children.

It is our hope that this book will serve as one important tool in early childhood teacher education. In addition to the information in this book, teacher education must provide a variety of strategies for teaching both novice and experienced early educators about working effectively with families and communities. Both undergraduate and graduate students who study about working with families must have field experiences and field assignments so that they can practice skills and adopt attitudes such as compassion, empathy, and tolerance.

Acknowledgments

We wish to acknowledge those who so ably assisted with this writing project. Rebecca Pettit provided a thoughtful review and many excellent suggestions for relating current theoretical perspectives to practice in early childhood education. Patty Keer Weibley's comments from her perspective as a parent with a young child, as well as a professional teacher, added clarity and authenticity. Anne Nickles, director of Shippensburg Head Start, provided us with many sources of invaluable information related to the family involvement component of Head Start. And she allowed us to keep the materials longer than we should have. Shippensburg University supported a semester-long sabbatical leave for Donna. Without this support for time to write, this book could not have been done in a timely manner. Our neighbor Arlene Keer provided a continuous listening ear and many empathic responses on morning walks during the sabbatical. We are grateful for the photographs submitted by Barbara Bartels and Gay Jones, and by the Szeles and McDaniel families. We are also grateful to Nancy Dymond, Teri Hilbinger, Beth Wachter, and Dr. David Lovett for providing parent voices in the second edition, and to Louanne Burt for additional family stories. Pattabhiram Marapudi was especially helpful in checking Web sites and Heather Waybright contributed greatly in her literature searches for the second edition. The teachers, staff, and parents at Rowland School lent their stories, support, and concern to this project for well over one school year.

Our families demonstrated patience with our work on this book as we missed visits and events over the past two years. We are grateful to many extended family members for their interest in this project. The staff at Delmar Learning who have worked with us include Erin O'Connor Traylor, Pat Gillivan, and Melissa Riveglia. Their quick responses to our requests for information were appreciated.

The authors of this textbook began collaborating on projects in 1983. We worked together as friends and colleagues through 1994. Since then, we continue to collaborate in our work for children, families, and schools as spouses. Living together through the challenges and blessings of family life has influenced our understanding of the importance of family and community involvement in early education.

Donna Couchenour
Kent Chrisman

Reviewers

The authors would like to thank the following reviewers, enlisted by Delmar Learning, for their helpful suggestions and constructive criticism.

Davia Allen
Western Carolina University
Cullowhee, North Carolina

Alice Beyrent
Hesser College
Manchester, New Hampshire

Marie Brand
State University of New York—New Paltz
New Paltz, New York

Mary Lou Brotherson, Ed.D.
Barry University
Miami, Florida

Robin Hasslen, Ph.D.
St. Cloud State University
St. Cloud, Minnesota

Margot Keller
Lima Technical College
Lima, Ohio

Judy Lindman
Rochester Community and Technical College
Rochester, Minnesota

Linda Hall Richey, Ph.D.
Middle Tennessee State University
Murfreesboro, Tennessee

UNDERSTANDING FAMILIES

OUTLINE

CHAPTER 1

A Theory-based Approach to Family Involvement in Early Childhood Education

OBJECTIVES

After reading and reflecting on this chapter, you should be able to:

- Relate the importance of families to young children's development according to three theoretical perspectives.

- Understand the scientific basis for including family involvement in early childhood education.

- Consider the categories of internal and external developmental assets necessary for optimal child development.

- Apply principles of developmentally appropriate practice (DAP) and the family support movement in meaningful ways.

The Importance of Families in Children's Lives

During the course of the 1996 U.S. presidential campaign, an ideological debate was begun about whether it takes a "village" or a family to raise a child. This was a debate that never should have happened. Professionals who work with young children are well aware that children need both families and communities. Furthermore, families and communities need children. Margaret Mead noted, "Of course we need children. Children are our vehicles for survival—for in them there is hope, and through them what has been, and what will be will not only be perpetuated, but also united."

Recent research by associates of the Search Institute (http://www.search-institute.org) has led to the establishment of a framework of **developmental assets**, or critical factors, necessary for children's healthy development. Even though scholars are continuing to test and refine this framework, current child development understanding supports the assets as listed at this point in time. The list of forty assets for each period of development (infancy, toddlerhood, preschool, elementary school age, and adolescents) demonstrates the importance that families, schools, and various community groups play in the lives of children. For each developmental level, twenty external assets and twenty internal assets are postulated. Figure 1–2 lists the four categories of external assets and the four categories of internal assets.

> *"It takes a village to raise a child."*
> —African proverb

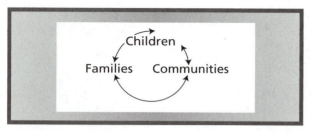

Figure 1–1   Children, families, and communities rely on each other.

Contextualist Theories

Three **contextualist theories**—bioecological, dialectical, and family systems—demonstrate relationships among children, families, and communities that are crucial to effective family involvement in early childhood education. When early childhood teachers apply these theories, their family involvement practices will be more authentic and supportive.

In this book, early childhood education is defined comprehensively as any program of care and education for children from birth through eight years of age. Early childhood educators, whether child care staff, preschool teachers, kindergarten teachers, or primary teachers, are a critical part of a healthy community for both young children and their families. Healthy communities rely on families to perform a variety of functions for their children. When families cannot or do not perform these functions, communities may sometimes "pick up the slack" for the good of the children. As society changes, the expected functions of families and communities shift.

T. Berry Brazelton and Stanley I. Greenspan (2000) discuss the **irreducible needs** of children in their book of the same title (Figure 1–3). These two pediatric medical specialists note that over the course of the 20th century, families with young chil-

---

FOUR EXTERNAL ASSETS

Support.   Children need care and love from families, neighbors, community groups.

Empowerment.   Children are empowered when communities value them, and keep them safe and secure.

Boundaries and Expectations.   Children need to know what is expected of them. Limits should be clear, realistic, and responsive.

Constructive Use of Time.   Children need to have opportunities to play safely. Choices should be provided with many varied activities. Both developmental level and individual differences should be considered.

FOUR INTERNAL ASSETS

Commitment to Learning.   Families and communities encourage children to be lifelong learners.

Positive Values.   Children are exposed to examples of caring, fairness, social justice, integrity, honesty, responsibility, and healthy life choices.

Social Competencies.   Children have opportunities to learn how to get along with others, to celebrate similarities and differences, and to peacefully resolve conflicts.

Positive Identity.   Children have positive role models and responsive nurturing so that they can develop a sense of self-worth and caring for others.

Figure 1–2   Categories for Developmental Assets.
Source: http://www.search-institute.org

dren face more and different stresses than in the past. They emphasize the need that young families have for support from sources outside the immediate family in order to best nurture their children. Our society, they believe, is in grave danger of failing our children. And when children do not get what they need for optimal development, society often pays the price. The premise that all children have a right to sensitive nurturance and that no citizen has a right to ignore children's needs is the common thread throughout much of the work of Brazelton and Greenspan. This current and critical work splendidly echoes the old African proverb "It takes a village to raise a child."

The roles that children serve and the expectations families hold for their children have evolved dramatically in the past 150 years. Moving from an agrarian society through the industrial revolution and into the information age has caused flux in all societal institutions. We have moved from seeing children as property of the father to individuals who have responsibility for themselves, from miniature adults having no rights to developing human beings possessing legal rights and needing societal safeguards (deMause, 1974). For many, changes in

> *"Many things can wait. Children cannot. Today their bones are being formed, their blood is being made, and their senses are being developed. To them we cannot say tomorrow. Their name is today."*
> —Gabriela Mistral, Chilean poet.

the family, so much easier to observe and critique compared to changes in larger societal institutions, signal doom. Thus, some people deny the need for families to rely on the larger community for support. The "village" becomes an enemy. This is faulty logic and can harm young children as well as their families by denying children and their families needed sources of support.

Good early childhood teachers have always known that frequent, effective communication with families is imperative in the provision of quality care and education for the youngest children. "The emphasis on parents in the settlement house movement of the 1880s, the nursery school movement of the 1920s, and the early intervention movement

Early childhood education teachers are a critical component of a community for both young children and their families.

All children must have the following needs met in order to grow and thrive:

- ongoing nurturing relationships
- physical protection, safety, and regulation
- experiences that consider individual differences of children
- experiences that are developmentally appropriate
- appropriate limits, predictable structure, and reasonable expectations
- a stable, supportive community
- cultural continuity.

Figure 1–3 The Irreducible Needs of Children. (Brazelton & Greenspan, 2000)

of the 1960s is exemplary of the parent participation tradition in early childhood education" (Powell, 1989, p. 1). Teachers have used traditional forms of communication such as newsletters and conferences when they are effective, but teachers also have created new and different strategies for individual circumstances such as interactive journals and portfolio parties.

Since the 1970s when society saw an increase in the number of very young children in out-of-home care, a preponderance of early childhood literature supporting the need for family involvement has been written. As time passes, we are seeing the need as even greater than we did in the beginning. The latest research on early brain development reinforces our somewhat intuitive notion about the importance of teacher-family partnerships, emphasizing again that parents are not only children's first teachers, but probably also their most important teachers.

The concern for continuity of children's experiences is widely held as a rationale for positive and sustained relationships between early childhood teachers and family members (Powell, 1989). Early childhood literature and practice have assumed that continuity is necessary and good for children. Though little research exists to document this as an absolute, some theories offer substantial support for the importance of continuity in young children's lives. In early childhood education, the best way to provide continuity is to develop strong home-school bonds.

> "The reality is that learning does not begin when kids are age five. Learning begins well before they enter the schoolhouse. And what happens to children in their early years has profound impacts on the kind of entering students they will be."
>
> **Sharon Lynn Kagan, Professor at Teachers College, Columbia University, and past President of NAEYC.**

Bronfenbrenner's Bioecological Theory

Urie Bronfenbrenner's (1979) **bioecological theory** provides substantial support for upholding practices of involving families in early care and education. This theory emphasizes the developmental notion that biological predispositions and environmental influences interactively affect human growth. Bronfenbrenner has provided details about environmental systems that take our understanding beyond the effect of the immediate environment on children's behavior and development.

> Urie Bronfenbrenner's Theory
> **http://www.psy.pdx.edu/PsiCafe/
> KeyTheorists/Bronfenbrenner.htm**

Bronfenbrenner poses five environmental systems.

1. Microsystem is the setting in which the individual lives or the near environment. This includes the home, school, and community. Often, in a study of home-program relationships, only this system is considered.

2. Mesosystem is defined as the relationships between contexts in the microsystem. The relationship or the connection between two forms of microsystems actually influences children's behavior and development. For example, a telephone call from the teacher regarding a child's difficulties at school may affect parental treatment of the child at home.

3. Exosystem is a system removed from direct access of the individual, and has an indirect rather than direct effect on her. Examples of exosystems include parental work sites, extended family, and mass media.

4. Macrosystem is the culture in which an individual lives. Values and beliefs of a culture or subculture affect children and families. Western culture is more individualistic whereas many non-Western cultures are collectivistic.

5. Chronosystem is the time or the sociohistorical context. The era in which one lives her life affects behavior and development.

Taking each of these systems into account in the process of development certainly indicates the complex nature of ecological effects on children. Many experts believe that when professionals understand the nature of such effects, more appropriate and effective strategies for optimizing children's development will be incorporated such as the basis for strong connections between children's families and early education programs.

These systems are most frequently understood as a series of concentric circles, with the individual at the innermost circle (Figure 1–4). Based on this theory, Bronfenbrenner has written frequently about what children need from their families and what families need from the larger society.

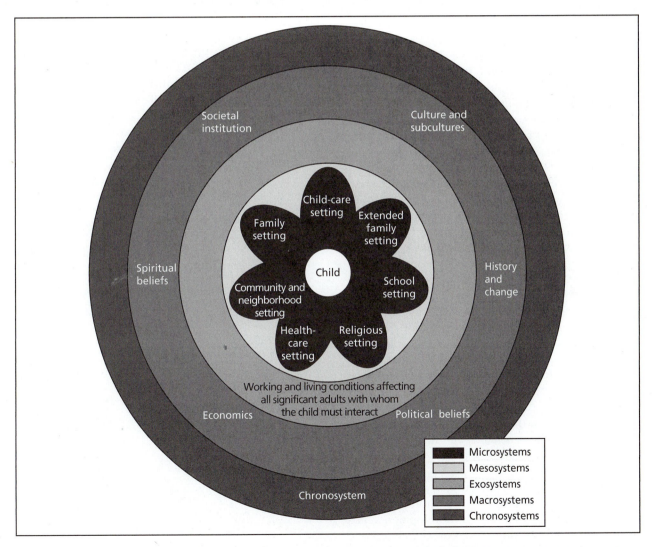

Figure 1–4 Concentric circle model of bioecological theory. (Adapted with permission from Kostelnik, M. J., Whiren, A. P., Soderman, A. K., Stein, L. C., & Gregory, K. [2002] [4th ed.]. *Guiding children's social development.* Clifton Park, NY: Delmar Learning)

Although many early childhood teachers are capable of and committed to providing excellent educational climates for young children, they do not have responsibility for each child throughout the child's entire life. Thus, even when teachers' functions are similar to parents' functions, a major difference exists. This shows us that even though high-quality early education is extremely important for children's development, the family is even more important. For Bronfenbrenner, the importance of families for children goes beyond caregiving. He states unequivocally that parents are more capable of providing for the physical and psychological needs of a child when they have a third party who admires and loves them for their caregiving. So a parent who has a loving relationship with another adult can more easily provide for children's needs. He summarizes human development as occurring "in the context of an escalating psychological ping pong game between two people who are crazy about each other" (1990, p. 31).

The converse is that single (or unattached) parents do not always get the fuel they need from other adults to provide optimally for their children. Multiple sources exist for single parents to feel loved and admired; any of these sources that are healthy can be supportive of that parent's caregiving. Some examples are found in grandparents or other extended family, faith communities, or friendships.

Further, workplace policies affect family relationships. As more families than ever have all adults working outside the home, the effects of the workplace conditions are felt by children. Flexible hours, part-time positions *with* benefits, and availability of quality child care offer tremendous support for families with children. Such jobs are not readily available for many workers in the current economy. Many jobs are part time, without benefits, and hours change at the whim of the employer or manager rather than to meet family needs.

As a theorist, Bronfenbrenner is unusual in his advocacy for changing social policy in ways that will positively influence children's development. His recognition that the culture does make a difference in children's lives as expressed in his definition of the macrosystem has led to his call for national ac-

tion in both public and private sectors to demonstrate our care for children and support of their families.

Vygotsky's Dialectical Theory

Early childhood educators have increasingly looked to the work of Lev Vygotsky in their attempt to better understand the determinants of children's development. Certain aspects of this **dialectical theory** are parallel to Bronfenbrenner's explanation of the importance of the external social world for a child's development (Tharp & Gallimore, 1988).

Vygotsky postulated that human knowledge is derived from culture. This means that much of what we "know" comes from our families and larger society. The holidays we celebrate and the ways we celebrate them exemplify knowledge based on culture. The food we eat, the way we prepare and serve it, and even our table manners result from experiences within our culture.

For young children, much of their behavior is rooted in family expectations. Some four-year-olds

A child's development is dependent on both high-quality early education and the quality of family life.

have learned at home that "hitting back" is an acceptable solution to problem situations with peers or siblings. It will be important for early childhood teachers to realize that not only must they teach the child a new set of rules for getting along at school, but also they must communicate with parents and solicit their support for behavior that is acceptable at school.

On the other hand, early childhood teachers sometimes must accept differences of behavior in children and accommodate the classroom to meet these differences. For example, teachers should support children's development of their home language. This practice demonstrates respect for a family's primary language and communicates that the early childhood staff values the family's culture. Further, children who speak more than one language have an asset that will serve them well in future endeavors.

> Position Statement on Linguistic and Cultural Diversity
> http://www.naeyc.org/resources/position_statements/psdiv98.htm

Another premise from Vygotsky is that thinking is determined by social and historical assumptions. For example, social assumptions related to limited gender roles influence thinking, even when one claims to be logical or unbiased. Many couples find that before they had children, it was easier to maintain an egalitarian relationship. However, after having children, the added responsibilities seem to affect the egalitarianism, and many fathers take more traditional roles as breadwinners whereas many mothers take more traditional roles as homemakers.

Historical assumptions that are inaccurate may also cloud our thinking. An excellent example of this is the one so many practicing teachers were taught as students: Columbus discovered America. Could Columbus have discovered America when there were already people living here? We know now that there are more accurate ways of describing Columbus's explorations.

> Lev Vygotsky's Theory
> http://www.psy.pdx.edu/PsiCafe/KeyTheorists/Vygotsky.htm

Of course, it is possible that our assumptions may also reflect greater accuracy than the above examples illustrate. Accurate social and historical assumptions affect our thinking in useful and productive ways.

For Vygotsky, the **zone of proximal development** (ZPD) is the mechanism by which development occurs. The ZPD has four stages:

Stage 1: Performance is assisted by others who are more capable in the particular task.

Stage 2: Performance is assisted by the child herself as she moves towards self-regulation.

Stage 3: The child has internalized the task to a point that assistance would interrupt development. Performance is beyond both social and self-control; it is automatic and without self-consciousness.

Stage 4: Lifelong learning requires that the learner make recursive loops back to Stage 2 in order to improve or maintain skills (Vygotsky, 1962).

An example of the first three stages of the ZPD is noted in the following anecdote.

Chelsea, age three, loves to sing and learns words to songs with ease. With this knowledge, her aunt sang a popular nonsense song to her one day: "Willaby, Wallaby, Wee, an elephant sat on me, Willaby, Wallaby, Woo, an elephant sat on you, Willaby, Wallaby, Welsea, an elephant sat on Chelsea." (stage 1) The child responded at first by staring and smiling. Her aunt continued with other names in the family: Christopher, mommy, daddy, and Bryan. Soon, Chelsea started to sing the words that were familiar to her such as "an elephant sat on Christopher" (stage 2 begins) and later that day she was singing

"Willaby, Wallaby, an elephant sat on mommy" (more stage 2). She did not use the unfamiliar words that rhyme with a name and begin with a "w" such as "wommy" or "waddy" but listened carefully when her aunt did. Five days later, Chelsea had another visit with her aunt. Now she was singing the entire phrase and filling in names of her family (more stage 2). Several days later, Chelsea was singing the Willaby, Wallaby song without much effort or conscious thought as she played with blocks (stage 3).

It is too soon to tell whether Chelsea might engage in the recursive loop if she forgets the words at a later date.

Family Systems Theory

Supporting Bronfenbrenner's notion that children develop in context, Lerner (1989) notes "the family is *not* a context within which a child's ontogeny merely unfolds. Instead, the family is a dynamic context, one wherein a child is both transformer and is transformed. In addition, the child-family relation is reciprocally related to interactions with other key contexts of life, for example, the school and the peer group" (p. 18). This point of view, developmental contextualism, evolved from an effort to connect human developmental theories that espouse a strong biological foundation and family sociology theories that emphasize the family as the central social institution.

In addition to the developmental contextualist theory that has grown out of studies of human development across the life span, family sciences has also emphasized a *systems* approach. "In the **family systems theory**, everything that happens to any family member is seen as having an impact on everyone else in the family. This is because family members are interconnected and operate as a group, or system" (Olson & DeFrain, 1994, p. 16).

Several family systems models have been developed. The **circumplex model**, created by Olson and others, intends to demonstrate how all family members are interconnected. Following are three concepts that are critical to this model.

1. **Cohesion.** This refers to the feelings family members have for one another, as well as the amount and kind of time they spend together. The four levels of cohesion range from very low (disengaged) to low/moderate (separated) to moderate/high (connected) to very high (enmeshed).

2. **Flexibility.** This refers to the ability of family members to change roles and amounts of power they hold over time. The four levels of flexibility range from very low (rigid) to low/moderate (structured) to moderate/high (flexible) to very high (chaotic).

3. **Communication.** The purposes of communication in families are to establish and maintain cohesion, and to assist families to change and adapt over time by creating shared meanings.

In order to explain the processes involved in family communication, the circumplex model was devised by crossing the axis of cohesion with the axis of flexibility (Olson & DeFrain, 1994) (Figure 1–5).

The Circumplex Model of Family Systems

HIGH COHESION

Enmeshed

Connected

Rigid   Structured   Flexible   Chaotic

LOW   HIGH
FLEXIBILITY   FLEXIBILITY

Separated

Disengaged

LOW COHESION

Figure 1–5   Flexibility and Cohesion Axes.

Measures of these three dimensions can lead family scientists or therapists to classify a family in one of three ways:

1. balanced families who have balance on both the cohesion and flexibility dimension

2. midrange families who are extreme on one dimension but balanced on the other

3. extreme families who are extreme in both cohesion (either too close, enmeshed, or too far apart, disengaged) and flexibility (either too loose, chaotic, or not flexible enough, rigid) (Olson & DeFrain, 1994).

> Research with the Circumplex Model
> http://www.lifeinnovation.com/fip.html

From these concepts, a total of sixteen family variations can occur. Four types of balanced families are flexibly connected, structurally connected, flexibly cohesive, and structurally cohesive. Eight types of midrange families are chaotically connected, chaotically cohesive, flexibly disengaged, structurally disengaged, flexibly enmeshed, structurally enmeshed, rigidly connected, and rigidly cohesive. And the four types of extreme families are chaotically disengaged, chaotically enmeshed, rigidly disengaged, and rigidly enmeshed (Olson & DeFrain, 1994).

Because families are dynamic, this family systems theory points to the importance of the family's ability to change over time. For example, family cohesion is often higher in young couples and in families with young children than in families with adolescents. Teens' need to separate from their parents and find their own identities often leads to less cohesiveness during this stage of family life. Not surprising, families with young children often find that they become less flexible than they were before the first child was born and then become more flexible when the children become adolescents (Olson & DeFrain, 1994). Families with young children often have such tight daily schedules that flexibility lessens out of necessity.

Using a model similar to Bronfenbrenner's, the family systems model espoused by Carter and McGoldrick (1989) employs a concentric circle model with the addition of arrows for **horizontal stressors** (those that occur over time) and for **vertical stressors** (those that are embedded in particular families' patterns of relating). Family systems theory examines the family unit whereas human development theory focuses on the individual (Carter & McGoldrick, 1989).

Carter and McGoldrick also emphasized the importance of the family life cycle in order to best understand families. A **family life cycle** approach considers how families typically change over time. Relationships among family members take priority over family functions in this theory. Intergenerational relationships account for a great deal in how families move from one stage to another of the family life cycle process.

Most of the research and theory-building done in this area is applicable to middle-class families in the United States. Families that differ culturally and economically from this group will most likely not follow the same developmental cycle. This may also be true for families with various structures such as single parents and blended families. For early childhood educators, the primary implication from this theory is that child development occurs within the context of the family life cycle.

Although there are several models of the family life cycle, some having as many as twenty-four phases, the work of Carter and McGoldrick includes the following stages:

1. Leaving home: single young adults

2. Marriage: the new couple

3. Families with young children

4. Families with adolescents

5. Launching children

6. Families in later life

Because the emphasis in this text is on families with young children, this stage will be discussed further. Interestingly, this stage is referred to as the "pressure cooker" phase of the family life cycle

(p. 12). It may be helpful for early childhood educators to keep this idea in perspective as they try to understand and work with families of the young children they teach. This period often requires immense adjustment by both parents. They are moving in terms of the family life cycle from a concern for themselves as a couple to trying to balance child care, household responsibilities, and increasingly, each one holding a full-time job. Because care of children is a primary effort during this stage, when any part of this balancing act goes awry, it may cause their children's caregivers or teachers to feel the effects of the couple's apprehension.

The balance depends on many factors: well children, job security, quality and affordable child care, housing, working conditions of home appliances, and reliable transportation. When any one of the factors is out of the ordinary or not expected, the balance is threatened. Thus, when an early childhood teacher requests a conference or schedules a parent meeting, parents of young children often are immediately aware of all the complications an addition to their "pressure cooker" schedule might cause. Further, when parents do attend a conference or

Parents may have concerns about balancing a full-time job and caring for their child.

group family meeting, it is important that the time is planned carefully, with the starting time and ending time communicated in advance, and that the time be well organized and used to benefit all concerned.

Because moving to the young children phase of the family life cycle requires so much adjusting for new parents and other family members, rituals are often seen as a support for the family. Both extended family and community are often involved in such celebrations. Some of the common rituals marking this phase include baby showers, handing out cigars, posting lawn signs announcing the baby's gender, sending birth announcements, and newspaper announcements of births. Some rituals are based on religious tradition such as baptism, christening, and bris.

There have been a number of social changes over the past generation that affect tasks and responsibilities across the family life cycle in the United States. Some of the important changes include a lower birth rate, longer life expectancy, the changing role of women, relocation of young families for jobs or education, and the increasing divorce and remarriage rate. Divorce is now so common that many social scientists see it as a normative event.

Specific implications for early childhood educators that can be culled from family systems theory include the following:

1. Teachers and caregivers need to remember the influence of all family members on children's behaviors. Influence may affect family members regardless of geographic distance or even after the death of some members. For example, one family member may insist to the parent that the child should have a structured reading program emphasizing phonics. This causes the parent or other primary caregiver to question the school's whole language reading program.

2. Each family member may play a role in a child's life that may remain consistent or may vary, depending on the family's situation. For example, a grandparent may become more actively involved if a parent dies, divorces, or has a job change.

To demonstrate recent changes in families, please do the following:

1. Write down the number of children your parents have, the number of children that were in each of your parents' families as they grew up, and the number of children in your grandparents' families as they grew up. Add the total for each of the three generations. What did you find?

2. Ask about the ages at which any of your deceased relatives died. Note that current life expectancy for middle-class people in the United States is about 74 years. What did you find about earlier generations in your family?

3. What was your mother's role in the family related to working outside or inside the home? What were your grandmothers' roles? What roles do women in your own generation play? How have these changed over time? What are the reasons the roles have changed?

4. What was your father's role in the family related to working outside or inside the home? What were your grandfathers' roles? What roles do men in your own generation play? How have these changed over time? What are the reasons the roles have changed?

5. Has divorce and/or remarriage been an aspect of your immediate family? Your extended family? How has divorce or remarriage affected your family's life cycle process?

6. Do you live near your extended family? Have you ever moved with your immediate family? How does living near or far away from other family members affect relationships with grandparents, aunts, uncles, and cousins?

7. What is your family's philosophy regarding children? Speculate on how this philosophy might have changed over the generations.

"It is widely recognized that children vary on every measurable characteristic. Youngsters demonstrate individuality related to genetic, cultural, and contextual factors. Despite the rhetorical acceptance of such variability, conventional definitions of early development and learning have been more attentive to genetic and/or developmental variation than to cultural or contextual variation. Such a focus on genetic and developmental variability has had important and often negative consequences. In some cases, access to differing educational opportunities has been determined by assessments that ignore cultural competence and that use majority-culture norms to determine competence on a single dimension . . . Developmental equivalencies are often not understood, and variation within cultures is often neglected. Individual, cultural, and contextual variables influence how children present themselves, understand the world, process information, and interpret experiences . . ."

—Kagan, Moore, & Bredekamp, 1995

3. Stress in the family may change the child's role and relationships with other family members. Death of a parent or divorce may result in a child's greater role in emotional support of the remaining parent.

4. The function of myth may affect the child's behavior while at school. An example of one family myth, "We don't let anyone push us around," may influence the child so that she hits in response to conflict.

Implications for Practice in Early Childhood Education

Guidelines for Developmentally Appropriate Practice (DAP)

"**Developmentally appropriate practices** derive from deep knowledge of individual children, and the context within which they develop and learn. The younger the child, the more necessary it is for professionals to acquire this knowledge through relationships with children's families" (Bredekamp & Copple, 1997, p. 22).

Position Statement on Developmentally
    Appropriate Practice
**http://www.naeyc.org/resources/position_stat
    ement/daptoc.htm**

Bredekamp and Copple (1997), in their book *Developmentally Appropriate Practice in Early Childhood Programs,* list eight guidelines to help professionals establish reciprocal relationships with families of children in early education programs.

1. Mutual respect, cooperation, shared responsibility, and negotiation of conflicts toward achievement of shared goals are requirements for effective family and school partnerships.

2. Collaborative partnerships require regular, frequent, two-way communication with the child's family.

3. Roles for parents include decision-making about children's care and education, as well as observation, participation, and decision-making regarding the program.

4. The teachers' role includes sensitivity to families' wishes and respect for their preferences while maintaining professional responsibility to children.

5. Teachers and family members share their knowledge of the child through day-to-day communication and planned conferences. Teachers provide support to families to promote strengths and competence of family members.

6. Family members are involved in assessing and planning the program for individual children.

7. The program links families with services and resources based on the concerns and priorities of program staff and families.

8. All professionals who have information about the child will share that information with the family as children pass from one level or program to another (p. 22).

These guidelines form the basis for excellence as early education programs devise their own design for family involvement. When questions arise and decisions must be made, use of these guidelines ensures that program staff will acknowledge the importance of reciprocal relationships with families. Each program may develop unique ways of implementing the DAP guidelines.

Key Characteristics of Early Childhood Programs Practicing

Inclusion

1. Inclusive early childhood programs enroll typically developing children and children with identified disabilities.

2. Staff members are well trained and competent in providing a high-quality early childhood program.

3. The same daily schedule is available to all children.

4. The curriculum is developmentally appropriate and meets the needs of individual children.

5. All children have the support they need to participate actively in the program.

6. Adaptations and modifications are provided for individual needs. Specialized services are provided as needed.

7. All children are supported to engage in successful peer interactions.

8. Family members are active participants in various ways.

9. Staff members and families collaborate to provide the best educational program for each young child (Schwartz, Sandall, Odom, Horn, & Beckman, 2002).

National Accreditation Guidelines

Based on these guidelines for reciprocal relationships with families, the National Academy of Early Childhood Programs (NAECP) devised requirements for specific practices related to staff-parent

> Position Statement on Accreditation Criteria
> http://www.naeyc.org/resources/position_stat
> ements/psacc98.htm

interaction for **accreditation** (National Academy of Early Childhood Programs, 1991). This national accreditation system is voluntary. Early childhood programs serving children five and under may choose to apply for accreditation by completing a self-study and documenting how they meet the criteria designed by leaders in early childhood education. The program director then schedules a validation visit with the NAECP office. Trained volunteers observe and document criteria as submitted in the self-study. All paperwork is then reviewed by commissioners, and a decision to accredit or defer is made. Programs that are deferred receive information to assist them in meeting all criteria and may reapply.

Public service announcements and community task forces often share information about accredited centers with families of young children. Some communities have support (such as staff training or funding for educational materials) for child care centers to work toward accreditation. Many times, parents who are seeking quality care for their young children choose an accredited program over another one.

Following are accreditation requirements for partnerships with families:

> *"The purpose of the National Academy of Early Childhood Programs is to improve the quality of care and education provided for young children in group programs in the United States. The Academy achieves its purpose by developing training resources, disseminating public information about high quality programs, and administering a national, voluntary accreditation system for early childhood programs."*[50]
>
> —**Accreditation Criteria and Procedures**

1. Information about the program is given to new and prospective families, including written descriptions of the program's philosophy, operating procedures, and plans for meeting children's nutritional needs.

2. A process must be developed for orienting children and parents to the program, which may include a pre-enrollment visit, parent orientation meetings, or gradual introduction of children to the program.

3. Staff and parents communicate frequently about child-rearing practices in the home and at the program in order to minimize potential conflicts and confusion for children. Staff members give parents specific ideas for promoting children's healthy development and learning at home.

4. Parents are welcome visitors in the program at all times (for example, to observe, eat lunch with a child, or volunteer to help in the classroom). Parents and other family members are encouraged to become involved in the program in various ways, taking into consideration working parents and those with little spare time.

5. A verbal and/or written system is established for sharing day-to-day happenings that may affect children. Changes in a child's physical or emotional state are reported regularly.

6. Conferences should be held at least once a year and at other times, as needed, to discuss children's progress, accomplishments, and difficulties at home and at the program.

7. Through newsletters, newspaper articles, bulletin boards, and other appropriate means, parents are informed about the program and the curriculum, about policy or regulatory changes, and other critical issues that could potentially affect the program and/or the early childhood profession.

8. Staff and parents communicate to ensure that children experience smooth transitions from one program to another during the day. Staff and parents communicate to ensure that the

programs from which children come and to which they go from one year to the next provide continuity over time.

Responsiveness to Family Cultures, Values, and Languages

The Division for Early Childhood (DEC) of the Council on Exceptional Children has recently approved a position statement regarding the importance of individualized approaches for serving young children with special needs and their families (www.dec-sped.org.positions/positionculture.htm/). In order to best individualize services and to meet the legislated requirements for serving young children with special needs, relationships among staff and family members must demonstrate respect and appreciation for each family's culture, values, and language. Characteristics expected of professionals who work with these young children and their families include:

- respecting the values and practices of all family members.
- encouraging multiple viewpoints.
- increasing professional competence with regard to respecting differences in culture, values, and language.
- seeking meaningful representation and participation of people from different backgrounds.
- using and supporting dissemination of resources that address differences in families.
- attending professional development sessions that incorporate the impact of cultures, values, and languages in all early childhood services.

> The Division for Early Childhood of the Council on Exceptional Children
> http://www.dec-sped.org/

Family Support Movement

Since the mid-1970s, the interdisciplinary family support movement has evolved from an emphasis on program development to providing principles for national efforts in work with families. The essence of this movement constitutes "a fundamental change in the traditional belief systems, reflecting a change from assuming that the role of government is to be a resource for families in crisis to recognizing the responsibility of our society to promote the well-being of all families" (Weissbourd, 1994, p. 37). This movement clearly is an application of Bronfenbrenner's theory, emphasizing the importance of various systems as they relate to children and families.

At the heart of family support is community-building. The best way to improve the lives of children and families is through caring communities. This movement sees such community support for all families as an "inherent responsibility of a democracy" (Weissbourd, 1994, p. 41).

Leaders in the **family support movement** have created a set of principles to be used in defining effective family-school relationships. Bowman (1994) notes the following principles:

- promoting family health and well-being
- inspiring parental confidence and competence
- responding to family cultural preferences and values
- providing concrete help for real-life problems
- giving information tailored to parental needs
- empowering relationships between individuals and between families and helping institutions
- encouraging voluntary participation by parents

This perspective recognizes "that families are responsible for their children's development, and that no family can function alone" (Kagan & Weissbourd, 1994, p. xxi). Family support points to the absolutely critical need that children and families have for continuity between home and school. From this movement, early childhood educators must become advocates not only for young children but also for the families and communities from which those children come.

A child gains her identity and sense of self from her family. When family strengths are recognized and needs are met through the community, families do better and children do better. Bowman (1994) ex-

A child gains her identity and sense of self from her family.

plains how the family support movement changes our paradigm "from a prevention to a promotion model" (p. 41). This means we have evolved from seeing families primarily with deficits and our task as intervening to prevent problems, to seeing families essentially as having strengths and our task as providing resources to support family well-being.

Family Focus
http://www.collaboratory.nunet.net/itrc/ff/
Family Support America
http://www.familysupportamerica.org
Institute for Responsive Education
http://www.resp-ed.org/

Summary and Conclusions

The information about theory and best practices in this chapter indicates to early childhood practitioners that children do not arrive at early childhood programs having had the same experiences or come

from families who value the same experiences. A contextualist framework permits professionals in early childhood education to understand concepts, then to apply those ideas especially to the setting in which they work with young children and their families.

Young children do not enter educational programs on a level playing field. As members of families, they come to us with all of the positive, negative, and neutral experiences of their families' lives. Children have learned much about what to expect in their own social world before we see them in early childhood education programs. It is an increasingly important responsibility of early childhood educators to understand the importance of families in children's lives and to include various components from all families' lives in early education.

Key Terms

developmental assets	**developmental**
contextualist theories	**contextualism**
irreducible needs of	**family systems theory**
children	**circumplex model**
bioecological theory	**cohesion**
microsystem	**flexibility**
mesosystem	**horizontal stressors**
exosystem	**vertical stressors**
macrosystem	**family life cycle**
chronosystem	**developmentally**
dialectical theory	**appropriate practices**
zone of proximal	**(DAP)**
development (ZPD)	**inclusion**
	accreditation
	family support movement

Chapter One Applications

1. Using information from at least one theory discussed in this chapter, respond to the following comments from early childhood teachers or administrators:

   a. "My job is to teach the children, not to provide a shoulder for parents to cry on."

   b. "There are not enough hours in the day to plan, implement, and evaluate a family involvement program for my classroom."

c. "I enjoy working with children, but not adults. That's why I wanted to teach."

d. "How can I include a child with special needs in my center?"

2. Using information from at least one theory discussed in this chapter, respond to the following comments from family members who have children enrolled in early childhood programs:

a. "I send my child to preschool so that she can learn. The teacher's job is to make sure she does. I resent being asked to volunteer in the classroom."

b. "I did not like school when I was a student. I am not comfortable being in the classroom."

c. "I don't want those teachers at my daughter's child care center telling me how to raise my children. I won't go to any of the parent meetings as long as they're telling me what to do."

3. Using information from at least one theory discussed in this chapter, respond to the following comments from community members who do not have young children:

a. "I don't want my tax money going to support preschool programs in the schools. Parents should take care of their own children."

b. "Good parents don't put their kids in child care. I will never do that to my children."

c. "Families don't care about children like they used to. They want the community to build parks and to provide recreation so they can send their kids out of the house and ignore them."

Questions for Reflection and Discussion

1. When you think about teaching young children, how do you envision your role with families? How have your expectations changed since reading and reflecting on this chapter?

2. When you think about teaching young children, what do you think about the community's involvement or influences on children? How

have your ideas changed since reading and reflecting on this chapter?

3. What is your understanding of the role of each of the following theories in developing exemplary family involvement programs in early childhood education?

a. bioecological

b. contextualist

c. family systems

4. Using each of the three theories explained in this chapter, critique the guidelines for developmentally appropriate practice, national accreditation, and family support.

Field Assignments

1. Interview several early childhood teachers or administrators about the role families and community members have in their programs. Consider interviewing early childhood professionals in the following types of programs: Head Start, child care, public school, family center, and early intervention. Compare and contrast family involvement in each kind of program.

2. Interview some parents or other family members about their involvement in their young children's educational program. Consider interviewing family members who have children enrolled in various types of programs as mentioned in Assignment 1. What similarities and differences did you find?

References

Bowman, B. (1994). Home and school: The unresolved relationship. In S. L. Kagan & B. Weissbourd (Eds.), *Putting families first: America's family support movement and the challenge of change.* San Francisco: Jossey-Bass.

Brazelton, T. B., & Greenspan, S. I. (2000). *The irreducible needs of children: What every child must have to grow, learn and flourish.* Cambridge, MA: Perseus.

Bredekamp, S., & Copple, C. (1997). *Developmentally appropriate practice in early childhood programs* (rev. ed.).

Washington, DC: National Association for the Education of Young Children.

Bronfenbrenner, U. (1979). *The ecology of human development: Experiments by nature and design.* Cambridge, MA: Harvard University Press.

Bronfenbrenner, U. (1990). Discovering what families do. In D. Blankenhorn, S. Bayme, & J. B. Elshtain (Eds.), *Rebuilding the nest: A new commitment to the American family.* Milwaukee, WI: Family Service America.

Carter, B., & McGoldrick, M. (1989). The changing family life cycle: A framework for family therapy. In B. Carter & M. McGoldrick (Eds.), *The changing family life cycle.* Boston: Allyn & Bacon.

deMause, L. (Ed.) (1974). *The history of childhood.* New York: Psychohistory Press.

Kagan, S. L., Moore, E., & Bredekamp, S. (Eds.). (1995). *Reconsidering children's early development and learning: Toward common views and vocabulary.* Washington, DC: National Education Goals Panel.

Kagan, S. L., & Weissbourd, B. (1994). *Putting families first: America's family support movement and the challenge of change.* San Francisco: Jossey-Bass.

Lerner, R. M. (1989). Individual development and the family system: A life-span perspective. In K. Kreppner & R. M. Lerner (Eds.), *Family systems and life-span development.* Hillsdale, NJ: Lawrence Erlbaum Associates.

National Academy of Early Childhood Programs. (1991). *Accreditation criteria & procedures.* Washington, DC: National Association for the Education of Young Children.

Olson, D. H., & DeFrain, J. (1994). *Marriage and the family: Diversity and strengths.* Mountain View, CA: Mayfield.

Powell, D. (1989). *Families and early childhood education.* Washington, DC: National Association for the Education of Young Children.

Schwartz, I. S., Sandall, S. R., Odom, S. L., Horn, E., & Beckman, P. J. (2002). "I know it when I see it": In search of a common definition of inclusion. In S. L. Odom (Ed.), *Widening the circle: Including children with disabilities in preschool programs.* New York: Teachers College Press.

Tharp, R. G., & Gallimore, R. (1988). *Rousing minds to life.* New York: Cambridge University Press.

Vygotsky, L. (1962). *Thought and language.* Cambridge, MA: MIT Press.

Weissbourd, B. (1994). The evolution of the family resource movement. In S. L. Kagan & B. Weissbourd (Eds.) *Putting families first: America's family support movement and the challenge of change.* San Francisco: Jossey-Bass.

OUTLINE

Understanding Family Diversity

Contextualist Theories and Family Differences

Bioecological theory (Bronfenbrenner, 1979) informs teachers that differences in children's microsystems will account for differences in children's behaviors and development. The social environment provided to children by their families is directly driven by the family's identification with race, culture, and ethnicity. Other factors that influence the microsystem include economics, gender, religion, and geographical region of residence.

Vygotsky's contextual theory emphasizes the notion that knowledge derives from culture. Teachers observe differences in behaviors of children and their family members based on their culture's view of what is appropriate. Such knowledge cannot be disputed in favor of a teacher's or other

dominant view. A child's very definition, and thus knowledge, of family is rooted in his culture.

Family systems theory (McGoldrick, 1989) places great importance on ethnicity and culture as a factor in a family's beliefs, practices, and values. Income level of a family is likely to influence many aspects of family decisions and behaviors. For example, professional women often celebrate the arrival of their first child at about the same age (31 to 35) that some lower-income women celebrate their first grandchild. Females and males are likely to experience family quite differently, from everyday behaviors to rituals and celebrations. "Religion also modifies or reinforces certain cultural values. Families . . . whose religion reinforces ethnic values, are likely to maintain their ethnicity longer" (p. 70). Families who live in close proximity to others of the same ethnic, racial, and cultural background are more likely to maintain the same norms; those who

This child's knowledge of family is rooted in her culture.

African American Internet Links
http:/clnet.ucr.edu/Afro.links.htm]
Asian American Resources
http://www.ai.mit.edu/people/irie/aar
Index of Native American Resources on the Internet
http://www.hanksville.org/NAresources
Latino Resources
http://www.latinoweb.com
http://latino.sscnet.ucla.edu
Multicultural Pavilion
http://curry.edschool.virginia.edu/go/multicultural
New American Studies Web
http://cfdev.georgetown.edu/cndls/asw/aswsub.cfm?head1=Race%2C%
http://20Ethnicity%2C%20and%20Identity

move away may become more homogenized or more influenced by a dominant culture.

Ways in Which Families Are Different

Families define themselves as a family. Membership in a family can be decided only by each member of that family. Thus, it is the role of early childhood educators to be aware of who constitutes each child's family. It is never the role of an early childhood educator to define the child's family for him. *That is, teachers should not attempt to alter a particular family's view about membership in that family.* Some factors that make families different from one another include ethnicity, race, culture, economics, gender roles, religiosity, and geographic regionalism.

It is important that these differences are considered in order to increase understanding on the part of early childhood teachers. It is common for each of us when we hear the word "family" to think of our own familial experiences and to ignore differences.

Ethnicity, Race, and Culture

"Ethnicity refers to a concept of a group's "peoplehood" based on a combination of race, religion, and cultural history, whether or not members realize their commonalities with each other. It describes a commonality transmitted by the family over generations . . . it is more than race, religion, or national and geographic origin . . . It involves conscious and unconscious processes that fulfill a deep psychological need for identity and historical continuity (McGoldrick, 1989, p. 69)."

Family ethnicity is sustained through "unique family customs, proverbs and stories, celebrations, foods, and religious ceremonies" (p. 110). Differences have been noted between the notions of self-concept and ethnic identity. Families often find it difficult to instill ethnic pride in their children in our pluralistic society (Stauss, 1995, citing Harriett McAdoo). Effects of racism affect beliefs and practices in nonmajority ethnic groups (McDade, 1995).

It is this deep psychological need for identity that must be taken into account by early childhood professionals. The degree to which ethnicity is important to a given family varies. Understanding these differences will help early childhood teachers view each family's individuality as a strength and support children's sense of connection to their ethnic group.

Chelsea is a three-year-old daughter of European-American parents. Her family portrait includes a picture of her mother, Stacey; her father, Jay; herself; and her five-month-old brother, Christopher. These family members live together in the same home in a small town in eastern Ohio. Living nearby, her paternal grandmother has almost daily contact with Chelsea's family. Her maternal grandparents live about fifteen miles away, and visits between them and Chelsea's family occur weekly.

Jamal is the five-year-old son of Janice. They live in St. Louis with Janice's mother, Dianne, and her long-time partner, Samuel. Jamal's family portrait includes his mother; grandmother; Samuel; and Samuel's teenage daughter, Jalisa. Jamal calls his grandmother "Mamma" and his mother "Janice." Frequent family visitors include Dianne's mother and father who live in the same city, and Samuel's mother who travels from Chicago twice a year for a month-long stay.

Robin, seven years old, is the youngest child in her Japanese-American family. She lives in Seattle with her parents, her maternal grandfather, and two

Understanding ethnic differences will help early childhood teachers support children's sense of connection to their ethnic group.

older brothers. Her family portrait includes her mother, Marcia; her father, Paul; her grandfather, Ito; and 13-year-old twin brothers, Rodger and Raymond. Last year, Robin's family traveled to Kyoto, Japan, to visit her paternal grandparents.

For family events in early childhood programs, teachers and other staff should not only be prepared for a variety of family members, not just parents and siblings, but also plan for and welcome them. Early childhood educators must go beyond traditional work with parent involvement to a more timely approach of family involvement. Welcoming grandparents, aunts and uncles, and even family members who have no official title based on bloodline can be a critical factor for building successful family-school relationships.

Teachers too often talk of children who come from good homes and those who have troublesome families. Often, the meaning of a "good home" is synonymous with the teacher's own family and the meaning of a less than good home is one that is different from the teacher's. Knowledge about cultural differences is a key to changing teacher perspectives about diverse families.

"The first thing to remember about the American family is that it doesn't exist. Families exist. All kinds of families in all kinds of economic and marital situations, as all of us can see . . . The American family? Just which American family did you have in mind? Black or white, large or small, wealthy or poor, or somewhere in between? Did you mean a father-headed, mother-headed, or childless family? First or second time around? Happy or miserable? Your family or mine?"

—**Louise Kapp Howe (1972)**

1. Draw a picture of your family at the time you were born. 2. Next, draw a picture of your family when you were a preschooler. 3. Draw your family when you were in elementary school. 4. Draw your family during your middle school or junior high years. 5. Draw your family as it was when you graduated from high school. 6. Draw your family as it is today. 7. Draw your family as you expect it to be five years from now. Reflect on the following: How did your family change over time? How do you define family? On what did you base your expectations of your family in the future? Compare and contrast your drawings and reflections with others in your class.

What is Culture?
http://www.wsu.edu:8001/vcwsu/commons/topics/cultur/culture-index.html/

Is the idea of family values one that is reasonable? Mellman, Lazarus, and Rivlin (1990) found in their research a high degree of consensus on love and emotional support, respect for others, and taking responsibility for actions. Perhaps these are the characteristics we should look for when we want to label a family as having a "good home."

Ethnic differences go beyond race. The term race, based on physical differences, is often noted to be scientific in nature as opposed to the sociocultural nature of ethnicity. In this regard, most sources tell us that three races exist in the world: Negroid, Mongoloid, and Caucasoid. Each of the three races is defined by very specific characteristics such as skin tone, facial structure, and geographic origin. However, in authentic work with children and families, early childhood educators often realize that emphasis on race alone is not very helpful. This is seen most clearly in children of interracial families. The question of "What race are you?" is often both confusing and irrelevant in the United States today. It is more helpful for early childhood educators to understand individuality within diversity in families.

Wardle (1987) notes that we know little about interracial families. However, one point made strongly is that children from interracial families cannot choose to identify with the race of one parent over that of the other. This misconception is an oversimplified attempt to understand the unique difficulty that interracial children have with their need for identity.

Wardle suggests that teachers work closely with parents (or other family members) to "feature cultural customs of both (or all) races represented in each interracial child, as well as create ongoing experiences for all children in which multicultural diversity is celebrated" (p. 58).

Culture refers to the unique experiences and history of various ethnic groups. Cultural differences often indicate differences in views on the family and the community, differences in expectations of children, differences in child-rearing, and differences in the value placed on education.

Carol Brunson Phillips (1995) notes that early educators need to have an understanding about both how culture is transmitted and how it is not transmitted. She has formulated six concepts to help with this understanding.

1. *Culture is learned.* Culture is not biological; teachers cannot identify a family's culture by how the family members look. Instead, each individual learns his culture's rules through daily living. Examples include table manners, interpersonal interactions, and ways of demonstrating respect.

2. *Culture is characteristic of groups.* An individual's characteristics are both cultural and individual. Unique personality traits are not culturally based. Cultural behaviors are rooted in groups. Some cultures may place greater emphasis on individuality or conformity than others.

3. *Culture is a set of rules for behavior.* "The essence of culture is in the rules that produce the behaviors, not the behaviors themselves" (Phillips, 1995, p. 5). So, culture is an influence on behavior, often a sweeping influence, but the behaviors alone are not culture. Behaviors commonly influenced by culture include types of clothing and flavors in foods.

4. *Individuals are embedded to different degrees within a culture.* Some families and individuals place more emphasis on cultural traditions than do others. Some Irish families may "act" more Irish than others; some Vietnamese families may "act" more Vietnamese than others; some African families may "act" more African than others. These are individual variations within cultures. Teachers should not expect all people of one culture to be equally involved with their cultural rules. Understanding of both cultural rules and individual differences in people of the same or similar culture is important.

5. *Cultures borrow and share rules.* Over time, cultures have influenced one another. Culture is not stagnant. As people from two or more cultures interact, cultures are affected and may undergo transformations.

6. *Members of a cultural group may be proficient in cultural behavior but unable to describe the rules.* Because young children begin to learn their culture in their own home environments, behaviors seem natural to them. Not only can they not tell you why they engage in these behaviors, it is also likely they are not conscious of all of the behaviors they have learned from their culture. When one northerner spent her first Thanksgiving in the deep south, she asked the cook, "Why do you put boiled eggs in the gravy?" Certain that there must be some interesting story or superstition related to this practice, she was surprised at the response: "I don't know. That's the way my mother did it."

In their work to include families, teachers of young children would find it more profitable to consider not only race, but also ethnicity and culture. It is more likely that knowledge of sociocultural factors would provide greater understanding to teachers than information about physical differences noted in definitions of race. Thus, including understanding of racial differences is most useful in the context of cultural and ethnic differences as well.

According to contextualist theories, the roles that nuclear families, extended families, and communities play vary. One important factor in these variations is related to culture and ethnicity. It is frequently noted that in the United States, ethnic groups that are not dominant in the culture are more strongly influenced by extended families (McDade, 1995). Further, the macrosystem and chronosystem for cultural groups differ. Figure 2–1 illustrates differences in parenting characteristics and value placed on education for a variety of cultural groups.

Sometimes, teachers unintentionally emphasize differences among groups of people, and the effect is assaultive rather than respectful toward diversity. One step to avoid this with preschool-age children is to "focus on the people in the child's world of today, not a historical world. *The goal with preschoolers is not to teach history, but to inoculate them against racism*" (Clark, DeWolf, & Clark, 1992, p. 8).

James A. Banks (1997) also reminds us that "An individual's identity with his or her ethnic group varies significantly with the times in his or her life, with economic and social status, and with the situations and/or setting." This statement should guide us as we work with families to focus on who they are right now; and that, in turn, will help us focus on children's needs and interests. Trawick-Smith (1997) states, "Only through a full understanding of parental beliefs, socialization practices, and family relationships can teachers meet the unique needs of individual children."

Economic Differences in Families

In the contemporary United States, children and families have vastly different experiences related to income and other resources. The Children's Defense Fund has reported that in 1998, 22.7 percent of children under age six in the United States lived in

Consider each of the six concepts for understanding culture. Share an example of a behavior or expectation in your culture that relates to each concept. Reflect about how your actions or thoughts may be culturally based.

African-Americans

Parenting: Discipline often appears to be severe and punitive. Many parents emphasize high achievement and a strong work ethic. Boys and girls are socialized similarly, with emphasis on adaptive coping ability and emotional strength necessary for dealing with hostile environments (McDade, 1995).

Education: Traditional educational strategies may not meet the needs of some children in this culture. Research suggests that some males are particularly not well-served through the feminine orientation of most elementary classrooms (Hale, 1986). Many African-American parents emphasize education as the way to greater economic success.

Asian-Americans/Pacific Islander Americans

Parenting: Typically, children are encouraged to be independent and to respect authority. It is expected that they will be unquestionably obedient to their parents and often, they are expected to put the needs of their parents before their own. Parents desire children to be emotionally controlled, self-disciplined, and logical thinkers (McDade, 1995).

Education: These families typically emphasize education and high levels of achievement in their children (Hamner & Turner, 1996). The emphasis on the value of conformity may help children to adapt to expectations in U.S. schools.

Hispanic/Latino

Parenting: The family may take precedence over individuals and the expectation is for the family to be self-reliant. However, individual achievement or responsibility is not valued in some families, but social skills are given a high priority.

Education: Hispanics as a group are increasing their educational achievement. Mexican-Americans are less likely to complete high school, however, than other Hispanic populations, with 56 percent of Mexican-Americans having less than a high school education (Hamner & Turner, 1996).

Native Americans

Parenting: Although there are differences by tribe, some common values are found related to parenting. Children are generally valued by adults, and this is shown in their inclusion in all social events as well as in very gentle styles of discipline. Important characteristics to foster in children include loyalty, humility, respect for elders, reticence, and diminished emphasis on personal gain and private ownership (McDade, 1995).

Education: Few Anglo teachers seem to understand tribal culture, and often, Native American children and families see a lack of cultural relevance in schools. Because silence is valued in tribes, children are comfortable with not answering questions in class, especially avoiding the risk of an incorrect answer and taunting by classmates. There is some movement to have education under tribal control (Hamner & Turner, 1996).

Figure 2–1   Variations in parenting and educational values. These descriptions are based on evidence from research and are not necessarily indicative of individual families. For further reading and understanding of the research see *Early Childhood Development: A Multicultural Perspective* by Jeffrey Trawick-Smith and *Teaching Strategies for Ethnic Studies* by James A. Banks.

poverty. For various ethnic groups, this proportion is even higher (Figure 2–2).

In 1996, federal legislation was passed that included time limits for which adults could receive aid. Under the Temporary Assistance for Needy Families (TANF), parents must go to work after receiving welfare for a maximum of two years, and families are limited to a lifetime total of five years' cash assistance. States may exempt up to 20 percent of their cases from the five-year limit. Because this legislation gave states the responsibility of implementing the mandates, a variety of designs has been put into place. Marian Wright Edelman, head of the Children's Defense Fund, notes that Minnesota stands out because it has "made it a goal to move families with children not just off welfare but out of poverty" (CDF Reports, 1997, p. 3). Further, Edelman writes, "There is no mystery about how to help families off welfare

Percent of Children Living in Poverty	
White	13.0
Black	30.9
Hispanic	28.0
Asian/Pacific Islander	14.5
In families headed by single women	39.8
In working families	77.6

Poor Children Defy the Stereotypes
7.3 million are white
3.5 million are Black
3.3 million are Hispanic

Figure 2–2 Rates of child poverty.
Source: Children's Defense Fund

and out of poverty. States must provide the education, training, and work experience that parents need to compete for jobs with decent wages. States also need to remove the obstacles that often prevent parents from leaving welfare for work: lack of health care, transportation and child care" (p. 3).

Early childhood teachers often take on the role of advocating for children and families with young children. Advocates understand that families must be able to earn a living wage; have access to health care; have reliable transportation; and have access to affordable, quality care for their children during the hours that they are required to work.

Frequently, educators' understanding of diversity does not include differences by family income or the traditional term, social class. Yet financial re-sources have a tremendous impact on families, their practices, and their values. All parents are aware that poverty is a threat to children. Families living with scarce resources have had to learn the importance of meeting children's most basic needs.

Cheal (1996) notes that as a society, we have several reasons for concern about families and their risk for poverty. He highlights three reasons:

1. The risk of poverty is highest in early childhood.

2. Families with children do not reap enough benefits from government redistribution of income.

3. Current political views about the role of government do not allow for assisting poor families in meaningful ways.

Even after President Johnson's "War on Poverty" in the 1960s, into the 1980s and 1990s, young children continued to have the highest risk of living in poverty. This has been especially true for those children living in families headed by women. The economic picture for these families remains bleak. Even when women are employed, they typically do not make enough money to provide reliable transportation to their jobs, pay for high-quality child care for their children, and maintain a safe and healthy home environment. "The risk of poverty among women has often depended heavily on the nature of their relationships with men"

The U.S. Census Bureau (2000) reported that the poverty line for a family of three was below $13,290 per year in 1999, or less than $1,108 per month. Investigate costs in your locality for housing, food, health care, transportation, and other necessities. Comment on your findings.

Children's Defense Fund
http://wwwchildrensdefense.org
National Center for Children in Poverty
http://cpmcnet.columbia.edu/dept/nccp/
National Center for Policy Analysis: Welfare
http://www.ncpa.org/iss/wel/
University Research on Families
http://www.childwelfare.com/kids/ university_research.htm
U.S. Census Bureau—Poverty
http://www.census.gov/hhes/www/ poverty. html

(Cheal, 1996, p. 55). Further, traditional gender roles have been discarded for these single mothers. Often, mothers have not been expected to be employed, but rather it has been socially desirable for them to stay home and raise their children. This belief is no longer held in regard to women on welfare (Cheal, 1996).

The American dream for modern times included the notion that children should not have to rely on "the luck of the draw;" that is, their happiness and productivity should not rely simply on being born into one economic level of family versus another one. With this view came the political notion that government would make an attempt to redistribute societal resources so that all children might benefit. However, from 1978 to 1987, government expenditures on children decreased by 4 percent while those for the elderly increased by 52 percent (Danziger & Weinberg as cited in Cheal, 1996). Public school was one way of attempting to even out children's lives. The notion that all children would have equal access to good, effective education was one way of equalizing the chances for poor children (Cheal, 1996). One issue that faces education today involves seeking strategies for parity to those school districts having fewer resources.

The predominant political view about poor families is that they must be moved from welfare to work, and for the most part, they must do it on their own. Individual responsibility is valued and expected. However, in the 1930s, at the time of the Great Depression, it was understood that poverty was not the result of individual failings, but rather the economic structure of society played a very large part in family financial losses. Few policy makers today are willing to include societal explanations or responsibilities in their views on the poor (Cheal, 1996). Some child and family advocates believe that these political views contain hints of both racism and sexism. Because many poor families are composed of women and children, and because a huge majority of policy makers are white and male, this is a very real possibility. In his extensive analysis about systemic causes of poverty, David Cheal (1996) notes that "the poverty of children is not accidental. It is the fixed position of children in a carefully graded system, in which the youngest children have the highest risk of poverty" (p. 182). He is correct when he refers to this planned system as "perverse."

Early childhood professionals often criticize families for lack of interest in their children's education or a reluctance to volunteer in the education program. A complete understanding or appreciation of the minute-to-minute stresses of families living in poverty may not be possible. However, an effort by the teacher to accept each family must be visible. Further, early childhood educators must support all families at the place they are. Wishing away family stress caused by a lack of resources does not work. Helping to meet their pressing needs is the first step to forming partnerships with some families. Sometimes, teachers of young children feel frustration when families do not send money or notes back to school as the teacher requested. Rather than assuming that the parents or responsible family members are apathetic or hostile, it is helpful to keep in mind that the family may be dealing with other needs that were more pressing such as keeping the heat turned on or a medical appointment. In such instances, teachers must call on their own compassion and understanding. Use of gentle reminders and a call of concern will be much more fruitful than accusations.

Many studies have shown that economic hardship puts many children at very high risk in the United States. Negative outcomes for children include difficult peer relationships, school problems, and low self-esteem (Bolger, Patterson, & Thompson, 1995; Brooks-Gunn, Klebanov, & Duncan, 1996). The stress of poverty makes parenting more difficult. The threat of violence in immediate neighborhoods is increasing in some communities. Involvement in children's lives seems to be impossible for some parents living in such desperate circumstances.

Families who live in poverty are often called on to pool their resources throughout their extended families and neighborhoods. Their very survival may depend on sharing child care arrangements and meals as well as lending money. Addresses may change frequently as families move in with others, and when finances get a little better, attempt to move out on their own. In this need for mutual support, some rely on friendship networks as much as on extended family (Zinn & Eitzen, 1987).

Prejudice against families who receive "welfare" abounds. "For most Americans, the words *welfare recipient* evoke the image of a good-for-nothing freeloader who drives a Cadillac, uses food stamps to buy sirloin steak, or watches soap operas all day. It is a classic icon of American culture, routinely projected upon all who are receiving public assistance" (Rank, 1994, p. 2). In an effort to describe the lives of welfare recipients, including their strengths and their problems, Rank's research includes information from interviews with people about their lives. What he found is, ". . . like most families, the parents in my sample want what is best for their children. Their frustration comes from not being able to provide it" (p. 70).

Planning for the future is not something that poor families can easily do, whether the reference is to the immediate future, or months or years from now. Unplanned or unexpected events such as illness, unreliable transportation, or requests from children's school for field trip money often have a serious consequence on a family's financial plans.

Working-class families often rely heavily on extended family. Siblings, parents, aunts, uncles, and cousins make up the primary social network in working-class families (Zinn & Eitzen, 1987). When adults in these families have economic stability, their lifestyles may appear much more like the middle class; however, when jobs are not stable, these families teeter on the brink of poverty. Many of these families are one or two paychecks away from the welfare rolls. A married mother of two children relates her feelings about applying for welfare.

We felt like it was a shameful thing to be doing, basically. And I remember when the in-take worker was going over our form and wanted to know what our income had been for the previous month, and we said, it was something like two hundred and fifty dollars. And she looked at us and she said, "Uhh, this can't be right, you couldn't live on this." And we said, "That's right, that's why we're here!" (Laughter.) I think we felt grateful that it was there. But it was a real blow to our pride. We had all kinds of . . . I mean . . . the way the public generally views welfare people, we had a lot of those same views.

And it was really a hard thing for our pride to put ourselves in that position, and join that category of people (Rank, 1994, p. 40)

People in the working class who are most likely to be affected by poverty are adults of childbearing age (25 to 44 years), the elderly (65 years and over), and children, especially under one year of age. The following percentages relate the likelihood that various age groups in the working class are living in poverty (Cheal, 1996):

Children, under 1 year	*53%*
Children, 1–4 years	*50%*
Elderly, 65+ years	*48%*
Adults, 25–44 years	*29%*
Young adults, 15–24 years	*24%*
Middle-aged adults, 45–64 years	*21%*

On the other end of the spectrum, affluent, professional, or middle-class families with young children may supply children with basic needs and amenities. But these families, too, may fall prey to situations that may be harmful to their young children. From concern for their progeny's success, parents may get caught up in the "superkid syndrome." David Elkind (1987) has written about "the hurried child" and those who are "miseducated." "Parents today believe that they can make a difference in their children's lives, that they can give them an edge that will make them brighter and abler than the competition" (p. xiii). Families with this goal for children pose another kind of challenge to early childhood teachers who try to plan for a developmentally appropriate educational experience for children, but are often confronted with parental requests to move their child up a grade or place them in accelerated groups.

Gender Role Identity

An individual's **gender role** is "a set of expectations that prescribe how females or males should think, act, and feel" (Santrock, 1994). People's understanding of themselves as male or female, and what that means in their particular environment, is influenced by biological, social, and cognitive factors. Within any given family, the roles specified for males and females may be rigid or fluid. Families with rigid stereotypes are likely to view males as independent, aggressive, and power-oriented, whereas females are seen as dependent, nurturant, and uninterested in power. Research regarding the interaction of ethnicity and gender on traditional gender roles has shown that expectations for males and females vary according to ethnicity (McGoldrick, 1989).

In the pluralistic culture of the United States, many variations on gender roles exist. A feminist perspective on gender indicates that women and girls are competent in their own right. This conflicts with the traditional view of female existence as important only in relation to males.

Because early childhood teachers work with both female and male family members, it will be important that the teacher is aware of his own views about gender roles. It may be a challenge to accept and support the role, whether it be traditional or feminist, that a particular parent has taken. For example, how would you react to the following situations, noting your own biases and preferences?

- In Suzanne's (age four years) family, Mr. Jaworski stays home with Suzanne and her younger brother, Tucker. Suzanne's mother, Dr. Stoner, who kept her maiden name, has a very successful career and travels on business at least six times a year.

- In Peter's (age seven years) family, Mrs. Jordan is a full-time homemaker. Peter and his two older brothers are enrolled in the elementary school in which you teach. Mr. Jordan has been in danger of losing his job because of cutbacks in his corporation.

- Debra's (age two-and-a-half years) mother, Ms. Meyer is employed as an administrative staff member on a local university campus. She has insisted that you not call her "Mrs. Meyer." Debra and her mother live with Ms. Kennedy who works on the grounds crew at the same campus.

Mother-headed families often have very different needs than father-headed, single-parent families. First of all, there are many more of them in existence. It is estimated that as many as one-half of all children will spend some of their childhood years in a family headed by a single woman (Garfinkel & McLanahan, 1989). Single-parent families headed by women are much more likely to be poor than are those headed by men. Reasons for the poverty include little or no support from fathers, limited earning capacity of mothers, and the difficulties that come with trying to juggle the roles of sole breadwinner and sole caregiver (Burns & Scott, 1994).

As social and economic climates change, women have been increasingly able to get reasonable employment. But comparisons with a number of

> "Women have always played a central role in families, but the idea that they have a life cycle apart from their roles as wife and mother is a relatively recent one, and still is not widely accepted in our culture. The expectation for women has been that they would take care of the needs of others: first men, then children, then the elderly. Until very recently, 'human development' referred to male development and women's development was defined by the men in their lives. They went from being daughter, to wife, to mother, with their status defined by the male in the relationship . . ."
>
> —Monica McGoldrick (1989)

Gender Development
http://www.psy.pdx.edu/PsiCafe/Areas/Developmetal/GenderDev/
Sexual Orientation and Gender Identity
http://www.aclu.org/issues/gay/GLSEN.html

other countries, most notably Sweden, show that in addition to access to employment that pays a living wage, mothers must also have access to affordable, highquality child care as well as other family support services, and must be able to collect child support from the noncustodial parent (Burns & Scott, 1994). One mother who attempted to leave public assistance noted how crucial good child care is:

> *Well, I had two little bitty babies. And I was working at the time I got pregnant. So I tried going back to work when Stacy was about, say, two months old. And the lady that I got to baby-sit for me just didn't come up to par for me. And with me having the two babies, one was just walking and one was an arm baby, I made the decision that it's best for me to try to be here with them. And I know they were taken care of like I would have wanted them to be taken care of. So that's when I applied for aid (Rank, 1994, p. 42).*

Many educators have concerns about children of lesbian families. However, existing literature gives no support that these children are worse off than other children (Burns & Scott, 1994). The common view that children will suffer from the lack of a father is not substantiated when children have relationships with multiple adults who have somewhat of a parenting role: friends, grandparents, and/or biological father. When lesbian mothers have social, economic, and personal resources, "chosen, father-free parenthood" can meet children's needs (McGuire & Alexander, 1985). Further, comparisons of characteristics of lesbian mothers with women in general show the following for lesbian mothers (Figure 2–3 provides additional commentary):

- higher levels of education and professional training
- scored as more normal on psychological tests
- had more support and practical help from cohabiting partners than wives receive from husbands
- mother-child relationships were closer
- cognitive and social competence was normal or high

- sex role behavior was normal
- daughters chose more prestigious/masculine careers
- daughters reported higher popularity (McGuire & Alexander, 1985)

Concern about lack of father involvement in families or specifically with their very young children does not exist only when fathers are living out of the home. A British study by Jane Ribbens (1994) shows that contemporary child-rearing remains in the domain of women:

> *. . . issues of childcare, presumptions about the needs of children, and decision-making about how to deal with and relate to children are major preoccupations in women's everyday lives. Furthermore, a consideration of how women perceive, understand and resolve some of these issues around childrearing is essential to any analysis of gender relationships, divisions of labour and distributions of resources within households. (p. 29)*

Further, Ribbens notes that it is generally the responsibility of the mother to create "the family." In this task, two processes are involved: (1) work on internal cohesion, making certain that the family members form a meaningful unit; and (2) work on external boundaries, making certain that there are clear separations of the family from other social units.

> *Within the apparently "conventional" families in my own study, images of family togetherness did not always correspond to how things worked out in everyday interactions. While the women living with their husbands were quick to tell me their good qualities as fathers, in the details of their accounts strains could also become apparent in constructing "the family" with an involved father. Much of the care of pre-school children occurs in women's worlds, either within or outside the home, and men are marginal to these worlds (Ribbens, 1994, p. 64).*

After analyzing the information provided by the mothers in her study, Ribbens goes on to say that much of the mother-child time together did not

Family Pride Coalition
Mother's Day Guest Commentary
by C. Ray Drew and Kate Kendell

Until just recently, the existence of lesbian and gay parents went almost unrecognized in our culture. Much of our society simply believed that being a gay or lesbian parent was a contradiction in terms, and numerous negative myths promulgated that position. Heterosexist laws denied the possibility of parenting for openly gay/lesbian people, and penalized anyone with children from a prior heterosexual relationship with loss of visitation or custody.

The last ten years have changed this landscape dramatically. We now find ourselves in the middle of a "gayby boom" as countless thousands of lesbians and gay men choose to become parents. We have countered the Radical Right's argument that a family consists only of a heterosexual father, mother and children, with our community's family values of love, diversity, respect, caring and pride. We have proudly stated to the world that "love makes a family."

But is love enough? What happens when the "love" between a lesbian couple fades or sours? In recent years we have experienced a threat to our community's families as alarming as the Radical Right's hate campaign. In surging numbers, we have seen an insidious increase in the number of custody battles within the community involving lesbian couples, as biological mothers deny visitation to their former partners.

No one is at their best when a couple splits up. It is a time of serious emotional crisis. It is a time when it is easy to rationalize that a former partner's behavior is a reflection of a poor parenting bond with the child. Friends and family may feel protective and support the biological mom in her dismissal of her former partner. In the absence of laws to the contrary, it is tempting to redraw the family construction around heterosexist laws, take the child and cut the partner out of the family picture forever.

But can we use the heterosexist, anti-gay laws to assure that a former partner is denied the right to see her child and simultaneously demand that others recognize our family commitments? While together, a couple may have lamented the fact that their family was discriminated against by IRS laws, insurance regulations, social security policies and numerous laws that denied the legal recognition of their family. Sadly, after dissolution of the relationship, the biological mother can use those very laws to deny that the other parent was EVER a "real" parent.

In the legal world of non-gay married couples, an elaborate court system is ready to decide custody and visitation issues when the parents cannot do so. Even if one parent was only marginally involved the court nevertheless recognizes their status as parent. In the absence of identified harm to the child, even the less involved or marginal parent is granted some visitation. The community and court standards reflect the parental rights and obligations of both parents.

When a lesbian couple breaks up, without a legally sanctioned relationship or legal recognition of their family, who decides what is in a child's best interests? Couples, who had a clear, unambiguous agreement that they would be equal parents to this child, suddenly become very unequal in the face of divorce. The biological mother has absolute power in these cases to determine the fate of the child and the privileges of the non-biological mother. In case after case, the biological mother has denied that her former partner is even a parent. Some courts have agreed, denying the non-biological mother's right to her day in court to seek any legal redress, much less be granted visitation with her child.

Are legal protections important? Of course they are. We need the protection for our families that legally sanctioned marriage provides. We need the protection of second-parent adoptions in the absence of marriage.

But more important than these legal protections we need to honor our agreements and our intentions with one another. Family is a social construction as much as a legal entity. If we are to truly have permanent parental and family relationships, we need a social ethic that says they are permanent. We need a consistent community value, which says that a commitment to parenting is lifelong. If we want our children to grow up secure in who they are and who their family is, they need to see a community with a strong sense of family, a community that maintains that standard even when couples break up.

Does love make a family? You bet. And when love doesn't last forever, the "family" still does. It is our commitment that will signal to society and our children just how seriously we take our own families.

Kate Kendell is the Executive Director of the National Center for Lesbian Rights, a legal resource and advocacy public interest law firm. C. Ray Drew is the Executive Director of the Family Pride Coalition International, an international LGBT family advocacy organization. Kendell can be contacted at NCLRsf@aol.com and Drew can be contacted at GLPCI@GLPCI.org.

Figure 2–3 Commentary of lesbian and gay parenting. (With permission from C. Ray Drew and Kate Kendell. Mother's day guest commentary [On-line].)

occur within families at all, but rather in variations of networks of other women and their children. This finding brings the researcher to the conclusion that observational studies are needed of mothers and their young children as they participate in "semipublic" settings such as play groups.

Within families, fathers play very different roles from mothers. It is only since the mid-1970s that much attention has been given to research on fathering. Contemporary society sees fathers essentially in two ways: either as increasing their involvement with their children, or as absent with little emotional or financial responsibility for their children. Furstenberg (1988) refers to this as the "two faces of fatherhood." Early childhood teachers may observe these vast differences in fathers of children in their care. Sometimes, fathers are so removed that children have not met them or barely know them. Adults are often under the mistaken assumption, then, that the children's closeness to another adult male, grandfather or uncle, simply replaces their relationship with fathers.

Erna Furman (1992) writes about young children who have been "deeply affected by the loss of their father through death or family breakup" (p. 36). She notes that even though the loss of a father may cause long-term hardship, those children who never had relationships with their fathers should also be our concern. She tells of two such children. Felicity, at three-and-a-half years, had never met her father. Her mother never talked about him and was certain that Felicity at this young age did not even think about her father. Felicity's behaviors such as thumb-sucking and unceasing demands, however, were determined by a therapist to be related to her desire to know her father. With this information, Felicity's mother tried to prepare her for possible disappointment and contacted her father to let him know of their daughter's wishes. In this case, the father responded and came to spend some time with his daughter. Even though their contact was sporadic, the trust between mother and daughter was seen as a very positive outcome in this situation.

In a second scenario, Ben had not met his father. When his toddler class was planning visits by their fathers, his mother asked the teacher if Ben's

beloved grandfather might come with him instead. When the teacher suggested that mom ask Ben his opinion, mom was surprised. And when she asked Ben, she was surprised again. Ben initially refused to have his grandfather go to school with him. Because he had never mentioned his absent father, Ben's mother assumed that meant he never thought about who his father might be. Once it was revealed that Ben did have questions about his own dad, his mother was able to explain that he lived far away and could not visit. Ben, then, was willing to have grandfather accompany him to school.

So many teachers assume that because it is now common for children to live in homes without their fathers, that children accept it or do not even notice it. Furman (1992) points out that when teachers observe carefully, they report situations with children that contradict this viewpoint. She says "there are no easy answers to these human dilemmas, but respecting our children's thoughts and feelings has much to do with respecting ourselves and with building a

Fathers can be competent caregivers of children.

community in which we all learn to respect one another. Respect, like charity, begins at home" (p. 37).

In his review of the research literature related to fathers and families, Parke (1995) notes that a great deal of research supports the fact that fathers spend less time with their children than do mothers. This is true from infancy through adolescence. Other consistent findings from research are that fathers are competent caregivers of their children when they need to be, and fathers interact in qualitatively different ways with children than do mothers. Whereas mothers are more verbal and directed and use toys in their interactions, fathers are more physical and tactile with children. It seems reasonable to believe that both styles of interaction will stimulate children and that children will benefit from such differences.

What is it that determines how involved fathers are in their children's lives? A variety of factors have been shown to contribute to any given father's interaction with his children. Parke (1995) uses empirical data to demonstrate that the following considerations are related to father involvement. It is evident that father involvement is based on a complex system of in-home and out-of-home variations.

- *Fathers' relationships with their own parents.* Those men who had positive interactions with their own fathers may model those with their children. However, there is also some evidence that men who view their relationships with their fathers as negative sometimes make an effort with their own children to increase positive feelings and interactions.

- *Fathers' belief systems about the roles of mothers and fathers.* Some men have more stereotypic ideas about what each parent should do with chil-

dren. Others are more willing to be flexible in meeting their children's needs.

- *Attitudes of the mother.* Some mothers believe that they are the more important and competent parent, and restrict father involvement in various ways. As more mothers enter the workforce full time, they may be more willing to encourage a greater level of father involvement with their children.

- *Marital relationships.* When mothers provide support to fathers in their caregiving roles, fathers gain competence and confidence in relating to their children.

- *Timing of fatherhood.* Males who become fathers when they are adolescents tend not to be highly involved in their children's lives. Sometimes, these fathers rarely even visit their children. Men who become fathers later in their lives often appreciate their children more and have greater self-confidence in their parenting. On the other hand, men who became fathers "on time" were more likely than older fathers to be physical with their children.

- *Family employment patterns.* Fathers typically spend a greater amount of time with their children when mothers are employed outside the home. It also may be that the quality of father-child relationships changes when mothers are employed outside the home.

- *Work quality.* Difficult or stressful work conditions may cause fathers to be more disengaged with their children when they are at home. It is also believed that positive workplaces can enhance the quality of the father-child relationship.

Those who advocate for higher levels of father involvement do so in part because they believe there will be positive outcomes for children. Parke (1995) also discusses the research related to this area of interest. Following are some of the findings related to children whose fathers do not live with them:

- little effect of father contact on well-being of children 11 to 16 years

- no relation between father contact and children's social and cognitive development for children five to nine years

Dads and Daughters
**http://www.dadsanddaughers.org/Research/
Fathering/NFIFacts.htm**
Family Support and Father Involvement
http://npin.org/library/pre1998/noo288.html

These findings are somewhat surprising in light of the emphasis on father involvement in children's lives. One explanation, however, is that father presence during the first three years may be the most important time. Several studies seem to support this point of view. Further, quality of interaction seems to be important to father-child relationships, not just quantity of time spent together.

One way that quality has been observed is related to fathers' physical play and positive affect with their children. Young children whose fathers exhibit these two characteristics have been found to be more popular and have a higher degree of social acceptance from other children (Parke, 1995).

As with mothers, individuals in our society typically assume that all fathers are heterosexual. This is obviously not true. It is difficult to obtain a count of the number of gay fathers in the United States today. The primary reason for this is that the prejudice and discrimination against these fathers threaten their relationships with their children. It is believed that the largest group of children of gay fathers today are those who were born in heterosexual relationships of their biological parents before one or the other parent had identified themselves as lesbian or gay. It is common that gay fathers do not have custody of their children nor do they often live in the same home as their children. There remains a great deal of bias in the legal system against gay fathers getting custody of their children. At times, they may even be denied visitation rights based on the notion that they are negative influences on their children (Patterson, 1995).

Research on gay fathers is sparse. Patterson (1995), in her review of the literature on gay fathers, notes that they report differences in their parenting in comparison to heterosexual fathers. Gay fathers reported both greater warmth and responsiveness to their children, and more limit-setting. Some attention has been given to comparisons between gay fathers and gay men who are not fathers. These fathers reported higher levels of self-esteem and fewer negative attitudes about homosexuality than did the nonfathers.

One of the concerns that is sometimes stated—and sometimes not—is whether the sexual identity of gay fathers' children will be affected. At this time,

there is no research evidence to support the notion that children of gay fathers will necessarily be homosexual in their orientation (Patterson, 1995).

As early childhood educators, our greatest concern for children from gay or lesbian families may be for their psychological and physical safety. However, this concern is not created within the family, but rather from the bigotry and hate that these families may receive from society.

Families and Religiosity

Due in part to the legal aspects of the separation of church and state, much of education has been silenced about religion. But ignoring the understanding of the importance of religiosity in families is as erroneous as ignoring culture or economic status. It is true that some teachers and schools place religion within a family's culture, but because there has been so little attention given to family and individual differences related to religion in education, the authors have chosen to accent it in this chapter.

Religiosity refers to the amount of emphasis religion has in families. With differences in various religious practices, it is not always evident to early childhood professionals just how religious a family is or is not. Some families may discuss their religion with teachers due to specific classroom practices such as holiday celebrations. Others may have unexpressed concerns and still others may have no need to be open with their child's teacher about their religious views.

Black churches have historically provided a great deal of family support. Because members of these churches were often denied access to other forms of family support in the United States, church members intervened to assist with survival. Caldwell, Greene, and Billingsley (1994) note that black churches have had a social service role since their inception in the late 1700s. During the civil

---

Religiosity
http://www.wikipedia.com/wiki/religion

rights movement of the 1960s, black churches took on a political activist role. In the 1980s, when drastic cuts were made in public funding for social programs, these churches once again reached out to their communities to provide support to families. It is believed that family and church are "strong interactive institutions that are mutually enhancing in their influence on African American communities" (p. 142). Further, "Black churches are mediators that buffer and enhance the relationship between

the family's informal social network and the larger formal societal network" (p. 143). One aspect of this "larger formal societal network" is the educational institution.

Janice Hale (1986), a scholar in the area of African-American child development, speaks about the differences in black churches and Anglo churches. She notes that from very early ages, African-American children are active during church services. The expectation is not to sit still and quiet

---

Forget the home-run race. Litigation has now surpassed baseball as America's favorite national pastime.

The latest example of how quick we are to "call a lawyer" comes from Ohio, where a school district may face a lawsuit for closing school on Rosh Hashana and Yom Kippur (Sept. 21. and Sept. 30 respectively).

School officials argue that absenteeism is too high on those days to hold classes in any meaningful way. Some 15% of the students in the district are Jewish and most of them stay home or attend synagogue for two of Judaism's most significant holy days. In some schools, absences ran as high as 21%.

A group of parents—with the ironic name of Parents for Fairness—objects, claiming that closing the schools these two days would favor the Jewish faith over other faiths in violation of the First Amendment.

Who's right?

It's true that the First Amendment's establishment clause requires that public school officials be neutral among religions and between religion and nonreligion. The school board can't close the schools on Jewish holy days because it wants to favor Judaism

But school officials have a good civic (or secular) purpose for their action: Too many students would be absent those days to conduct a normal school day. The closings are meant to serve the educational needs of all the students, not to advance a particular religion. Just because the policy also benefits Jewish kids doesn't make it unconstitutional.

It would be different if the district had a much smaller Jewish population. In that case, the best approach would be to allow Jewish students to be excused for services and require them to make up the missed work.

Beyond the legal issues, Parents for Fairness might want to think more about what they mean by "fairness." After all, the school calendar already favors the majority faith since no classes are held on Sunday and Christmas is a national holiday. Most Christians don't need to worry about the school schedule.

By contrast, minority faiths have to work around the existing calendar. Jews who observe the Sabbath have a problem participating in Friday night ball games and Saturday activities. Muslim students who wish to attend community prayer mid-day on Fridays sometimes have a hard time getting released from school.

This built-in advantage should be all the more reason for school officials to be sensitive to the religious needs of students from minority faiths. Of course, that rarely means closing school. But it does mean finding ways to accommodate requests where possible.

Rosh Hashana, by the way, is the Jewish New Year, a time of celebration but also of judgment. According to Jewish tradition, during the 10 days following Rosh Hashana, God examines the deeds of the people. For Jews, this is a time of profound self-examination and repentance.

At the end of this period, on Yom Kippur—the Day of Atonement—God makes a final judgment and forgives those who have truly repented. Many Jews fast for 25 hours and spend much of the day in the synagogue, praying for forgiveness.

Repentance, judgment, forgiveness. Nowadays a little time off for these things seems like a very good idea.

Figure 2–4   All faiths should be fairly treated in schools. (With permission from Charles C. Haynes, Senior Scholar, Freedom Forum First Amendment Center. *Public Opinion*, Chambersburg, PA, September 1998)

as so often happens in Anglo churches. Imagine the shock when these children come to school where they are inappropriately expected to be still and quiet!

Variations in religious beliefs and practices must be respected, just as teachers respect differences in culture, ethnicity, gender, and abilities. One source that helps to explain the differences is *How to Be a Perfect Stranger: A Guide to Etiquette in Other People's Religious Ceremonies* (Magida, 1996). Knowledge about these differences is often the first step to understanding. (Figure 2–4 provides additional commentary.)

A few years ago, Marian Wright Edelman voiced a call to all communities of faith to "Stand for Children." On June 1, 1996, more than 300,000 child advocates attended a rally at the Lincoln Memorial in Washington, DC. Since that time, June 1 continues to be a day to "Stand for Children." Many religious communities use materials provided by this division of the Children's Defense Fund.

Geographic Region

Some individuals have tried very hard to identify what it means to be an American family. Perhaps those who have relocated to other geographic regions can understand best some of the differences that exist in families, even of similar ethnicity, culture, economic class, and religiosity. Regional differences even affect expectations by gender (Figure 2–5).

Family poverty rates for the nine Census geographic divisions for 1994 demonstrate regional differences (Triest, 1997). The highest rate was 15.8 percent in the west south central region. Others above the national average of 11.6 percent include

east south central, California, and New York. The lowest family poverty rate was in New England—8.2 percent—with north central, middle Atlantic, south Atlantic, mountain, and Pacific below the national average.

Various stereotypes exist about people from different regions of the United States. Terms such as "salty New Englander," "southern belle" and "southern gentleman," "hillbilly," "farmer's daughter," and so on reflect images held by many living in other parts of the country. As with other stereotypes, a small part of the image may be based on reality, but the picture is far too narrow and limits our real understanding of differences in people. The differences we experience from one region to the next are based on many factors including climate, terrain, proximity to waterways, economy, industry, and history.

Sometimes, differences in dialect, slang, or variations in manners will lead to degrading others. Understanding expectations from various regional

Consider some of the notions you have about the people from one or two of the following regions: northeast, southeast, midwest, southwest, northwest, and Pacific. On what are your ideas based? What experiences have you had with people from regions other than your own?

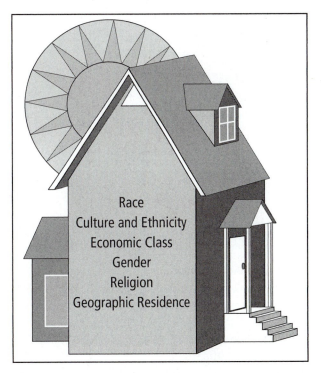

Figure 2–5 All of these pieces interact for individuality.

Race
Culture and Ethnicity
Economic Class
Gender
Religion
Geographic Residence

groups can help in having positive interactions with them. One child moved from the northeast part of the country to the south. He soon learned that his teachers expected him not to reply with his standard "Yes" or "No" but with "Yes, ma'am" or "No, sir." The child explained that this was difficult for him to learn because typically, when "ma'am" or "sir" was added to his speech in the past, it was not considered good manners, but rather sarcasm. Although teachers can expect respectful interaction from their students, it will be important to understand such regional differences, especially in terms of one's intent.

In examining characteristics of Appalachian mountain families, Klein (1995) noted that connections between generations are critical for these families. Further, spirituality is emphasized over financial success. Because of an emphasis on humility, people of the Appalachians are often viewed as "dull" and lacking self-esteem. After discussing a number of characteristics that set this group apart from others, the author notes that educators must consider not only racial and ethnic differences but also those related to community and cultural heritage.

Alliance for Full Acceptance
http://www.affa-sc.org
Erase the Hate
http://www.usanetwork.com/functions/nhday/
   nohateday.html
Facing History and Ourselves
http://www.facinghistory.org/facing/fha02.nsf
Museum of Tolerance
http://www.wiesenthal.com/mot/
Teaching Tolerance
http://www.Tolerance.org
Tufts University Child and Family Web Guide
http://www.cfw.tufts.edu
50 Multicultural Books Every Child Should Know
http://www.soemadison.wisc.edu/ccbc/
   50mult.htm#repro

Application to Early Childhood Education Programs

Celebrating Diversity

People celebrate for many different reasons. Some people celebrate the same holiday but do it quite differently. Others celebrate completely different holidays. Celebrations and rituals are an important part of the human experience. One way to share about differences in the way we celebrate is to have families come to early childhood programs to share their particular ways of celebrating. In an effort to move to anti-bias approaches, some early childhood educators have done away with all celebrations. This is not necessary and may not even be desirable. Instead, be sensitive to all ways of celebrating and consider creating some celebrations unique to your classroom for special events such as new siblings, lost teeth, and other common developmental occurrences in families with young children (Figures 2–6 and 2–7).

Inclusiveness

The goal for understanding diversity in early childhood education is ultimately to provide an *inclusive* environment, one in which each child and family can feel a sense of belonging, no matter what commonalities or differences they have with others in the group. This is quite a lofty goal, and because of many societal factors, may not be easy to achieve.

As teachers plan for their groups of children, and as they set their classroom rules and policies, checking for **inclusiveness** must be a part of the

"When we make choices about what to celebrate, let us be very conscious of who we are doing it for . . . If we are doing it for the children, let us be conscious of all the subtle messages inherent in what we do and choose things to celebrate that are meaningful, developmentally appropriate, and healthy for them."

—Bonnie Neugebauer, 1990

Various Faiths and Practices
**http://dir.yahoo.com/Society_and_Culture/Reli
gion_and_spirituality/Faiths_and_Practices**
(Atheism, Buddism, Christian, Hindu, Humanism,
Islam, Native American Religions, New Age,
Shinto, Taoism, Wicca, and more)
Eastern Orthodox Church in America
**http://www.oca.org/pages/orth_chri/calen-
dar/index.htm**
Jewish Holidays
http://www.bnaibrith.org/caln.html
Jehovah's Witness
http://www.jwic.com/home_e.htm
Mormon
http://www.lds.org
Scientology
**http://www.foundingchurchdc.org/dc/ref/cree
d/index.htm**

Figure 2–6 Various religious celebrations and
traditions—selected Web sites.

process. Even the most sensitive and knowledgeable
teacher may err in this process; however, the important fact is what teachers do when they realize that
their classrooms are not inclusive. A compassionate,
effective early childhood teacher will collect information, ask for guidance, and make changes so that
the sense of inclusiveness prevails.

Ethical Considerations

Relating Diversity to Developmentally Appropriate Practice (DAP)

The DAP handbook (Bredekamp & Copple, 1997)
includes the two primary components for appropriate practices in forming reciprocal relationships with
families:

- Caregivers form partnerships with parents
  through daily communication, building mutual trust, working to understand parents' pref-

Kwanzaa is celebrated by many African-Americans between December 26 and January 1. It is meant to be a
time of reaffirming for African-American people for
focusing on their ancestors and culture. Traditions
include the following:

Nguzo Saba: 7 guiding principles
Kinara: candleholder for 7 candles
Mkeka: straw or cloth place mat
Vibunzi: ears of corn, one for each child in the
family

One guiding principle is applied to each of the seven
days of celebration:

- Umoja (OO-MO-JAH): Unity of family and
  community
- Kujichagulia (KOO-GEE-CHA-GOO-LEE-YAH):
  Self-determination
- Ujima (OO-GEE-MAH): Collective work and
  responsibility
- Umjamaa (OO-JAH-MAH): Cooperative
  economics
- Nia (NEE-YAH): Purpose (to set personal goals to
  benefit community)
- Kuumba (KOO-OOM-BAH): Creativity
- Imani (EE-MAH-NEE): Faith

Kwanzaa Information Center
http://www.melanet.com/kwanzaa/

Figure 2–7 Kwanzaa.

erences, and respecting cultural and family
differences.

- Members of each child's family are encouraged to be involved in ways in which they feel
  comfortable.

Relating Diversity to Programs for Children with Special Needs.

The mission statement of the Division for Early
Childhood (DEC) of the Council on Exceptional
Children (CEC) includes ". . . promoting policies and
practices that support families . . ." http://www.dec-
sped.org

The DEC goals include:

- respecting families' diverse values, culture, and linguistic background
- promoting parent-professional collaboration

Accreditation Guidelines

Criteria from the accreditation guidelines compiled by the National Academy of Early Childhood Programs (1991) related to family involvement are:

- The goal for staff-parent interaction is that parents are well-informed about and welcome observers and contributors to the program
- The staff will respect cultural diversity
- The staff will include all children in all opportunities, speaking favorably about variations in physical characteristics and cultural heritage (see Appendix B)

The Code of Ethical Conduct for Early Childhood Education includes the following in the category of ethical responsibilities to families:

- to respect the dignity of each family and its culture, customs, and beliefs
- to provide the community with high-quality, culturally sensitive, early childhood programs and services

Early childhood education staff should respect, encourage, and foster cultural diversity in the classroom.

Family Support Principles

The family support principles that are particular to the information in this chapter include the following:

- to promote family health and well-being
- to respond to family cultural preferences and values
- to provide concrete help for real-life problems
- to give information tailored to parental needs

To listen to a father speak about the need for diversity education, go to the on-line resource at www.earlychilded.delmar.com.

This father of four discusses the need for diversity education to support his children's understandings of themselves and of others. He discusses some of the reasons that diversity is important and gives examples of what that might look like in school in this on-line voice.

Summary and Conclusions

Families are different in many ways. It is crucial that early childhood teachers work to increase their understanding of differences in families and interact sensitively with these differences in mind. Lifelong learning is a requirement for teachers in this regard. For as society changes, so will families change.

Celebration of diversity leads to inclusive practices in early childhood education. Teachers' acceptance of differences in families is essential for each child to feel a sense of belonging in early education programs. Welcoming all families is a prerequisite for effective family involvement. Family members who view themselves as very different from teachers and other school personnel are less likely than other families to be involved in their children's education. It is the responsibility of early childhood teachers to foster a climate that encourages various types of family involvement so that all children may reap the benefits known to occur from home and school partnerships.

Key Terms

ethnicity

race

culture

Temporary Assistance for
Needy Families (TANF)

gender role

religiosity

inclusiveness

Chapter Two Applications

1. A primary grade teacher, your colleague, tells you that because she has only one child who does not celebrate Christmas in her classroom and twenty-three who do, that she goes with the majority. For most of December, the class is involved in projects related to Christmas. How do you respond?

2. A mother of one of your kindergarten children tells you that you must not celebrate her son's birthday. Additionally, he may not attend any birthday celebrations because of religious beliefs. What do you do about your tradition to celebrate each child's birthday?

3. When you request photos of each of your preschoolers' families for your bulletin board project, one child brings a picture of herself and two men. The child tells you that this is her with Daddy and Daddy's roommate, Ron, when they were on vacation at the beach. What do you do with the picture?

Questions for Reflection and Discussion

1. Consider the various forms of diversity discussed in this chapter. Discuss your experiences with each type of diversity.

2. Give an example of an experience from your past when you did not feel a sense of belonging or included in the situation. What do you think were the factors related to your feeling excluded?

3. Recall some common celebrations that you have observed in early childhood settings, either when you were a child or more recently. Identify some situations that were not inclusive. What are some ideas that you have for making the celebrations more inclusive?

Field Assignments

1. Interview a Head Start director or family coordinator about the benefits that quality early education has for low-income families.

2. Observe in a child care center, preschool program, kindergarten, or primary grade classroom. Note situations that you feel were examples of a good understanding of diversity in families. Also, note situations that were exclusive for some children or families.

3. Interview a staff member of a religious community. Ask about programs that are offered that support families.

References

Banks, J. A. (1997). *Teaching strategies for ethnic studies* (6th ed.). Needham Heights, MA: Allyn and Bacon.

Bolger, K. E., Patterson, C. J., & Thompson, W. W. (1995). Psychosocial adjustment among children experiencing persistent and intermittent family economic hardship. *Child Development, 66,* 1107–1129.

Bredekamp, S., & Copple, C. (1997). *Developmentally appropriate practice in early childhood programs* (rev. ed.). Washington, DC: National Association for the Education of Young Children.

Bronfenbrenner, U. (1979). *The ecology of human development: Experiments by nature and design.* Cambridge, MA: Harvard University Press.

Brooks-Gunn, J., Klebanov, P. K., & Duncan, G. J. (1996). Ethnic differences in children's intelligence test scores: Role of economic deprivation, home environment, and maternal characteristics. *Child Development, 67,* 396–408.

Burns, A., & Scott, C. (1994). *Mother-headed families and why they have increased.* Hillsdale, NJ: Lawrence Erlbaum Associates.

Caldwell, C. H., Greene, A. D., & Billingsley, A. (1994). Family support programs in black churches: A new look at old functions. In S. L. Kagan & B. Weissbourd (Eds.), *Putting families first: America's family support movement and the challenge of change.* San Francisco: Jossey-Bass.

Cheal, D. (1996). *New poverty: Families in postmodern society.* Westport, CT: Greenwood.

Children's Defense Fund. (2002). Every child deserves a fair start. http://www.childrensdefense.org/fairstart-faqs.htm

Clark, L., DeWolf, S., & Clark, C. (1992). Teaching teachers to avoid having culturally assaultive classrooms. *Young Children, 47*(5), 4–9.

Division for Early Childhood. Mission of DEC. http://www.dec-sped.org

Elkind, D. (1987). *Miseducation: Preschoolers at risk.* New York: Knopf.

Furman, E. (1992, May). Thinking about fathers. *Young Children, 47*(4), 36–37.

Furstenberg, F. F., Jr. (1988). Good dads—bad dads: Two faces of fatherhood. In A. J. Cherlin (Ed.), *The changing American family and public policy* (pp. 193–218). Washington, DC: Urban Institute Press.

Garfinkel, I., & McLanahan, S. (1989). *Single mothers and their children: A new American dilemma.* Washington, DC: Urban Institute Press.

Hale, J. (1986). *Black children: Their roots, culture, and learning styles* (rev. ed.). Baltimore: Johns Hopkins University Press.

Hamner, T. J., & Turner, P. H. (1996). *Parenting in contemporary society.* Needham Heights, MA: Allyn & Bacon.

Howe, L. K. (1972). *The future of the family.* New York: Simon & Schuster.

Klein, H. A. (1995). Urban Appalachian children in northern schools: A study in diversity. *Young Children, 50* (3), 10–16.

Magida, A. (Ed.). (1996). *How to be a perfect stranger: A guide to etiquette in other people's religious ceremonies.* Woodstock, VT: Jewish Lights.

McDade, K. (1995). How we parent: Race and ethnic differences. In C. K. Jacobson (Ed.), *American families: Issues in race and ethnicity.* New York: Garland.

McGoldrick, M. (1989). Ethnicity and the family life cycle. In B. Carter & M. McGoldrick (Eds.), *The changing family life cycle* (2nd ed.). Needham Heights, MA: Allyn & Bacon.

McGuire, M., & Alexander, N. J. (1985). Artificial insemination of single women. *Fertility and Sterility, 43,* 182–184.

Mellman, M., Lazarus, E., & Rivlin, A. (1990). Family time, family values. In D. Blankenhorn, S. Bayme, & B. Elshtain (Eds.), *Rebuilding the nest: A new commitment to the American family.* Milwaukee, WI: Family Service America.

National Academy of Early Childhood Programs. (1991). *Accreditation criteria and procedures.* Washington, DC: National Association for the Education of Young Children.

Neugebauer, B. (1990). Going one step further—No traditional holidays. Child Care *Information Exchange, 74.*

Parke, R. (1995). Fathers and families. In M. H. Bornstein (Ed.), *Handbook of parenting, volume 3: Status and social conditions of parenting* (pp. 27–63). Mahwah, NJ: Erlbaum.

Patterson, C. J. (1995). Lesbian and gay parenthood. In M. H. Bornstein (Ed.), *Handbook of parenting, volume 3: Status and social conditions of parenting* (pp. 255–274). Mahwah, NJ: Erlbaum.

Phillips, C. B. (1995). Culture: A process that empowers. In P. L. Mangione (Ed.), *Infant/toddler caregiving: A guide to culturally sensitive care* (pp. 2–9). Sacramento, CA: California Department of Education.

Rank, M. R. (1994). *Living on the edge: The realities of welfare in America.* New York: Columbia University Press.

Ribbens, J. (1994). *Mothers and their children: A feminist sociology of childrearing.* Thousand Oaks, CA: Sage.

Santrock, J. W. (1994). *Child development.* Madison, WI: Brown & Benchmark.

Stauss, J. H. (1995). Reframing and refocusing American Indian family strengths. In C. K. Jacobson (Ed.), *American families: Issues in race and ethnicity.* New York: Garland.

Trawick-Smith, J. (1997). *Early childhood development.* Upper Saddle River, NJ: Merill-Prentice Hall.

Triest, R. K. (1997, January-February). Regional differences in family poverty. New England *Economic Review,* 3–18.

Wardle, F. (1987). Are you sensitive to interracial children's special identity needs? *Young Children,* 42 (2), 53–59.

Zinn, M. B., & Eitzen, D. S. (1987). *Diversity in American families.* New York: Harper & Row.

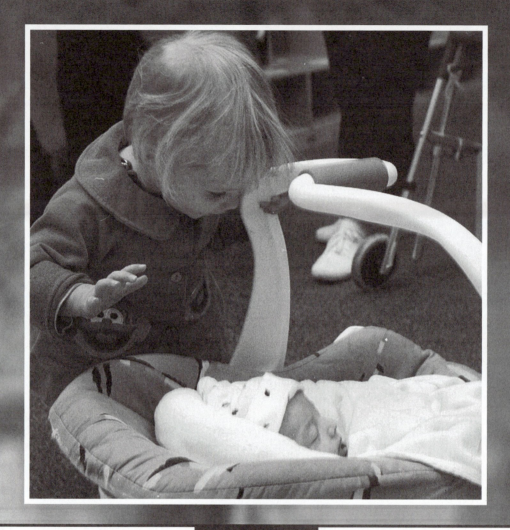

OUTLINE

Developmental Issues in Families with Young Children

Theoretical Foundation

Bioecological Theory

According to Bronfenbrenner's (1990) bioecological theory, the family environment provided for young children has a powerful effect on them. Proposition I of this theory states the importance of "reciprocal activity, on a regular basis over an extended period in the child's life, with one or more persons with whom the child develops a strong, mutual, irrational, emotional attachment, and who is committed to the child's well-being and development, preferably for life" (p. 29). Proposition II emphasizes that "the informal education that takes place in the family is . . . a powerful prerequisite for success in formal education from the primary grades onward" (p. 33). But more than this is needed for the optimal development of children.

The child and caregiver "depend in substantial degree on the availability and involvement of another adult, a third party who assists, encourages, spells off, gives status to, and expresses admiration and affection for the person caring for and engaging in joint activity with the child" (p. 33). Those families that have two parents who happen to be in love with each other provide one option for this provision. However, other possibilities also exist. For example, some single parents have friends or a family member who admire and care for them and their children. With the increasing stress from hectic day-to-day life, many parents may find it difficult to have stable, consistent, meaningful relationships with other adults (pp. 34–35). Bronfenbrenner points out how important such relationships are for parents to be at their best.

Further, the child is influenced by ongoing patterns of open, effective communication and trust between the settings where the child spends the most time: home and child care and/or school. Finally, the parents' workplace stress is a major factor in what happens at home. The premise of an extensive study conducted by Parcel and Menaghan (1994) is that conditions in parents' workplaces affect the home environments these parents create for their young children. And home environments affect children's cognitive and social development. Findings that support this premise are discussed later in the Work and Family section.

Other systems such as public policy and practices (p. 37) influence child-rearing within families, and thus, child outcomes. Families that have support, outlets for frustration, and caring others can do more positive parenting.

Family Systems Theory

Family systems theory notes, "... becoming a parent shares the common characteristic of a change of membership and a change of function of its members" (Bradt, 1989, p. 235). The changes necessary in the family system with the birth of a first child are immense. For both new mothers and new fathers, balance between work and home undergoes a dramatic shift. Adults are challenged continuously about

Children are influenced by ongoing patterns of open communication and trust at their school.

> *"Being a parent, whether father or mother, is the most difficult task humans have to perform. For people, unlike other animals, are not born knowing how to be parents. Most of us struggle through."*
>
> —Karl Menninger

whether they have the capacity to live up to the responsibility for nurturing this new generation (Bradt, 1989). New parents may meet this challenge in very different ways, some insisting that there is nothing to rearing children and others becoming increasingly focused on their children. Most likely, there is some middle ground between these two perspectives that is a healthy response to meeting the challenge.

Family Issues

Transition to Parenthood

A study in 1957 (LeMasters) revealed that 83 percent of new parents had experienced a serious amount of family distress following the birth of their first baby. Whereas the ideal in American family life is that a baby celebrates the love of the married couple, this idealism quickly turns to exhaustion from efforts to meet the nonnegotiable needs of the baby (La Rossa & La Rossa, 1981). Few new parents feel well prepared to meet the constant needs of newborns. Further, most new parents are surprised by the stress that is added to their lives. This indicates that little support is available for couples as they become parents.

Men and women report some differences in their **transition to parenthood**. Although both clearly feel the loss of nearly all free time, women are more likely to value their relationships with the baby. Fathers are more likely to act as if their babies are things to show to others, and they see babies as less competent than do mothers. Even egalitarian couples begin to split family responsibilities in the direction of more traditional gender roles (LaRossa & LaRossa, 1981).

Historical Changes
http://www.happinessonline.org/MoralDrift/p.
6htm

Rocking the Cradle—and the Marriage
http://seattletimes.nwsource.com/news/lifesty
les/html98/tran_19991024.htm.

New mothers report that they see it as their responsibility to create a family, "to produce a different sort of social unit" (Ribbens, 1994, p. 59) when the first child is born. Having a family, to most people, means having and caring for children. Even at this point in history, with so much emphasis on gender equality, it is seen as the mother's role to ensure the formation and integration of the family unit.

One reason for this move toward "traditionalization" is that larger systems in society—that is, the exosystem and macrosystem—do not support gender equity in parenting (LaRossa & LaRossa, 1981). So even when couples attempt to make a deal about shared parenting, the workplace, extended families, and other social institutions often do not provide the necessary support. With so many parenting tasks to complete, tired new parents often do not see gender equity as the battle that they can afford to fight. Thus, they give in to the system.

One point of concern related to research on the transition to parenthood is that most studies have used middle-class or upper middle-class families. If these families are noting this much stress, what happens in families with fewer resources, human or material? Based on ecological theory, we can only hypothesize that a single mother with a low income will face even greater crises in this transition.

The Cowans (1995) make an important point: it is clear that families need interventions to assist them in this critical transition. When parents adjust more easily, their relationships with their children are of higher quality. This relationship is a critical factor in the child's development, and central to the child's success as a preschooler and elementary student. It is primarily for this reason that early childhood educators must be aware of the importance of

various forms of support for couples in their transition to parenthood. Parents face a tremendous challenge with their first babies, but each new birth changes the family system and requires added support. As we celebrate births, we must also be prepared to help families receive the help and care they need to reduce the negative outcomes associated with the transitions.

Sibling Relationships

As families grow, new relationships must be negotiated. As the first child becomes the big brother or big sister, parental roles also change. Attention to **sibling relationships** becomes a new challenge for parents who are often just beginning to feel more confident of their abilities. What are the typical ways in which young children react to the announcement about the coming of a new baby? Certainly, these vary by development and individual differences in temperament. Chelsea, at age two and a half, responded to her parents' announcement about a new baby by stating, "No baby. Doggie." For young preschoolers, this may seem like a reasonable, desirable, and logical variation to the family composition.

Child developmentalists believe that sibling rivalry is to be expected. For parents who are in the middle of these rivalries, and have essentially caused the situation, understanding the "normalcy" of the phenomena does little to alleviate their concern.

Early childhood teachers have frequent experiences with children whose behaviors change at school when a new baby is expected or has arrived in the home. In the above example, Chelsea seemed to adapt to the notion of having a new baby in the family. By the time baby Christopher was born, she was three years old and commenting frequently, "He's so nice." One day, however, Chelsea heard her mother refer to herself as "Christopher's mommy, too." The mother was surprised to realize that Chelsea had gotten used to the idea of the baby living in their house, but she was not prepared to share her mother! For young children, there is so much to figure out about family relationships. Faber and Mazlish (1987) give an example in their book to help parents understand some of the feelings of rivalry children may experience with the introduction of new siblings. They suggest that parents might have greater understanding if they try out the feelings they would have if their spouse brought in a new spouse to be added to the family!

Hernandez (1993) discusses details related to growing up in larger families versus smaller families. The median family size decreased from 6.6 in the 1890s to 2.9 in the 1940s. During the baby boom (1946–1964), median family size rose to 3.4. Most recently, during the "baby bust," median family size has decreased to 2.1 (Figure 3–1). Fewer siblings in the house means a marked change in the typical family's microsystem. Generally, young children today have fewer relationships within the family and a greater number of people with whom they interact in additional microsystems.

Hernandez's analysis indicates that the reasons for declines in family size are related to social, economic, and political changes. The first issue Hernandez (1993) addresses is that having many siblings is a mixed blessing: there is the opportunity for caring sibling relationships but less attention is available from parents. Hernandez points to a second issue raised by this data: children from larger families receive less education, thus move on to lower-status occupations and less income. Further, a great deal of research has pointed to the fact that when children

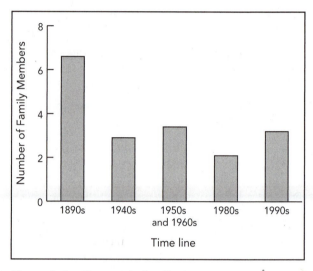

Figure 3–1   Changes in family size.

have increased interactions with parents, it leads to gains in verbal ability and school success. Smaller families provide a better possibility that children will have more interactions with their parents. This is likely one reason that young children currently have higher levels of language development when they enter preschool or kindergarten than did children in the past.

Many studies regarding the characteristics of only children have demonstrated that they are very similar to other children or somewhat advantaged (Falbo, 1992). Conventional wisdom in U.S. society points to a desire for two or three children, down from a generation or two ago. And conventional wisdom opposes planning for having only one child. Even adults who were reared as only children note that they wish they had grown up with brothers and sisters. Falbo notes that it is rare for an only child to have "strong positive feelings about his or her status because it is and continues to be nonnormative" (p. 77).

In her review of literature regarding only children, Falbo (1992) notes that only children scored higher than others on achievement motivation and self-esteem. They were not unique in many personality traits including dominance, generosity, autonomy, anxiety, and popularity. In childhood, the home lives of only children have been more likely to encourage intellectual activities including reading, music,

---

Children with Disabilities: Understanding Sibling Issues
http://www.kidsource.com/NICHCY/sibling.issues.dis.all.3.1.html

Helping Children Adapt to a New Sibling
http://www.nncc.org/Guidance/cc45_new.sibling.html

How Foster Children Impact Sibling Relationships
http://www.fostercare.net/reportack.htm

Sibling Relationships
http://npin.org/pnews/1999/pnew599/int599b.html

Siblings in Adoption—Expanded Families
http://www.pactadopt.org/press/articles/sibattach.html

dance, and travel outside the country. In school, only children were not more likely than others to cause trouble or have special needs, but they were less inclined than others to demonstrate antisocial behavior, hyperactivity, dependency, or social withdrawal.

The primary reason for the decline in **family size** is a desire of individuals and couples to increase their social and economic standing or to keep from falling behind in their economic standing (Hernandez, 1993). The cost of having children has increased and the economic benefit to having children has all but disappeared. As society has shifted from an agrarian emphasis to an industrial and technological one, each child's needs for housing, food, and clothing was no longer provided directly by the family, but rather families had to pay for goods and services. Not only was child labor restricted but also school attendance became mandatory. The quality of living is now tied to increased numbers of goods and services; parents need more time for their own careers and recreation. Typically, parents feel that their resources are too stretched to have more than one or two children. Essentially, changes in the exosystem, macrosystem, and chronosystem have affected decisions about the size of the family in the microsystem. Childhood within the family context has experienced a "revolutionary shift" (Hernandez, 1993) from large to small families within the past 100 years. The downside of this shift is that children have fewer siblings who are potential companions throughout childhood and adulthood; the benefit is that children today receive more attention and resources from their parents.

Sibling relationships often challenge parents. Faber and Mazlish (1987) provide many examples from parents of such challenges. It seems that some sibling rivalry is inescapable within the family context. Parents claim that it is not only hard to understand why their children express such dislike for one another but also that it is difficult to live with. Parents believe in the same paradigm used by researchers: that siblings are companions, friends for life. But children's actions rarely support this view.

Researchers interested in studying sibling relationships note that these interactions and emotions cannot be meaningfully studied outside the context of family and peer relationships. Further, research into

Sibling rivalry is to be expected.

sibling relationships may dispel the notion that parent-child relationships are the only significant ones in the processes of socialization (Buhrmester, 1992).

Children with siblings who are mentally retarded or have other disabilities may face unique challenges in their relationships. It is not unusual for children to be taunted or teased about a disability of a sibling. Gath (1992) notes that a useful strategy for parents is to provide an understandable explanation to children regarding their sibling's disability. There is some evidence that "life may be easier for a brother or sister when there is another normal (sic) child in the family" (p. 103). Also, "the presence of other normal (sic) children in the family is a great comfort to the majority of parents, but conversely, the arrival of a second handicapped child in the same family increases the grief many times over and the presence of two children with mental retardation or other long standing disability in one family adds up to very much more than twice the burden of one" (p. 102). Other challenges to families who are rearing siblings with and without disabilities include issues of fairness in terms of expectations about behavior and opportunities, as well as overcoming sadness and distress about a child's disability.

Anderson and Rice (1992), in their study of sibling relationships in nondivorced, divorced, and remarried families, found that some personality traits of siblings differed by gender. Girls demonstrated more positive behavior such as empathy and support toward brothers and sisters than did boys, but they also showed equal amounts of aggression and hostility as boys. Generally, the findings in this study supported the family systems notion that increased family transitions contributed to conflict or ambivalence in sibling relationships. Negative sibling relationships were more common in stepfamilies and divorced families than in nondivorced families. These researchers emphasize that despite the conflicts among siblings, children in all types of families demonstrated a great deal of positive behaviors toward their siblings.

Even if this is true, parents who have shared their stories in workshops with Adele Faber and Elaine Mazlish make it clear that sibling rivalry is difficult to live with. Hetherington (1992) notes that "sibling relationships are unique because they combine the affective intensity and reciprocity of peer relationships with many of the complementary processes associated with parent-child relationships . . ." (p. 11). She goes on to say that sibling relationships have both an intense emotional component and high levels of supportive and antagonistic behavior.

Faber and Mazlish, basing their suggestions on the work of Haim Ginott (1965), offer strategies for the following:

- communicating feelings in acceptable ways
- knowing when and how to stop children's hurtful actions toward each other
- avoiding negative *and* positive comparisons of children
- understanding the differences between equal treatment and meeting each child's legitimate needs
- intervening in rivalries when one sibling has a disability
- setting limits on fighting
- managing tattling
- viewing sibling relationships as important across the life span

One of the most moving parts of the Faber and Mazlish book is the last chapter in which stories are shared from parents who are trying to impact their children's relationships in a positive way. Some of these parents tell about contacting their adult siblings and using the strategies to repair or rebuild their own sibling relationships.

Work and Family

Families and Work Institute
http://www.familiesandwork.org
Institute for Child and Family Policy
http://www.childpolicy.org/

The current state of the economy is such that many families feel the need for two full-time incomes. This has caused a dramatic change in the functions that families can and do perform. Many who are concerned about children and families have called on employers to incorporate **family-friendly work policies** for their employees.

Along with other members of contemporary society, many early childhood professionals have strong opinions about when and whether mothers of young children should be in the workforce. Only each family can decide this issue for itself. For some, it's a matter of simple arithmetic (the amount of income necessary to keep them afloat); for others, it's the notion of career paths. As we move into the 21st century, we are more accepting of "Mr. Moms" but still tend to think of the female as the one who should be willing to consider various work options. Many see this issue as more political than economic.

Married couple families in the United States have undergone changes in work patterns over the past generation. As can be seen below, dual-career couples are the most common, and wife as breadwinner with husband as homemaker remains the least common (Cheal, 1996).

Dual-career couples	30%
Husband provider, wife coprovider	24%
Husband breadwinner, wife homemaker	19%

One partially employed	8%
Both partially employed	6%
Wife provider, husband coprovider	5%
Nonworking	5%
Wife breadwinner, husband homemaker	2%

Both family life and work life are changing at a very rapid pace. From 1992 to 2001, the percentage of mothers with infants under one year of age in the labor force increased from 51 to 55. During the same period, employment rates for mothers with children under three years of age increased from 54.5 percent to 60 percent. Employment rates for mothers with children under six years of age varied by marital status: 60 percent of married mothers and 68 percent of single mothers were employed (Employment Characteristics of Families in 2001, 2002). Obviously, mothers of children are less readily accessible to them than in the recent past (Figure 3–2).

Stress in the workplace is on the rise. **Downsizing** often means that each person is required to do the work formerly done by at least two people. Both males and females report working longer hours than they would like. Emotionally, they are torn, grateful to have a job but stressed by the workload and expectations. Workers who have children report increased levels of stress and are coping less effectively than those without children. Fifteen percent of employed parents say they rarely or never do anything for fun with their children (Galinsky, 1994).

Many believe that **maternal employment**, that is, mothers working outside the home, is always negative for both the women and their families. Galinsky points out that this is not always the case. In many dual-earner families, women bring home 40 percent of the total income. This is a significant proportion

Year	% of Mothers in Workplace
1975	34.0
1992	54.5
2001	60.2

Figure 3–2 Changes in rate of employment for mothers of children under three years of age.

of household income, and it can be assumed that families would suffer a much lower quality of life without this income. For decades, many believed that if women would just return to caring for their young children, both families and the economy would be better off. Researchers since the early 1970s have examined the effects of maternal employment, and the conclusions are that other variables are more important for children's welfare than just whether or not the mother is working outside the home. Some of these variables include variations in home life, effects from the specific work environment, and the availability of quality child care. So essentially, employed moms who have a satisfying family life, a supportive work environment, and access to quality care for their children provide positive outcomes for children. It is clear that segments from both the exosystem and macrosystem can affect families in either positive or negative ways.

In a study of the relation of maternal employment to mothers' and teachers' ratings of children's temperament and social behavior, Farver, Couchenour, and Chrisman (1998) found that young children's mothers who were dissatisfied with their work status, whether they worked outside the home or stayed at home, rated their children as more problematic in terms of difficult temperament. Also, mothers who were younger, and had less education and lower incomes, were more likely to rate their children as difficult than older, more educated, higher income mothers. Further, teacher ratings of the children's behavior yielded some important results.

Teacher ratings of preschool children's behaviors by the categories in Figure 3–3 were examined in relation to mothers' working full time, part time, or not working outside the home. Each of the high end scores are marked with an asterisk. Keep in mind that high scores indicate difficulty relating to the characteristics of the preschool children. For mothers not working outside the home, only the category of Hesitant was noted as significantly troublesome by preschool teachers. It is possible that children whose mothers are not employed outside the home have had fewer external social experiences, and thus, demonstrate hesitancy in social encounters in preschool. For mothers who worked part-time, only

	Not working	Working Part Time	Working Full Time
Sociable		*	
Difficult			*
Hesitant	*		
Aggressive			*
Prosocial			*
Asocial			*
Hyperactive/ Distracted			*
Anxious/Fearful (No significant findings)			
Excluded (No significant findings)			

FIGURE 3–3 Mothers' work status by teachers' ratings of children's behavior.

sociability was noted as troublesome. One possibility for this finding is that some children experience inconsistency in their caregiving arrangements and other aspects of the daily schedule when mothers work part-time, thus leading to the possibility of difficulties in getting along with others. Teachers noted more areas of difficulty in children whose mothers worked full time: difficult temperament including slower to accept new experiences and a greater frequency of negative emotional responses to others, higher levels of aggression, fewer prosocial interactions and more asocial behaviors, and greater levels of hyperactive/distracted behaviors.

One of the important concepts demonstrated in this study is the complexity of children's behavior and the outcomes of maternal employment. It is important to use information such as this in ways that will positively affect all children and families in children's school experiences. For example, early childhood teachers can plan ways to support children who are socially hesitant in preschool. Another example is to redirect aggressive behaviors so that these children can have more successful social experiences.

It is important to note that this study does not show causal relationships between children's social characteristics and maternal employment. That is, one cannot stipulate from this study that maternal employment causes preschoolers to be aggressive or asocial. It is possible that families sometimes choose for children

to attend various types of preschools (including full day child care) because they have assessed that their children would benefit from more social experiences with other children. This view might lead parents to make the choice for mothers to be employed outside the home. Additionally, there are other external factors that were not examined in this study such as presence or lack of family-friendly characteristics in the workplace, extended family or other social supports for the family, special needs of children or siblings, marital satisfaction, and many more variables. More research needs to be conducted using a variety of factors before one can conclude that maternal employment causes particular social characteristics in children. This is an important caveat since so often, the media publicizes studies such as this and suggests causal results that are not supported by the research.

One of the primary stressors for working parents is a breakdown in their child care arrangements. Often, this happens when children are ill or their caregiver has an emergency. Further, a lack of empathy and negativism from the child's caregiver has a negative effect on both the mother's and the child's well-being. One of the most severe causes of distress for employed mothers and their children is inconsistency of caregivers.

In addition to child care worries, a variety of characteristics of work sites also take a toll on employed moms. Most notably affecting both marriage and children's development are overly demanding jobs, heavy workloads, job insecurity, long hours with no flexibility, lack of autonomy and lack of control over work schedules, unsupportive supervisors and coworkers, an unsupportive social atmosphere, and the perception of discriminatory practices. While long hours and demanding jobs are typically problematic, many fathers and mothers with complex, challenging jobs that they like have been found to be warmer, more responsive, and firmer with their children (Galinsky, 1994).

Parcel and Menaghan (1994) note the importance of examining information regarding both parents' employment rather than studying maternal employment alone. The title of their work, *Parents' Jobs and Children's Lives*, represents their primary research question: How does parental employment affect children's cognitive and social development? Results of this study show complex ways in which children are affected by employment of their parents. Some of the more remarkable conclusions follow.

At ages three to six years, children's verbal facility, including vocabulary development, was related to both maternal and paternal characteristics as well as to the home environment. Verbal facility was higher when the mother's work was complex and she received a good salary; verbal skill was also higher when the father had higher hourly wages. When either or both parents clocked overtime work, children's verbal ability was likely to be hindered. Married mothers with fewer children were likely to have preschoolers who had greater verbal skills.

Later reading and math achievement of children ages six to eight years was also related to some parental characteristics and the home environment. Level of education, as well as hourly wages for both parents, was positively related to children's reading ability. Children who had higher reading achievement scores were likely to have mothers who were employed in more complex work. One exception to this situation was evidenced. In cases where family size was increasing and mothers had complexity in their jobs, reading skills of young children were negatively affected. Children whose fathers worked less than full time were negatively affected in their reading ability. Math skills were positively related to mothers' age and education but had no relation to fathers' age or education.

As with reading skill, math achievement was higher for children whose parents had higher hourly wages and when mothers' work had greater complexity. Some additional characteristics were noted for families of children who had higher math skill: one level of maternal part-time employment (21 to 34 hours per week) showed a positive association and another level of part-time employment (35 to 40 hours per week) showed a negative association. The researchers speculate that when mothers work 21 to 34 hours per week, they may actually have less spousal support for home and family responsibilities, and/or inconsistent child-care arrangements. Both of these circumstances may increase stress and cause a less positive home environment for children. It is not clear why these employment patterns did not affect

reading achievement in the same way. Finally, math achievement was also higher in stable marriages and lower when a marriage ended, or the family head was stably single. It seems that young children's math skill is more dependent on various home and family characteristics than is reading achievement.

Behavior problems were also examined in relation to parental characteristics, employment, and the home environment (Parcel & Menaghan, 1994). Mothers with positive self-concepts and higher levels of education were less likely to have children who manifested behavioral problems. Further, higher maternal wages, stable marriages, and stronger home environments were negatively associated with children's behavior problems.

Over and over again, this research points to the fact that maternal employment alone is not responsible for children's academic achievement or social development. Rather, complex interactions help to explain the child outcomes. In summary, when parents are too stretched, often due to both work and family situations, then children are likely to be hindered. However, when employment provides satisfaction and an increase in resources for the family without stretching parents too far, children are likely to benefit.

It is true that companies are increasingly providing more work-family assistance to help families with the balance of job and family responsibilities. Even though more programs are offered such as child-care assistance, flexible time, and part-time and leave policies, it is typically those with higher job status who have more choices and greater access to these programs. Thus, white, upper middle-class employees are receiving the bulk of these forms of support from employers. Although families that receive such supports from employers find them to be extremely helpful, there is concern that this is yet another way the gap is increasing between the haves and have-nots in today's society (Galinsky, 1994).

Much of Ellen Galinsky's research at the Families and Work Institute points to increasing family support programs in the workplace. It seems that corporations go through stages in their understanding of what types of family support programs will be good for families and good for companies. Two areas of current interest are greater training for supervisors about how to be supportive to employee family needs and creation of a family-friendly culture in the workplace.

Galinsky (1994) notes that as a society our beliefs about work need to change if we are going to support families to a greater degree. Some of the traditional "deep-seated beliefs" that she says must change include the following:

- Time equals commitment.
- Presence equals productivity.
- People have to sink or swim.
- People issues and work issues are different.
- If it isn't unpleasant, it isn't work.
- If you give employees an inch, they'll take a mile.
- Employees must sacrifice their personal needs to get ahead.
- There is no connection between the work-family problems of employees and the company's productivity (p. 132).

- Some beliefs that should replace these are the following:
- It is better to focus on work tasks than work time.
- People perform better when they are not hampered by personal pressures.
- Flexibility is a competitive issue and a management tool.
- Manage by empowering, rather than controlling (p. 132).

When workplaces provide more support to families, children will reap those benefits. When children have greater opportunities for optimal development, all of society will benefit.

Ellen Galinsky (1999) has more recently turned her research endeavors to asking children what they think about parental employment. One aspect of this research was concerned with children's views of the parenting they were receiving such as "good values," "Someone I can talk with," "appreciates me," and "is involved with my school." No differences were found in responses from children whose mothers were or were not employed outside the home. Other areas that this study examined included amount of time spent with parents, child care, and the effects of parents' jobs on children and child development. Results included the finding that children who spend more time with their parents when their parents were relaxed and calm saw them in a more positive way. Both quantity and quality of time matter to children. More children reported too little time with their fathers than reported too little time with their mothers.

Only half of the children in the study believed that their child care experiences were positive. Those who believed that their child care experiences were positive generally also felt that child care was good for their development. The problem here seems to be that too little high-quality child care exists to meet the needs of all children (Galinsky, 1999).

When children see their parents being tired and stressed from their jobs, they often tend to worry about them. Even though parents in this study seemed to be out of sync with children's feelings, the children reported that the one thing they would change if they could is that their parents would be less stressed and less tired. Further, it was found that parents often do not share much about their jobs with their children; they seem to see work as a competitor with children. This observation led some children to believe that parents did not like their jobs, when in fact, those parents reported liking their jobs (Galinsky, 1999).

This study broke new ground regarding the assumptions that adults make about work and children. Understanding the view of children can certainly lead adults to behaviors that will yield more positive outcomes for children. Some of these behaviors seem to be spending a good amount of high-quality time with children, finding ways to reduce job stress, getting enough rest, understanding how to choose high quality child care, and talking some about the joys and challenges in their work.

Child Care

High-quality, affordable child care is not readily accessible to many families. The most common form of out-of-home child care used by families that need it is provided by friends or relatives in their home. In 1982, this was true for 63 percent of families needing

> *"We have to ask whether this nurturance is possible in settings where caregivers are caring for four or more babies (and later six or more toddlers), are paid minimal wage, and given little training and little incentive to avoid staff turnover (among those who can get better jobs.)"*
>
> —Brazelton & Greenspan, 2000, pp. *xiii-xiv*

out-of-home care (Hofferth as cited in Greenman, 1984). But the number of child care centers and family day homes has increased dramatically in the past three decades.

A variety of forms of nonparental or out-of-home care are possible. For many families, coming up with the perfect or best child care arrangement is a huge challenge. Families often decide from among the following choices: care by another family member, employing someone to come into the home (a nanny or au pair), family home child care, center care, or many different combinations of these. States require child care centers to be licensed, and many require family home caregivers to register or be licensed. To best advocate for children, parents must understand the importance of licensed care. Essentially, a state license has only minimum requirements for health and safety of children. All children deserve at least this amount of protection.

A lot of attention has been given to the **child care "trilemma."** How can we balance quality of care, compensate child caregivers fairly, and keep quality care affordable for families? The importance of good quality care for children was mentioned previously in the section on families and work. Parents are more productive when they feel good about their children's care. A great deal of research on the outcomes of child care for children shows that when the care is of high quality, children flourish; but when the care is not good, it may be harmful to children's development. Quality child care has several components: responsive adult-child interaction including positive guidance strategies, developmentally appropriate curriculum and authentic assessment, family involvement, staff prepared in early childhood education or child development, and small group sizes and adult-to-child ratios. All of these components must be considered when quality care is desired for young children.

Quality care is not cheap. Currently, in our society, parents are generally required to pay tuition. To make child care affordable for families, too often, quality is compromised. One of the most serious problems with maintaining quality care is the high staff turnover. Turnover is high primarily because wages are low. It is not uncommon for child caregivers to earn minimum wage and to be employed part time without benefits. Parking lot attendants are usually paid better than child caregivers.

The Children's Defense Fund recently surveyed child care centers in cities and rural areas across the country (Schulman, 2000). A typical range of $4,000 to $6,000 per year for child care for a four-year-old was found; this means over $300 to $500 per month. Some child care costs as much as $10,000 per year for a four-year-old. Infant care is much more expensive that care for a preschooler, due in part to the smaller ratios of caregiver to child. Infant care was found to generally cost about $1,100 more per year than care for a four-year-old, or over $400 to nearly

Center for the Child Care Workforce
http://www.ccw.org/home/
Child Care Aware
http://www.childcareaware.org/
National Association for Family Child Care (NAFCC)
http://www.nafcc.org
National Association for the Education of Young Children—Accreditation
http://www.naeyc.org/accreditation/default. org
National Child Care Information Center
http://nccic.org/
National Network for Child Care
http://www.nncc.org/
Wheelock College Institute for Leadership and Career Initiatives
http://institute.wheelock.edu

> Survey several centers in your region to calculate costs of child care for one year for a four-year-old child and a 12-month-old child.

$600 per month. Cost for child care was a little less in rural areas, ranging from $3,000 to $6,000 per year for a four-year-old. The average cost for infant care in rural areas was over $4,500 per year. In many cities around the country, four years of child care cost more than four years of public college tuition. This reality hits a working family's budget quite hard, with many families above the poverty level spending about 7 percent of their income for child care for one child.

While it is necessary to keep the cost of care affordable to families, this means there is little money to pay caregivers. Often, caregivers of young children have little or no preparation for understanding children's development, yet they are entrusted with our youngest children. Poor pay causes many individuals to leave child care. When they stay for low wages, they are essentially subsidizing families for the care of their children. Because child care providers are available to provide child care for a small hourly wage, family members are free from child care responsibilities and can earn more. Some corporations provide on-site care for children of employees. One site charges tuition to employees at a rate that is about 60 percent of the typical cost of care. However, a caregiver at the center with a state certification in early childhood education is paid a maximum of $8 per hour. This is not a good situation for that caregiver.

Although states require that minimal standards be met, there has been ongoing concern about the number of poor quality centers providing care to children. In 1987, the National Academy of Early Childhood Programs began a process of voluntary accreditation. Since that time, many centers across the country have become accredited and are being challenged to maintain the high quality of care offered for children and their families. It is recommended that parents looking for good care for their

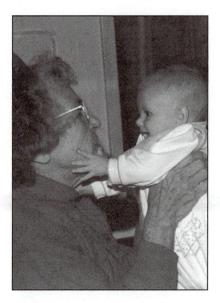

Extended family relationships, especially those of grandparents, are frequently overlooked.

children ask whether the center is accredited by this branch of the National Association for the Education of Young Children (NAEYC). See Appendix C for accreditation criteria.

Extended Family Relationships

With the prevalence of the nuclear family image as the ideal for today's society, **extended family relationships**, especially those of grandparents, are frequently overlooked. Unlike the family configuration of two generations ago in the United States, most children do not live in homes with both their parents and grandparents. Because the quality of living has gone up quickly for young families, it has been expected that they would form their own households. This often means that "vital connections" (Kornhaber & Woodward, 1981) between grandparents and grandchildren go unrealized. These researchers note that missing these connections is a detriment to both the children and the aged in a family.

In their study of about 300 grandchildren ages five to eighteen years, Kornhaber and Woodward (1981) noted that only about 5 percent of them had an intimate connection with at least one grandparent. This emotional closeness was fostered mostly by spending time together; no other factor was as critical to forming vital connections. Grandchildren who are given the gift of grandparents form emotional bonds second only to those they have with their parents. Because the parent-child relationship can be overcome with conflict at various times in the family life cycle, the grandchild-grandparent bond can serve a very different purpose in the emotional life of children. With grandparents, children often feel unconditional acceptance and warmth.

When children do not have a grandparent-like relationship, it is noted in this study, it is an emotional loss to these children: ". . . grandparents and grandchildren are naturally at ease with each other while both have intense emotional relationships with the middle generation . . . grandparents and grandchildren do not have to do anything to make each other happy. Their happiness comes from *being* together" (p. *xiii*).

The emphasis on the nuclear family has often brought about a view of grandparents as "meddlers" or "child spoilers" rather than as people who can help to support the family (Kornhaber & Woodward, 1981). With this view and the feeling of being unneeded, many grandparents move away from their grandchildren at the time of retirement. About 90 percent of grandchildren in this study had sporadic contact with their grandparents, and the children and grandparents did not really know much about each other. In addition to relocations at the time of retirement, divorce of children's parents also is a factor in children not having intimate contact with at least some of their grandparents. Grandparents, parents, and grandchildren all seem to believe that a lack of grandparenting relationships in children's lives is not a tremendous loss. But today's families are overlooking history: "For

the 40,000 years that humankind has been known to exist, children have typically been raised in tribes, clans, and variously extended networks of kin" (p. *xix*).

If grandparents have lost their social significance in the United States, the research by Kornhaber and Woodward demonstrates that they remain an important emotional attachment for grandchildren. "Society . . . cannot change what a grandparent means to a grandchild" (p. 167).

. . . the real experts on the aged are children. Only children understand what elders are for, and only they can meet the real need of the aged: the need to be needed. Children need grandparents and grandparents need children, whether they are their own flesh and blood kin or surrogate grandchildren. And until these mutual needs are acknowledged and supported, the aged will never achieve more than begrudging respect, much less outright affection, as elders in American society (p. 167).

Arthur Kornhaber (1996) has continued to collect data for the Grandparent Study that he and his associates began in the 1970s. Current results confirm prior findings of the "existence of a unique emotional relationship between grandparent and grandchild" (p. 36). An important positive characteristic of effective grandparent-grandchild relationships is a feeling of joy and fun. The following anecdote is one example of those feelings between a grandmother and her granddaughter.

Four-year-old Chelsea, who lives next door to her grandmother, frequently calls ahead to schedule play time with her. They play games together as well as engage in some messy play such as finger painting. Chelsea's grandmother, Dee, admits to trying to avoid the mess of finger painting one evening by reminding Chelsea that the plastic clothing protector that came with the finger paints had torn. Knowing the resourcefulness of her grandmother, Chelsea countered with, "You can find something to cover my clothes, Mumma." Sure enough, they found an old towel and the finger painting activity was on! Both parties reported having fun.

Foundation for Grandparenting
http://www.grandparenting.org
Grandparents Rights Center
http://www.grandparentsrights.org

The Grandparent Study shows that roles are changing for women and men. Many contemporary women, having experienced the world of work outside the home, are striving for more balance in their lives. One way many of them are attempting to do this is to reduce work hours and increase time spent with family members. This seems to be good news for grandchildren. Grandfathers who may have had little time to spend with children earlier in their lives also seem to be setting priorities that involve their grandchildren. One grandfather who worked two full-time jobs for many years found a great deal of pleasure in time spent with his preschool-aged grandson. This relationship changed as the grandson grew to adulthood from playful interactions to one of genuine friendship. Other family members noted through the years how this pair seemed to really like being together.

While role changes in contemporary society seem to contribute positively to grandparenting, some changes in families today certainly contribute to complications in the grandparenting role. In instances of divorce and remarriage, the complexity of relationships or the sheer number of children and parents involved may interfere with children spending time with grandparents. The increase of variations in family structure also contributes to confusion about roles and identities. Following are some of these variations:

- an increase in single-parent families
- single grandparents
- blended families
- grandparents serving as parents
- gay and lesbian partnerships (Kornhaber, 1996)

The research noted above and another study by Kivnick (1982) both examined the effects that grandchildren have on grandparents. Grandparents noted the following:

- recall of their own parenthood experiences as they anticipate birth of their first grandchild
- feelings of joy about arrival of grandchild, even when the timing of that birth was wrong for social reasons
- wandering thoughts of immortality, connections, spirituality

- impulse to see, hold, hear, care for, and indulge baby
- grandparent role central to their lives
- enjoying role as valued and esteemed elder in family

Kivnick (1982) found that grandparents attached a great deal of meaning to their roles with grandchildren and that the strength of this value was connected to the mental health of grandparents. The role of grandparent seemed to enhance the quality of life for the aging, thus contributing to positive mental health.

Research makes clear how important grandchildren and grandparents can be to each other. Some attention must be given to the middle generation, the parents, so that they, too, might see the benefits of grandparents in their children's lives. The need that young parents have to be independent in this society detracts from the real support that grandparents can give, especially to their grandchildren. Although much of the research emphasizes the biological connection, especially from the view of the grandparent, there is enough information to support the value of the grandparent role for children and the grandchild role for the aging so that programs for surrogate grandparenthood and grandchildhood make sense.

The following factors mentioned by Kornhaber and Woodward (1981) apply to surrogate situations as well as biological ones:

- young children are in awe of the elderly and can delight them
- the young and old have more time "to be;" parents are at an age where they must produce
- grandparents and grandchildren are relatively free of emotional conflict with each other
- grandparents are voices out of other times
- grandfathers are especially important as male figures for today's children who are so frequently missing those in their lives

To know the value of grandparents to children, observe some interactions between young children and their grandparents, reflect on some of your own experiences with grandparents, and ask people of all ages about their relationships with their grandparents.

At age three, Chelsea was given an assignment in her preschool class to draw a picture of something for which she was thankful. She drew some*one*: her grandmother. Several months after Thanksgiving and that assignment, the drawing still has a special place on the grandmother's refrigerator (Figure 3–4).

Neugarten and Weinstein devised five styles of grandparenting in 1964, a classification that continues to be useful to researchers and practitioners (Smith, 1995):

- formal—using prescribed roles for differentiating grandparents from parents
- fun seeker—viewing grandchildren as satisfying, and a primary role is to have fun with them
- surrogate parent—providing care for grandchildren
- reservoir of family wisdom—dispensing guidance, skills, or points of view to grandchildren
- distant—little contact with grandchildren, usually only for ritual occasions

It is likely that the style of grandparenting one possesses will influence the relationship with grand-

Figure 3–4   "I am thankful for Mumma."
Preschooler's drawing.

children. In addition to grandparents' personal preferences for style, other factors may come into play as relationships are formed. For example, grandparents' ages and health affect their activity with grandchildren.

The most common source of child care for single parent families is grandparents (Kennedy & Keeney as cited in Smith, 1995). While this is true for all families, African-American grandmothers have long served as surrogate parents, often being more active in the parenting role than fathers who were present in the home (Pearson, Hunter, Ensminger, & Kellam as cited in Smith, 1995). Grandparents who assisted teen mothers with their children under two years of age were studied by Oyserman, Radin, and Benn (as cited in Smith, 1995). Although grandmothers in this study had little measured effect on children, the role of grandfathers as male role models for "nurturance and cooperation" was noted. It is generally seen as a positive for young children to have grandparents assist with parental roles.

Smith (1995) discusses two areas of practical conern related to grandparenting in contemporary society.

1. Workshops for effective grandparenting, with the purpose of helping to strengthen family relationships and communication.
2. Legislation in all fifty states providing grandparents with visitation rights when parents of their grandchildren divorce.

The existence of these two phenomena suggests that grandparents see their roles as relevant to the lives of their grandchildren. And as the research shows, grandchildren and grandparents often benefit.

Practical and Ethical Considerations

Family Support Principles

Family support principles that are particularly relevant to information about developmental issues in families with young children include the following:

- promoting family health and well-being
- inspiring parental confidence and competence

- giving information tailored to parental needs
- encouraging voluntary participation by parents

Code of Ethical Conduct

Following are the items in the NAEYC Code of Ethical Conduct for early childhood education that relate particularly to content in this chapter and programs of early childhood education:

- to acknowledge and build on strengths and competencies as we support families in their task of nurturing children
- to respect families' child-rearing values and their right to make decisions for their children
- to interpret each child's progress to parents within the framework of a developmental perspective, and to help families understand and appreciate the value of developmentally appropriate early childhood programs
- to help family members improve their understanding of their children and to enhance their skills as parents
- to participate in building support networks for families by providing them with opportunities to interact with program staff and families

Summary and Conclusions

Although families are different in many ways, families rearing young children are likely to face many similar situations. Family systems theorists point to this period in the family life cycle as a "pressure cooker." Very often, parents with young children are in the early stages of their career or work life. Jobs may be less stable and incomes may be inadequate. Solutions for balancing family and work are complicated and not easily found. Concerns related to caring for children, both in and out of the home, abound. New parents must establish new identities, seeing themselves as mothers and fathers for the first time. Relating to extended families and in-laws may be challenging.

All families with young children need support. This support may come from other family members, friends, neighbors, and community groups. Families with too little support may require more from their children's early childhood programs. Teachers must be aware of all the demands and pressures made on family members as they rear their young children. This knowledge serves as a foundation for incorporating practices into early childhood education that support families at this stage of the life cycle.

Key Terms

transition to parenthood	maternal employment
sibling relationships	high-quality, affordable
family size	child care
family-friendly work	child care "trilemma"
policies	extended family
downsizing	relationships

Chapter Three Applications

1. The societal concern about the negative effects of maternal employment on young children was not echoed in the welfare reform legislation (as discussed in Chapter Two). Comment on why you believe the concerns were ignored in this legislation.

2. Plan and implement a way to disseminate information to parents of young children about the components of quality child care as provided in the National Accreditation Criteria.

3. Review and discuss the Faber and Mazlish model for parents to use in limiting sibling rivalry.

Questions for Reflection and Discussion

1. How would you explain the notion of family transitions to someone who has not read this chapter? What do family transitions mean for children in your care?

2. Can you provide examples from your own life of ways in which the macrosystem and exosystem have affected you?

3. What does the term "trilemma" mean in the child care discussion? Give an example from a real-life or hypothetical family situation.

4. Of what importance to your career in early childhood education is the discussion about grandparents?

Field Assignments

1. Interview some grandparents of young children (birth to eight years) about the role they have in their grandchildren's lives. Ask about their satisfaction with their role; would they change anything about it if they could?

2. Interview parents of young children about changes they made in their work and family life after the birth of their first child. What factors have facilitated their transition to parenthood? What factors have served as barriers? What work and family situations do these parents suggest would have been helpful?

3. Interview an early childhood educator about the effects she believes that maternal employment might have on the lives of young children.

4. Observe an early childhood program that has been accredited by the National Academy of Early Childhood Programs. Using the accreditation criteria highlighted in this chapter, note evidence of the criteria during the time of your observation.

References

Anderson, E. R., & Rice, A. M. (1992). Sibling relationships during remarriage. In E. M. Hetherington & W. G. Clingempeel (Eds.), *Coping with marital transitions: A family systems perspective. Monographs of the Society for Research in Child Development*, 57 (2–3, Serial No. 227, pp. 149–177).

Bradt, J. O. (1989). Becoming parents: Families with young children. In B. Carter & M. McGoldrick (Eds.), *The changing family life cycle*. Boston: Allyn & Bacon.

Brazelton, T. B., & Greenspan, S. I.(2000). *The irreducible needs of children: What every child must have to grow, learn and flourish*. Cambridge, MA: Perseus.

Bronfenbrenner, U. (1990). Discovering what families do. In D. Blankenhorn, S. Bayme, & J. B. Elshtain (Eds.), *Rebuilding the nest: A new commitment to the American family*. Milwaukee, WI: Family Service America.

Buhrmester, D. (1992). The developmental courses of sibling and peer relationships. In F. Boer & J. Dunn (Eds.), *Children's sibling relationships: Developmental and clinical issues* (pp. 19–40). Hillsdale, NJ: Lawrence Erlbaum Associates.

Cheal, D. (1996). *New poverty: Families in postmodern society*. Westport, CT: Greenwood.

Cowan, C. P., & Cowan, P. A. (1995). Interventions to ease the transition to parenthood: Why they are needed and what they can do. *Family Relations, 44*, 412–423.

Employment characteristics of families in 2001. Bureau of Labor Statistics. Accessed October 19, 2002, http://www.bls.gov/cps.

Faber, A., & Mazlish, E. (1987). *Siblings without rivalry: How to help your children live together so you can live too*. New York: Avon.

Falbo, T. (1992). Social norms and the one-child family. In F. Boer & J. Dunn (Eds.), *Children's sibling relationships: Developmental and clinical issues* (pp. 71–82). Hillsdale, NJ: Lawrence Erlbaum Associates.

Farver, J., Couchenour, D., & Chrisman, K. (1998, July). The relation of maternal employment to mothers' and teachers' ratings of children's temperament and social behavior. Research poster presented at the Biennial Meeting of the International Society for the Study of Behavioural Development. Bern, Switzerland.

Galinsky, E. (1994). Families and work: The importance of the quality of the work environment. In S. L. Kagan & B. Weissbourd (Eds.), *Putting families first: America's family support movement and the challenge of change*. San Francisco: Jossey-Bass.

Galinsky, E. (1999). *Ask the children: What America's children really think about working parents*. New York: Morrow.

Gath, A. (1992). The brothers and sisters of mentally retarded children. In F. Boer & J. Dunn (Eds.), *Children's sibling relationships: Developmental and clinical issues* (pp. 101–108). Hillsdale, NJ: Lawrence Erlbaum Associates.

Ginott, H. G. (1965). *Between parent and child: New solutions to old problems*. New York: Macmillan.

Greenman, J. (1984). Perspectives on quality day care. In J. T. Greenman & R. W. Fuqua (Eds.), *Making day care better: Training, evaluation, and the process of change*. New York: Teachers College Press.

Hernandez, D. J. (1993). *America's children: Resources from family government and the economy.* New York: Russell Sage Foundation.

Hetherington, E. M. (1992). Coping with marital transitions: A family systems perspective. In E. M. Hetherington & W. G. Clingempeel (Eds.), Coping with marital transitions: A family systems perspective. *Monographs of the Society for Research in Child Development, 57* (2–3, Serial No. 227, pp. 1–14).

Kivnick, H. Q. (1982). *The meaning of grandparenthood.* Ann Arbor, MI: UMI Research Press.

Kornhaber, A. (1996). *Contemporary grandparenting.* Thousand Oaks, CA: Sage.

Kornhaber, A., & Woodward, K. L. (1981). *Grandparents/ grandchildren: The vital connection.* Garden City, NY: Anchor Press.

La Rossa, R., & La Rossa, M. M. (1981). *Transition to parenthood: How infants change families.* Beverly Hills: Sage.

LeMasters, E. E. (1957). Parenthood as crisis. *Marriage and Family Living, 19,* 352–355.

Parcel, T. L., & Menaghan, E. G. (1994). *Parents' jobs and children's lives.* New York: Aldine De Gruyter.

Ribbens, J. (1994). *Mothers and their children: A feminist sociology of childrearing.* Thousand Oaks, CA: Sage.

Schulman, K. (2000). The high cost of child care puts quality care out of reach for many families. Children's Defense Fund. htttp://www.childrensdefense.org/ pdf/highcost.pdf.

Smith, P. K. (1995). Grandparenthood. In M. H. Bornstein (Ed.), *Handbook of parenting, volume 3: Status and social conditions of parenting* (pp. 89–112). Mahwah, NJ: Lawrence Erlbaum Associates.

OUTLINE

CHAPTER 4

Family Strengths, Family Functions, and Family Structure

OBJECTIVES

After reading and reflecting on this chapter, you should be able to:

- Discuss the meaning of family strengths, family structure, and family functions.

- Describe the factors that are related to change in family strengths, family structure, and family functions.

- Apply understanding about strengths, structure, and functions of families to work in early childhood education.

Introduction

Defining Family Strengths, Functions, and Structure

Scholars in family studies attach a great deal of importance to the meaning of **family strengths**, **family functions**, and **family structure**. The meaning of each of these terms as well as research supporting each term is discussed in this section of the textbook.

It is important for early childhood teachers to know what makes families strong. A great deal of study on this topic has occurred over the past two decades. Those factors that routinely seem to be related to strong families include **family pride** and **family accord**. Characteristics of family pride are mutual respect, trust and loyalty within the family, optimism, and shared values. A family's impression of competency in dealing with conflict is the critical aspect of

family accord (Olson, McCubbin, Barnes, Muxen, Larsen, & Wilson, 1989). For example, families that have ways of acknowledging and respecting differences among their members often demonstrate higher levels of accord. To create harmony, families may accept differences among members or use strategies for compromise. The family is the essential unit for meeting several functions. It has been common for family sociologists to refer to seven traditional functions of the family (Eshleman, 1988) (Figure 4–1):

1. Economic
2. Prestige and status
3. Education
4. Protection
5. Religion
6. Recreation
7. Affection

Economic—Families met their own economic needs; they produced what they needed to consume.

Prestige and Status—The family name was important.

Education—The family provided education, especially in the form of job training and household tasks.

Protection—Adults provided safety for children, and adult children took over this role as parents aged.

Religion—Religious practices in families included grace at meals and daily scripture reading.

Recreation—Home provided relaxation and physical activity for enjoyment.

Affection—Love was shared between spouses and through procreation of children.

Figure 4–1 Ogburn's family functions. (*Source: Eshleman, 1988. Original list from Ogburn, W. F. [1938]. The changing family. The Family, 139–143.*)

These functions have been viewed as important since at least the 1930s. As society changes, the precise view of each family function also changes. For many, these changes demonstrate the perspective that the diminished importance of family functions indicates the demise of the family, and perhaps of all society.

Today, family science experts still view the seven functions as important for maintaining strong family units. However, the descriptions and examples for each of the functions have changed over time. These changes are delineated in Figure 4–7.

In reality, families are able to meet the functions in a variety of ways. For example, specific demonstrations of affection frequently vary. One family may express its love with words and another more with actions. Some families show love through kisses and others through helping with chores. Further, families of a variety of structures can meet

the functions as fully as any other family. It is possible for single parents to meet all of the functional needs for their families just as it is possible for a two-parent family or a blended family. Essentially, the structure of the family does not indicate whether or not family functions are or will be met.

Another dimension of understanding families is structure. Structure refers to family membership. Some cultures define the family more in terms of the **nuclear unit**: parents and their children. Others emphasize the **extended family**, including additional generations from both parents' families, their **families of orientation**, as well as siblings and their **families of procreation** (Figure 4–2).

Bioecological Theory

Bronfenbrenner's theory points to the importance of extended families as well as of larger social institutions. Individuals are affected, both positively and negatively, by their microsystem or nuclear family. Further, larger social units affect the nuclear family. As society changes, the functions of the family also change. Take a look at the economic function of the family. As society has changed from

Nuclear Family—Any two or more persons of the same or adjoining generation related by blood, marriage, or adoption sharing a common residence.

Extended Family—A family in which two or more generations of the same kin live together (extension beyond the nuclear family).

Family of Orientation—The nuclear family into which one was born and reared (consists of self, siblings, and parents).

Family of Procreation—The nuclear family formed by marriage (consists of self, spouse, and children).

Figure 4–2 Terms related to family structure. (Definitions from Eshleman, 1988)

having an agrarian emphasis to an industrial emphasis to a technological emphasis, the family maintains an economic function, although the nature of the function has changed. One clear difference is that most families do not produce all of their own food; instead, it becomes a function of contemporary families to purchase food from grocery stores, butcher shops, and specialty markets. Families are likely to pay for food with money rather than with labor.

Family Systems Theory

Early childhood teachers are most likely to be working with families who have young children, though not all families fit into one stage quite so neatly. The family structure of those with young children changes dramatically with the birth of each new child. Sometimes, loss of family members, either by death, divorce, or separation, also occurs during this stage. Such losses affect the structure of the family as well as the way the members perform the various functions. When educators understand some of the common dynamics of families with young children, they can be better prepared to create positive partnerships with families.

Family systems theorists emphasize the stressors related to particular points along the family life cycle. Carter and McGoldrick (1989) note that there are three changes in family status that are required of families as they transition to parenthood. These family status changes are written for two-parent families; however, new parents who are single and parents who are blending families may find that with only some small differences, they, too, must negotiate similar status changes in their families.

- First Family Status Change. In two-parent families, it is typical that a couple will have to create space for children in the system that they have already established. Figure 4–3 provides some details about this change.
- Second Family Status Change. Two-parent families find that they must negotiate tasks related to nurturing children, consider new

---

Family Space for Children
(Carter & McGoldrick, 1989)

1. Children may be born into a family that has:
   a. no space for them.
   b. space for them.
   c. a vacuum for children to fill.
2. Contemporary families have an emphasis on work outside the home, and devalue events and situations in the domestic sphere, including child-rearing.
3. Young parents often relocate and children then do not have strong ties to extended family members. Fewer available adults leads to less space for children in families.
4. At the other extreme is the child-focused family in which a child fills a vacuum left by a marital partner or the loss of parents' parents.
5. Changes in women's roles have affected family space for children. Women in the workforce are able to time children with more effective birth control methods than in the past. However, many families ignore the "greater complexity of tasks and relationships" (Carter & McGoldrick, p. 242) that the new baby brings. (Bradt, 1989)

Figure 4–3   First family status change.

expenses and ways to manage finances, and balance house and family work with employment responsibilities. Figure 4–4 illustrates some details regarding these tasks that families need to regulate.

- Third Family Status Change. Two-parent families find that they need to have new understanding of themselves as parents and of their own parents as grandparents. As their roles are transformed, parents frequently deal with the issues listed in Figure 4–5.

Regulation of Tasks
(Carter & McGoldrick, 1989)

Nurturing children
- parents must make an emotional adjustment for others to care for their children
- couples arrange work schedules to provide for child care, and rarely see or interact with one another
- adjustment if one parent stays home to provide full-time care, leaving the workforce

Financial management
- cost of child care
- changes in income related to caring for baby
- decision-making related to new expenses for child

Housework
- balancing work and home responsibilities
- societal expectations and gender roles for mothers and fathers
- conflicts about who has each responsibility (Bradt, 1989)

Figure 4–4   Second family status change.

Transforming Relationships
(Carter & McGoldrick, 1989)

Parents
- What does it mean to be a mother? A father?
- How do past experiences influence these views?
- Taking roles and responsibilities of adults
- Must be available to nurture children

Grandparents
- Which set of grandparents is more involved and has more influence with their grandchild?
- How do grandparents affect the marital relationship?
- How much contact do new parents have with their child's grandparents? Has it changed since the birth of the baby?
- How do new grandparents see themselves providing for family continuity over the generations? (Bradt, 1989)

Figure 4–5   Third family status change.

Family Strengths

What Makes a Family Strong?

Several studies in the 1970s were the first to examine family strengths. Nick Stinnett (1979) and his associates found the following factors to be present in strong families:

- appreciation
- spending time together
- open communication
- commitment
- high degree of religious orientation or spirituality
- ability to deal with crises in a positive manner

The family strengths approach provides information about what makes a family healthy. Olson and DeFrain (1994) note that many of the strengths just listed can be placed in context with the three dimensions from the family circumplex model. Commitment and spending time together are related to family togetherness or cohesion; ability to deal with crises and spirituality help with a family's flexibility; and appreciation for one another and effective interaction are aspects of the communication dimension. Early childhood teachers should note that research supports the presence of all of these characteristics in strong families. It is not the place of teachers to criticize families for lacking in any of the strengths, but rather to best use this information by supporting families who engage in activities that exemplify these factors. For example, in some communities, many families attend religious services on a particular night of the week. When teachers are aware of this, homework might be assigned in ways that support this practice.

Olson (1989) notes characteristics of functional (versus dysfunctional) families (see Figure 4–6 for explanations).

What Factors Support Family Strengths?

Because we know that young children are so dependent on their families and that families have a tremendous impact on child development, it behooves early childhood professionals to foster ways in which the larger society might support these specific factors related to strong families. Further, the family support movement (Kagan & Weissbourd, 1994) emphasizes that all families have strengths and all families need support. Looking for and supporting the strengths, even in troubled families, can be a useful strategy for early childhood teachers.

Family pride—Families are unified and loyal; they view their family positively and cooperate with one another.

Family support—Families spend time together and provide love and support to each member for a growth-producing environment.

Cohesion—In addition to cooperating with each other, members respect one another's individuality. Family members are interdependent without being too dependent or too independent.

Adaptability—In the face of change, families can adapt. Tasks may rotate or are completed by those who have time and skill.

Communication—Both sharing of self and careful listening to others is important.

Social support—Family members accept responsibility for supporting community endeavors.

Values—Families who function well know their values and they work to practice and live by them.

Joy—Families know how to have fun together.

Figure 4–6 Characteristics of functional families.

Building Family Strengths
http://fyd.clemson.edu/building.htm

Creating a Strong Family
http://www.ianr.unl.edu/pubs/family/nf498.
  htm

Family Support and Children's Mental Health
http://www.rtc.pdx.edu/

From Family Stress to Family Strengths
http://www.edc.gov/nasd/doc1300/d001269/d
  001269.htm

Resilient Children

Since the mid-1980s, researchers have concluded that some children, even in the face of great adversity, somehow overcome the odds. These **resilient children** exhibit "good developmental outcomes despite high-risk status, sustained competence under stress, and recovery from trauma" (Werner, 1995, p. 81). Most of the research in this area consists of studies of children from one or more of the following situations:

- families of chronic poverty
- parent(s) suffering from serious psychopathology
- families that broke up in various ways
- children lacking nurturing (Werner, 1995)

Center on the Family
http://uhfamily.hawaii.edu/index.asp

Family Resilience
http://outreach.missouri.edu/extensioninfo-
    line/youth&family/family_resilience.htm

Family Works, Inc.
http://www.familyworksinc.com/

Project Resilience
http://www.projectresilience.com/

By reviewing several longitudinal studies, Werner (1995) notes factors that seem to be consistent for **at-risk children** who proved to be resilient. A very important element appears in the resilient child's temperamental makeup. They are easy children: active, affectionate, and good-natured. These children seem to bring forth positive responses in the adults who care for them, and they learn early to cope through both self-sufficiency and asking for help when they need it (Werner, 1995).

In addition to the child's temperament, family and community components also offer protection for at-risk children. A child who lives with a great deal of family discord but somehow builds a relationship with at least one family member who is emotionally competent, stable, and willing to nurture that child, is more likely to become resilient. Further, community members, especially teachers, are often seen as a source of support when at-risk children are facing crises. Characteristics of these teachers are that they ". . . listened to the children, challenged them, and rooted for them . . ." (Werner, 1995, p. 83). Early childhood teachers are often in a prime position to assist and support children who live with so much adversity. Note that characteristics of teachers who have helped resilient children listened to them and demonstrated concern in their ongoing role as educators. Best educational practices in early

Teachers have helped children by listening to them and demonstrating concern.

childhood education call for such behaviors in teacher-child relationships.

Family Functions

Historical and Contemporary Purposes of Families

Beliefs about family functions are often based on history or tradition. As society changes, the ways in which families fulfill functions also change. Consider the function of education. In earlier times, the family was the primary educator, not only for infants and very young children but also frequently for adolescents who were taught the family business or trade, as well as caring for the home and family. Today, more than half of all families rely on out-of-home care for their babies during the first year of life. Many families seek some form of preschool education for chil-

> Children, Youth & Family Consortium
> **http://www.cyfc.umn.edu**
> Forum on Child and Family Statistics
> **http://www.ChildStats.gov**

dren between the ages of three and five years, and nearly every child who is eligible attends kindergarten. Although there is a home schooling movement in the United States, the vast majority of school-age children receive their elementary and secondary education at public or private schools. Further, many adolescents and young adults receive their career training outside the home. And arguably, little attention or priority is given to youth regarding skills needed to care for homes and families.

Even though the specific tasks of the education function have changed over the past several generations, families still have a function to seek and provide

Strong families enjoy one another's company and express affection for one another.

education for their children. When families need child care services for their infants and toddlers, they must choose from available options what best suits the needs of the family and the child. Some families choose to live in particular cities or neighborhoods because of the schools their children would attend. And frequently, parents and other family members pay for or assist and support students in their post-secondary education. Thus, many families continue to fulfill their function as their children's educators, but the ways in which they do so are very different from the ways of families in the past.

Galinsky and David (1988) quote Urie Bronfenbrenner regarding the connection between child care, families, and work: "One of the most important elements of good quality and one that is not usually discussed, is the importance of linkages between the family, the day care, and the world of work. If the child care enhances the power of family, there are excellent results for the child. If the family is undermined, then the outcome is not beneficial for the child" (p. 420). This comment makes it clear that systems of work, family, and child care affect one another, and that the outcomes for children are very predictable. When workplaces and educational settings hold families in high regard—and let them know it in a variety of ways—children benefit. It is also important to note, however, that children may be harmed when families are not honored.

Many early childhood programs include the idea of empowering parents as a goal in their family involvement plan. The Cornell Empowerment Group defines the term in this way: "Empowerment is an intentional, ongoing process centered in the local community, involving mutual respect, critical reflection, caring, and group participation, through which people lacking an equal share of valued resources gain greater control over those resources" (Dean, 1991, p. 10). One program that was led by this group for child caregivers and parents of children in child care instructed participants in effective interpersonal communication using skills such as active listening, assertiveness, and conflict resolution (Dean, 1991). The development of effective interpersonal skills is an important process for empower-

ing parents. More information about interpersonal communication is discussed in Chapter 8.

Some ways that each of the expected family functions have been met in the past and how they are likely to be met currently are shown in Figure 4–7.

Causes of Change in Family Functions

As changes occur in the systems beyond the microsystem, families find a need to accommodate to the larger society. For example, economic changes in the United States have affected many families such that there is a need for two incomes. Along with the economic changes, a social change has occurred: young adults expect to have many of the luxuries with which they grew up and credit is readily available. At the same time, child care is more available than it was a generation ago. The complexity in interaction of all these changes has affected the decisions that families make about work as well as care and education of their children.

Family pride is shown in portraits.

Economic

Past—provided for all needs, goods, and services

Present—purchase many goods and services

Prestige and Status

Past—family name

Present—profession, job responsibility, promotions, social opportunities in community

Education

Past—taught children at home, especially for vocational and household responsibilities

Present—provide access to education, pay for it, advocate for and attain special services, form partnerships with educators

Protection

Past—fathers especially were to keep the family physically safe

Present—choice of neighborhood, related to economic function

Religion

Past—practices in the home

Present—greater responsibility of religious institutions and society to instill spirituality and morality

Recreation

Past—activities and fun planned at home with families

Present—community-oriented sports, arts, nature, parks, and other activities

Affection

Past—love shown through nurturance

Present—love shown by providing of "wants" and through various means of caring

Figure 4–7 Family functions past and present.

Family Law

In *The Rights of Families*, Guggenheim, Lowe, and Curtis (1996) provide current interpretations and details regarding family law. Included in this guidebook are the following topics: divorce and child custody, child support, property division, gay and lesbian families, adoption, and child abuse and neglect. In the introduction, the authors make an important point regarding the unique American viewpoint of those who advocate for public policies that support young children and families. They note that even more critical to the well-being of children and families, both historically and today, is the notion of being "free from unjustified governmental interference" (p. xv). Guggenheim, Lowe, and Curtis go on to explain:

This is, in essence, a "hands off" view of family law, one that focuses heavily on a family's procedural rights. It is very different from other countries' conception of family rights, which reflect their society's commitment to the well-being of children and their families. Unlike the United States, many countries around the world believe that families need positive support in the form of paid childcare leave, national health insurance, subsidized day care, free universal preschool, child allowances, child support assurance, and free (or low-cost) higher education. The absence of such substantive rights for families in the United States is the subject of ongoing debate. (p. xv)

It is interesting to note that the U.S. Constitution makes no mention of children and families, yet

In addition to the economy, availability of credit, and the existence of child care, what other factors can you attribute to recent changes in family functions? How have functions changed just since you were a young child? Interview those in the previous two generations to gain firsthand information about how family functions have changed over that period of time. Speculate about some of the causes of these changes, especially those that occur beyond the microsystem.

Family Support America
**http://www.familysupportamerica.org/
content/home.htm**

courts have upheld rights of families. Two concepts that have been held in high esteem by the legal system include **right of family integrity** and the **primacy of parental rights**. The right of family integrity includes the legal basis for parents to bear and rear children, and to guide those children according to their own beliefs. The primacy of parental rights upholds the strict limits of the Constitution to interfere with family life (Guggenheim, Lowe, & Curtis, 1996).

Family Structure

Family structure refers to the makeup of a family. Who are the members of a particular family? Traditionally, in our culture, when families are depicted, it is common to see a mom, dad, son, daughter, and perhaps a pet or two (Figure 4–8).

Variations in Family Form

We tend to assume that Figure 4–8 is a realistic depiction of a traditional family. Consider some other possibilities: the adult male is the mother's brother;

As you prepare for your career in early childhood education, consider the list of services mentioned in the quote on page 73 (paid child care leave, national health insurance, and so on). If each service was available to families in the United States, note advantages and disadvantages. Interview a variety of citizens about their viewpoints related to one or more of these services. Analyze the responses you receive from your interviews. Do your responses support the notion of individuals wanting to be free from governmental interference?

Figure 4–8   People tend to assume that this is a realistic depiction of a traditional family.

the adult female is the father's sister; the children are cousins being reared in the same home; the family is blended. The possibilities are endless. How many more possibilities can you produce? The same is true for the members of families depicted in Figure 4–9.

The reality is that we cannot be sure of the roles or relationships of various family members just by looking at the structure. Sometimes in our judgments about individual families, we forget this truth. The traditional family form is often idealized in our society. That is, we consider this family form, no matter who the individuals are, to always be best for everyone. A case in point follows. One primary grade teacher had the responsibility to assign children in the first grade among four classrooms. In her own classroom, she placed only children who were living with both of their biological parents. One might say that she was aware of the research indicating that children who live in single-parent families are at greater risk for intellectual problems (National Commission on Children, 1993) and that she held an idealized view of traditional families. The surprising

Figure 4–9 Structures of families take many forms.

point in this story is that this teacher herself had been a single parent and reared a successful son. Discuss concerns about ethical issues that you might relate to this particular situation.

Although it is true a strong marriage is often a good place for raising children, it is not the only good place. And while it is true that children in single-parent families are at greater risk, many of them have nurturant parents who are meeting their needs (National Commission on Children, 1993). Four important components of family structure have been identified by family researchers, regardless of the presence of a married couple (Ihinger-Tallman & Pasley, 1987).

1. Division of labor. Who is responsible for each family function?

2. Rules of behavior. What are the expectations for interacting with family members in everyday life?

3. Family roles. What behavior is expected for each position in the family? What does the mother do? The father? Each child?

4. Power hierarchy. Adult family members typically have more power than children. What happens when this is not so?

> For each of the four components listed, give examples from your family of origin. For each of the four components, give examples from your family of procreation or your expectations for your future family. Share your examples in a small group. Discuss commonalities and differences you find within your group.

The Meaning of Birth Order

One segment of family structure that has been of interest to researchers, families, and early childhood educators for many years is that of birth order of siblings. "When differences in **birth order** are found, they usually are explained by variations in interactions with parents and siblings associated with the unique experiences of being in a particular position in the family" (Santrock, 1994, p. 446).

Some behaviors have been found to apply more to firstborn children, regardless of the number of siblings that have followed that child's birth:

- more adult-oriented
- more helpful

- more conforming
- more anxious
- more self-controlled
- less aggressive

There is general consensus that the presence of these characteristics is related to the demands and expectations placed on children by their parents. Being in the first position seems to be related to both higher achievement and higher guilt, probably because the parents have some time to focus only on this firstborn. Research on only children has dispelled the popular myth that they are typically bratty and self-centered, and has found that most often, only children have the positive characteristics of firstborns (Santrock, 1994).

Although there are some popular notions about how middle children and youngest children are expected to behave, many researchers believe that birth order alone is not a sufficient cause for variations in behavior. Following are some factors that are not considered in oversimplifying the birth order explanation for behavior:

- number of siblings
- age of siblings
- spacing of siblings
- gender of siblings
- temperament of siblings
- individual characteristics of siblings such as talents, skills, interests
- health of siblings such as chronic conditions, disabilities, or life-threatening or terminal illness

Considering all of the possible factors, it is best to not blame or credit a child's birth order for a set of behaviors. There is little need to do so. Although it is oversimplifying our understanding of children's behavior to use birth order explanations, it is important that we understand the importance of family dynamics. Sibling relationships are an important factor in understanding children and their families.

Birth Order Affects Career Interests
**http://www.acs.ohio-state.edu/
researchnews/archive/birthwrk.htm**
Birth Order and Its Effects on Self-Esteem
**http://www.citadel.edu/citadel/otherserv/psyc
/scholar2.html**
Birth Order and Personality Differences
**http://www.encouragingleadership.com/Birth
_Order.htm**
The Effect of Birth Order on Intelligence
**http://www.mwsc.edu/psychology/research/ps
y302/fall95/lowery.htm**

When adults in the family provide loving care to children, it matters little whether they are parents, grandparents, aunts, uncles, or friends.

Application of Chapter Information

Family Support

It is important that we use research information on family strengths, family functions, and family structure when planning for family support policies and programming. Being aware of the risk at which divorce places children, we might be tempted to judge parents who divorce as self-centered and uncaring about their children. Even if this were accurate, judging of families by early childhood teachers does nothing to help children.

In the booklet *Strengthening and Supporting Families*, the National Commission on Children (1993) notes, "Decisions about marriage, divorce, childbearing, and parenting are intensely personal, but they are also influenced by cultural messages and by friends, family, and social institutions" (p. 20). Consider the bioecological systems in Bronfenbrenner's theory. We see evidence in the preceding quote that all of society has some responsibility for supporting families. For early childhood educators, the most important reason for this societal support is that we know that all children need and deserve homes filled with love and support.

When we do not take all of the systems into consideration, it is easy to complain about and blame individual families for their inability to maintain a marriage or provide the best home for their children.

It is crucial that we understand the effect of larger systems on families and children. One of the most important of these larger systems is the economic system. Women with college degrees continue to earn less than men with high school diplomas. "Children in one-parent families are six times more likely to be poor than children who live with two parents" (National Commission on Children, 1993, p. 20). After a divorce, women are worse off economically and men are significantly better off. Taking all of these facts into consideration, it is clear that divorce alone is not the reason for so many young children living in poverty. Inequality in the economic system must be factored into our understanding of this gloomy picture.

Early Childhood Programs

When early childhood teachers understand that all families have strengths and all families need support, they will realize that family structure is less critical than the accomplishment of family functions. Young children can be nurtured in many variations of family

> *"Building and maintaining positive relationships with families must resonate throughout programs—in the physical environment, in activities, in administrative and policy guidelines, and in programmatic features."*
>
> —Barbara Bowman, 1994

structures. When adults in the family provide loving care to children, it matters little if they are parents, grandparents, aunts, uncles, friends, or others.

As specifics about how families fulfill the requisite functions evolve, so will the role of early childhood educators. In all early education settings, professionals must provide both care and education. As the saying goes, "We cannot educate young children without caring for them and we cannot care for young children without educating them." In support of this creed, both Bettye Caldwell and Magda Gerber have used the term "educare" for the primary function of early childhood education programs.

Partnership for Family Involvement in Education

Under the auspices of the United States Department of Education, the Partnership for Family Involvement has a mission that involves increasing home-school-community partnerships to strengthen schools and improve student achievement. It is likely that families, too, benefit from participating in some of the initiatives of this organization (Figure 4–10).

Partnership for Family Involvement in Education
http://pfie.ed.gov

The Partnership for Family Involvement in Education

"Better Education Is Everybody's Business"
—U.S. Secretary of Education Richard W. Riley

The Partnership's Mission

- To increase opportunities for families to be more involved in their children's learning at school and at home.
- To use family-school-community partnerships to strengthen schools and improve student achievement.

Our Partners   Thousands of partners pledge their support for student learning to high standards through this growing grassroots movement. Partners belong to one of four groups: Family-School Partners, Employers for Learning, Community Organizations, and Religious Groups.

Together, partners support efforts to:

- Strengthen family-school partnerships through good communication and mutual responsibility for children's learning;

- Adopt family- and student-friendly business practices;
- Provide before- and after-school learning activities for children;
- Make effective use of facilities—schools, community buildings, churches—for children and families; and
- Give parents the resources, training, and information they need to help children learn, and teachers and principals the tools they need to engage families.

continues

Figure 4–10   Partnership for Family Involvement. (Reprinted with permission from the Partnership for Family Involvement in Education)

The benefits of joining include:

- Connecting with other groups to share and learn from one another;
- Working together to strengthen and improve efforts to help children learn;
- Keeping up with the latest information and activities nationwide; and
- Receiving recognition for visible commitments at the local, state, and national levels

Activities of the Partnership   In addition to the numerous local activities in which Partnership members are involved, many participate in nationwide activities such as the following:

READ*WRITE*NOW!   As part of the America Reads Challenge, this activity focuses on reading during the summer months. Participating children read and write for thirty minutes every day, and teenagers and adults share a love of reading as **reading partners to young children.**

America Goes Back to School.   During the months of August through October, join Americans across the country as they go back to school to share their talents and experiences. Make a year-long commitment, starting in the fall, to help improve education and to help students learn.

Think College Early.   Help increase awareness and support for middle and high school students to take the courses needed to enter college and to be prepared financially through this new initiative.

Priority on After-School Extended Learning.   Partner members have placed new emphasis on the importance of providing before- and after-school activities that extend learning for children in a safe, drug-free environment.

The Partnership for Family Involvement in Education

Partner Registration

To register and receive your Partnership Promise Certificate, enter the information requested and then press the submit button at the bottom of the form. Also, you can print the form and mail to Partnership for Family Involvement in Education, 400 Maryland Avenue, SW, Washington, DC 20202-8173 or fax to 202-205-9133.

The registration must include a contact person and phone number in order to be processed. The information you provide may be made available by the U.S. Department of Education on the web, and, in any event, is subject to the Freedom of Information Act, and will be made available to requestors upon request.

We would like to become a member of the Partnership for Family Involvement in Education. We commit to family-friendly practices and will work with others to form partnerships that support children's learning.

Name of Partner group or school

Address line 1

Address line 2

City	State	Zip

Telephone	Fax

URL

continues

Figure 4–10   (continued).

Head of Organization

Contact Person

Email

Is your organization a(n) (Please check one.)

☐ Family-School Partner   ☐ Community Organization
☐ Employer for Learning   ☐ Religious Group

According to the Paperwork Reduction Act of 1995, no persons are required to respond to a collection of information unless it displays a valid OMB control number. The valid OMB control number for this information collection is 1860-0505. The time required to complete this information collection is estimated to average 5 minutes per response, including the time to review instructions, search existing data resources, gather the data needed, and complete and review the information collection. If you have any comments concerning the accuracy of the time estimate or suggestions for improving this form, please write to: U.S. Department of Education, Washington, DC 20202-4651.

Figure 4–10   (continued).

Summary and Conclusions

Early childhood practitioners must understand both family functions and family structure. Whereas many functions of the family have remained stable over time, the nature of those functions changes as society changes. It is because of such changes in society that many families now search for quality early childhood programs before their children are of traditional "school age." Family structure, the makeup of a family, influences how families manage their responsibilities. Single-parent families, by their nature, manage differently than most two-parent families. Blended families face challenges not known to original families of procreation.

Research points to certain characteristics that relate to strong families. When early childhood teachers apply their knowledge about these characteristics, program decisions and policies will then support families. It behooves professionals in early childhood education to provide support for the strengths in all families. Such support will lead to a greater likelihood that partnerships between home and school will be successful.

Key Terms

family strengths	family functions
family structure	family pride
family accord	nuclear family
extended family	family of orientation
family of procreation	resilient children
at-risk children	right of family integrity
primacy of parental rights	birth order

Chapter Four Applications

1. Review the information about family strengths in this chapter. Thinking about a family that is familiar to you, comment on each of the strengths in relation to that family.

2. List ten families you know. Create a representation of each family's current structure or the structure when you had contact with them. Compare and contrast the family structures. How do you believe the variations in structure in these families has affected specific functions of the family as discussed in this chapter?

3. How will you, as an early childhood educator, help ensure positive relationships with families (in the words of Barbara Bowman) through the physical environment, in activities, in administrative and policy guidelines, and in programmatic features?

Questions for Reflection and Discussion

1. How is knowledge about family strengths, functions, and structures useful to early childhood teachers?

2. How do you understand families differently after reading this chapter?

3. How will your teaching of children and working with families differ after reading about and reflecting on family strengths, functions, and structure?

Field Assignments

1. Interview five people in your own generation. Ask them questions about how they view recent changes in the family. Note their comments. Critique the comments based on what you have learned about how changes occur in various levels of societal systems.

2. Create at least ten different representations of various family structures. Ask five adults to speculate about the relationships among the family members. Share your findings in class.

3. Interview an early childhood teacher about variations in family structure he has observed in the past three years. Ask the teacher to give you approximate percentages of the types of family structures currently in his classroom.

Request comments from the teacher about any special or unusual circumstances. *Please note:* no names of families should be elicited for this assignment. Respect confidentiality.

References

Bowman, B. (1994). Home and school: The unresolved relationship. In S. L. Kagan & B. Weissbourd (Eds.), *Putting families first: America's family support movement and the challenge of change.* San Francisco: Jossey-Bass.

Bradt, J. O. (1989). Becoming parents: Families with young children. In B. Carter & M. McGoldrick (Eds.), *The changing family life cycle.* Needham Heights, MA: Allyn & Bacon.

Carter, B., & McGoldrick, M. (1989). Overview: The changing family life cycle: In B. Carter & M. McGoldrick (Eds.), *The changing family life cycle: A framework for family therapy.* Needham Heights, MA: Allyn & Bacon.

Dean, C. (1991, March). Bringing empowerment theory home: The Cornell parent-caregiver partnership program. *Networking Bulletin: Empowerment & Family Support, 2,* 10–13.

Eshleman, J. R. (1988). *The family: An introduction.* Needham Heights, MA: Simon & Schuster.

Galinsky, E., & David, J. (1988). *The preschool years: Family strategies that work from experts and parents.* New York: Times Books.

Guggenheim, M., Lowe, A. D., & Curtis, D. (1996). The rights of families: *The authoritative ACLU guide to the rights of family members today.* Carbondale, IL: Southern Illinois University Press.

Ihinger-Tallman, M., & Pasley, K. (1987). *Remarriage.* Newbury Park, CA: Sage.

Kagan, S. L., & Weissbourd, B. (1994). *Putting families first: America's family support movement and the challenge of change.* San Francisco: Jossey-Bass.

National Commission on Children (1993). *Strengthening and supporting families.* Washington, DC: National Commission on Children.

Olson, D. H. L. (1989). *Families: What makes them work.* Newbury Park, CA: Sage.

Olson, D. H. L., & DeFrain, J. D. (1994). *Marriage and the family: Diversity and strengths.* Mountain View, CA: Mayfield.

Olson, D. H., McCubbin, H. I., Barnes, H. L., Muxen, M. J., Larsen, A. S., & Wilson, M. A. (1989). *Families: What makes them work.* Newbury Park, CA: Sage.

Santrock, J. (1994). *Child development.* Madison, WI: Brown & Benchmark.

Stinnett, N. (1979). In search of strong families. In N. Stinnett, B. Chesser, & J. DeFrain (Eds.), *Building family strengths: Blueprints for action.* Lincoln, NE: University of Nebraska Press.

Werner, E. E. (1995, June). Resilience in development. *Current Directions in Psychological Science,* 81–85.

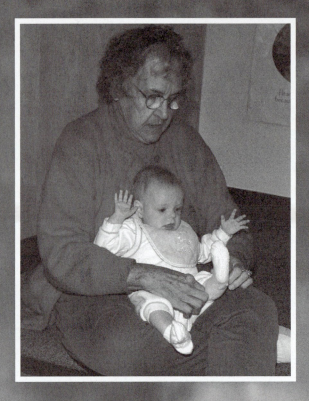

OUTLINE

Parenting

Bioecological Theory

What Affects Parenting?

What makes a parent? The most obvious answer is one based on biology. But beyond the biological connection that most parents have to their infants and children, what contributes to a mother or father's development as a parent? Bioecological theory would explain this in terms of the systems surrounding the parent, both past systems and current systems.

A great deal of research on **parenting** style and skills shows that parents are very likely to parent the way they were parented. Thus, parents who were given appropriate nurture, care, and guidance have had positive models for parenting their own children. On the flip side, parents who were denied nurturance and care, as well as effective guidance, will have to work very hard to overcome their experiences to provide a more appropriate environment for their children.

Microsystem Effects. Parental microsystems, both past and present, affect parents' behaviors with their children. Love and support from the other parent and significant others enable parents to do their best for their children.

Exosystem and Macrosystem Effects. The exosystem and macrosystem also affect parenting. Extended families, workplace stresses and pleasures, neighborhoods, and faith communities can contribute to challenges and successes of parenting. The economy, the government, and the political climate certainly affect much of what parents are able to do for children. A recent report from the Children's Defense Fund (2001) lists the amounts spent on raising a child to age eighteen for two-parent households at various income levels (Figure 5–1).

Income	Spent on Child
< $38,000	$121,230
< $38,000–$64,000	$165,630
> $64,000	$241,770

Figure 5–1   Differing costs to raise a child to age 18.

Public policies set by federal or state governments can affect parenting. Recent trends to cut welfare from mothers who stay home to rear their children indicates a change in viewpoint about the role of parents. A generation ago, welfare policies were based on the premise that mothers should stay home to rear their young children. As societal expectations have changed about mothers in the workplace, the viewpoints about welfare have changed as well.

"... the United States also takes the lead, among developed nations ... with respect to poverty ... the data are consistent with the general trend among economically developed nations: children and families in the United States experience greater environmental stress. Further, many of the problems facing American families are not restricted to particular ethnic or economic subgroups. Rather, these conditions are pervasive, applying across the population spectrum."

—Urie Bronfenbrenner

Chronosystem Effects.   Clearly, the chronosystem or era in which one is parenting affects parents and their children. In the 1950s and 1960s, most mothers with young children not only stayed home with their children but also were expected to do so by society. Currently, 62 percent of mothers with children under six years of age work outside the home (Children's Defense Fund, 1998). This change not only makes parenting very different, it also makes the kinds of family support needed very different. Many functions that were once accomplished in the home now require external support, most notably care for young children while any and all adults in the home spend most of their day in the workplace.

Parents introduce their young children to community activities.

Ways to Parenthood

Biological and Fertility Alternatives

The most common way in which people become parents is through sexual intercourse. Sometimes, becoming a parent in this way is planned, and sometimes pregnancies are unplanned. Although advances have been made in contraception, no method is 100 percent reliable. When sexual partners are married and conceive a child, most assume that a child was planned. When partners are not married, many assume that the child was not planned.

In addition to a woman conceiving a child through sexual intercourse, another method of conception is through **artificial insemination,** whereby a woman decides on a medical procedure to impregnate her with sperm from a donor, possibly her sexual partner. It is most likely that educators would not be aware that this procedure was chosen by the parents of a child in the early childhood classroom.

Advances in medical technology are providing a vast array of options for people who want to become parents but who, for a variety of reasons, do not do so through the more traditional means. In the 1970s, the possibility of test-tube babies seemed amazing. The first successful in vitro fertilization occurred in England in 1978. Since that time, more than 500,000 births from this procedure have occurred around the world. The number of births from in vitro fertilization has increased greatly in the United States from 257 in 1985 to 11,342 in 1995. Even with the cost at approximately $10,000, this alternative has become quite popular with couples who experience fertility problems (Miracle babies, 1998).

The popularity of this alternative fertilization procedure has increased with its greater acceptance.

When Louise Brown was born at Oldham Hospital near Manchester, England, in July 1978, the world reacted as if she were a creature of science fiction. The first child conceived by in vitro fertilization— that is by uniting sperm and egg in a glass container—she was instantly known as the test-tube baby. Such was her notoriety that after leaving the hospital she had to be fed at midnight in a car on an empty street near the family's home in Bristol, since throngs of reporters made it impossible to reach the front door. For years neither she nor her working-class parents, Lesley and John Brown, could escape the global spotlight. The unrelenting scrutiny once prompted Brown, now a preschool nurse in Bristol, to admit, "Sometimes I wish it wasn't me." Despite the attention, she has emerged as a healthy, happy young woman. (Miracle babies, 1998, p. 62)

There are more alternative methods to becoming parents than once thought possible. While many ethical questions persist, those whose dreams of be-

coming a parent have been answered through medical technology remain appreciative. Technological advances seem to provide new hope for those wishing to conceive a child.

Blended Families

With greater frequency, both men and women are parenting children they conceived, as well as those of their new spouse or partner. This is the case in **blended families**. Each partner in a blended family may bring their biological children to the new marriage. The parents in that household then are attempting to provide care, nurturance, and guidance to children who may have very recently been parented by someone else. Of course, parents do not always live in the same household with their children; many parents are carrying out their responsibilities with the added challenge of residing elsewhere.

Hanson, McLanahan, and Thomson (1996) note their puzzlement that the existing research regarding children in "stepfamily households" shows the absence of "a remarriage benefit." That is, that even though financial and other resources are greater than those in single-parent families, children are not better off. This concern led to the speculation that perhaps children in blended families experience higher levels of conflict than children in two-parent biological families. Their study examined eight variables related to the child's well-being: school performance, grade point average, school behavior problems, loss of temper or bullying others, sadness or withdrawing from others, sociability, initiative, and a global measure of quality of life. Children in their original two-parent families scored significantly higher on all areas of well-being except for grade point average. While these results are not surprising, it was unexpected that children in blended families would not be doing better than those in single-parent families, including in the areas of school performance and behavior problems. Children in single-parent families were significantly more sociable than those in reconstituted families. In an attempt to explain these results, the researchers studied parental conflict. Their results indicate that children in blended families experience higher levels of parental conflict than do other children. This is because they encounter more "intrahousehold" conflict than children in original families as well as "interhousehold" conflict, thus having two sources of possible family conflict. This is likely to increase their stress levels and lead to concern about the negative outcomes regarding child well-being noted by the researchers.

Adoption

Some who want to be parents choose **adoption**. Adoption is a legal process creating a nonbiological parent-child relationship. Following the adoption, adoptive parents assume all of the legal rights and responsibilities held by biological parents (Guggenheim, Lowe, & Curtis, 1996). This path to parenthood was popular from 1950 to 1970 but has decreased in popularity since then, due, in part, to greater acceptance by society of single women keeping and raising their children. Available statistics show that from 2 percent to 4 percent of families include an adopted child (Guggenheim, Lowe, & Curtis, 1996; Rosenberg, 1992). In the United States, a little over half of all adopted children are parented by adults who are related to them (Stolley, 1993).

It has been commonly believed that adoption of children offered perfect solutions for both the relinquishing family and the adoptive family, as well as for the adopted child. All needs are met, and family life can proceed with ease, happily ever after. Elinor Rosenberg (1992) has, however, shown that differences exist between biological families and the adoption circle. Attention to these differences can assist healthy adjustment by all of those in the adoption circle: the birth parents, the adoptive parents, and the adopted child.

Birth parents do not typically see their decision to give up their child as an easy one. They often take advice from others or see adoption as their only real alternative. Further, they continue to have life cycle issues related to this decision throughout their lives. Some of these issues include secrecy, anniversary dates such as the child's birthday or the day on which the legal process was concluded, relationships to children born either before or after the adoption,

intimate relationships, guilt, and lack of an official or social process for mourning the loss. It is certain that birth parents do not just relinquish their child and then never look back. Throughout their lives, they may question the decision they made. Rosenberg notes that even into old age, they may wonder about the existence of unknown grandchildren. Today, we hear beautiful stories about reunions between birth parents and the children they relinquished. Not all of these stories have such happy endings, however. Sometimes, lives become so complicated that families are unable to cope with such reunions.

Although early childhood teachers may not be aware of birth parents who have relinquished their children, they are likely to be aware of families who have adopted a child. Although this may be a sensitive issue for families to share with teachers, due to the differences in biological family and adoptive family issues, it is helpful for teachers to have this information. One of the most common situations for adoptive parents is that they have had to come to the realization that they were not able to have biological children. (Although this is not always the case, it is true for most adoptive parents.) Coming to terms with this loss is not always easy, and the pain may surface from time to time, especially if their adoptive child is having some difficulty.

Rosenberg (1992) has created five phases for adoptive parents from the decision to adopt to the time that their children reach school age. Each phase has one or more developmental tasks associated with it. In the first phase, the decision for the adoption to take place, developmental tasks may include acceptance of inability to reproduce, deciding to parent children outside of the bloodline, and deciding on the type of adoption that will be undertaken. The second phase is the adoption process. Tasks for this stage involve making both social and legal arrangements. Social arrangements are those relating to family and community. The third phase is the actual adoption, with the primary developmental task the acceptance of a new member into the existing family. The fourth phase occurs during the child's preschool years. Developmental tasks for parents include acknowledging adoption as a fact in their family and deciding who, when, what, and how to tell. During the child's school-age years, the fifth phase requires adoptive parents to acknowledge adoption in the larger community.

Adopted children also have some issues that are different from biological children. It is common now to tell children the story of how they came to be a member of their family. These stories vary greatly for biological children who hear about how they grew inside a special place in their mother's body, and for adopted children who are told they were so special that their parents selected them. It can be safely said that all adopted children wonder about their birth parents; some of them are articulate and curious enough to engage their adoptive parents in discussion about this, and others are less inclined to be open about their questions, concerns, or desire for information.

There may be variations in these issues for both parents and children in cases of racial or ethnic differences between adoptive parents and adopted children. In a newspaper editorial, Julie Higginbotham, a European-American mother of a Chinese-American daughter, commented on the insensitivity shown by strangers who ask questions and make comments about her daughter that are really none of their business. She has fielded questions such as: "Is she adopted?" "Where is she from?" "Was it really expensive?" The last paragraph of this editorial helps teachers and others to understand how adoptive parents feel about questions or comments that demonstrate such a lack of concern for parents' and children's feelings. "Alice was adopted, once upon a time. But now she is simply my child and our hearts are knit as tightly as any parent and child's can be. Alice is not a public exhibit. She deserves to be protected from adult questions that subtly invalidate her family's right to exist" (Higginbotham, 1998).

As teachers of young children, it is important to be sensitive to issues of adopted children and their families. Concern about terminology should be noted by teachers. Rosenberg (1992) tells about one preschooler who understood the common term "put up for adoption" to mean that all of the children who were available for adoption were placed on a shelf and waited for their adoptive families. Teachers of young children must understand that as adopted children and their families proceed through the life cycle, new issues are likely to arise that will require understanding on the part of professionals who work with them.

Grandparents as Parents

There are an increasing number of grandparents providing all or most of the parental responsibilities. In the recent past, it was not uncommon to have at least one grandparent living in the home with parents and children, in an extended family living arrangement. Many children, though, now live with only one or two grandparents, and the parents are not part of the child's daily life. Since 1980, this number has increased by 40 percent; there are about 3.2 million children in the United States whose grandparents are parenting them (Doucette-Dudman & LaCure, 1996).

Parenting grandchildren poses some complications to daily living. In addition to caring for the grandchild, or as often is the case, grandchildren, grandparents frequently work to create or maintain a relationship between the birth parent(s) and the child. Some experts believe that this is a crucial task for the healthy development of the children. Legal issues related to grandparents and their grandchildren vary from state to state, and in many cases, are not very clear. Some grandparents seek custody or adoption of their grandchildren, but many believe they are serving as temporary caregivers and that as soon as they can, the birth parent(s) will assume the parenting responsibilities. The truth is that even when the arrangement is temporary, it often stretches into years. When grandparents assume parenting roles, frequently birth parents have been involved in alcohol or drug abuse, or in physical, emotional, or sexual child abuse. The children may also be HIV positive. These desperate situations are often the catalyst for grandparents to attempt to save their grandchildren (Doucette-Dudman & LaCure, 1996).

In our society, some helping professionals and policy makers view it as odd that grandparents would want to parent or adopt their grandchildren. Some seem to be concerned that the relationships will be confusing to the children: for example, their aunts and uncles, and maybe even their birth parents, take on sibling roles. As a grandmother raising her granddaughter, Doucette-Dudman makes an important point:

> *This is Sabra's life, she has known no other, she is not confused in any way. We have explained and will continue to elaborate on, her family connections. We (grandparents) are her parents because we parent. She also has birth parents, just like any other adopted child. Sabra loves them, too, but they do not parent. . . . Biological designations are practically irrelevant (pp. 143–144).*

Not only are grandparents discouraged from seeking full custody or adopting their grandchildren, but also there are few resources available to them. In many situations, if grandparents did not assume the care of children, foster care would be necessary. The existing social service system allows for financial payments and medical insurance to those providing foster care, but grandparents are not eligible for these resources. Reverend Eduardo Yarde is quoted in *Raising Our Children's Children* (Doucette-Dudman & LaCure, p. 88):

> *With welfare reform, this is where the churches are going to play a crucial part. That's one sector that's been neglected. My philosophy is that these grandparents have already raised their kids, they are under no obligation to raise more kids. And to me they are doing us, society, a favor. They are doing the State a favor. They should be rewarded for that. If we can't see that, we surely have lost sight of everything. The State really looks the other way, "Oh, that's grandparents." They don't even consider giving them some sort of support, nothing. And it's hard.*

As grandparents raise their grandchildren, a number of difficulties have been documented (Kornhaber, 1993).

1. Without formal custody, grandparents have difficulty getting either preventive or emergency medical care for children.

2. Typically, insurance companies will not permit grandchildren to be included as dependents on policies.

3. Schools may not admit children who do not live with their parents and often deny authority of grandparents.

4. Social Security benefits for the children are available to grandparents only if they legally adopt.

5. Financial assistance from social service agencies is typically not available, not even resources available to foster families.

6. Housing regulations of grandparent residences may not allow children, or zoning laws may exclude grandchildren in the definition of single-family dwellings.

Having some knowledge about the stress that grandparents deal with in raising their grandchildren can help early childhood teachers to be sensitive to needs of "parents" and children in these families. It is common for children being raised by grandparents to have special needs because of their biological parents' substance abuse or child abuse. Education systems are in a position to ease the stress of grandparents; when educators and social service agency personnel work together, children and families will benefit. Doucette-Dudman and LaCure issue a plea for teachers to have some understanding and concern for grandparents who, out of "love and devotion," are nurturing their grandchildren.

Peggy Tuter Pearl (2000) suggests the following for teachers when grandparents are the primary caregivers:

- Modify language in notes, letters, requests for signatures

- Know who the primary caregivers of their students are

- Allow extra time during conferences

Dianne Rothenberg (1996) includes a list of school strategies intended to help grandchildren in an article entitled "Grandparents as Parents: A Primer for Schools." Listed below are excerpts from this list. For a complete version and more information, go to http://www.ed.gov/databases/ERIC__Digests/ed401044.html.

- Anticipate transitional or adjustment difficulties, and act to minimize them.

- Look for children's strengths and build on them.

- Try not to single out children because of their family status.

To listen to a grandparent's voice, go to the online resource and listen to "Nancy." Nancy is a grandmother who is parenting her two grandsons (ages 9 and 14). She describes some of the issues in her role as both grandmother and parent in the personal online voice including legal, medical, and daily realities.

Responsibilities of Parenthood

Economic

Parents have the ultimate responsibility for all of their children's needs. In the United States, most people believe that parents bear the financial obligation for their children's expenses, which include health care, child care, shelter, food, and clothing. This belief is so strong in our culture that we often assume all parents are capable of providing basic needs for their children. We ignore societal preferences and biases. For example, parents who have full-time jobs are more likely to have medical insurance for themselves and their children, and, thus, access to both preventive and emergency health care. Those in entry-level, lower-paying jobs, even if they are full time, are less likely to have their insurance paid for by employers. A concern for the well-being of children who do not have health insurance has led many states—as well as the federal government—to provide plans for young children. Although medical expenses are still seen as a parental responsibility, some policy makers have noted that healthy children really will cost society less in the future (Figure 5–2).

Nurturance and Child Care

Another responsibility of parents is to provide care and nurturance for their children. Traditionally, we have referred to this as "mothering" children. Even though many two-parent families currently find that two incomes are required, mothers are still seen as

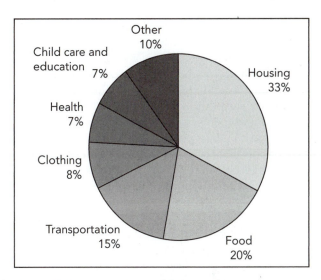

Figure 5–2   Percentages of estimated annual expenditures on a child by husband-wife couples with incomes of less than 38,000. (*Source:* Children's Defense Fund, Washington, DC. What it costs to raise a child. http://www.childrensdefense.org/factsfigures_costchild.htm).

the parent who is responsible for and more capable of caring for children. "The research evidence clearly indicates that husbands share very little of the burden of raising their children and caring for their homes" (Hamburg, 1995, p. 11). Most single parents who are the primary caregivers for their children are mothers. In fact, only about 10 percent of all single-parent families are headed by fathers (U.S. Bureau of the Census as cited in Hamner & Turner, 1996).

Bioecological theory emphasizes the need for parents to have a system of social support in order to do their best at nurturing children.

The establishment and maintenance of patterns of progressively more complex interaction and emotional attachment between caregiver and child depend in substantial degree on the availability and involvement of another adult or a third party—spouse, relative, neighbor, or formal service provider—who assists, encourages, spells, gives status to, and expresses admiration and affection for the person caring for and engaging in joint activity with the child (Bronfenbrenner & Neville, 1994, p. 14).

Note that early childhood teachers may serve as the "third party" to provide support to parents in their role as nurturers. This is a critical understanding in planning for the family involvement component in any program of early childhood education.

Child care outside the home continues to be viewed as a women's issue rather than a family or societal concern. Many policy makers continue to voice the opinion that if mothers stayed home with their young children, there would be no need for child care centers. Oddly enough, these same people often call for "welfare mothers" to go to work.

It remains the parents' responsibility to choose child care for their young children. Many parents, in reality, have little choice. Accessibility and affordability are two areas of concern. Parents tend to rely on care that is close to home and that costs the least. Often, this means that parents sacrifice quality of care of their children for what they can afford. Current interest and concern for this issue at the federal level and initiated by Hillary Rodham Clinton is welcomed by many child and family advocates. High-quality child care costs more than most families can afford. Further, it is difficult to find.

Early childhood education teachers may serve as the "third-party" to provide support to parents in their role as nurturers.

Attachment and Socialization

The third area of parents' responsibility is related to their children's psychological well-being. Forming emotional attachments is crucial for children's healthy development in all domains. Attachment to parents is necessary for healthy physical, cognitive, social, and emotional development. Figure 5–3 shows the relationship of attachment to all areas of child development.

Parents are the child's link to society. Early socialization experiences, including communication, play, and teaching behaviors, all happen within the context of the home. These early attachment and socialization experiences are thought to be a strong influence on children's development. Current research on brain development indicates that social interaction in the first three years of life creates important neuron connections for later learning. Parents are a child's first and foremost teachers, even if they employ other forms of care for their children at very young ages.

Healthy attachments in infancy can lead to the following outcomes for preschool children:

Physical development—brain development, physical health

Cognitive development—skillful in problem-solving, seeking maternal assistance when challenged, curious about new things

Social development—leaders with peers, self-confidence, sympathetic to others, competent in peer interactions, well-liked by others, considerate

Emotional development—ability to tolerate frustration, expression of positive emotions such as joy

Figure 5–3   Relationship of attachment to the child's development: physical, cognitive, social, and emotional.

Building and Maintaining Relationships

It is those in the parental role who introduce others into the lives of their children. Extended family members, especially grandparents but also aunts, uncles, cousins, neighbors, friends, and siblings, become a part of the child's world. Parents sometimes rely on some people on this list to help with child care or just to socialize with their children. Families include others in varying ways, partly depending on their culture or ethnicity, and partly depending on their individual views. For some families, cousins are almost like siblings, and for others, cousins are hardly known. These individual variations are most often decided and put into effect by parents.

Character Education and Spirituality

Spirituality, in various forms, is seen as a parental responsibility. For many families, spirituality is dealt with in the form of organized religion. It is the responsibility of families to see to it that their beliefs are shared with their children. Many parents count on the church or temple to at least assist with this duty. Religion, along with other factors, influences "the kind of activities the family engages in, the limits set and the controls placed on children's behavior, and the set of expectations that parents hold for their children" (Hamner & Turner, 1996, p. 21).

For other families, morality is of higher value than religiosity. Moral behavior is often related in some way to spirituality or the meaning of life (Coles, 1990). Lickona, Schaps, and Lewis (1998) note that school programs of character education should state in the mission statement, "Parents are the first and most important moral educators of their children" (p. 55). In addition to this critical point, Lickona and his associates go on to say,

> . . . each program should take pains at every stage to communicate with parents. To build trust between home and school, parents should be represented on the character leadership committee that does the planning. The program should actively reach out to "disconnected" subgroups of parents: All parents need to be informed about—and have a chance to contribute, react, and consent to—proposed core values and plans for implementing them. Finally, programs and families will enhance effectiveness of their partnership if they recruit the help of the wider community—business, religious institutions, youth organizations, the government, and the media—in promoting the core ethical values (p. 55).

> *"Clearly we can all agree about the importance of teaching our children, both as individuals and as members of society, the importance of common values such as respect, responsibility, trustworthiness, and citizenship."*
>
> —Richard Riley,
> **Former U.S. Secretary of Education**

Collaborating with Societal Institutions

A newer responsibility of parents is that of relating to societal institutions and helping their children to do so, including early childhood settings. This is often a difficult responsibility for parents because they have had no models. This responsibility is related to the very topic of this textbook: how can early childhood education and families form partnerships that benefit not only children but also parents and teachers? For parents working with their children's teachers often means finding effective means of resolving conflict. There are times when parents and teachers seem to value different activities or behaviors for children. It is imperative that both parents and early childhood teachers address such conflict in ways that will best help children, while still respecting the family and maintaining the educational program.

Parenting Styles and Beliefs

Diana Baumrind, in a series of studies (1967, 1971, 1977), has found three primary discipline styles of parents. These styles are identified as follows:

- Authoritative
- Permissive
- Authoritarian

Further, Baumrind has related children's behaviors to variations in disciplinary style. The outcome for each style points to a preference for the authoritative disciplinary style (Figure 5–4).

Authoritative

While it may be true that particular personalities of some parents may make it more likely that they will naturally use one style of discipline, it is clear that most parents must learn special skills that combine to form an authoritative style. These skills include the following:

- stating behavioral expectations to children
- knowing when behavioral change is called for
- understanding reasonable rules for development of child
- using personal messages
- reflection

Authoritative Parents—Consistent, loving, conscientious, secure in their ability to parent, set firm rules, communicate clearly, warm and unconditionally committed to their children

Associated Child Behaviors—More likely than other children to exhibit prosocial behavior such as sharing, sympathy toward others, and cooperation

Authoritarian Parents—Firm control over children, punitive, little warmth or support provided to children

Associated Child Behaviors—Because children typically have fewer possibilities to interact with others, they have less social competence. Often, children are anxious and do not initiate activities. They have poorer communication skills and some are overly aggressive

Permissive Parents—Insecure in parenting ability, expect little of children, indulgent to excess, set few or no limits, exert little control

Associated Child Behaviors—These children have fewer social opportunities than those of authoritative parents due to chaos or distraction, and so their social competence is also low. They lack self-control and self-esteem, and are often unfriendly and disrespectful

---

Figure 5–4   Parenting styles and child behaviors.

- description of adult's emotion
- giving an appropriate behavior alternative
- giving children reasons or explanations (Kostelnik, Stein, Whiren, & Soderman, 1998)

Permissive

Characteristics of permissive parents (Baumrind, 1966) include the following:

- nonpunitive, accepting, and affirmative
- allow child to self-regulate activities
- avoid exercising control
- externally defined standards not valued
- consult with child on family decisions
- exert few demands on child for responsibility and appropriate behavior
- use reason and manipulation rather than power

Maccoby and Martin (1983) further differentiated permissive parenting into two types: **permissive-indifferent** and **permissive-indulgent**. Characteristics of children from permissive-indifferent parenting include the following:

- social incompetence
- lack of self-control
- not knowing how to handle independence
- feel like "second fiddle" to other aspects of parent's life

Following are characteristics of children from permissive-indulgent parents:

- social incompetence
- lack of self-control
- not popular with peers
- disrespectful to others

Authoritarian

Authoritarian parents exhibit the following characteristics:

- restrictive
- punitive
- directive

- teach children to respect work and effort
- set firm limits with little verbal exchange allowed
- control all aspects of children's behavior

Effects noted on children of authoritarian parents include the following:

- social incompetence
- anxious about being compared with others
- fail to initiate activity
- poor communication skills
- sometimes overly aggressive

Trends in Beliefs about Discipline Strategies

Even as existing research shows support for authoritative parenting, that is stating expectations and providing explanations to children about reasons for expected behavior, there is a current trend in parental beliefs and behaviors that ignores the importance of balance between "guiding limits and loving compassionate care" for young children (Brazelton & Greenspan, 2000, p. *xviii*). Families who are so overwhelmed with responsibility are often attracted to simplistic discipline techniques that rely on punishments and rewards to control children's behavior. When used as a primary disciplinary method, these outdated approaches often lead children to either aggressive behavior or fearful, withdrawn behavior, neither of which will lead to children's optimal development. This "back-to-basics discipline ethic" does not consider children's need for sensitive nurturance and developmentally appropriate experiences (Brazelton& Greenspan, 2000).

Mothers and Fathers

Differences in Parenting

Even though we have come to accept the term "parenting," most families and teachers are aware that we have different expectations for mothers and fathers.

One single mother reports an occasion when her mother commented on what a good job a particular single father who had custody of his son was doing. Conversation between the single mother and her mother went like this:

Mother: "John works so hard at his job and still is such a good father for Joshua."

Daughter: " I work hard, too. And, I think I'm a good mother."

Mother: "Of course you're a good mother. Women know how to take care of young children. It's natural for them."

Daughter: "Working full time and being a mother is not easy."

Mother: "Women have been having children and taking care of them for generations. It's not new for women your age."

It is safe to say that many people in our society believe that any woman who has a child knows how to be a mother but not all men with children know how to be fathers. This belief sets quite a double standard for our expectations about parental responsibilities.

Generally, women experience greater fulfillment in their parental roles than men do, but they also see being a parent as more of a burden. Mothers feel restricted in other aspects of their lives due to their parenting duties (Goetting, 1986). Both of these feelings held by many mothers of young children are easily traced to societal expectations. At very early ages, many girls play with dolls, and when asked what they want to be when they grow up, they say "a mommy." Boys, on the other hand, play with toys that are symbolic of the world beyond the home and want to be pilots, police officers, or firefighters. They expect to be employed outside of the home, not to be restricted in their occupations by parenting duties.

In the 1950s, Parsons and Bales (1955) classified the role of mothers as "expressive" and the role of fathers as "instrumental." By this, these early scholars meant that mothers provided the care and love, and fathers' direct role in caring for children was minimal. A father's position allowed him to be the tie the family had with the outside world. Although times have changed and more mothers of children under six work outside the home, we still observe vestiges of this perspective. When one parent does stay home to care for children, it is still most often the mother. And when parents divorce, mothers are still more likely to get custody of the children.

Capabilities of Mothers and Fathers

Current research has examined how mothers and fathers interact with their babies and young children. Many studies have found that mothers are more likely to provide the physical care such as feeding, bathing, and diapering, and fathers are more likely to play with their children. Also, mothers, whether they work outside the home or not, spend a great deal more time with their children than do fathers. Perhaps this accounts for why mothers find parenting more fulfilling *and* more restrictive.

It is interesting to ask children (if they are old enough to respond) who takes care of them in various ways such as who prepares their food, washes their clothes, makes doctor appointments, and plays with them. Children's perceptions are often quite accurate in terms of understanding which parent performs which duties. One school principal tells of waiting in the deli line at a grocery store when a four-year-old boy asked him, "Where is the 'girl' who lives with you? Why isn't she doing the shopping?"

> To check this information with families that you know, interview several families with young children and ask the following questions:
>
> 1. Who provides physical care of your children, including preparing meals, bathing, making certain of clean clothes, and so on?
> 2. If a child is ill, who stays home from work with the child? How is this decided?
> 3. Who makes medical appointments?
> 4. Who plays with the children?

Stay-at-home Fathers

As of 1996, it was estimated that there were approximately two million stay at home fathers in the United States. Frank and Livingston (2000) state that "Stay at home fathers recognize that caring for children and family is not emasculating; as their children become older they are likely to remain intimately involved with their children, aware of their friends, schoolwork, and activities, and active as the on-call parent who responds when the child is sick at school."

If this description is accurate, then teachers will need to actively invite and welcome fathers, and become aware of the role(s) they play in the life of their child. This awareness will also help teachers understand the family's caregiving arrangements.

Parenting Beliefs

Parenting is one of the most important roles a person can perform. Yet, it is expected that parenting skills will come naturally. Because so many people do become parents in one way or another, this role is different from many others. Five differences have been noted (Bigner as cited in Hamner & Turner, 1996).

1. Women receive more pressure to become mothers than men do to become fathers.
2. Parenthood is not always voluntary.
3. Parenthood is irrevocable.
4. Parents receive very little preparation or guidance.
5. Parents develop and accommodate their parenting strategies as their children develop.

> Consider the five parental roles. State your agreement or disagreement with each belief. Give real-life examples to support your view.

Child Development and the Role of Children in Families

The ZERO TO THREE National Center for Infants, Toddlers and Families conducted a study that focused on the following questions: "How much do parents of babies and toddlers know about their children's intellectual, social, and emotional development at the earliest ages?" and "What are parents doing to encourage healthy development of their babies in these interrelated domains?" (Melmed, 1997, p. 46).

Results of this study are reported in nine points.

1. Parents know that early childhood is important but they do not understand the full significance of this period to human development.

2. Parents believe that they can impact emotional development moreso than intellectual or social development of their young children.

3. Parents see the first three years as not so important for the area of social development.

4. Parents emphasize nature over nurture when it comes to their children's intellectual development.

5. Parents play down the effect that outside child-care arrangements have on their children's development, especially if a stable home life is provided.

6. Parents are learning about children's needs as they parent rather than before they become parents.

7. Parents want information about early brain development, and specific information about what it means and what they should be doing for their children.

8. Parents emphasize their role in keeping their children safe, and seem not to know ways to match activities for and interactions with the development, interests, temperament, and moods of their children.

9. Parents desire to spend more time with their children.

Interactions with Early Childhood Educators

This study leads to many implications for early childhood teachers. One realization is that parents may deemphasize the importance of quality care outside the home, especially two-parent families who can provide well for their children. Those working in early care and education can feel devalued with this attitude. However, it will be important that early childhood professionals build on the importance of the family to children. Parents are vital to the young child's development, so finding areas of common ground and agreement between parents and educators is important. For this reason, it is essential that early education address all aspects of the child's development: physical, cognitive, social, and emotional.

Melmed (1997) suggests two parental needs that early childhood educators can help meet:

- Information for understanding their particular children's feelings or needs, especially for difficult situations

- Creative ways that they can spend more quality time with their children

What ideas do you have for each of these two ways to meet family needs?

While the ZERO TO THREE study emphasizes some similarities in parental beliefs about early development, Trawick-Smith (1997) outlines differences in beliefs about children related to cul-

It is important that early education address all aspects of the child's development: physical, cognitive, social, and emotional.

ture, poverty, and oppression. Culture affects beliefs about childhood through daily life and expectations; some see childhood as a carefree time to play and explore, others as a time to teach serious responsibility. Often, families and cultures who have endured great adversity in their lives have quite different belief systems than those who were fortunate to receive advantage and privilege.

As you review the nine points from the ZERO TO THREE study, consider how these statements might guide parent-teacher conferences and discussions. Understanding and appreciating parents' beliefs and knowledge of child development can help teachers and caregivers plan effective communications and interactions. Providing clearly worded statements about program goals and expectations can also help parents match their beliefs with the program's goals and expectations. Listening to parents can also help programs change and evolve to meet different expectations while still being grounded in developmentally appropriate practice.

Summary and Conclusions

Many parents have children through biological means. Others become parents in various ways. No matter how one becomes a parent, there are many responsibilities involved in this family role. All parents need support in providing the best for their children. Traditional mother and father roles continue to be common in today's society. Children can thrive in alternative family forms, including single-parent families, gay and lesbian families, and families headed by grandparents. An authoritative parenting style is most effective in fostering children's optimal development.

Parents have legal rights as well as responsibilities. It is very important that early childhood teachers understand the primacy of the family in the lives of young children. This understanding lends support for active family involvement in early childhood education. Teachers must initiate partnerships with family members. Whether the role of parents is being played traditionally or nontraditionally, early childhood professionals will increase children's opportu-

nities for academic success by involving those adults who are parenting young children in their programs.

Key Terms

parenting	permissive-indulgent
artificial	parenting
insemination	expressive role
adoption	public policies
attachment	blended families
spirituality	nurturance
authoritative parenting	socialization
permissive parenting	authoritarian
permissive-indifferent	parenting
parenting	instrumental role

Chapter Five Applications

1. Consider the results of the ZERO TO THREE study. Discuss the significance of each of the nine findings. How might early childhood teachers or administrators support families in each of these areas?

2. How might the way in which parents come to their parenting role affect their parenting philosophy and strategies? For example, how might adoptive parents differ from biological parents, and so on?

3. Discuss how specifics about each of the parenting roles have changed in the past generation or two. Also, discuss ways in which parents vary in carrying out each of the roles.

Questions for Reflection and Discussion

1. How will you involve all members of a family in your classroom? Will you differentiate requests for fathers and mothers?

2. How will you implement content from this chapter in your interactions with parents?

3. In what way is it helpful to understand variations in parenting styles and behaviors?

Field Assignments

1. Interview three mothers and three fathers about their interactions with their children.

Compare the responses to research findings in this chapter.

2. Interview a parent from a blended family who is parenting both his or her biological child(ren) and a child or children of his or her spouse. Ask about both challenges and joys.

3. Interview two early childhood professionals about ideas they have for creative ways parents can spend more quality time with their children. Share these ideas in class. Compose a class list of the best ideas to keep for a resource.

References

Baumrind, D. (1966). Effects of authoritative parental control on child behavior. *Child Development, 37,* 887–906.

Baumrind, D. (1967). Child care practices anteceding three patterns of preschool behavior. Genetic *Psychology Monographs, 75,* 43–88.

Baumrind, D. (1971). Current patterns of parental authority. *Developmental Psychology Monographs, 4*(1, Pt. 2), 1–103.

Baumrind, D. (1977). Some thoughts about childrearing. In S. Cohen & T. J. Comiskey (Eds.), *Child development: Contemporary perspectives.* Itasca, IL: F. E. Peacock.

Brazelton, T. B., & Greenspan, S. I.(2000). *The irreducible needs of children: What every child must have to grow, learn and flourish.* Cambridge, MA: Perseus.

Bronfenbrenner, U., & Neville, P. R. (1994). America's children and families: An international perspective. In S. L. Kagan & B. Weissbourd (Eds.), *Putting families first: America's family support movement and the challenge of change.* San Francisco: Jossey-Bass.

Children's Defense Fund, (1998, January). What it costs to raise a child. *CDF Reports, 19*(1). http://www.childrensdefense.org/factsfigures_costchild.htm.

Coles, R. (1990). *The spiritual life of children.* Boston: Houghton Mifflin.

Doucette-Dudman, D., & LaCure, J. R. (1996). *Raising our children's children.* Minneapolis, MN: Fairview Press.

Goeting, A. (1986). Parental satisfaction. *Journal of Family Issues, 7*(1), 83–109.

Guggenheim, M., Lowe, A. D., & Curtis, D. (1996). *The rights of families: The authoritative ACLU guide to the rights of family members today.* Carbondale, IL: Southern Illinois University Press.

Hamburg, D. (1995). *The challenge of parenthood.* The challenge of parenting in the '90's. Queenstown, MD: The Aspen Institute.

Hamner, T. J., & Turner, P. H. (1996). *Parenting in contemporary society.* Boston: Allyn & Bacon.

Hanson, T. L., McLanahan, S. S., & Thomson, E. (1996). Double jeopardy: Parental conflict and stepfamily outcomes for children. *Journal of Marriage and the Family, 58,* 141–154.

Higginbotham, J. S. (1998, November 12). *Adoption and privacy.* Harrisburg Patriot-News.

Kornhaber, A. (1993). Raising grandchildren. *Vital Connections, 14,* 1–4.

Kostelnik, M. J., Stein, L. L., Whiren, A. P., & Soderman, A. K. (1998). *Guiding children's social development.* Clifton Park, NY: Delmar Learning.

Lickona, T., Schaps, E., & Lewis, C. (1998, November/December). Eleven principles of effective character education. *Scholastic Early Childhood Today,* 53–55.

Maccoby, E. E., & Martin, J. A. (1983). Socialization in the context of the family: Parent-child interaction. In P. H. Mussen (Ed.), *Handbook of child psychology* (4th ed., vol. 4). New York: Wiley.

Melmed, M. (1997). Parents speak: Zero to Three's findings from research on parents' views of early childhood development. *Young Children, 52*(5), 46–49.

Miracle babies. (October 12, 1998). People.

Parsons, T., & Bales, R. (1955). *Family, socialization, and interaction process.* Glencoe, IL: Free Press.

Pearl, P. T. (2000). Grandparenting. In L. Balter (Ed.), *Parenthood in America: An encyclopedia.* Denver: ABC CLIO.

Rosenberg, E. B. (1992). *The adoption life cycle: The children and their families through the years.* New York: Free Press.

Rothenberg, D. (1999). Grandparents as parents: A primer for schools. (Report: EDO-PS-96-8). Urbana, IL. ERIC Clearinghouse on Elementary and Early Childhood Education, ERIC Digest (073). (ERIC Document Reproduction No. ED(401044).

Stolley, K. (1993). Statistics on adoption in the United States. *The Future of Children: Adoption, 3*(1), 26–42.

Trawick-Smith, J. (1997). *Early childhood development: A multicultural perspective.* Upper Saddle River, NJ: Prentice-Hall.

OUTLINE

CHAPTER 6

Family Stress

OBJECTIVES

After reading and reflecting on this chapter, you should be able to:

■ Relate the effects of various unpredictable stressors in the lives of families with young children.

■ Understand some of the societal beliefs that are at the root of various forms of family violence.

■ Explain the grief process involved in a family's sense of loss.

Family Systems Theory

The Circumplex Model and Family Coping

Some families are better able to cope with stress than others. Olson and his associates (Olson, Russell, & Sprenkle, 1989) found that of the three types of families categorized by the circumplex model (**balanced**, **midrange**, and **extreme**), balanced families have more resources that they use for coping. Some of these resources are good financial management skills, appreciation for personalities of other family members, strong support from family and friends, and satisfaction with their quality of life. Further, balanced families are more likely to deal with stressors rather than deny them; they are more effective communicators and they have better problem-solving strategies.

Boss (1988) defines **family coping** as "the management of a stressful event or situation by the family as a unit with no detrimental effects on any individual in that family. Family coping is the cognitive, affective, and behavioral process by which individuals and their family system as a whole manage rather than eradicate stressful events or situations" (pp. 60–61). This definition implies that passively coping with traumatic situations may be detrimental to family functioning. Sometimes, giving up is required for a family to change. Boss (1988) notes that "even though it looks like failure when a family fails to cope, the failure itself can be positive" (p. 64). Thus, when families place too heavy an emphasis on coping, they may not adapt or change in ways that could increase their quality of life.

Horizontal Stressors

Chapter 3 addressed the developmental issues typical for young families or families with young children. These situations are referred to in family systems theory as developmental stressors. Another type of horizontal stressor in this theory is one that is unpredictable for families, regardless of the stage in the family life cycle (Carter & McGoldrick, 1989). The nature of these unpredictable stressors makes them difficult to cope with and to resolve.

Families and Unpredictable Stressors

Examples of unpredictable events include family violence, effects of substance abuse, homelessness, disabilities, various illnesses, and immigration.

Family Violence

Violence is prevalent in the lives of families in the United States. The very institution that should be providing love and nurturance is also the one in which violence is too often perpetrated. It is important that early childhood teachers have some understanding of the rate of violence as well as ideas about why it is so common. Women and children are at greater risk of being victims of abuse than are men.

Straus (1991) discusses five social causes of **family violence**:

* High level of conflict inherent to family life
* Gender inequality
* Norms that allow violence in the family
* Early training in violence within the family
* Multiple risk factors such as alcoholism, poverty, and societal violence

High Level of Conflict Inherent in Family Life.

Some of the inherent conflicts in families arise from gender and age differences, involuntary membership in the family, insulation or privacy, and the relationship of violence to conflict. These factors are considered to play at least some role in family violence. Any of the factors by itself would not be viewed as the sole cause or reason for violence. Understanding the complexity of causes of family violence is important; one cannot predict that violence will

exist in a given family based on the presence of one or more of these factors.

Gender and Age Differences.

Most families are made up of both males and females, and have members of various ages. A great deal of research points to gender differences in values, priorities, interests, and notions about power. These differences lead to male-female differences in families. Some areas of difference include amount of income, activities and interests, and even television programming. In most families, these differences do not lead to violence, but when other factors are present, such differences seem to result in harm against females, younger children, or older family members. Although abuse can be committed against males, they are less likely to be physically hurt by it. The generation gap also creates a number of areas of conflict. Different generations have different preferences for music, clothing styles, and how they spend their leisure time.

Involuntary Membership.

Family members did not necessarily choose each other. Even though marriage partners in the United States are likely to have at one time chosen each other, many factors influence these choices, including the belief that they had many areas in common with one another. Marriage and parenthood often squelch some of those common interests. Responsibilities tend to take over each person.

Family Preservation and Child Welfare Network
http://www.familypreservation.com
Family Violence Prevention Fund
http://endabuse.org/
National Clearinghouse on Child Abuse and
    Neglect Information
http://www.calib.com/nccanch/index.cfm
National Coalition Against Domestic Violence
http://www.ncadv.org/
National Council on Child Abuse and Family
    Violence
http://www.nccafv.org/
National Domestic Violence Hotline
http://www.ndvh.org/

Children and parents do not typically choose each other. Rather, they get the "luck of the draw." Some children are fortunate to have parents who nurture and understand their needs without reverting to violent methods of child-rearing. Others are less fortunate. The very fact that many family members are put together by circumstance rather than choice can cause tension among members. The old adage "You can choose your friends, but not your relatives" has more meaning than many realize. This factor carries over to relationships with in-laws and stepchildren.

Family Privacy.   Families are often insulated and have strong beliefs about being self-sufficient. The notion of privacy in the family can often be taken to an extreme. Spouses may speak to each other and their children in ways they would not want anyone else to hear. Behavior that is not observed by outsiders is less likely to be civil or humane, especially in the face of conflict. It is this factor—family privacy—that is overlooked by many when a pillar of the community is accused of spousal or child abuse. Family privacy, while of tremendous value, can also lead to family secrets: "It's nobody's business."

Increasing Conflict Leads to Violence.   As the amount of conflict increases in a variety of areas within a family, violence becomes more likely. Family privacy, sexism, and physical power increase the likelihood that a person believes that he is right to use fists to settle conflict. There is little chance of getting caught and a good beating is believed to have the capacity to stop the behavior that is causing conflict.

Gender Inequality.   Many people believe that husbands are and should be the heads of households. This belief is supported in many informal ways throughout our society. Legal documents often list male names first, even in the case of co-ownership or joint income tax returns. Sometimes, this leads to a belief in male dominance, that men have ultimate responsibility for all decisions and practices in their families. Research shows that "the greater the departure from gender equality, the greater the risk that physical force will be used to maintain the power of

the dominant person" (Straus, 1991, p. 26). This is true even when females agree that males should be dominant. Now, even though male dominance is a factor in family violence, it is important to understand that most male-dominant marriages are not violent. This **gender inequality** is one factor that makes violence more likely.

Society's Sanction of Violence.   Parents are both permitted, and in some communities, expected to use physical punishment on their children. When child abuse laws were passed in the 1970s, most laws indicated that the intent was not to take away parental authority or the rights of parents to use physical punishment. A vast majority of parents use physical punishment, especially with young children. Fully 90 percent of parents support the use of such methods as necessary for child-rearing.

Just as our cultural norms support spanking and other forms of physical punishment of children, they also frequently support hitting in marriage. Even though many say they oppose violence generally, large numbers of adults still note that there are some instances when spouses can and should be hit, especially those related to extramarital sexual affairs. But it is never permissible to strike a colleague in the heat of disagreement, nor is it socially acceptable to use violence in any other social setting.

Early Training in Family Violence.   In families, violence is carried out by loving parents who are genuinely concerned about their children. The use of physical punishment for even small infractions teaches children that hitting within families is okay. "The problem is that these actions also teach the child the principle that those who love you are those who hit you" (Straus, 1991, p. 29). Research has shown that the more adults were physically punished as children, the greater the chance that they will hit their spouses as adults (Straus, 1983).

Multiple Causes.   In addition to the factors already mentioned, other factors that increase the probability of violence in families include alcoholism and other forms of substance abuse, poverty, and other types of stress on families. None of these factors necessarily predicts family violence. Even though violence occurs at an alarmingly high rate, there are more nonviolent families than violent ones, even when several factors are in place. However, having several factors in a family places that family at a much higher risk. When factors were placed in a checklist format, as the scores on the checklist increased, so did violence increase (Straus, Gelles, & Steinmetz, 1980).

Research indicates that family violence is not committed by only a few very sick individuals. It is much more widespread than many people believe. Early childhood teachers must take seriously any indication that children in their care may have been abused. This is true even when the teacher tends to doubt the possibility of abuse because the child comes from a "good family."

A Particular Form of Family Violence: Child Abuse

The Child Abuse Prevention and Treatment Act of 1974, PL 93–247, defined **child abuse and neglect.** This law described abuse and neglect as "the physical or mental injury, sexual abuse, negligent treatment, or maltreatment of a child under the age of eighteen by a person who is responsible for the child's welfare under the circumstances which indicate that the child's health or welfare is harmed or threatened thereby" (U.S. Department of Health, Education, and Welfare, 1975, p. 3). Individual state statutes are based on this federal law and are available from county courthouses, state legislators, or state legislative libraries (Iverson & Segal, 1990).

Early childhood educators and child advocates often question the causes of child abuse. They wonder about the type of person who could hurt small children. Concern about safety and best placements for children whose family members have abused them is common. Although many believe that only someone with a severe mental disorder would harm a small child, reality does not bear this out. Historically, children, viewed as property of parents, could be legally harmed or killed by parents. This perspective affected both attitudes and behaviors toward children.

Until the 1974 law was passed, there were few safeguards for children whose parents maltreated

them. In contrast, cruelty to animals was outlawed at least a century earlier. It was the Society for the Prevention of Cruelty to Animals (SPCA) that advocated for Mary Ellen in a widely publicized case of severe child abuse in 1874. This brief historical review demonstrates that abuse of children has been an acceptable practice based in part on the low status of children in families and in society (Inverson & Segal, 1990).

Research over the past thirty years has demonstrated the ill effects of abuse and neglect on children. Early childhood educators are aware that these effects on children ultimately affect classroom dynamics. Based on ecological theory, Garbarino (as cited in Iverson and Segal, 1990) notes two primary causes of abuse as parental psychopathology and societal approval of physical punishment of children. It follows that preventive efforts must focus on both of these causes. Family support services must include attention to mental health needs in families as well as alternatives to physical punishment of children.

Some family characteristics have been shown to be related to abuse of children. In their review of literature, Iverson and Segal (1990) note the following factors:

- Parental experience includes models parents have for child-rearing, especially from their own families and in their own cultures; skills for parenting; and understanding of child development.

- High levels of stress caused either by children or environment; poverty is especially stressful.

- Some characteristics of parents who abuse their children include physical or medical problems, intellectual deficits, lack of ability to form healthy parent-child relationship, marital problems, low self-esteem, immaturity, neuroses, dependency, and depression.

- Teen parents are more likely to possess the characteristics of parents who abuse because of their developmental levels. Because of their developmental stage, teens are consumed with themselves and often financially dependent.

These characteristics place them at higher risk for abusing their children.

Although the characteristics listed above place families at higher risk for child abuse, not all teen parents or those with intellectual deficits will harm their children. Understanding the risk factors should help professionals provide appropriate resources for preventing neglect and abuse of children. For example, parenting programs for those at risk might include not only information about what is best for their children but also child care for teen parents so that they are able to complete their education. Those living in poverty will benefit from high-quality child care so that they can finish school or take advantage of job training opportunities.

Effects of abuse and neglect on children are listed in Figures 6–1 and 6–2 (Iverson & Segal, 1990).

Infants and Toddlers
attachment disorders
aggressive toward peers and caregivers
not responsive to friendly overtures

Preschoolers
physically and/or verbally aggressive
destructive behavior
angry outbursts
less socially mature than nonmaltreated children
play alone or watch others from a distance

School-agers
angry
aggressive
less impulsive than maltreated preschool children

Figure 6–1 Effects of abuse and neglect on children.

Physical Characteristics of Maltreated Children

Physical Abuse
Bruises, lacerations, welts, abrasions, fractures, or burns as follows:

Unusual Location	• cheeks, lips, mouth, earlobes
	• back, buttocks, back of legs
	• external genitalia
	• burns on soles of feet, palms of hands, back, or buttocks
Unusual Appearance	• clustered or patterned
	• resembling the shape of an instrument
	• on several different surface areas
	• cigar or cigarette burns
	• immersion (glove- or sock-like) burns
	• rope burns (especially on neck)

Suspicious Circumstances	• no explanation
	• explanation does not fit injury
	• patterns to the occurrence of injuries (e.g., after absences from school)
	• repeated injuries or injuries in various stages of healing

Whiplash syndrome in infants
Nonorganic failure to thrive

Neglect
Underweight, malnourished
Poor hygiene
Fatigue, constant falling asleep
Bald spot on infant's head
Unattended physical problems or medical needs:
  • chronic anemia

continues

Figure 6–2 Indicators of abuse and neglect. (With permission from Iverson, T. J., & Segal, M. (1990). *Child abuse and neglect: An information and reference guide.* Table 4–1, p. 72, Table 4–4, p. 95, and Table 4–6, p. 106)

Physical Abuse
- severe diaper rash
- skin rashes
- tooth decay/gum disease

Neglect
- head/body lice
- ringworm

Nonorganic failure to thrive

Sexual Abuse

Swelling, bruising or irritation around
- genital areas
- anal areas
- mouth

- Torn, stained, or bloody underclothing
- Pain/discomfort in walking or sitting
- Genital pain or itching
- Difficulty in urination

- Vaginal discharge
- Anal ulcers
- Venereal diseases
- Pregnancy

Emotional Abuse

Physical symptoms of anxiety:
- psychogenic skin disorders
- pain with no physical basis
- ulcers
- unexplained vomiting

Common Descriptions of the Interpersonal Behavior of Maltreated Children

Physical Abuse	Neglect	Sexual Abuse	Emotional Abuse
Aggression	Aggression	Sexually aggressive or preoccupied	Aggressive
Withdrawal	Withdrawal	Overly compliant	Suspicious
Avoidance	Suspicious/distrustful	Seductive	Avoids eye contact
Fearful of others	of others	Distrustful	Unable to make friends
Angry	Unresponsive	Fearful of opposite sex	Overly compliant
"Frozen watchfulness"	Hostility	"Role reversal"	Overly noncompliant
Hostility		Withdrawn	Bizarre or inappropriate
		Isolated	interpersonal behavior

Behavior Sequelae of Maltreatment

Physical Abuse	Neglect	Sexual Abuse	Emotional Abuse
Self-abusive behavior	Irregular school	Excessive daydreaming/fantasizing	Self-abusive behavior
Lying	attendance	Excessive sexual play/masturbation	Hoarding food
Stealing	Begging, stealing, or	Self-abusive behavior	Referral to self in the third
Truancy	hoarding food	Truancy	person
Tics	Lying	Running away	Thumb-sucking
Stuttering	Theft	Regressive/infantile behavior	Nailbiting
Unpredictable	Vandalism	Suicidal gestures	Habit disorders—
	Running away	Insomnia	sucking, biting, rocking

continues

Figure 6–2   (continued)

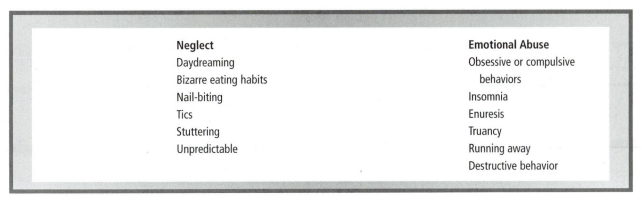

Neglect	Emotional Abuse
Daydreaming	Obsessive or compulsive behaviors
Bizarre eating habits	Insomnia
Nail-biting	Enuresis
Tics	Truancy
Stuttering	Running away
Unpredictable	Destructive behavior

Figure 6–2 (continued).

Early childhood teachers have a legal responsibility to report any suspected case of child abuse. For this reason, it is important that professionals be familiar with indicators of physical, sexual, and emotional abuse and neglect of children. Knowledge of such factors is extremely useful as teachers take notes and document reasons they have to suspect abuse. Reporting an instance of possible child abuse is not intended to punish families, but rather to help them receive the interventions they need to help with managing their children and their lives.

Many states have hot lines for reports of child abuse. If you do not know your hot line or who to call, contact your State Department of Human Services. These departments have a variety of names including Public Welfare, Human Resources, Family Services, and Child and Youth Services. Check the social service agency listings in your local telephone directory for help. Please note that even though schools and child care centers often create procedures for teachers to report suspected cases of abuse or neglect through principals or directors, many states list teachers as those who are required to report to state officials.

When you call to report a case of suspected child abuse, it is likely that the individual taking your call will ask the following information:

- From where are you calling?
- What is your name? (You may choose to remain anonymous, depending on circumstances.)
- What have you observed that led to this call?

- What is the child's name?
- How old is the child?
- What are the child's parents' names?
- Where does the child go to school?
- Provide a description of the child.
- What is the child's address?
- Have you discussed your observations with the child or family members?

It is important for educators to understand that reports are made to child protective service workers, but that ultimately, it is the legal system—the courts—that decides the outcome for abused children and their families. Although agencies and courts have critical roles in attacking the problem of child abuse in our society, teachers of young children have an increasingly important role.

When the 1988 reauthorization of funding bill for the National Center on Child Abuse and Neglect was legislated, the importance of increased school involvement in the prevention, identification, and treatment of child abuse and neglect was noted (Cicchetti, Toth, & Hennessy, 1993). This recommendation came about from the research evidence that maltreated children will have their learning processes interrupted or otherwise negatively affected. To optimize learning for children who have been abused and neglected, Cicchetti and his associates offer several suggestions for educators, details of which can be found in Figure 6–3.

The following recommendations are from the work of Cicchetti, Toth, and Hennessy (1993).

1. Assessments of maltreated children must include not only those for cognitive development and academic achievement but also those for the social and emotional domains. Because many abused children act out in school, too often the emphasis is on the behavior only and not on the emotional disturbance caused by abusive situations.

2. Intervention efforts must begin as soon as identification of maltreatment occurs. Schools may be the only setting in which such interventions can occur. Thus, courts and agencies must work with educators for positive outcomes. At this time, often interpretations of confidentiality procedures exclude educators and schools from appropriate levels of participation in intervention. Educators must increase their understanding of the importance of confidentiality in instances of abuse so that they can share appropriately in intervention efforts.

3. Early childhood teachers who are involved in intervention efforts should involve parents and other relevant family members. This creates the greatest possibility of continuity between environments.

4. The curriculum for maltreated children must be developmentally appropriate. Including all areas of child development in curriculum goals is essential so that these children have a greater chance for adjustment throughout their lives. Special planning and instructional support may be necessary for children to gain abilities and attitudes for cognitive, social, and emotional growth.

5. Specific training for teachers is necessary in regard to styles and strategies that are conducive to optimizing development of maltreated children. Teachers must recognize and avoid "any physically or emotionally abusive interchanges with children." The use of physical punishment must be forbidden. Too few teachers are trained in early childhood special education, especially in the area of emotional support. Research suggests that an extrinsic, behaviorally focused system for these children may interfere with their motivation. Thus, behavior modification programs should not be used with abused and neglected children. Instead, plans should include strategies for increasing the children's internal motivation while dealing with their emotional distress.

6. Teachers of young children are very important figures in children's lives. A positive relationship based on trust is important. Some current practices such as multiage grouping and looping are useful for abused children in that they may continue to build positive relationships with the same teacher or teachers for longer than one school term.

7. Since identification of abuse and neglect must come before any educational intervention can be offered, teachers and schools must improve their knowledge regarding recognizing and reporting instances of maltreatment. Having the attitude that reporting is required to help the child, not to punish the family, is also an important understanding.

8. Training must be provided so that child protective services workers and educators work together. Little progress has been made in this area and unfortunately, these groups of professionals often see the other group as problematic instead of working collegially toward more effective interventions. To be fair to individuals, the human services system and the educational system have not typically fostered these working relationships.

Figure 6–3 Policy implications for schools educating maltreated children. (*Source:* Cicchetti, D., Toth, S. L., & Hennessy, K. [1993]. Child maltreatment and school adaptation: Problems and promises. In D. Cicchetti and S. L. Toth [Eds.], *Child abuse, child development, and social policy* [pp. 301–330]. Norwood, NJ: Ablex)

"Children have neither power nor property. Voices other than their own must speak for them. If those voices are silent, then children who have been abused may lean their heads against windowpanes and taste the bitter emptiness of violated childhoods. Badger every legislator from every county . . . . let no editor or reporter sleep, until the remedy you want is granted. For you are the only voices of the violated child. If you do not speak, there is silence."
—Justice Francis T. Murphy. Cited in Doucette-Dudman & LaCure, 1996

Resources for Information about Child Abuse and Neglect.

National Center on Child Abuse and Neglect (NCCAN)
63 Inverness Drive East
Englewood, Colorado 80112–5117
(303) 792–9900
http://ojjdp.ncjr.org/pubs/fedresourcest110 ag-05.html

National Committee to Prevent Child Abuse
332 S. Michigan Avenue, Suite 1600
Chicago, Illinois 60604
(312) 663–3520
http://www.casanet.org/library/abuse

National Association of Counsel for Children
205 Oneida Street
Denver, Colorado 80822
(303) 322–2260
http://naccchildlaw.org/

Substance Abuse in Families

When family members use illegal drugs, or misuse alcohol or prescription drugs, children often suffer great difficulties. Parents who are addicted to drugs and/or alcohol typically cannot provide consistent nurturing for their children. Further, economic well-being of the family is compromised when adults lose their jobs because of behavior related to substance abuse.

Center for Interventions, Treatment and Addiction Research
http://www.med.wright.edu/citar
Center for Substance Abuse Treatment
http://www.samhsa.gov/centers/csat2002 csat_frame.html
Center on Addiction and Substance Abuse
http://www.casacolumbia.org/

Prenatal use of alcohol and drugs may have dire consequences for newborns that last throughout life. Drinking alcohol during pregnancy may lead to babies having Fetal Alcohol Syndrome (FAS); the safe level of drinking during pregnancy is not known. Some of the characteristics of FAS include central nervous system disorders, growth lags, and facial deformity (Olson, 1994). Effects of maternal drug use on infants and young children include neurological immaturity, which is manifested in poor sleeping and eating patterns, poor self-control, inconsolability, hypersensitivity to the environment, and decreased ability to interact with others (Poulsen, 1994).

Addiction to any substance (or condition) points to personality characteristics, disabilities, or impairments, each of which may have significant implications for an adult's ability to parent a child, and may predispose an adult to adopt an authoritarian, overcontrolling, or underinvolved style of parenting. Moreover, all substances of abuse alter in varying degree an individual's state of consciousness, memory, affect regulation, and impulse control, and may become so addictive that the adult's primary goal is to be able to supply his or her addiction to the exclusion of all else and all others in his or her life. These types of alterations likely influence markedly at any given moment the adult's capacity to sustain contingent, responsive interactions with an infant and young child (Mayes, 1995, p. 105).

Children who are growing up in homes in which one or more adults are addicted to drugs or alcohol are likely to be affected in one or more of the following ways:

- child reverses roles with parent
- fearful, angry, mistrusting, guilty, and sad
- either overresponsible or underresponsible
- chronic grief or depression
- isolated from others
- academic problems
- learning disabilities (Krestan & Bepko, 1989)

Children living in families with alcoholism or drug abuse frequently need more support than classroom teachers can provide. Referring children to guidance counselors or other mental health professionals may be helpful.

"Numerous barriers stand between women, especially mothers, and drug treatment. For example, women often resist entering treatment programs because they must release their children to someone else's care and fear never seeing them again. Despite this reality, only a handful of residential drug-treatment programs accept women with their children. Treatment programs need to be developed that treat parents, especially mothers, in the context of their families."

—Zuckerman & Brazelton, 1994, p. 82

Marital Transitions and Single Parenting

Divorce and remarriage have become so common in our society today that some family experts believe that they may be developmental stressors rather than unexpected ones. However, since the consequences of divorce and remarriage for young children are often stressful, attention will be given to these transitions in this section of the text. The prevalence of divorce and remarriage may cause teachers and parents to disregard or discount the significance of these occurrences in the lives of children. Although children may benefit from knowing other children and families in similar circumstances, by and large, the changes in family structure are likely to lead to some concerns for all family members.

In the United States, the divorce rate began to rise in the 1960s. Currently, almost 50 percent of marriages end in divorce. Most people who divorce will eventually remarry. Remarriages in which children from previous relationships are present have a 50 percent rate of dissolution than those without children from previous relationships (Fields & Casper, 2001).

The number of single-parent families has also increased since 1970. In 2000, there were 10 million single-mother families compared to 3 million in 1970. The number of single-father families also increased during the same time period from 393,000 to 2 million. Compared to single-father families, single-mother families are more likely to have more than one child, to live below the poverty level, and to have never married. As the proportion of married couples has decreased, the proportion of U.S. families that are led by single mothers has increased. Single-parent families have increased both as a result of the divorce rate and a rise in the number of births among single women. Birth rates among single women continued to increase throughout the 1990s even as the divorce rate has begun to level off. Some experts predict that the divorce rate may soon fall to 40 percent (Emery, 1999; Fields & Casper, 2001).

Disagreement persists among scholars about the effects of divorce on children. Even though many studies have been completed in this area, so many variables in families have impeded researchers from declaring conclusive results. Robert Emery (1999), in his extensive review of research literature, has compiled "four global facts about consequences of divorce for children" (p. 35).

1. Divorce causes stress for children. Such stress is often related to the loss of frequent contact with one parent. Another common cause of stress has to do with the economic hardship families face as they divide one household into two.

2. Children whose parents divorce are at an increased risk for psychological difficulties, both internalized (depression, anxiety) and externalized (behavioral, conduct) problems.

3. Despite children's increased risk for psychological problems when their parents divorce, they are resilient in their coping.

4. Even with this ability to cope, children remain emotionally vulnerable when parents divorce. Even well-adjusted adults whose parents divorced when they were children report the existence of painful feelings, unhappy memories, and ongoing distress.

One topic that is perplexing about divorce and children has to do with cause and effect. It might be that children who display serious consequences seemingly from parental divorce may actually have had some distress or difficulties before the divorce. Sometimes, divorce exacerbates children's behaviors, or it may be the reason that family members or educators take notice of concerns regarding children. Children's difficulties may have sources other than parental divorce such as troubled parents, relationship issues, parents who lack parenting skills, or parents who have mental health-related issues. It is possible that these situations lead to parents being more likely to divorce and to having troubled children (Emery, 1999).

The resilience of children has been documented in research about divorce. Even though children from divorced families have more difficulties than children from married families, "time does appear to help divorced families to heal" (Emery, 1999, p. 61). Support and concern from caring adults is helpful to children experiencing divorce; however, the passing of time is an important consideration. Researchers have found that most children show significant improvement in their adjustment two years after the divorce (Emery, 1999).

> *"Perhaps what is most insensitive and unjust is to arrive at the conclusions about divorce and its effects on children without carefully considering what we know, not just what we believe."*
> —**Robert Emery, 1999, p.1**

A key question for early childhood teachers when examining the effects of divorce on young children is "What factors help children reach a healthy adjustment as their family structure changes?" Parents can implement some strategies that will help to support children's increased adjustment to the new family structure. Galinsky and David (1988) share this advice for parents:

Explain the separation to the children and provide as much consistency as possible. Tell them where they will live, who will care for them, and when and how they will visit the noncustodial parent. Keep them updated on changes in advance of new situations.

Explain that the separation is not the child's fault and that it might take a while to feel better about it. Young children often believe that they caused the separation or divorce because of inappropriate behavior or a one-time wish. Parents most likely will need to frequently remind children that they were not the cause. Sharing feelings, both sad and optimistic, will be important for the healing process.

Encourage children to continue the discussion when they have concerns or questions. In addition to authentic conversations, children's books and media can provide a basis for discussion. Invite children to initiate conversation with you.

Provide support for children and yourself. Children and adults need various forms of social, emotional, and sometimes physical support as they adjust to new circumstances involved in divorce. Both personal (family and friends) and professional support is helpful.

Avoid promises, uncertain assurances, surprises, and extravagances led by guilt. Focus on what is real. Have fun together. Delight in the joys that exist in the relationship with your child.

Teachers and other community members can be excellent sources of support for children and parents as they adjust to their new living arrangements. Early childhood teachers can share the above advice for parents through newsletters or the establishment of special interest parent groups. Further, schoolwide groups for children have been found to be effective in supporting their adjustment to divorce. Children not only share their feelings

To listen to a mother speak about single parenting go to the online resource.

This single parent of two discusses the day-to-day responsibilities and relationships she has with her children. she also emphasizes the need for the school's support in helping her care for and educate her children in this insightful online voice.

and experiences but also discuss their changing family relationships. Strategies to support children in these discussions through various marital transitions such as separation, divorce, remarriage, or other blended living arrangements are helpful. Effective programs teach children specific appropriate skills for problem-solving, communication, and expression of emotions including fear and anger (Emery, 1999).

Adjustment Tasks for Stepfamilies
**http://www.stepfamilyinfo.org/09/
sf-task1.htm**
Divorce education and Mediation Program
**http://www.hamiltontn.gov/Courts/Circuit
Clerk/education.htm**
Helping children to Understand divorce
**http://www.muextension.missouri.edu/xplor/
hesguide/humanrel/gh6600.htm**
Primary Project
**http://www.childrensinstitute.net/programs/
primary/htm**

Homeless Families

The number of **homeless** individuals in the United States today is increasing. Precise statistics are difficult to come by because of the elusive nature of homelessness; one estimate from 1990 indicates that 500,000 to 750,000 school-age children are homeless and that this number is growing (National Coalition for the Homeless as cited in

Kling, Dunn, & Oakley, 1996). Many advocates agree that all young children have the right to a safe space to live. Much of our understanding about the optimal development of the whole child assumes physical and emotional safety. "The average homeless family includes two to three children under age five" (p. 3). It is believed that a common reason for homelessness is an inadequate supply of affordable housing along with declining family incomes, even when the adults in the household are employed. In short, there is too little money to pay for available housing.

The effects on children of being homeless are vast. Among the difficulties are language and motor delays and unmet health needs. Behavioral problems and emotional disabilities are frequently found in children who live in shelters. In addition, many of the children's parents also are plagued with mental health problems (Hamner & Turner, 1996).

Living conditions among homeless families vary: some live in a shelter, some have lived in several shelters over a period of months, and others live with friends or extended families. When homeless families move in with another family, conditions are frequently overcrowded and offer no privacy. Stays may last for only weeks or a few months, and the family may move in with other friends or family members. For children in early childhood programs, these relocations often mean that they either drop out of the program (before mandatory school age) or change schools. These disruptions may come suddenly and are difficult transitions for young children.

Education of Homeless Children and Youth
http://nch.ari.net/edchild.html
Futures for Children
http://www.futuresforchildren.com/
Homeless Children's Network
http://www.hcnkids.org/
Homes for the Homeless
http://www.homesforthehomeless.com/
The Reading Connection
http://www.thereadingconnection.org/

Following are some characteristics of homeless children:

- sleep disturbances
- nighttime anxieties about possessions, even wearing their shoes to prevent theft
- lethargy and inattention at school
- children may hoard food at school
- nutritional deficiencies
- delays in immunizations
- insecurity
- trouble playing with other children and making friends
- aggression
- anxiety
- language and other developmental delays (Kling, Dunn, & Oakley, 1996)

When parents are not able to provide shelter or security for their children, they often feel guilty and helpless. If they are not even competent enough to provide their children's basic needs, how can they possibly assist their children academically? Self-esteem of parents in homeless families is likely to be very low. Understanding these characteristics of homeless families and children can help early childhood teachers act sensitively toward them.

Early childhood educators must look for strengths of the homeless, just as they look for strengths in other families. Research shows that although these families have almost no material possessions, they do have "the desire and the will to maintain the family unit regardless of continual changes in their life circumstances" (Kling, Dunn, & Oakley, 1996, p. 7). All children need consistency in classroom schedules and routines, but children without homes need this consistency even more. They are also likely to need some alone time at school because they often live in crowded situations.

Parents in homeless families may not be able to participate as active partners in their children's education. Just getting their children to school is a huge accomplishment. Special invitations to homeless parents to be included in ways they feel comfortable may be a huge boost to their self-esteem. Following are

Reading materials about child development, family services available in the community, and free activities for parents and children to do together will assist early childhood educators who are working with homeless families.

some suggestions for early childhood educators who are working with homeless families:

- Set up a parent lounge where support groups might form.
- Provide reading materials about child development, family services available in the community, and free activities for parents and children to do together.
- Set up a toy lending library.
- Formulate a plan for homeless children to borrow toys from school to take to the shelter.
- Provide banks for clothing, food, and first aid materials.
- Maintain appropriate confidentiality while helping families get available services.

Early childhood educators should also be aware of the Stewart B. McKinney Homeless Assistance Act of 1987, which provides some funding to states for serving homeless families. Teachers should contact their State Department of Education to find out what programs for homeless families are operating in their state (Kling, Dunn, & Oakley, 1996).

Resources for Working with Homeless Families

The Homeless Information Exchange
  1830 Connecticut Avenue, NW
  Washington, DC 20009
  (202) 462–7551
  http://ericeece.org/pubs/digests/1993/goins93.
    html
National Alliance to End Homelessness
  1518 K Street NW, Suite 206
  Washington, DC 20005
  (202) 638–1526
  http://www.neh.org/
National Coalition for the Homeless
  1439 Rhode Island Avenue, NW
  Washington, DC 20005
  (202) 659–3310
National Law Center on Homelessness and Poverty
  918 F Street, NW, Suite 412
  Washington, DC 20004
  (202) 638–2535
  http://www.nlchp.org/

Families and Children with Disabilities

"Children may be born with one or more **disabilities**, and they may acquire disabilities later in life because of accident or disease" (Hamner & Turner, 1996, p. 315). When a baby is identified with a disability at birth, parents often react with disbelief. It is likely that many parents will proceed through the grief process because any baby who is not perfectly healthy can be perceived as a loss, certainly a lost dream if not a lost life (Figure 6–4). Although parents grieve in individual ways, some conditions of grieving seem to be common (Moses, 1983):

- denial
- anxiety
- guilt
- depression
- anger

> "What's supposed to be the best day of your life turns out to be like a funeral."
> —Robin Simons, 1987

Denial—Parents who are informed that their child has a disability are so overwhelmed by shock and fear that denial is one way to cope. They are likely to look for complete cures for their child's condition, even when none exist.

Anxiety—Constant concern for the child, as well as for their entire family, often leads parents to feel extreme pressure and worry. Arrangements for the child's medical care and further testing often overwhelm already busy parents. Sleeplessness, irritability, and other symptoms associated with anxiety may become prevalent.

Guilt—"If only I had eaten better;" "If only I had had earlier prenatal care;" "If only I. . . ." Parents attempt to assess what they did wrong and how they are at fault for the child's condition.

Depression—Parents may feel overwhelming sadness about the loss of what their child might have been. Dreams have been shattered. Parents focus on the disability.

Anger—At whom should parents direct their anger? Not the child, not the medical staff, not each other, not families or friends. Sometimes parents blame others who have no responsibility for their situation because there is no logical place to direct the anger.

Acceptance—With warmth and support from professionals, family, and friends, many parents of children with disabilities come to accept not only their child, but also their situation. They begin to focus on the child's gains instead of their own loss at what might have been.

Figure 6–4 Explanations for each of the conditions of grief.

Some factors are known to affect parental grief over the birth of a child with a disability. These include culture; religion; economic status; the nature of the disability; the family's ability to cope; the stability of the marriage; the number, gender, and age of other children in the family; and the availability of support systems. Consider two or three of these factors and tell how you believe they might affect families who have a new baby that has been identified as having a disability.

Children with Disabilities
http://www.childrenwithdisabilities.ncjrs.org/
ERIC Clearinghouse on Disabilities and Gifted
    Education
http://ericec.org
Exceptional Parent Magazine
http://www.eparent.com/
Federal Resource Center for Special Education
http://www.dssc.org/frc/index.htm
Free Appropriate Public Education Site
http://www.fapeonline.org/
A Guide to Children's Literature and Disability
http://www.kidsource.com/NICHCY/
    literature.html
Individualizing Inclusion in Child Care
http://www.fpg.unc.edu/~inclusion/
National Information Center for Children and
    Youth with Disabilities
http://www.nichcy.org/
Special Child
http://www.specialchild.com/index.html

Even when parents are coping well, families who have a child with disabilities have greater challenges than other families with young children. All infants and young children have many caregiving needs. Anyone who has cared for one healthy infant knows that it seems to be a full-time job. But children with disabilities have even greater needs, which consume much more time than typically developing children. Further, it is often difficult to find substitute care so that parents can have a much needed respite. Often, substitute caregivers do not feel that they have the additional knowledge or skills necessary to care for the child's special needs.

In addition to the challenge of caregiving demands, a second difference in families who have a child with disabilities is the level of stress. Hamner and Turner (1996) discuss the following causes of stress in these families:

- the need to feel "normal"
- lack of information about the child's condition
- concern about what the future holds for their child
- increased financial needs
- lack of sufficient support systems
- single parenthood

> *"I've heard this period called 'nothingness' and that's exactly how you feel. You can't move, can't think, can't do anything but feel—leaden, like a rock. There's nothing there—but that disability."*
> —**Robin Simons, 1987**

The one factor that seems to make a difference in helping families of children with disabilities to make a positive adjustment is the presence of informal support. Support from one's spouse is especially crucial. Families who have both sharing of tasks from inside the family as well as formal and informal support external to the family seem to cope best (Trivette & Dunst, 1992). Some planned programs for parents who have a child with a disability can include:

- Helping all children to understand and relate to a child who is differently-abled.
- Helping parents to help their children to respond to teasing or comments about his disability.
- Helping parents know how much to expect from their child's academic and social progress.
- Helping parents with strategies to advocate for their children's optimal education.
- Helping parents to know how and when to foster independence in their children with disabilities (Hendrick, 1998).

Since 1975, federal legislation mandates free public education for children with disabilities between

> *"I talk to other parents. There's no substitute for that. You find out you're not alone. You're not the only one with those concerns."*
> —**Robin Simons, 1987**

the ages of three and 21 years. In 1986, additional legislation required that all states provide preschool programs to all children between three and five years who have been identified as having a disability. Thus, many early childhood teachers are working in education settings that include young children with disabilities (Figure 6–5). Before the Education for All Handicapped Children Act of 1975 (PL 94-142) was passed, most children with identified disabilities were not served by public schools or were served only in special classes. Some children were able to attend special schools for children with similar disabilities such as blindness or deafness, but many children did not receive appropriate education or related services.

One of the major pieces of the 1986 legislation is the emphasis placed on the importance of the whole family of children with disabilities. Instead of requiring an Individual Education Plan (IEP), this law requires an Individualized Family Service Plan (IFSP). Attention is given to the needs of the child's whole family. Given the research on the special challenges felt by families of children who have a disability, this approach is believed to be much more effective than planning only an educational program for the child (Figure 6–6).

In addition to the parent involvement requirements for typically developing children and their families, Head Start requires even more of the staff who are working with families who have children with disabilities. The following standards, included by Head Start, are excellent guidelines for all early childhood educators:

- Support parents of children with disabilities.
- Provide information to parents on how to foster development of their child with disabilities.

PL 94-142 (1975) The Education for All Handicapped Children Act renamed in 1990 to the Individual with Disabilities Education Act (IDEA)

To assure "that all handicapped children have available to them . . . a free appropriate public education which emphasizes special education and related services designed to meet their unique needs, to assure that the rights of handicapped children and their parents or guardians are protected, to assist states and localities to provide for the education of all handicapped children, and to assess and assure the effectiveness of efforts to educate handicapped children."

Also, states were required to establish "procedures to assure that to the maximum extent appropriate, handicapped children, including children in public and private institutions or other care facilities, are educated with children who are not handicapped, and that special classes, separate schooling or other removal of handicapped children from the regular educational environment occurs only when the nature or severity of the handicap is such that education in regular classes with the use of supplementary aids and services can be achieved satisfactorily."

PL 99-457 (1986) The Infants and Toddlers with Disabilities Act (ITDA), now in IDEA

"ITDA requires provision of coordinated, multiagency, multidisciplinary services necessary to 'enhance' the development of infants and toddlers with disabilities. In addition to enhanced development, the law seeks to minimize the potential for developmental delay of children; eventually to reduce the need for special education and related services, and thereby reduce the cost of education for these children; to reduce the need for institutionalization and to 'maximize' their potential for independent living in a society; to work with families to assist them in meeting children's needs; and to assist the state and localities in meeting the needs of populations which are often underrepresented, for example, children living in poverty" (Guernsey & Klare, 1993, p. 250).

Figure 6–5   PL 94–142 and PL 99–457.

Each Individual Education Plan (IEP) and Individual Family Service Plan (IFSP) must contain:

1. Present levels of child's performance
   a. academic achievement
   b. social competence
   c. pre-vocational and vocational skills
   d. psychomotor skill
   e. self-help skills
2. Annual goals for child to achieve by end of school year
3. Measurable short-term instructional objectives that will assist the child in achieving the stated annual goals
4. Specific educational services needed by child including all special education related services, type of physical education program, and special instructional media and materials
5. Dates for services to begin and length of time to be provided
6. Description of how child will be included in regular education programs
7. Justification for type of educational programs prescribed
8. List of those responsible for various aspects of the IEP or IFSP
9. Objective assessment, at least annually, must be specified for measuring achievement of short-term goals
10. Teachers and parents must work together to decide on goals and how they should be achieved

Figure 6–6 Contents of IEPs and IFSPs. (*Source:* Federal Register, 41 [252], pp. 56966–56998)

- Provide observation opportunities for parents so that they can see activities described in child's IEP.
- Provide follow-up assistance to carry over program activities into the home.
- Refer parents to support groups or other parents whose children have similar disabilities.
- Inform parents of their legal rights.

"Sometimes I feel overwhelmed. How can I evaluate this program? How do I know this is best? Then I remember it's a team approach. I'm not in it alone. It's just my job to get the specialists I trust to talk to each other about it. I remind myself that they know programs, and I know my child."

—**Robin Simons, 1987**

- Inform parents of community resources available to them and help them to access the services.
- Identify needs related to the disability of siblings and other family members.
- Provide information regarding prevention of disabilities for younger siblings.
- Build parent confidence and skill in advocating for their children with special needs (Head Start program performance standards and other regulations, 1993, pp. 313–314).

To listen to a mother of a child with a disability discuss her relationship with a school, go to the online resource.

Teri is the mother of a child with autism. She briefly describes the history of her son's development and her role as his advocate. Teri discusses the school's role in his development and the need for a team effort in this personal online voice.

Families and Children with Serious Illness

Just as families with children who have disabilities face a major crisis at the time they are informed of their child's condition, so do families of children with a **serious illness**. Hilton Davis (1993) explains the intense feelings of families as they receive information concerning their child's illness. The diagnosis "brings with it irreversible change. The world is instantly transformed in a nightmarish way. The sudden need to adapt to dreadful circumstances is

Caring for Babies with AIDS
http://www.caring4babieswithAIDS.org/

Children's Memorial Hospital (Chicago)—
    Neonatology
http://www.childrensmemorial.org/depts/-
    neonatology

Chronically Ill Children: How Families Adjust
http://www.nurseweek.com/ce/ce565a.html

STARBRIGHT Foundation
http://www.starbright.org

forced upon the parents, their child, and indeed the whole family. Potentially they have to change their whole way of life, amid the terrible pain or anguish implied by the words above. Their vision of the world, their values, their ambitions, their whole philosophy will be altered by this one event" (p. 1).

Medical advances have made it possible for more children to survive even with serious illnesses or disabilities. Not only are children surviving but also efforts are made to have them live as normal a life as possible. Thus, such children appear in greater numbers than ever before in early childhood educational programs. Each child's particular illness or disease will affect his special educational needs. Thus, it becomes important for early childhood teachers to have some knowledge of the child's illness, as well as information about the child and family members (Figure 6–7).

Some serious illnesses cause greater concern than others in early education settings. Currently, children who are infected with HIV or have AIDS are among those who bring about the greatest apprehension. Often, children with these conditions are ostracized from society because of fears based on inaccurate understanding of how the disease is transmitted. Additionally, families of infected children face incredible strains on their resources (Hamner & Turner, 1996) (Figure 6–8).

Policies among early education programs vary widely on how they accept and deal with children with serious illness and their families. Generally, it is important that administrators and teachers understand the needs of all children and their families, and that

"HIV is a retrovirus that infects white blood cells, the brain, the bowel, the skin, and other tissues. Transmission of the virus occurs through sexual or parental blood contact, or from an infected mother to her fetus or infant. Infection results in a wide spectrum of illness and a high fatality rate. The most severe manifestation of HIV infection is acquired immunodeficiency syndrome (AIDS). . . . AIDS cases among children have increased rapidly since the first reports in 1982" (Simonds & Rogers, 1992).

Children contract the virus from their mother in three ways:

1. in utero as a fetus
2. during birth
3. by breastfeeding

Not all children born to HIV mothers contract the virus; estimates are that about 25 percent to 40 percent do.

Children with AIDS commonly have other illnesses and disorders including pneumonia, serious bacterial infections, skin disease, diarrhea, developmental delays, and neurological dysfunction. Most children with HIV develop AIDS in three to three-and-a-half years, and for most of these children, the disease is fatal.

Treatment is typically through drugs, and new treatments are evolving.

Figure 6–8   HIV/AIDS.

they work with families to help them receive appropriate services. Although many variations exist in policies for dealing with seriously ill children, confidentiality and the rights of children and their families must be the first priority in any policy. It will be necessary for teachers to comply with policy and to take precautions for their own safety such as wearing gloves when coming into contact with children's body fluids.

Davis (1993) offers four guidelines for those who are working with families of ill children:

1. Respect the parents.

Juvenile-Onset Diabetes—When too little insulin is secreted by the pancreas, juvenile-onset diabetes results. Needs: precise balance of diet, exercise, and insulin by injection. Close monitoring of sugar levels necessary 2–3 times daily. Snacks may be required during the school day.

Asthma—A chronic lung disease with bronchial sensitivity to many different stimuli. Wide variation in needs of children with mild cases to those with severe cases. Modifications in environment may be necessary to reduce allergens and irritants. Children with severe cases may have a lot of absences and need home-based educational services.

Spina Bifida—Improper closure of spinal column prenatally leads to spina bifida. Difficulties with movement in the lower body; child may not be able to move legs, and have little or no control of bowel and bladder. May need a wheelchair, braces or crutches; retardation is possible. Schools must provide accessibility to all educational programs.

Cleft Palate and Other Craniofacial Anomalies—Degree of these problems varies from minimal to great. Disfigurement of child's face is difficult issue for child and family to deal with. Some anomalies easily corrected by surgery; others more complicated. Children have a high risk for ear infections and hearing loss.

Congenital Heart Diseases—There is a wide variety of structural anomalies in the development of the heart. Surgery often helpful; it is very expensive; may help problems, not typically a total cure. Child has restrictions on daily activities after surgery and must be carefully monitored. Uncertainty about survival.

Leukemia—Most common childhood cancer begins with anemia, weight loss, and sometimes bleeding. An excessive number of white cells in the blood. Child is frequently hospitalized, receives a large amount of medication, and radiation therapy with major side effects. Uncertainty regarding remission and survival.

Hemophilia—Genetic disease in which blood clotting factor is absent and leads to uncontrolled bleeding. Nearly all affected are male. Often, bleeding occurs without an injury present. Painful arthritis may accompany disease; may require surgery or strong medication. Some treatment with blood products may now be done at home or school; requires fewer hospitalizations.

End-Stage Renal Disease—Extremely severe complication of variety of conditions affecting kidneys. Treatments include dialysis and transplants. When disease begins in infancy, high rate of failure to grow. Survival rate for these children increasing.

Sickle Cell Anemia—Results from abnormality in structure of hemoglobin. This affects shape of cells, and these cells have trouble passing through veins and smaller blood vessels. Risks include lack of oxygen to any body organ and to certain kinds of bacteria which cause bone infections and meningitis. Symptoms include anemia, diminished growth, and late onset of puberty. Children are hospitalized frequently and need strong pain medication.

Cystic Fibrosis—Children with CF have major chronic lung disease and frequent lung infections. Great strides have been made in treating this disease. Diagnosis is usually made in the first two years of life based on poor weight gain and frequent lung infections. Children need equipment for respiratory care, medications, and special diets.

Muscular Dystrophy—More common in boys, this disease involves progressive weakness of large muscles in legs first, and then extends to other muscles of the body. Diagnosis does not usually happen until about age five or six years, even though cause is genetic. Treatment is very limited.

Figure 6–7 Description of some chronic illnesses of children. (*Source:* Perrin, J. M. [1985]. Introduction: Severe and chronic illness in childhood. In N. Hobbs, J. M. Perrin, & H. T. Ireys [Eds.], *Chronically ill children and their families.* San Francisco: Jossey-Bass)

Early childhood education teachers should speak in short sentences and simple words to help immigrant children understand.

Education of Immigrant Children in New York City
http://www.ed.gov/databases/ERIC_Digests/ ed*402399.html

Health Coverage for Legal Immigrant Children
http://www.cbpp.org/10-4-00health.htm

Identifying and Serving Immigrant Children Who Are Gifted
http://ericae.net/edo/ED358676.HTM

Immigrant Children Exceed Expectations
http://www.ilw.com/lawyers/column_article/ articles/2001,0627-AILF.SHTM

Research Matters
http://www.researchmatters.harvard.edu/ story.php?article_id=233

Stages of Adaptation for Immigrant Children
http://members.aol.com/lacillo/immigrant. html

2. Parents have the major role in dealing with their child's illness.

3. Professionals work *with* and *for* families, not *on* or *instead* of them.

4. The most important thing for professionals is to really listen to family members as they confer.

Immigrant Families

Immigrant families often feel divided between two sets of emotions. On one hand, they are sad about losing their country of origin and leaving behind family, friends, familiar ways of doing things, and the ease of communicating in their native language. On the other hand, they are hopeful about the new opportunities that living in the United States brings, and look forward to improving the quality of life for themselves and their children. (Lieberman, 1995, p. 28)

As teachers welcome **immigrant families** into their programs, it is important for them to remember these dual emotions. It is easier for teachers to understand the joyfulness and excitement about coming to the United States.

As immigrant families enter their new country, change is sudden and all-encompassing. Language barriers may be difficult to overcome. This causes great stress, which may lead to anxiety or depression (Lieberman, 1995). As children are immersed in a new culture, families may be concerned about a loss of family values and traditions. Teachers can help reduce some of the stress that these families face. Following are some ways that early childhood teachers can help:

• Consider the language difference. Speak and write in ways that the family can understand. Use short sentences and simple words to ensure that they understand.

• Explain the daily schedule and routine activities. Take time to explain what happens in the program, and to listen to parent questions or comments.

• Acknowledge that there may be some tension between the family and the staff. It is most likely not personal, but rather based on cultural differences. Think about what you can do to communicate more effectively with the family.

• Ask questions about the family and their expectations for their children. Avoid getting too personal and do not give advice. Instead, listen carefully so that you can learn about the family.

- Establish a warm and trusting environment for all families and children. If you have concerns about the child or practices of the family, a trusting relationship will allow for ways to express the concern and for you to work in partnership with the family (Lieberman, 1995).

Migrant Families

Migrant families move from one location to another and from one job to another for financial reasons (Chavkin, 1991). And yet, migrant families are among the poorest in the United States (Lopez, Scribner, & Mahitivanichcha, 2001). It is difficult to estimate the number of migrant families in the United States, but there may be as many as 1.5 million migrant farmworkers (Shotland, 1989). Although little information is available about migrant families, it is known that there is diversity among their lifestyles (Chavkin, 1991). Some of this diversity might be related to the three primary geographic migration routes: East Coast, Mid-continent, and West Coast (Shotland, 1989).

Ethnicity and culture also contribute to the diversity of migrant families. Those farmworkers who migrate through the southern states and along the eastern seaboard are most often African Americans, Mexican Americans and Mexican nationals, Anglos, Jamaican and Haitian blacks, and Puerto Ricans. Those who migrate through south Texas and move through the midwestern and western states are most often Mexican Americans and Mexican nationals, as well as some Native Americans. Migrant workers who travel the West Coast through California to Oregon and Washington are also most often Mexican Americans and Mexican nationals. Some of these farmworkers are also southeast Asians (Shotland, 1989).

Factors including continuous relocation, extremely low wages, hard work in the fields, unsafe farm equipment, poor nutrition, and lack of consistent medical care often lead to poor health in both adults and children in migrant families. Huang (1993) discusses health problems related to prenatal care, agriculture as a dangerous occupation, and poverty. Poverty conditions contributing to ill health are numerous. Among them are malnutrition and poor sanitation in substandard housing that lacks indoor pluming for toilets or drinking water. These risk factors contribute to health related problems in many segments of the population but migrant families are susceptible to an extremely high number of them.

Many of those who migrate for economic reasons speak only their native language or they may have limited use of English. Along with their frequent relocations, language barriers obstruct their access to many human service programs available to others in the United States (Chavkin, 1991). These characteristics also impact the children's ability to succeed in school as well as families' involvement in their children's education (Menchaca & Ruiz-Escalante, 1995; Martinez & Velazquez, 2000).

Teachers of young children from migrant families must emphasize strengths that the children bring from this lifestyle. Since they have lived and traveled in several states and often in at least two countries, children have information and perspectives to share that differ from those of other children (Gonzales as cited in Menchaca & Ruiz-Escalante, 1995). When teachers respect and celebrate all cultures in the classroom, including those of migrant children, all children have a greater chance for success. Further, teachers must make all children feel welcome as members of the classroom community of learners no matter the length of their stay (Huggins as cited in Menchaca & Ruiz-Escalante, 1995). Moving from one school to another is a challenge for young migrant children, and early childhood teachers can support them by leading efforts to include them and making the classroom a safe place for all.

For all young children, family involvement in education contributes to academic success. It may be necessary for teachers to redefine their views about family involvement beyond a traditional view of participation in parent groups, attendance at school functions, and helping children with homework into a broader view that will encourage marginalized families "by building on each family's cultural values, beliefs, and economic positionality" (Lopez, Scribner, & Mahitivanichcha, 2001, p. 257). Some examples of ways that teachers can support migrant family involvement include:

- placing needs of families as the number one priority
- developing meaningful, authentic relationships with parents
- empowering parents by valuing their essential nature to children's success in school
- genuinely welcoming family members in a personal way to school function
- providing specific educational services to help migrant children and families
- collaborating with agencies in order to effect families' basic and health needs, as well as academic needs (Lopez, Scribner, & Mahitivanichcha, 2001).

Anchor School Project
http://www.anchorschool.org;

Migrant Education Program
http://www.ed.gov/offices/OESE/MEP/

Migrant Head Start
http://www.acf.dhhs.gov/programs/opu/facts/ headst.htm

Children of Incarcerated Parents

About two million children in any given year have at least one parent who in **incarcerated in a state or federal prison, or in a local jail** (Bilchik, Seymour, & Kreisher, 2001). Since the rate of incarceration has been continually growing throughout the decade of the 1990s and into the 21st century, greater numbers of children will be affected in the future. The number of children with incarcerated parents has grown by over 50 percent since 1991 (Federal Resource Center for Children of Prisoners, n.d.). Fathers are most likely to be incarcerated, but there has been an increase in female incarcerations. About eight percent of the two million children have mothers who are incarcerated (Bilchik, et al., 2001).

Little information exists about the specific effects experienced by children whose parents are imprisoned. However, since it is known that these families are more likely to be living in poverty and/or affected by substance abuse and violence, the effects are complicated by a number of negative environmental factors. When parents are taken into custody, children are confused and their world becomes immediately chaotic. Many children believe that they might be responsible for their parents going to jail. The separation that children experience, especially if the incarcerated parent is a primary caregiver, is traumatic.

Common responses from children with incarcerated parents include a variety of emotional and behavioral difficulties such as withdrawal, aggression, anxiety, and depression. These children are likely to do poorly in school, and beyond early childhood they are at risk for abusing illegal substances and committing crimes (Bilchik et al., 2001). Because of the trauma associated with a sudden separation from a parent, children may suffer from post traumatic stress disorder (PTSD), which includes symptoms such as withdrawal, hyperalertness, sleep disturbances, guilt, and impaired memory and concentration (Jose-Kampfner as cited in Young & Jefferson-Smith, 2000).

In addition to emotional and behavioral risk factors, children are also likely to feel embarrassed and isolated about having a parent in prison. They may attempt to keep others from knowing about the incarceration, either through silence or covering up the truth. Although the very nature of incarceration in our society is to punish the perpetrators of crime, care must be taken so that children of incarcerated parents are not unduly punished because of their parents' illegal acts.

A common pattern of dealing with children whose parents are incarcerated has been to help support the children without dealing with their concerns about their parents or the issue of incarceration. Often, no one mentions the parent or the imprisonment in conversations with these children. Even incarcerated parents in reaction to their own guilt may distance themselves both physically and emotionally from their children. However, these responses only cause children to feel isolated and rejected. Children, not understanding parents may be acting out of guilt or embarrassment, see the parents behavior as a lack of love of interest in them, and perhaps caused by something that they did (Young & Jefferson-Smith, 2000).

Programs for children whose parents are incarcerated are being created in many cities and states, and with input from organizations that have called attention to the needs of children in this situation. Families in Crisis provides a program for school-age children with both educational and therapeutic interventions. Services are provided to both children and parents in order to support strong family bonds that help children cope successfully (Bilchik et al., 2001). Girl Scouts Beyond Bars is a partnership program between correctional departments and Girl Scout councils, and was created to continue relationships between young girls and their incarcerated mothers (http://www.ncjrs.org/txtfiles/girlsct.txt).

Although fewer women are currently incarcerated, a greater number of programs seem to exist to support them in their parenting role both as they are imprisoned and on their release. Perhaps since women are often in the role of primary caregiver, these programs have been more widespread. However, Mendez (2000) makes the point, supported by his research, that incarcerated men also have an interest in their children and in increasing their parenting skills.

Fathers and Children Together (FACT) is another program supported by Families in Crisis. Young fathers between the ages of 18 and 21 who are about to be released from the Manson Youth Institute in Connecticut are provided with services to encourage them to be supportive fathers to their young children (Bilchik et al., 2001).

Caregivers and teachers of young children may find it difficult to know how to support children of incarcerated parents. The first step for those who are working with young children is to understand the confusion and trauma they have faced. Further, early childhood teachers should be prepared to provide a sense of security at school by listening to children's concerns and by providing unconditional nurturance. Answer children's questions in the best and

---

Families in Crisis
http://www.Familiesincrisis.org
Child Welfare League of America Center for children of Prisoners
http://www.cwla.org/programs/incarcerated

---

most honest way possible, respect the significance of family bonds, and seek assistance from the family and other professionals as necessary. Be sure to maintain confidentiality regarding sensitive information (Reilly & Martin, n.d.). Finally, early childhood educators should use the knowledge base from existing research and family support programs to advocate for greater numbers of appropriate interventions that will serve to keep family bonds strong, reduce the likelihood that parents will return to prison, or that their children will also go to prison, and decrease severe emotional challenges for children whose parents are or have been incarcerated.

The Role of Early Childhood Educators

As early childhood teachers prepare to work with an ever-increasing number of children with serious health concerns, several criteria must be included in their professional preparation:

- knowledge of legal requirements for each special need
- knowledge of health requirements for each special need
- understanding of family systems effects on children
- practicing effective strategies to support families as well as planning high-quality early education for the children
- advocating for needs of all children and families
- expansion of capacity to demonstrate compassion

It is the teacher's ethical obligation to exercise the idea of lifelong learning.

Although it is true that a teacher preparation program for entry-level teachers cannot possibly anticipate every situation the novice teacher might encounter, it seems evident that more emphasis should be placed on understanding various needs and strengths of families in stress. Even under difficult circumstances, many families find ways to cope or to adapt. Furthermore, as teachers face a variety of challenging situations, it is their ethical obligation to exercise the idea of lifelong learning to ensure the best early education for each child and appropriate support for each family.

Summary and Conclusions

All families face stressful events. Some forms of stress can be predicted such as the birth of a new baby or a planned relocation. Other stressors, however, are unique, and may be unexpected in families with young children. Violence in families causes stress to all members, whether or not they are being abused. Some stress is caused by economic factors; in extreme situations, families may lose their homes and all of their possessions. Serious illness or disabilities

in young children lead to many chronically stressful situations.

Some family stress may be the result of poor planning or dysfunction in families. However, much of this stress is unpredictable and perhaps unavoidable. Families cope in different ways. Those who have support and resources may find it easier to function at the time of a crisis. Others find it very difficult to adapt.

Early childhood teachers can offer support by listening and showing compassion when families need support. Sometimes, it may be necessary to refer children or families for additional or alternative services. Guidelines for ethical behavior require that early education practitioners form partnerships with all families based on trust and positive regard.

Key Terms

balanced families	**marital transitions**
midrange families	**homeless**
extreme families	**disabilities**
family coping	**serious illness**
family violence	**immigrant families**
gender inequality	**migrant families**
child abuse and neglect	**incarcerated**
substance abuse	

Chapter Six Applications

1. Review the information on factors related to family violence in U.S. society. Give an example from your life experiences that helps to explain or support each of these factors.

2. Consider the information provided in this chapter about various serious illnesses experienced by families with young children. Which of these illnesses do you know something about from experience?

3. When a young child is born with or acquires a disability, it affects the entire family. Considering the information in this chapter along with your own life experiences, how will you view children with disabilities in your classroom? How will you view parents of children with disabilities as they voice their expectations to you?

What challenges and joys do you predict when working with young children with disabilities and their families?

Questions for Reflection and Discussion

1. When you think about working with families of young children who have a major source of family stress, what do you see as your strengths? What areas of concern do you have about your reactions to the various stressors?

2. How will you decide on the extent and limits to which you will be involved in families experiencing stress?

3. How might you best prepare yourself as an early childhood educator to deal with the types of unpredictable family stress discussed in this chapter?

Field Assignments

1. Call the administrator of a homeless shelter or women's shelter in your area. Ask about what the needs are, and how you might be able to help young children and families at the shelter. Consider a toy drive, clothing drive, food drive, or collection of supplies such as paper, markers, glue, or other items; tutoring school-age children; or reading to children.

2. Observe in an early intervention program. Note the activities, participation, family involvement, and forms of assessment. If possible, ask the administrator about roles for early childhood educators in such programs.

3. Interview a children's protective services agent. Ask about experiences with family members who have been identified as child abusers. Discuss ways in which early childhood teachers and protective services workers might collaborate.

References

Bilchik, S., Seymour, C., & Kreisher, K. (2001). Parents in prison. *Corrections Today, 63*(7), 108–111.

Boss, P. (1988). *Family stress management.* Newbury Park, CA: Sage.

Carter, B., & McGoldrick, M. (1989). Overview: The changing family life cycle: A framework for family therapy. In B. Carter & M. McGoldrick (Eds.), *The changing family life cycle.* Needham Heights, MA: Allyn & Bacon.

Chavkin, N. F. (1991). *Family lives and parental involvement in migrant students' education.* (ERIC Document Reproduction Service No. ED 335 174.)

Cicchetti, D., Toth, S. L., & Hennessy, K. (1993). Child maltreatment and school adaptation: Problems and promises. In D. Cicchetti and S. L. Toth (Eds.), *Child abuse, child development, and social policy* (pp. 301–330). Norwood, NJ: Ablex.

Davis, H. (1993). *Counselling parents of children with chronic illness or disability.* Leicester, England: British Psychological Society.

Doucette-Dudman, D., & LaCure, J. R. (1996). *Raising our children's children.* Minneapolis, MN: Fairview Press.

Emery, R. E. (1999). *Marriage, divorce, and children's adjustment* (2nd ed.). Thousand Oaks, CA: Sage.

Federal Resource Center for Children of Prisoners. (n. d.). Retrieved September 7, 2002 from http://www.cwla.org/programs/incarcerated/frccpabout.htm

Fields, J., & Casper, L. M. (2001, June). America's families and living arrangements. *Current Population Reports.* Washington, DC: United States Department of Commerce, Economics and Statistics Administration, United States Census Bureau.

Galinsky, E., & David, J. (1988). *The preschool years: Family strategies that work from experts and parents.* New York: Ballantine.

Guernsey, T. F., & Klare, K. (1993). *Special education law.* Durham, NC: Carolina Academic Press.

Hamner, T. J., & Turner, P. H. (1996). *Parenting in contemporary society.* Needham Heights, MA: Allyn & Bacon.

Head Start program performance standards and other regulations. (1993). Washington, DC: U.S. Department of Health and Human Services.

Hendrick, J. (1998). *Total learning.* Columbus, OH: Merrill.

Huang, G. (1993). Health problems among migrant farmworkers' children in the U.S. (ERIC Document Reproduction Service No. ED 357 907.)

Iverson, T. J., & Segal, M. (1990). *Child abuse and neglect: An information and reference guide.* New York: Garland.

Keeping incarcerated mothers and their daughters together: Girl Scouts beyond bars. (1995, October). Retrieved September 7, 2002 from http://www.ncjrs.org/txtfiles/girlsct.txt

Kling, N., Dunn, L., & Oakley, J. (1996). Homeless families in early childhood programs: What to expect and what to do. *Dimensions of Early Childhood, 24*(1), 3–8.

Krestan, J., & Bepko, C. (1989). Alcohol problems and the family life cycle. In B. Carter & M. McGoldrick (Eds.), *The changing family life cycle.* Needham Heights, MA: Allyn & Bacon.

Lieberman, A. F. (1995). Concerns of immigrant families. In P. L. Mangione (Ed.), *Infant/toddler caregiving: A guide to culturally sensitive care* (pp. 28–37). Sacramento, CA: California Department of Education.

Lopez, G. R., Scribner, J. D., & Mahitivanichcha, K. (2001, Summer). Redefining parental involvement: Lessons from high-performing migrant-impacted schools. *American Educational Research Journal, 38*(2), 253–288.

Martinez, Y. G., & Velazquez, J. A. (2000). Involving migrant families in education. (ERIC Document Reproduction Service No. ED 448 010.)

Mayes, L. C. (1995). Substance abuse and parenting. In M. H. Bornstein (Ed.), *Handbook of parenting, vol. 4: Applied and practical parenting* (pp. 101–125). Mahwah, NJ: Lawrence Erlbaum Associates.

Menchaca, V. D., & Ruiz-Escalante, J. A. (1995). Instructional strategies for migrant students. (ERIC Document Reproduction Service No. ED 388 491.)

Mendez, Jr., G. A. (2000). Incarcerated African American men and their children: A case study. *Annals of the American Academy of Political and Social Science, 569,* 86–101.

Moses, K. (1983). The impact of initial diagnosis: Mobilizing family resources. In J. Mulick & S. Pueschel (Eds.), *Parent-professional partnerships in developmental disabilities services* (pp. 11–34). Cambridge, MA: Academic Guild.

Olson, D. H. L., Russell, C. S., & Sprenkle, D. H. (1989). *Circumplex model: Systematic assessment and treatment of families.* New York: Haworth Press.

Olson, H. (1994). The effects of prenatal alcohol exposure on child development. *Infants and Young Children, 6*(3), 10–25.

Perrin, J. M. (1985). Introduction: Severe and chronic illness in childhood. In N. Hobbs, J. M. Perrin, & H. T. Ireys (Eds.), *Chronically ill children and their families.* San Francisco: Jossey-Bass.

Poulsen, M. (1994). The development of policy recommendations to address individual and family needs of infants and young children affected by family substance use. *Topics in Early Childhood Special Education, 14*(2), 275–291.

Reilly, J., & Martin, S. (n.d.). Children of incarcerated parents: What is the caregiver's role? Retrieved September 7, 2002 from http://www.canr.uconn.edu/ces/child/newsarticles/CCC743.html

Shotland, J. (1989). Full fields, empty cupboard: The nutritional status of migrant farmworkers in America. Washington, DC: public Voice for food and Health Policy. (ERIC Document Reproduction Service No. ED 323 076.)

Simonds, R. J., & Rogers, M. F. (1992). Epidemiology of HIV in children and other populations. In A. C. Crocker, H. J. Cohen, & T. A. Kastner (Eds.), *HIV infection and developmental disabilities: A resource for service providers.* Baltimore: Paul H. Brookes.

Simons, R. (1987). *After the tears: Parents talk about raising a child with a disability.* Orlando, FL: Harcourt Brace.

Straus, M. A. (1983). Ordinary violence, child abuse, and wife-beating: What do they have in common. In D. Finkelhor (Ed.), *The dark side of families.* Beverly Hills, CA: Sage.

Straus, M. A. (1991). Physical violence in American families: Incidence, rates, causes, and trends. In D. D. Knudsen & J. L. Miller (Eds.), *Abused and battered: Social and legal responses to family violence.* New York: Walter de Gruyter.

Straus, M. A., Gelles, R. J., & Steinmetz, S. K. (1980). *Behind closed doors: Violence in the American family.* Garden City, NY: Doubleday.

Trivette, C., & Dunst, C. (1992). Characteristics and influences of role division and social support among mothers of preschool children with disabilities. *Topics in Early Childhood Special Education, 12*(3), 367–385.

U.S. Department of Health, Education, and Welfare, Office of Human Development/Office of Child Development, Children's Bureau/National Center on Child Abuse and Neglect. (1975). *Child abuse and neglect: The problem and its management* (DHEW Publication No. OHD 75–30073).

Young, D. S., & Jefferson-Smith, C. J. (2000). When moms are incarcerated: The need of children, mothers, and caregivers. *Families in Society, 81*(2), 130–141.

Zuckerman, B., & Brazelton, T. B. (1994). Strategies for a family supportive child health care system. In S. L. Kagan & B. Weissbourd (Eds.), *Putting families first: American's family support movement and the challenge of change.* San Francisco: Jossey-Bass.

PART 2

PRACTICE

OUTLINE

A Family-based Philosophy in Early Childhood Education

Rationale for a Family-based Philosophy in Early Childhood Education

Families are children's first teachers. By the time children come to early childhood education settings, they have already had many experiences from which to learn. In optimal home settings, young children will have learned a great deal that prepares them for entry into early education. But when coming from less than optimal home settings, children will experience a lot of discontinuity in their lives when they go to school. Even after children begin formal early education—child care, preschool, or kindergarten—families continue to be the primary force in their development. With this understanding, it is imperative that programs of early childhood education adopt a family-based philosophy.

As we understand more about families in general as well as the families with which we work specif-ically, it is clear that family involvement must be var-ied and abundant. Opportunities for families to par-ticipate with their children in the support of their education should take into consideration the obliga-tions and strengths of each family.

The Example Set by Head Start

Since its inception in 1965, family involvement has been a component of Head Start's comprehensive ed-ucational plan for working with children of low-income families. Many leaders in early childhood education believe that the success of Head Start would not be so remarkable without the emphasis on families.

Currently, The Head Start Vision for Parent Involvement includes three primary goals:

- support for parents in their role as primary ed-ucator, caregiver, nurturer, and advocate for their children

- support for parents in their own personal development

- support for parents as decision-makers for themselves, their children, and their Head Start program (*Head Start Handbook of the Parent Involvement Vision and Strategies*, 1996)

In supporting parents as the first educators of their children, Head Start teachers are aware that parents have enrolled their children in the program so that their children receive the educational benefits provided. Appreciating efforts made by parents is important to this goal. Accepting that whoever is doing the parenting (mothers, fathers, grandparents, or others) will need support from early childhood teachers for this role will increase the possibilities for successful partnerships. The descriptions of the three goals and the following sample strategies have been taken from the *Head Start Handbook of the Parent Involvement Vision and Strategies* (1996). Some of the strategies that are used in Head Start programs to support parental nurturance include:

- providing opportunities for parents to learn about child development
- sharing developmentally appropriate activities that parents and children can do together at home
- encouraging parents to visit and participate in the classroom to observe and later discuss how children learn and develop
- fostering participation in decisions about the classroom
- involving parents of children with disabilities in developing their child's individualized educational plan

The purpose of the second goal, which is related to parents' personal development, is that their personal growth affects their children's development and learning. Setting goals for themselves ultimately benefits their children. Those Head Start decision-makers who put this goal into place understood the importance of the family system to children's development. Some areas for parents' personal development for which Head Start programs may provide assistance or resources are:

- increasing skills for everyday life such as planning and preparing nutritious meals

Head Start programs encourage parents to visit and participate in their child's activities.

- planning for family life together
- identifying strengths and skills that they already possess that might help in managing family life or in finding a job
- working on skills they would like to learn or improve, such as effective and appropriate discipline of their children, or how to use a computer
- learning how to reduce stress and increase wellness
- creating opportunities to interact with other parents of young children and to build friendships
- being involved in a community of others who value their language and culture
- working with teams of parents and Head Start staff to participate in community activities or to address community issues
- setting goals for themselves and making progress in the achievement of the goals

The preceding list of strategies offers many possibilities. Variations in programs and communities may restrict or increase these possibilities. Sensitive early childhood staff who understand the strengths and needs of parents may be able to assist them in choosing one or two of these areas as priorities. It is also possible that parents who are veterans of Head Start may be willing to serve as mentors to new parents as they work to meet their goals.

Head Start has been successful in creating a sense of community among its staff and clients. This works to benefit children, teachers, and families. One of the keys to this community-building effort is that parents—as partners with Head Start staff—are included in decision-making throughout all aspects of the program, including the following:

- the children's curriculum
- choices of health services available to children
- planning for parent involvement activities
- activities to work on at home with their children
- ways to volunteer for Head Start
- choices about which committees or groups on which to serve

Families in a Democracy

Powell (1989) notes three premises about the role of families in U.S. society that provide a purpose for an emphasis on family involvement in early education (Figure 7–1).

- The doctrine of parental rights
- Family influences on children
- Democratic principles

Rights and Responsibilities of Parents. In a democracy, citizens have both rights and responsibilities. Rights and responsibilities related to parenting have legal and cultural roots. Professionals must be certain to understand parental rights just as they insist on parental responsibility. In this light, teachers must respect the primacy of the role that parents have with their children.

Continuity

From Home to School. Besides the critical role of families in the lives of young children, early educators have long been concerned about the child's adjust-

Doctrine of Parental Rights—Parents have legal rights and responsibilities in regard to their children. As educators, we often note parental responsibility, especially when we judge that it is not being fulfilled. However, family involvement in education principles must include the importance of parental rights as well.

Family Influences on Children—There is no doubt that parents are children's first teachers. Current brain development research points us to the fact that the child's first three years are critical as a time of learning. Early childhood educators and others in the community must help to support parent efforts even before children come to school.

Democratic Principles—Families living in a democracy have the privilege of choosing how to rear their children. At the same time, with all of these choices come huge responsibilities for meeting children's needs. Early childhood professionals can provide information to parents so that they can make knowledgeable choices as they fulfill their responsibilities.

Figure 7–1 Description of each of the three premises.

ment as she enters a formal educational program. Many experts believe that continuity of experience is beneficial to children. The very nature of moving from home to school causes a great deal of discontinuity in a child's world. When family members have opportunities to communicate frequently with their child's teacher, some of the discontinuity might be bridged (Powell, 1989).

Carlos entered a part-day preschool program when he was just a little over two-and-a-half years. Each day, his mother, Gina, walked into the school with him and stayed with him while he explored in the block center and sometimes the sand table. As children were invited to the group time rug, Carlos reached for his mother's hand and tears streamed down his face. Gina hugged Carlos and told him that she would be back to pick him up later. Carlos joined the others for group time, singing and moving, participating fully. Carlos continued to cry each day for almost two weeks when it was time for his mother to leave. The school staff encouraged Gina to stay as long as she wanted. Suddenly, one day, Carlos walked with Gina to the group time rug with a big smile on his face, the moment this parent had been waiting for! As Gina left the school that morning, teachers noticed tears streaming down *her* face. When Gina returned to pick up Carlos later that morning, she told one of the teachers that she did not realize that she was going to feel sad when Carlos happily left her to join the other children.

Transitions during the Day. Continuity refers to both **linkages** and amount of **congruence** between educational programs and families of the children they serve. Linkages are the types and frequency of communication between home and school; congruence is the amount of similarity that schools and homes have in terms of values and goals for children, use of language, and adult-child interaction patterns (Powell, 1989).

To increase the continuity that children realize between home and school, it is the professional responsibility of early childhood educators to plan, implement, and evaluate the linkages they have with families. To be considerate of all families, teachers may need to use more than one type of communication; that is, written and verbal. Increased frequency of communication between home and school also increases continuity for children. Many early childhood education programs state in their policy manuals that they require one parent-teacher conference each year. It is important that the planned or formal conference be combined with other forms of more frequent informal communication with families. Further, communication must include some method of two-way communication, not just one-way communication from school to home. Teachers must also consider variations in nonverbal communication. Suggestions for a variety of strategies are included in Chapter 8.

Congruence of expectations and values between home and school is an important aspect of continuity. It does not take much experience for an early

childhood teacher to realize that her objectives will not always be viewed as equally important by children's families. Variations in educational and income levels and culture or ethnicity may lead to incongruence of expectations for children between home and school. Many other family factors discussed in the first six chapters of this text are also likely to contribute to differences in goals for young children.

One school district superintendent tells about a conversation he had with a parent of a first-grader. The superintendent, Dr. Clarke, explained to the parent that by using strategies deemed to be developmentally appropriate for young children, the teacher was encouraging children to think for themselves. He went on to explain that children would grow to love learning. The parent interrupted him by saying, "I don't want my daughter to think for herself. I want her to do what I say." This incongruence between the school's philosophy of encouraging a child's autonomy in learning and the parent's value of compliance is one that educators frequently observe. What family, cultural, and societal factors do you believe might have influenced this mother's viewpoint?

Although it has been assumed that young children benefit from greater continuity between home

"Schools have choices. There are two common approaches to involving families in schools and in their children's education. One approach emphasizes conflict and views the school as a battleground. The conditions and relationships in this kind of environment guarantee power struggles and disharmony. The other approach emphasizes partnership and views the school as a homeland. The conditions and relationships in this kind of environment invite power sharing and mutual respect, and allow energies to be directed toward activities that foster student learning and development. Even when conflicts rage, however, peace must be restored sooner or later, and the partners in children's education must work together."

—Joyce Epstein, 1995

and school, there is little research support for such a perspective. However, it is possible that when the discontinuity between the two settings is too great, children will fail at school (Powell, 1989). It is possible that there is an optimal level of discontinuity in which children will learn to adapt to a variety of settings and that such adaptation is beneficial to children. Powell (1989) discusses Lightfoot's (1978) distinction between creative conflict and negative dissonance. Viewing creative conflict as preferable to negative dissonance, the difference seems to lie in the balance of power or mutual respect between home and school. Some educators have been known to give up on the idea of family involvement when the sources of conflict become too great. However, a balance of power and demonstrations of mutual respect are likely to lead to positive outcomes, even in conflict.

It is important for early childhood teachers to understand that family involvement is not just about families helping the school. This perspective assumes the school or the teacher is the base of power. Establishing a philosophy that is family-based in early childhood education does not do away with conflict with families. However, the creative conflict that does

Communication with parents should be face-to-face, and the interaction should occur in a private place where confidentiality is maintained.

come about may lead to solutions that are more beneficial to children, families, and teachers.

Leah was a five-year-old kindergartner reading on the fifth-grade level. In the beginning of the year, her mother was very worried that she would learn nothing during the year in the developmentally appropriate kindergarten classroom. After two months of observing the teacher and the class, and having frequent heated discussions with the teacher and the principal, the mother finally confided to another parent that her child was very happy and was gaining many unexpected skills.

It is obvious from this example that sometimes, creative conflict is not resolved immediately, but rather is a process that may take some time.

When there are discontinuities between settings, Bronfenbrenner (1979) noted some assumptions that are likely to enhance the development of children and their families as they function in various settings. First, attempt to agree on goals. Schools can inform parents of goals for children in their early education program. Parents, as consumers, can consider various educational options that they have for their child. Second, supportive linkages are required between the two settings. Teachers should radiate support for all children and families in their classrooms. It is possible that the lack of such support or negative feelings about a child's family lead to unfavorable outcomes for the child. Third, it is helpful to have a parent or other close family member from the home setting accompany the child to school. This often means spending time with the child in the new setting and not just dropping the child into the new environment. Teachers will need to invite family members to do this because it is often not what families expect. Issue the invitation before the family members arrive at school so they can better plan their day around it. Work or other demands may not give some families easy flexibility to spend time with their child as they enter school. Fourth, communication strategies should be two-way, especially when the topic of communication is personal to the child or family; that is, rather than announcements for all children. And, finally, Bronfenbrenner points out that communication should be face-to-face whenever possible. This is especially true for sensitive topics, when teachers are tempted to take the easy way out by sending a note home with the child. If face-to-face contact is not possible in a timely way, a telephone conversation is better than a written message. Whether these contacts take the form of telephone calls or face-to-face discussions, it is imperative that the interaction occur in a private place and that confidentiality is maintained.

Transitioning from Preschool to Kindergarten.
Some early education programs have created both formal and informal activities for supporting children and their families as children move to kindergarten or first grade. Typically, this transition involves a new location, as well as many new people and vastly different expectations. Often, the essence of this kind of transitioning program is a scheduled meeting for parents, with one or more of the kindergarten teachers informing parents about what their children should know and be able to do in order to be ready to succeed in kindergarten. Such informational sessions can be somewhat helpful, but they typically do not provide children or families with support or resources for ensuring future success. More comprehensive programs with opportunities for greater communication are helpful.

Many Head Start programs have developed and maintained "networks and collaborative relationships within their communities . . ." in order to assist children and families as they transition "to the next stage of their lives in their communities, carrying with them the supports and strengths they have developed in Head Start" (Head Start Handbook, 1996, p. 13). In the Head Start transitioning program, staff attempt to provide opportunities to experience the next steps, not only to hear from the kindergarten teacher but also perhaps to schedule visits to the classrooms, and to observe the teacher and children in action.

A transition activity booklet, Connecting Head Start Parents to the Public School Setting, is provided by some Head Start programs to parents as their children prepare to enter kindergarten. Figures 7–2, 7–3, and 7–4 contain excerpts from this very useful guide.

1. Parents are the most important teachers their children will ever have.
2. Parents know their children better than anyone else.
3. Parents are responsible for their children.
4. Parents' attitudes affect their children's motivation to learn.
5. Parent involvement increases children's academic achievement and success in life.
6. Parents are in the best position to supervise children's leisure time. They should limit television watching and encourage homework, reading, and conversation.
7. Parents are the strongest advocates for their children.

Figure 7–2   Why parents should get involved in their child's education. (*Source:* Epps, W. J. [n.d.]. *Connecting Head Start parents to the public school setting.* Florissant, MO: Southern Research Associates)

Home Visiting.   Home visiting is one way some early childhood programs have found to be effective in helping children transition from home to school. Listed below are reasons to conduct home visits, procedures to follow, cautions to consider, and some guidelines for the visit.

Reasons to go
- helps child feel comfortable with a new adult
- helps teacher know child (and family) in their setting
- helps to build trust and communication
- lets teacher see child in home environment

Procedures
- check school procedure regarding home visiting
- confirm with administrator
- contact the family in advance to set time and date, and clarify directions

(*Note:* some families may prefer a public place such as a library or fast food restaurant.)

1. Read aloud to your child everyday.
2. Select television and video programs that serve specific purposes.
3. Give your child meaningful tasks/chores around the house that he/she will be responsible for carrying out.
4. Correct inappropriate behavior in a calm, meaningful way.
5. Take advantage of all family outings to teach your child something new or reinforce something already learned.
6. Practice identifying road and other safety signs with your child.
7. Make it an ongoing practice to engage your child in conversations about different topics.
8. Set aside a period of quiet time where everybody in the home is involved in silent reading or meditation.

Figure 7–3 What parents can do to help at home. (*Source:* Epps, W. J. [1998]. *Connecting Head Start parents to the public school setting.* Florissant, MO: Southern Research Associates)

Safety considerations

- Go with a coworker to make the visit.
- Take a cell phone.
- Leave if the situation appears to be unsafe.

What to do

- Introduce yourself.
- Ask about the family with questions such as how many children are in the family? How long have they lived at this residence?
- Briefly explain the school day to the children and the family.
- Ask if there are questions or concerns.
- Invite the family to visit you at school and give ways to contact you.

A Parent Guide for Parent/Teacher Conferences

1. Write down questions and comments you want to make a day or two before the conference.
2. Be sure you let the teacher know that you have come to the conference with some questions or concerns.
3. Share with the teacher your child's feelings about friends at school, school activities, transportation, meals, or other topics.
4. Listen carefully and take notes for the future.
5. Ask questions before accepting recommendations from the teacher about behavioral plans, special services, and other areas.
6. Be sure to let the teacher know if there are words, terms, or phrases that are not familiar to you, or if you are unsure of the meaning.
7. If more time is needed, request another conference.
8. Be sure to thank the teacher for her concern about your child.

Conference Tips for Parents

1. Be confident.
2. Be on time.
3. Be organized.
4. Be positive.
5. Be open and honest.
6. Be assertive, not aggressive.
7. Be on task; discuss your child, not other children or parents.

Figure 7–4 A parent guide for parent/teacher conferences and conference tips for parents. (Adapted from Epps, W. J. [1998]. *Connecting Head Start parents to the public school setting.* Florissant, MO: Southern Research Associates)

Family Support

Responsibilities of Home and School

"In the family support movement, families are viewed as the dominant support for children's development. Partnerships between families and helping agencies—including schools—must acknowledge families' primacy" (Bowman, 1994, pp. 52–53). The importance of the child's family to her development and education cannot be overstated. Further, if family needs are met and support is available, children have a much greater chance at success. When families are overburdened with stress from poverty, illness, or violence, they cannot meet their own needs or those of their children.

Bowman discusses four themes that are often used to justify differences in academic achievement among those who have lower income or are not members of the dominant culture.

1. Certain characteristics of the child such as ethnicity or lack of self-esteem are barriers to learning.
2. Values from home conflict with school-valued learning and skill development.
3. Discriminatory practices and inequality in the distribution of resources cause disadvantages to poor children and those who are not from the dominant culture.
4. School practices affect individuals and groups differently.

These themes show that, in fact, there is little agreement about why children of color do not do well in school. Teachers need to consider that different children are likely to need different programs to help them succeed (Bowman, 1994).

Listed below are examples of how teachers can plan different programs to meet the needs of more children.

1. Plan activities and projects that are not costly. When the cost of an activity (for example, field trips) is high, seek external funding.

2. Include a variety of resource guests from different careers, income levels, and racial-ethnic groups.
3. Plan for active/passive times each day to meet differing needs. Include music, movement, quiet, individual, and small group choices for various activities throughout the day.

Suggested school practice changes

1. When planning school-wide events, include participants from various racial-ethnic and income level groups throughout the year.
2. Invite a variety of racial-ethnic leaders to speak and participate in school activities.
3. When purchasing books and other instructional materials, always consider the racial-ethnic and income level representations in the visual images.
4. Plan for differing time and space needs to meet unique needs such as before- or after-school care, unique transportation arrangements, and unique language accommodations.

Two excellent resources for ideas to meet unique needs are:

The Anti-Bias Curriculum, Louise Derman- Sparks, NAEYC, Washington, DC

Starting Small (video and teacher's guide), Teaching Tolerance, Southern Poverty Law Center, Montgomery, AL

Empowering Parents

Well-educated, affluent parents typically have very different interactions with their children's teachers than do their less well-off counterparts. Schools are often criticized for having greater concern for the well-being of the school as an institution than for the individual children and families that are being served. It is possible that the family involvement model for empowering parents that has been so successful in the Head Start program is not the model that would best serve other populations. Considering that parents who have higher levels of education and income may already feel empowered and assert themselves easily with teachers and administrators, goals for family involvement should differ. In any case, authentic communication is necessary to foster growth-producing relationships between parents and teachers. Some family involvement activities that are traditional (such as open houses, conferences, fairs, and so on) may be effective, but assessing these activities on an annual basis is necessary to make sure that they have not become meaningless rituals.

Empowerment is identified by Coleman and Churchill (1997) as only one theme for guiding a program's philosophy of parent involvement. Additional themes considered by these authors are parenting, identifying and developing family strengths, preparation of children for future schooling, providing information about community resources, modeling appropriate learning opportunities for children at home, and improving interpersonal relations between professionals and families. As they assess the needs together, families and teachers may choose one or more of these themes and develop goals together for specific family involvement. New themes are likely to evolve as partnerships are formed and nourished.

> Add some other ideas for themes to the list generated by Coleman and Churchill. Discuss which family characteristics might be more suited to each theme.

Linking Parents and Teachers

Parents as Consumers of Children's Education

In tuition-based early childhood education programs, it is obvious that families are consumers. In public education, the parent as consumer is less obvious but no less true (Kostelnik, Stein, Whiren, & Soderman, 1993). Parents have made tremendous investments in their children and expect teachers to have some idea about just how important those children are (Figure 7–5). To practice a family-

> As my daughter begins her last semester of college, I am amazed at how quickly the years have flown and how time for both of us seems to be measured by school years. It all seemed so short: preschool, kindergarten, high school graduation, and now I even have lodging reservations for her college graduation weekend! Brief, almost fleeting, and yet, so many milestones have been accomplished. Overall, I am very pleased and even appreciative of the educational endeavors that she and I chose for her 16+ years of education.
>
> In the beginning, I placed her in a private school. She was almost four. Her years at the private school led to kindergarten and first and second grades. While there, she was exposed to lots of reading, typing, some Spanish, computers, and her two favorite pastimes to this day: drama and roller skating.
>
> Next came a culture shock for her: public school. This presented a larger class size, diversity, school spirit, and busing. She barely missed a beat in the adjustment. She was bused to an inner-city school. She adjusted well and even ran for school president and won! I was pleased with her elementary school experience. I was especially pleased with two teachers who recognized that special creative streak in her and rewarded her for her individuality.
>
> Looking back, there is very little that I would change. I have loved seeing her achieve, stretch, be challenged, and most of all grow into a lovely, well-read, very verbal individual. It was 90 percent education and encouragement and 10 percent community outlets, church, and her mom, grandmother, and beloved uncle.
>
> —Cindy Chrisman

Figure 7–5 A parent looks back.

based philosophy, early childhood teachers must begin to understand that they are serving both children and families. In a sense, the role of early childhood teachers and other staff members takes on several new perspectives when this idea is incorporated. This does not necessarily mean that teachers will agree with every request a family member makes, but it does mean that the teacher will respect and understand that those requests are often made in the best interests of the child. When conflict arises between teacher and parent, the teacher assumes a professional role in working to resolve the conflict.

Best Practice—Teachers work in partnership with parents.

School Policy—A variety of two-way communication strategies are used to meet needs of each family. Schools ask families about useful and preferred means of communication.

Best Practice—Teachers and parents work together to handle differences of opinion as they arise.

School Policy—A plan for conflict resolution is in place and shared with all parents. Family members work with staff to develop the plan.

Best Practice—Teachers solicit and incorporate parents' knowledge about their children.

School Policy—Assessment procedures require conferences with parents. Information is shared appropriately with parents before the time of the conference so that they are prepared to make meaningful use of the time with the teacher. Family members share information about their child that will be used by staff when assessing children.

Best Practice—Parents have opportunities to be involved in ways that are comfortable for them.

School Policy—Parents are informed about a variety of ways in which they can be involved with their children's education, both in and outside the classroom. And families share with staff their skills, interests, and preferences.

Figure 7–6 Examples of school policies based on best practices.

Supporting School Policy and Families

It is not impossible to support both school policy and families. Careful listening to parent concerns and reflective responses will often lead to creative problem-solving. When school policies are based on what education professionals believe to be best practices, teachers can explain the purpose of the policy to families (Figure 7–6). More details about effective interpersonal communication are included in Chapter 8 of this text.

The Partnership for Family Involvement in Education, U.S. Department of Education, has produced posters outlining seven good practices for families. Using the motto "Education is everybody's business!" the Partnership poster includes these practices.

1. *Take the time.*—Moments talking at evening meals and visiting the library, museum, or zoo make a difference.
2. *Read together.*—It's the starting point of all learning. Read with your youngsters.
3. *Use TV wisely.*—Limit viewing to no more than two hours a school day.
4. *Stay in regular contact with your child's teacher.*—Check homework every day.
5. *Meet with your child's teacher and principal.*—Compare your school program with standards of excellence so your children can reach their full potential.
6. *Know where your children are.*—Support community efforts to start after-school and summer programs.
7. *Talk directly to your children.*—Share the values you want them to have and about the dangers of drugs, alcohol, and tobacco. It could literally save their lives.

Early childhood teachers can share these practices with families in a variety of ways. Providing additional information, such as criteria for quality programs in early education based on guidelines for developmentally appropriate practice or national voluntary accreditation criteria, will give parents knowledge to appropriately evaluate their children's education. Many early education programs provide their goals for children and philosophy of teaching and learning in handbooks and orientation sessions for parents.

A Framework for School, Family, and Community Partnerships

In her theory-building work, Joyce Epstein (1995) notes the existence of overlapping spheres of influence in the lives of children. Her idea that home, school, and community are all important in each child's education has led her to discuss types of involvement as well as examples and practices.

> *The way schools care about children is reflected in the way schools care about the children's families. If educators view children simply as students, they are likely to see the family as separate from the school. That is, the family is expected to do its job and leave the education of children to the schools. If educators view students as children, they are likely to see both the family and the community as partners with the school in children's education and development. Partners recognize their shared interests in and responsibilities for children, and they work together to create better programs and opportunities for students (Epstein, 1995).*

In the preceding quote, one notes that Epstein's framework places children as central. When families, schools, and communities are truly partners, the possibility of a "caring community" exists. Epstein identifies the following terms as critical to understanding her framework for partnership:

- family-like schools
- school-like families
- community-minded families
- family-friendly schools and communities

> Before reading any further, note some characteristics that you believe to be important to each of the four terms above.

According to Epstein (1995), family-like schools recognize individuality in children and welcome all families; school-like families recognize children as students and learners, and encourage their success; community-minded families (including students) help their neighbors in a variety of ways; and family-friendly schools and communities consider the needs and realities of contemporary families (Figure 7–7).

Six types of involvement or caring have been recorded by Epstein: parenting, communicating, volunteering, learning at home, decision-making, and collaborating with the community. It is suggested that schools utilize all six types of involvement for balance in their partnerships with families and communities. Figure 7–8 explains each type.

Epstein and her associates make it clear that creating a comprehensive caring community takes a lot of time and a lot of hard work. Organization and planning are required. They suggest the appointment of an action team and at least a three-year plan. Thus, partnerships are a process, not events. Before beginning the work of the action team, it is important to gather information about the school's existing practices. One way to collect this information is through use of the standards listed in Figure 7–9.

National Standards from the PTA

The National Parent Teacher Association (PTA) has had as its primary goal for more than 100 years, "affirming the significance of parent and family involvement . . . in support of children and their education. . . ." With this in mind, and the increasingly powerful evidence from research to support family involvement in education, the PTA, using Epstein's six types of involvement, has created national standards.

"The purpose for the standards is threefold:

1. To promote meaningful parent and family participation.
2. To raise awareness regarding the components of effective programs.

Parent meetings are problem-focused	5 4 3 2 1
Parents are informed about classroom activities	5 4 3 2 1
Parents are viewed as a source of information	5 4 3 2 1
Parental input is valued	5 4 3 2 1
Parents come to school for positive reasons	5 4 3 2 1
Parent meetings are held at various times	5 4 3 2 1
Teachers discuss parents in a positive manner	5 4 3 2 1
Teachers avoid gossiping about families	5 4 3 2 1
Parents are informed when their children are doing well	5 4 3 2 1
Teachers make it a point to invite all parents to school functions	5 4 3 2 1
Are relationships between parents and teachers generally seen as positive?	5 4 3 2 1
Did most parents of children in the school succeed in school themselves?	5 4 3 2 1

Figure 7–7   Checklist for family friendliness in schools. (*Source:* Rosenthal, D. M., & Sawyers, J. Y. [1996, Summer]. Building successful home/school partnerships: Strategies for parent support and involvement. *Childhood Education,* pp. 194–200.)

1. Parenting—Assist families with parenting skills and setting home conditions to support children as students, and assist schools to understand families.
2. Communicating—Conduct effective communications from school to home and from home to school about school programs and children's progress.
3. Volunteering—Organize volunteers to support the school and students.
4. Learning at home—Involve families with their children in homework and other activities.
5. Decision-making—Include families as participants in school decisions and develop parent leaders.
6. Collaborating with the community—Coordinate resources and services from the community for families, students, and the school, and provide services to the community.

Figure 7–8   The keys to successful school-family-community partnerships. Six types of involvement. (*Source:* Epstein, J., Coates, L., Salinas, K. C., Sanders, M. G., & Simon, B. S. [1997]. *School, family, and community partnerships: Your handbook for action.* Thousand Oaks, CA: Corwin Press.)

3. To provide guidelines for schools that wish to improve their programs." (http://www.pta.org/programs/invstand.htm accessed 2/20/03).

For each of the six standards for family involvement, the National PTA has provided **quality** **indicators** in the form of a checklist for ease in assessing a family involvement program. Figure 7–9 summarizes the standards. On the World Wide Web, go to http://www.pta.org/ programs for the entire checklist, including quality indicators.

Standard I—Communicating

Communication between home and school is regular, two-way, and meaningful.

Standard II—Parenting

Parenting skills are promoted and supported.

Standard III—Student Learning

Parents play an integral role in assisting student learning.

Standard IV—Volunteering

Parents are welcome in the school, and their support and assistance are sought.

Standard V—School Decision-making and Advocacy

Parents are full partners in the decisions that affect children and families.

Standard VI—Collaborating with Community

Community resources are used to strengthen schools, families, and student learning.

Figure 7–9   Listing of standards from the National PTA. (*Source:* http://www.pta.org/programs)

Professionalism in Family-based Early Education

Professionalism in early education is enhanced when all staff uphold their responsibilities to children and families. Due to low pay, early childhood educators are often regarded as having low status in U.S. society. Still, it is imperative that these educators view themselves as professionals so that they see the need and responsibility to apply the knowledge, skills, and values of the discipline. Although it is true that much is expected of early childhood teachers and that they are typically not compensated fairly for their work, professionalism must be evident.

Following are some of the components of acting professionally in early childhood education.

- *Confidentiality.* Early childhood teachers must be able to maintain confidences shared by fam-

"Programs are only as good as the individuals who staff them."
—**Head Start Advisory Council on Services for Families with Infants and Toddlers**

ilies. The nature of the job frequently makes early childhood teachers privy to information that may cause embarrassment or harm to a family. Information gleaned through observation, as well as formal records, must be kept in confidence. Teachers should make it clear to family members that it is their professional responsibility to maintain confidentiality and that they will not share information unless the family authorizes them to do so.

Requests for sharing information should occur only for the purpose of providing assistance to the family or child enrolled in the program. Responsibility for safeguarding confidentiality includes obtaining family consent when sharing information, obtaining family consent when inviting others to

Professionalism in early education is enhanced when all staff members uphold their responsibilities to children and families.

team meetings, keeping files secure, never gossiping or talking casually about a family, and respecting confidences coworkers share with you (*Family Partnerships*, 1998). See the **NAEYC Code of Ethical Conduct,** Section II, Principal 2.8 and 2.9 found in the Appendix on page __ of this book for statements on written and verbal confidentiality for both children's and families' rights to privacy.

The **Family Education Rights & Privacy Act (FERPA)** is a federal law designed to protect the privacy of a student's education records. Under this act, parents have the right to inspect and review all of the students education records maintained by the school. Parents have the right to request that a school correct the records believed to be inaccurate or misleading. Generally, schools must have written permission from the parent or eligible student before releasing any information from a student's record. For more information about FERPA go to http://www.ed.gove/offices/Om/ferpa.html

- *Advocacy.* Advocating for children and families is also a professional responsibility. **Advocacy** can happen within your school or center, in a town or city, in regional or state government, and at the national or international level. Advocacy may be done in person, through e-mail or letters, and by telephone.

Early childhood professionals may advocate within both private and public agencies, as well as with elected and nonelected public officials. For a detailed description of advocacy methods and strategies, read *Advocates in Action: Making a Difference for Young Children* (Robinson & Stark, 2002).

- *Collaboration.* Professionalism with families also extends into the community through collaboration with other agencies and programs. Collaboration may be minimal (informing parent of opportunities), or more extensive (budgeting time and money for collaborative efforts). Collaboration may be necessary to improve or extend support for families, obtain services for children, or increase knowledge about certain conditions. For further information about family-community collaboration, read "New Directions for Parent Leadership in a Family-Support Context" (Langford & Weissbourd, 1997).

- *Understanding roles and boundaries.* Early childhood teachers should be familiar with the roles and tasks included in their job descriptions. Work with families and children is frequently done on a very personal level. Sometimes, some personal disclosure on the part of the professional is effective, but it is critical that teachers are aware of professional boundaries in their relationships with children and families. Demonstration of caring must be balanced with limits in professional relationships. When friendships develop with either families in the program or with colleagues, it is important that professional boundaries be maintained in the interest of fairness to all. Some strategies that can be helpful in managing professional roles and boundaries include having accurate job descriptions, adhering to policies and procedures, not taking sides in family disputes, skill in assertive communication, knowing how to delegate when a boundary conflict may occur, and respecting professional boundaries with colleagues (*Family Partnerships*, 1998).

- *Record-keeping.* Having accurate and current records about children as well as relevant family information is useful for assessment of children. Further, such documentation can be invaluable if referrals for additional or alternative services are necessary. All records must be kept in a locked cabinet so that they are confidential. Keeping notes about informal and formal conferences with family members can serve as a reminder when planning for the group or for individual children. Observations of children in the classroom and in other settings provide meaningful information when compiling evaluations.

Embracing Diversity

When early childhood educators attempt to form a family-based philosophy, a willingness to acknowledge and respect family differences is required. Cultural differences in families lead to very different approaches to parenting young children. Some families believe that children are fragile and that families are the protectors of children; other families believe that children are tough and independent, and that families are the trainers of children (Trawick-Smith, 1997). **Diversity** in families is part of the richness of our pluralistic culture.

Observing and Appreciating Differences

For any given teacher, one of the parenting approaches just mentioned may be the one they find more appropriate. It will be important that early childhood professionals work to understand and respect both points of view as well as those in between. Rather than judging the family, teachers can use the information to better understand the child in their care. When necessary, differences in practices and expectations between families and schools should be discussed. Open communication can lead to understanding of an opposing point of view. Teachers can offer to share resources when parents ask questions or seek help with some area of difficulty. Teachers also should realize that the child's family can be the greatest resource for understanding the child.

You will teach children who come from a variety of family structures. Encouraging members of the

It is important that early childhood educators acknowledge and respect cultural diversity.

child's family to participate in school functions is an important aspect of early childhood family involvement. Frequently, this might mean inviting a parent (or other family member) who does not live with the child to participate in ways that are comfortable for all family members. Sometimes, parents who do not live together, will both attend the same parent-teacher conference, or they may request separate conferences with their child's teacher. Keep in mind that each family defines itself. It is the role of the early childhood teacher to include all family members, not to judge who is a "real" mother or "real" parent.

Some barriers to implementing a multicultural framework in classrooms have been identified by Swick, Boutte, & Van Scoy (1996). The following factors serve as barriers when early childhood teachers do not engage in ongoing personal and professional development.

Barrier #1: Cultural stereotypes. People are stereotyped when others have minimal or inaccurate information about them. When those in the dominant culture have low self-esteem and are insecure, they tend to foster intergenerational prejudices.

Barrier #2: Social isolation. Having experiences with people from a variety of different cultures often helps to understand those cultures. However, those

> *"We live in an increasingly diverse world. As an early childhood educator you are almost certain to have close contact with people who have different racial, economic, cultural, and linguistic backgrounds and different lifestyles. This diversity offers challenges and opportunities. Although you may have moments of discomfort and self-doubt, you also have the possibility of gaining new appreciation and insights. Each bias and prejudice that you overcome brings you a step closer to helping all children to reach their potential"*
>
> —Feeney, Christensen, & Moravcik, **1996, p. 12**

who have social contact only with others who are similar in culture and beliefs may lack information necessary for understanding differences.

Barrier #3: Tradition. By continuing the same activities in the name of tradition, schools can create exclusionary practices. When traditions are not inclusive, they must be reevaluated and modified, or dropped. All forms of bias must be considered including racism, sexism, ageism, as well as unfair limits placed on those with disabilities.

Barrier #4: Excessive conformity. Expectations for all to conform to the majority are sometimes stated as democratic. However, this leaves out a crucial piece for democracy: that all have a voice and deserve to be represented. While in a vote, majority rules, this is not the case for everyday events in educational settings. Children can learn to celebrate differences.

> *"Schools also need to recognize the effect they have on children's multicultural development. Some teachers have limited understanding of their student's cultural backgrounds. The resulting erroneous beliefs must be transcended through staff development, personal reading and enrichment, and through personal growth experiences. Institutional practices of tracking, ability grouping and rigidly defined graded systems need to be replaced with more inclusionary strategies such as multiage grouping, cross-cultural peer learning and more personalized instruction. Unquestioned rituals and policies imprison culturally different children within an inequitable and insensitive environment. . . . Inappropriate and inaccurate labeling has led many children to years of academic failure."*
>
> —**Kevin J. Swick, Gloria Boutte, & Irma Van Scoy, 1996**

Strategies to overcome barriers

1. Repeatedly invite guests, speakers, and participants from a variety of cultures into the school program. Plan education and recreational activities together.

2. Use a variety of media to show different cultures and promote the celebration of differences. For example, display posters depicting many cultures and change them throughout the year, use children's literature with different racial-ethnic and socioeconomic levels represented in positive ways and use videos depicting a variety of cultures in positive ways.

3. Plan celebrations that involve diverse communities and include food, music, dance, visual, and language traditions throughout the year

Anti-Bias Curriculum. Louise Derman-Sparks and her associates (1989) have created a model approach for implementing curriculum goals related to understanding and respect for diversity in early childhood education. In the words of this group:

> *Anti-bias curriculum embraces an educational philosophy as well as specific techniques and content. It is value-based: differences are good; oppressive ideas and behaviors are not. It sets up a creative tension between respecting differences and not accepting unfair beliefs and acts. It asks teachers and children to confront troublesome issues rather than covering them up. An anti-bias perspective is integral to all aspects of daily classroom life (Derman-Sparks and the A.B.C. Task Force, 1989, p. x).*

Even though the emphasis of the anti-bias curriculum is on teaching and learning in early childhood classrooms, there are ways to consider this philosophy in work with families and communities. The authors of this curriculum dedicate an entire chapter to setting goals and working with parents. Including work with parents, they say, is "vital" to the effectiveness of this approach in early childhood education. The authors include the following goals:

- to establish genuine parent/teacher dialogue that opens up discussion of each other's points of view and seeks to gain clarity, understanding, and solutions agreeable to both teacher and parent

- to provide information that facilitates parent awareness of how young children develop racial-ethnic and gender identity, and the ways in which sexism, racism, and handicappism negatively affect healthy socioemotional and cognitive growth

- to create safe settings for parents to discuss with each other the issues raised by anti-bias work and to increase their ability to integrate anti-bias perspectives in their child-rearing.

- to facilitate development of children through joint parent/teacher problem solving and mutual support

- to involve parents in curriculum development, implementation and evaluation (Derman-Sparks and the A.B.C. Task Force, 1989, p. 97)

It is clear that carrying out these goals will challenge most, if not all, early childhood professionals. Value systems held by some families will be on a collision course with the values held by those who believe in an anti-bias approach to education. Some families will just not have given these ideas much thought, and although they may have some ideas based on political or religious ideology, they might begin to think about the importance of understanding and respecting those people with whom they come into contact on a regular basis; for example, in their child's school. There will be those families who agree with the importance of anti-bias curriculum but have not been actively sharing ideas with their children. And finally, early childhood teachers are likely to find that some families with whom they work have already embraced the philosophy of respect for all people.

For early childhood programs that are serious about implementing an anti-bias approach, the creators of this curriculum offer a nine-session plan for parent group meetings. Topics include the following:

1. Introducing Anti-Bias Curriculum
2. Gender Identity and Sexism
3. Creating Nonsexist Home Environments
4. How Children Develop Racial Identity and Awareness
5. Creating Antiracist Home and School Environments
6. Sexism and Racism in Children's Books

7. Talking with Children about Disabilities
8. Children's Books about Differently Abled People
9. Advocating for the Rights of the Differently Abled

Strategies and resources are suggested for each of the above topics. Although this outline is a useful beginning for informing parents about an anti-bias philosophy in educating young children, it is not exhaustive. Attention is not given to some specific groups that are oppressed, including low-income families, gay and lesbian people, overweight people, and older people. Clearly, it is the intent of this educational philosophy to eliminate all oppression and to advocate for fairness for all people.

Figure 7–10 contains suggestions for parents who seem to be reticent about involvement in their children's education (Lee, 1995).

Understanding that Many Ways of Interacting with Children Can Serve Them Well

Early childhood teachers work with both children and their families. We can best teach children by including their families in a variety of ways. As we provide quality early childhood education programs for young children, we are also supporting and caring for families (Feeney, Christensen, & Moravcik, 1996). Adults in families have many ways of nurturing and providing for their children; they have values that may differ from the teacher's values. When early childhood teachers can assess family strengths and not see these differences only as deficits, then it is more likely they will enjoy successful partnerships with families of children in their programs.

Evaluating the Family Involvement Component in Early Education

As with any other component in quality early childhood education, it is important that early childhood

Suggestions offered by parents who participated in the study about how to reach out to reticent parents who seldom take part in school activities.

1. Encourage active parents to stress the importance of participating in school activities.

2. Urge children to encourage and remind their parents to attend school activities.

3. Invite parents to visit school and observe their children any time, and reassure them that they will be given a friendly welcome when they come to school.

4. Clearly indicate to parents that a language difference need not be a primary concern for parents who are interested in getting involved at school.

5. Invite interpreters to come with parents for open-house and back-to-school-night activities, or encourage teachers to have interpreters present.

6. If two or more parents belong to the same Asian ethnic group, reassure them that they are free to speak in their own language to each other during parent meetings. This way, Asian parents who are able to communicate in English may help others to understand the discussions.

7. Reserve some time to communicate with Asian parents alone after the parent meeting (e.g., on back-to-school night) so that Asian parents do not feel that they have been ignored.

8. Visit reticent parents in their homes. In general, Asian parents respect teachers and feel honored when their children's teachers visit. Asian parents also view that teacher's willingness to come forward as a sign of sincerity (Shen & Mo 1993). Parents are more willing to be educational partners when they learn that teachers make an effort to reach out to them.

9. Sometimes, children inhibit parents' participation because they feel embarrassed by their parents' inability to communicate well in English. They sometimes wish their parents would not appear at school. Convey that a language difference is not a negative trait.

10. Provide an opportunity for parents in the same Asian group, whose children attend the same school, to get acquainted with one another.

11. Schedule parent-teacher conferences to enable parents from the same Asian group, with children in the same class, to visit school at the same time. This way, reluctant parents may not feel as threatened by the unfamiliar school environment and may be encouraged to communicate with the teacher.

12. Asian parents who speak English and are familiar with school procedures can give introductions regarding the following matters to reticent parents from the same Asian group: school registration procedures, immunization, school volunteer programs, parent-teacher conferences, school educational goals, grading and evaluation systems, etc. Holding meetings about these issues in a parent's home might provide a less threatening environment for the reticent parent. Schools may also conduct seminars in parents' native tongues to help them become familiar with basic features of the school system such as educational services and programs, extracurricular activities, and procedures for assessment and evaluation of children (Yao, 1988).

13. Send notes to parents from time to time. The note could be a one- or two-sentence progress report, or it may be something that would make parents smile such as, "Do you know what your child did today that gave us a good laugh?" or "Would you like to know what interesting thing your child did today?"

Figure 7–10   Strategies for involving reticent parents. (*Source:* Lee, F. Y. [1995, March]. Asian parents as partners. *Young Children, 50,* 4–7. With permission from the National Association for the Education of Young Children.)

teachers and administrators evaluate the success or effectiveness of family involvement. In planning for evaluation, it may be helpful to use the Continuum of Parent Involvement identified by Galen (1991) (Figure 7–11).

To evaluate this in a logical and consistent manner, a program must first identify its goals for family involvement. Both short-term and long-term goals may be identified. Some examples of goals, strategies, and methods of evaluation are provided in this

HIGH
- Parents, trained by teacher, assist in classroom in such learning activities as reviewing writing samples, assisting at learning centers, or helping with computer use.
- Parents in classrooms reinforce processes and concepts introduced by teachers.
- Parents in classrooms practice with children on vocabulary words, number facts; help them enter answers on computer cards.
- Parents read to children in the classrooms.
- Parents make classroom presentations or present hands-on activities in areas of expertise.
- Parents participate in committees that directly influence school curricula and policies. Committees consist of parents, teachers, and administrator(s).
- P.T.A. parents work on sponsorship and implementation of curriculum-related and family-oriented activities, e.g. cultural arts contests, displays, Family Fun Night.
- Parents make instructional materials for classroom use, as directed by teachers.
- Parents assist in school library, checking out and shelving books.
- Parents participate as room mothers or room fathers.
- Parents supervise on class trips or chaperone at school functions.
- Parents visit classrooms during American Education Week or Back-to-School Night.
- Parents attend classroom plays, presentations.
- Parents attend school assembly programs.
- Parents attend competitive games, athletic events at school.
- Parents attend promotion ceremonies.
- Parents attend parent-teacher conferences.
- Parents are encouraged to help children with homework at home.
- Parents are involved in P.T.A. fund-raising activities.
- Parents are asked to join P.T.A.
- Parents are encouraged to read school's handbook for parents.
- No parental involvement.

LOW

Figure 7–11 Continuum of parent involvement. (*Source:* Galen, H. [1991, January]. Increasing parental involvement in elementary school: The nitty gritty of one successful program. *Young Children, 46,* p. 19. With permission from the National Association for the Education of Young Children.)

section. Please note that this list is a sample and not indicative of a comprehensive family involvement plan for early childhood education.

Goal—providing program information regarding the philosophy of teaching and learning to all new families

Strategies—providing written brochures at the time of application, providing handbooks at the time of enrollment, personal explanations of program by director or other staff, teacher-led parent meeting that explains the program early in the year

Evaluation methods—noting that the program philosophy has been added to the handbook or a brochure, having parents sign that they have read and understand the philosophy, asking parents to submit questions or comments that will be addressed in a parent meeting to increase their understanding of program philosophy

Goal—creating an orientation to the program for both children and families

Strategies—classroom visits before school starts, making curriculum resources available to families, explanations or listings of all support services available

Evaluation methods—filing the plan for orientation including how and when orientations are conducted, ask participants to complete a checklist about the usefulness of the orientation, ask family members who have been in the program for at least a year for suggestions for orientation topics and formats

Goal—scheduling home-school conferences at least twice during the school term

Strategies—designing flexible schedules to meet family needs, including children when appropriate in conferences, involving other staff, other family members, or advocates when appropriate, giving parents a list of suggested questions they might ask during conferences

Evaluation methods—recording dates and times of conferences, collecting evaluations from family members about the usefulness of conferences and suggestions for improvement

Goal—making family members feel welcome as classroom volunteers

Strategies—matching family members' interests or skills with classroom needs, preparing materials and space in advance for parents, informing parents of daily schedule and exceptions to the schedule, consistently welcoming parents throughout the day, personally inviting each parent or family to participate in the classroom

Evaluation methods—request feedback from volunteers who frequent the classroom, send anonymous questionnaires to those who do not volunteer to request information about what the program staff can do to increase their comfort level, self-evaluate which families you feel most comfortable having in the classroom and how you might increase comfort level of others

The results of evaluation of family involvement activities will lead the program staff to be aware of their successes as well as areas that need attention. Program assessment should then lead to new goals that will continue to build partnerships with families.

Summary and Conclusions

To practice a family-based philosophy in early childhood education, teachers must have knowledge of families and value the primacy of families in children's lives. In early childhood education, Head Start has provided a model program for partnerships between programs and families. Since 1965, Head Start has had a primary goal of empowering parents to take responsibility for their lives and for those of their children. High expectations have been coupled with various forms of support for families. Teachers in family-based early education programs see themselves as support for children and their families.

Policies in early childhood education programs must incorporate current understanding about parents as their children's first teachers. Family involvement must be a priority for early education professionals. As programs for children are planned and implemented, the central role of families must be incorporated in a variety of ways.

Key Terms

parental rights	continuity
linkages	congruence
empowering	overlapping spheres of
quality indicators	influence
Family Education	diversity
Rights & Privacy Act	code of
(FERPA)	ethical conduct
advocacy	home visiting

Chapter Seven Applications

1. The most important aspect of family involvement in education is that parents spend time with their children. Describe some ways you can help to foster this, even when parents are not volunteering in the classroom.

2. Explain the concept of continuity in children's lives. Give examples of ways early childhood professionals can increase continuity for children.

3. How might a perspective of parents as consumers of early education affect parent-teacher relationships?

Questions for Reflection and Discussion

1. Make a list of topics that should be included in a family-based philosophy of early childhood education.

2. Which areas of practicing a family-based philosophy will challenge you? In which areas do you possess experience or strengths?

3. How will particular early education settings (e.g., child care, public school, Head Start, and so on) affect your philosophy about family involvement?

Field Assignments

1. Ask several parents of young children about care and education arrangements they have made for their children each day. Note the number of transitions some very young children deal with daily.

2. Interview three early childhood teachers about the responsibilities they believe parents have for their children's early education. What suggestions would teachers give to parents of young children related to these responsibilities?

3. Interview three parents of young children about responsibilities they believe early childhood teachers have for their children's early education. What suggestions would parents give to teachers related to these responsibilities?

References

Bowman, B. (1994). Home and school. In S. L. Kagan & B. Weissbourd (Eds.), *Putting families first: America's family support movement and the challenge of change*. San Francisco: Jossey-Bass.

Bronfenbrenner, U. (1979). *The ecology of human development: Experiments by nature and design*. Cambridge, MA: Harvard University Press.

Coleman, M., & Churchill, S. (1997, Spring). Challenges to family involvement. *Childhood Education*, 144–148.

Derman-Sparks, L., & the A.B.C. Task Force. (1989). *Antibias curriculum: Tools for empowering young children*. Washington, DC: National Association for the Education of Young Children.

Epps, W. J. (1998). *Connecting Head Start parents to the public school setting: A transition activity booklet*. Florissant, MO: Southern Research Associates.

Epstein, J. (1995). School/family/community partnerships: Caring for the children we share. *Phi Delta Kappan, 76*, 701–712.

Epstein, J., Coates, L., Salinas, K. C., Sanders, M. G., & Simon, B. S. (1997). *School, family, and community partnerships: Your handbook for action*. Thousand Oaks, CA: Corwin Press.

Family partnerships: A continuous process. Training guides for the Head Start learning community. (1998). Washington, DC: U.S. Department of Health and Human Services.

Feeney, S., Christensen, D., & Moravcik, E. (1996). *Who am I in the lives of children?: An introduction to teaching young children*. Englewood Cliffs, NJ: Prentice-Hall.

FERPA web-site address: www.ed.gov/offices/Om/ferpa.html

Galen, H. (1991, January). Increasing parental involvement in elementary school: The nitty gritty of one successful program. *Young Children, 46*, 19.

Head Start Handbook of the Parent Involvement Vision and Strategies. (1996). Washington, DC: U.S. Department of Health and Human Services.

Kostelnik, M. J., Stein, L. C., Whiren, A. P., & Soderman, A. K. (1993). *Guiding children's social development*. Clifton Park, NY: Delmar Learning.

Langford, J., & Weissbourd, B. (1997). New directions for parent leadership in a family-support context. In S. L. Kagan & B. T. Bowman (Eds.), *Leadership in early care and education*. Washington DC: National Association for the Education of Young Children.

Lee, F. Y. (1995, March). Asian parents as partners. *Young Children, 50*, 4–7.

National PTA. www.pta.org/programs/invstand/htm, accessed 3/9/99.

Powell, D. (1989). *Families and early childhood programs.* Washington, DC: National Association for the Education of Young Children.

Robinson, A., & Strk, D. R. (2002). *Advocates in action.* Washington, DC: National Association for the Education of Young Children.

Rosenthal, D. M., & Sawyers, J. Y. (1996, Summer). Building successful home/school partnerships: Strategies for parent support and involvement. *Childhood Education,* 194–200.

Starting Small. Teaching Tolerance Curriculum. Montgomery, AL: Southern Poverty Law Center.

Swick, K. J., Boutte, G., & Van Scoy, I. (1995/96, Winter). Families and schools: Building multicultural values together. *Childhood Education,* 75–79.

Trawick-Smith, J. (1997). *Early childhood development: A multicultural perspective.* Upper Saddle River, NJ: Prentice-Hall.

OUTLINE

Family–Staff Relationship

OBJECTIVES

After reading and reflecting on this chapter, you should be able to:

■ Discuss attitudes and practices necessary for effective communication between home and school.

■ Understand which communication strategies are most effective for various situations.

■ Apply effective conflict resolution practices in the family involvement component of early childhood education.

■ Familiarize yourself with useful Web sites to build and support family-staff relationships.

■ Learn strategies for responding to a variety of interactions with families.

Building Relationships

Attitudes

A perspective that views teachers and parents as partners in children's education is a very powerful one. The sense of common purpose and mutuality is a strength of the partnership notion (Swick, 1991).

Establishing a positive relationship with parents begins with the first phone call to the school or with the first visit. Creating a positive relationship with parents involves everyone in the school. For example, the person who answers the phone or greets the family on their arrival may set the tone for the entire visit. Incidental meetings with staff often provide useful information for families.

What makes a positive or healthy relationship? Clearly, any relationship depends on more than one person's attitudes and behaviors. However, it is also true that one person with certain understandings and skills can make a difference in the direction of a relationship. It is the duty of professionals to take this responsibility as they interact with family and community members.

Some characteristics are known to be related to healthy relationships. The following are included by Hanna (1991) in her discussion of this topic:

High self-esteem—Teachers who love and accept themselves are more likely to demonstrate caring and acceptance of others.

Freedom from co-dependency—Teachers who are not extremely dependent on others, serving them and sacrificing their own needs, possess a trait that is important for positive relationships.

Genuineness—Honest, open, authentic teachers avoid game-playing in relationships with others.

Warmth—Caring for others, even with their faults, helps to maintain healthy relationships.

Empathy—Trying to understand the behavior of others and the underlying meaning of that behavior is an important characteristic of building relationships.

Self-disclosure—Balancing how much and what you disclose about yourself with family and community members can be a challenge. A certain kind and amount of disclosing is related to other characteristics of healthy relationships such as genuineness, warmth, and empathy.

Fairness and dependability—Over time, teachers have the opportunity to demonstrate that others can trust them to be fair-minded and to follow through as they have have committed to do.

Energizing feelings—As teachers build relationships with families and their communities, they are likely to leave a situation feeling energized by the possibilities communicated. Experience with such situations is likely to positively influence teachers to work on relationships with parents and other community members.

Consider the characteristics of healthy relationships just mentioned. Think about a teacher that you had in the past who seemed to excel in one or two of those areas. Share some examples of teacher behaviors that you believe demonstrate these characteristics. Which of these areas do you see as your strengths? In which areas could you use some practice?

The U.S. Department of Education lists seven tips for building partnerships with families. These tips are work together, assess needs, survey resources, share information, seek out experienced collaborators, set goals, and decide on measures of success. A complete description of these tips may be found at http://pfie.ed.gov/.

Practices

Written Communication.   One of the initial contacts with parents is usually a letter welcoming their child to the school. Although this letter may be sent by the director or principal, it needs to include information and perhaps a greeting from the classroom teacher as well.

The content of all the written information sent home to parents needs to be clear and worded positively. Always proofread for correct spelling and grammar. The initial information should be covered

As teachers build relationships with families and their communities, they are likely to experience energized feelings.

in welcoming, supportive, and inviting ways. Written communications can include brochures about the early childhood education program including philosophy and goals for children, as well as school policies and information about the staff.

Communication In-Person.   When parents visit the school or center for the first time, it is important that both written and human resources are available.

Personal communication should include pleasant greetings, a tour of the building and grounds, introductions to teachers and other staff, and an opportunity to ask questions. Figure 8–1 provides one format for interviewing parents or family members who are new to the early childhood program.

Family involvement in early childhood education thrives in programs that practice an open door policy. In both written and personal communication, parents should understand that they are welcome at the school any time, that they are partners in their child's education, and that their voice is important to

1. Would you like to work with the children in the classroom?
2. What would you prefer doing in the classroom if you were to come?
3. Name something special that you can do or make, or something you know about that you would be willing to share with the children.
4. I'm going to read a list of items to you. Tell me if you have ever felt a need to know more about any of these items by answering either yes or no. (Interviewer: Please check appropriate category.)

		Yes	No
a.	How to teach my preschool children		
b.	Whether my child is developing appropriately		
c.	Services provided by community agencies to which I have a right		
d.	How to communicate better with my children		
e.	How to help my children interact better with others		
f.	How to discipline my children		
g.	How to make toys and other things for my children		
h.	How to tell whether my child is progressing in school		
i.	What to do when my children do things that I do not consider proper (temper tantrums, thumb-sucking, bad manners)		
j.	How to play with my children		
k.	Where to take my children so they can have a nice time and learn		
l.	How to help my children retain their cultural heritage		
m.	How to use and develop the talents and skills that I know I have		
n.	How to refrain from hitting my child		
o.	How to guarantee that my child will succeed in school		
p.	How to talk to teachers		
q.	How to help my child learn a second language when I don't speak a second language		
r.	How to extend language learning		
s.	How to use my home environment as a learning experience for my children		

5. What is your opinion of preschool parents coming together at least once a month to talk and learn more about the areas to which you answered "yes?"
6. If you felt that this parent meeting is a good idea, how can we make sure that the meetings are worthwhile for parents?
7. Would you be willing to help organize the first parent meeting?
8. Are there other ways you might be willing to help with the parent meetings?
9. Name something special that you can do or make, or that you know about that you would be willing to share with other parents.

Figure 8–1 Parent interview form. (*Source:* Hohmann, M., Banet, B., & Weikart, D. P. [1979] *Young Children in Action,* High/Scope Press. Reprinted with permission from the High/Scope Educational Research Foundation)

the school. Examples of ways in which families are involved in the early childhood program could be shared at this initial visit.

A handbook provided for parents at the time of orientation or initial enrollment has been found to be useful by many early childhood professionals. Parent or family handbooks are likely to include a philosophy of the educational program, goals or expected outcomes for children, information about family involvement opportunities, daily schedules, operating policies and procedures, and information about individual classrooms.

Ongoing Communication

One-Way Communication

The following strategies are examples of one-way communication from school to home.

Newsletters. Sending home newsletters from school is one way to help parents stay informed about and connected to school events. Having columns by teachers, children, administrators, and parents is a strategy that allows for a variety of voices and perspectives. This format makes it more likely that a larger number of parents will actually read the newsletter.

Suggestions for topics of interest and concern to families with young children include the following:

- the meaning of developmentally appropriate practice
- the importance of play for young children
- multiple intelligences
- the meaning of pretend play for young children
- early literacy
- nutrition
- understanding children's physical and motor development
- understanding children's intellectual development
- understanding children's social and emotional development

- appropriate strategies for moving from diapers to potty

Columns about these topics and many others are provided for use by early childhood programs in *Family-Friendly Communication for Early Childhood Programs* (Diffily & Morrison, 1996).

Especially important in a newsletter are dates of upcoming events and brief explanations or descriptions of school activities. Providing both a listing of current activities and those further into the future will remind parents and help them in planning busy schedules. A sample page from a newsletter is found in Figure 8–2. Figure 8–3 suggests content for newsletters to families.

The following ideas were selected from an article by Bob Krech entitled "Improve Parent Communication with a Newsletter" (1995):

- The main goal of the newsletter is to answer parents' questions before they ask them.
- Try to keep the newsletter to one page.
- Always remember to thank parents, at least once, in your newsletter.

Notes. Notes home to families can take a variety of forms and serve a variety of purposes. One form is the standard note sent to all parents in the school or class. This type of note is useful for occasions such as field trips, picture days, or activities for which parents need to either give permission or send items to school (Figure 8–4).

More personal notes include teacher-generated communications regarding a child's academic or behavioral progress. It is important to balance the types of notes and not use them for sending home only negative messages. Incorporating celebratory or congratulatory notes when something has been done well helps parents keep a balanced perspective about their child, the teacher, and even their own parenting. What experiences have you had with personal notes from teachers? What points of consideration do you believe to be important when drafting such notes? Critique the notes sent by teachers to families in Figure 8–5.

Announcements. Announcements need to be made in a variety of formats over different lengths of

What We Can Do to Help Our Children Learn:

Listen to them and pay attention to their problems.

Read with them.

Tell family stories.

Limit their television watching.

Have books and other reading materials in the house.

Look up words in the dictionary with them.

Encourage them to use an encyclopedia.

Share favorite poems and songs with them.

Take them to the library and get them their own library cards.

Take them to museums and historical sites, when possible.

Discuss the daily news with them.

Go exploring with them and learn about plants, animals, and geography.

Find a quiet place for them to study.

Review their homework.

Meet with their teachers.

Do you have other ideas?

For sale by the U.S. Government Printing Office Superintendent of Documents, Mail Stop: SSOP, Washington, DC 20402-9328

Figure 8–2 What we can do to help our children learn. (Reprinted with permission from the U.S. Department of Education)

Newsletter Columns and Sections Could Include:

Activities for home

for children to do alone or with siblings or peers

for parents to do with children

for family outings

Explanations of activities and routines at school

Announcements of child or family-related community activities

art, drama, music, films

Information about school staff

introductions

recent training

personal or biographical information

School changes or announcements

due to weather conditions

due to construction/repairs/maintenance

Articles on parenting, guidance, health, safety

Ideas for different seasons

travel guidelines and activities

developmentally appropriate toys for gifts for children

Reminders about

tuition due dates and other fees

change of clothes, diapers, and the like

field trips

closing times and related policies

Figure 8–3 Suggestions for newsletter topics.

time. Putting important dates in an annual calendar helps to keep everyone alerted in a timely way. Sending home schoolwide announcements with children is another strategy. Posting signs on doors and at pickup points helps remind families of upcoming events or activities.

Placing emergency announcements on the school's voice-mail system helps to get information to parents. Some schools have an information line that has a new recording each day, and family members can call for upcoming events. Placing long-term announcements in newsletters and discussing them at parent meetings reinforces dates and information.

Daily Information Sheets. Some centers use preprinted forms that are completed each day by classroom staff and sent home to families. Information that can be useful to parents is included on these sheets: what the child had to eat for each mealtime and snacks, sleep schedule, activities that the child particularly enjoyed, accomplishments or developmental milestones observed, and special comments or concerns.

November 13, 2003

Dear _____

     School pictures will be taken on Friday, November 20. Both individual packets of photographs and group photos for each classroom will be available for purchase. We expect all prints to be available by December 11. Individual packets are priced at $12.50 and class pictures are $2.50. All picture money is due by December 16. Please call your child's teacher if you have questions or concerns.

Stacey Blades
School Director

Figure 8–4 Sample note sent home to all families in the school or class.

Two-Way Communication

Frequently, strategies that involve **two-way communication** between home and school are essential. Two-way communication between families and early childhood teachers offers some distinct advantages over one-way strategies. These methods focus on developing ongoing communication "in which both parties are equals, contributing valuable information to the discussion" (Kagan & Cohen, 1997, p. 22). Some useful two-way communication techniques are discussed next.

Planned Conferences. Planned conferences need to be in a quiet place where information can be shared calmly and with confidentiality. The teachers need to have all notes, portfolios, and other necessary materials ready at the time of the conference. It is usually recommended that strengths of the child be reviewed first to give a complete picture before discussing any concerns or areas for improvement. Some recommend the use of a "compliment sandwich" in which the early childhood teacher begins and ends with a positive comment, and the middle of the conference is used as the time to discuss concerns of both teacher and family members. Another suggestion that is sometimes helpful is to begin with three positive areas before be-

Note #1

Dear _____,

     I just wanted to let you know that the work you've done to help Chris with his spelling words has paid off! He got 100% on his test this week. Congratulations to both of you!

Sincerely,
Kate Olijiwa

Note #2

Dear _____,

     Sara has been having some problems on the playground for the past three days. Please call me during my phone hours, Monday through Thursday from 2:45–3:15 so that we can discuss this.

Steve Elliott

Note #3

Dear _____,

     I wanted to let you know how much I appreciate your help in the classroom for the past three weeks. You are very good at supervising children during their learning centers time. I hope you will continue to come each week this school term. Thanks for your time and efforts in our classroom.

Martha Douglas

Figure 8–5 Sample personal notes to parents or families.

ginning areas of concern. It is important that the positive comments be authentic and meaningful, not just words to meet the guideline of three positives. When teachers need to conference with parents because of a particular concern, the preference for balance is often overlooked. The two strategies mentioned above aid in achieving such equilibrium.

A record of the conference needs to be kept, with brief documentation of the topics discussed. Some early childhood programs have duplicate forms that teachers use for preparation and holding conferences. It is useful for the forms to also include a place for follow-up by both teacher and parents after the conference (Figure 8–6).

Conferences should be planned at times that are convenient for all families. Many families have some flexibility if they know about times and dates for conferences in advance. Others will need to be able to request variation in scheduling times for conferences. Routine conferences are frequently quite short, fifteen to twenty minutes. This amount of time

Date _____

Time _____

Location _____

LIST OF TOPICS TO BE DISCUSSED:

_____

_____

_____

_____

Teacher comments

_____

_____

_____

_____

Parent comments

_____

_____

_____

_____

Action to be taken,

Type	By whom	Accomplished by (date)
_____	_____	_____
_____	_____	_____
_____	_____	_____
_____	_____	_____
_____	_____	_____

Signatures:

Teacher(s) _____   Parent(s) _____

_____   _____

_____   _____

Figure 8–6 Sample conference form.

is useful for a fairly quick overview of a child's progress, but more time is likely to be needed if serious concerns are to be shared.

Children may be included and involved in conferences when it is deemed appropriate. Following are some examples of appropriate topics for children to be included during conferences:

- reviewing portfolios
- discussing problem situations
- outlining a new plan of action
- sharing relevant information

Naturally, the age of the child, as well as any extenuating circumstances, would be considered when deciding whether to include him in the conference.

Involving other teachers and school staff is also recommended when others are involved in the topic of discussion. Following are examples of other staff who might be involved:

- counselors
- nurse
- director or principal
- itinerant teachers or other staff
- social service coordinator
- cafeteria or playground supervisor

Introductions of these staff members may be necessary if parents do not see these people on a regular basis. A brief explanation about the reason for attendance at the conference is also a good idea.

It makes sense to invite parents to bring others who are concerned about the child with them as well. Sometimes it is not possible for both parents in two-parent families to attend. In addition, single parents are likely to appreciate support from another concerned adult at conferences. Parents may want to invite the following:

- a friend
- grandparent of child
- child's caregiver
- significant other

Unplanned Conferences. Sometimes, a conference with parents or other family member needs to be arranged quickly. These conferences are likely to be held before or after school. Some guiding principles for unscheduled conferences are listed below.

1. Move to a quiet area away from other children and families.
2. Ask for someone else to supervise the children in your care, if necessary.
3. If the family member has initiated the conference, listen carefully to the concern before commenting or responding.
4. If you need more time to gather information, tell the family member you will contact him as soon as possible, and then do it.
5. If you have initiated the conference, thank the family member for agreeing to meet with you on such short notice and determine how much time is available.
6. Plan a follow-up to give direction or closure.

Phone Calls. Telephone calls are a convenient and sometimes necessary way to remain in contact with parents. Some teachers communicate to families at a time each week that is convenient for the family. Some

Telephone calls are a convenient and sometimes necessary way to remain in contact with parents.

teachers set a weekly time when they try to make short calls as follow-up related to earlier concerns throughout the week. Be sure to use the phone for sharing positive comments with families as well as a way to quickly check on a concern you might have. Keep in mind that some families may not be accessible by phone. Also, there are situations when phoning is not a reasonable alternative such as when there are differences in spoken language or many distractions in the environment. Listed next are some suggestions and guidelines for contacting families by phone.

Before phoning a family:

- determine whether it is agreeable to call a work number for a conference.
- consider advance scheduling for a phone conference.
- send information home ahead of time so that parents can prepare for the conference.

During the call:

- maintain confidentiality when making the phone call and after the phone call is completed (central offices or teacher work areas are not the best place for privacy).
- be polite and calm.
- try to maintain the time limit agreed on in advance.

- conclude the call with a follow-up plan.

After the call:

- make notes about the call.
- send a follow-up note to families. Include a positive or optimistic statement.

Journaling.   Maintaining a journal that is sent back and forth from parents to teacher and teacher to parent is a method of communication that is increasing in popularity (Figure 8–7). Journaling with a parent is an excellent communication mechanism under the following conditions:

- both the teacher and the family agree to and are committed to this type of communication
- confidentiality is required
- the families are literate and comfortable writing their comments
- frequency of writing should be established and agreed upon by both parties; frequency should be assessed occasionally during the school term and modified as deemed necessary
- a reliable courier process is established such as use of children's backpacks or wire notebooks, and routine days are planned for sending and returning journals

---

A concern about four-year-old Nicole's withdrawn and passive approach to activities at preschool

Journal for: <u>Nicole Williams</u>

From Teacher(s)	**From Parent(s)**
10/2 Nicole joined in play with other children a little more quickly than usual today. After scanning the room briefly, she walked to the art center and joined two others in their work on a mural for our farm theme.	10/2 I'm glad to hear about Nicole's artwork with the others. She actually seemed excited about the farm mural. Her grandparents live on a farm, and she has always enjoyed the animals and the machinery.
10/4 I didn't realize Nicole had so much farm experience. She has been more enthusiastic than ever with this topic. What other interests or experiences has Nicole had that we might use to build on this positive experience?	10/5 She likes babies; a new cousin visits us often. She also likes to watch the construction crew working at the end of our street. This summer, she started to be interested in various insects. Thanks for using information from us to help Nicole at school.

Figure 8–7 Excerpts from a journaling experience.

Electronic Mail. As computer networking becomes more readily accessible to many people in our society, it is possible that e-mail can be a very useful tool for maintaining communication with families of children in early childhood programs. A few guidelines and concerns about this type of communication are listed below.

- Be aware that e-mail communication may not be private. Avoid sharing highly sensitive information by this method.

- Employers may not want family members to receive personal e-mail at work. Be sure to check with parents about this before sending e-mail to their workplace.

- Many families still do not have access to e-mail. This method should not be used in a way that would exclude them.

Home Visits. Early childhood programs with very strong family involvement components often include home visiting as one aspect of their efforts to create strong partnerships between families and teachers. For example, the Head Start performance standards require that teachers make at least two visits to homes of all enrolled children, unless the parents decline. Reasons given for requiring home visits are as follows:

- making connections between the home and program settings

- learning more about parent-child interactions

- developing positive relationships, which allow parents and staff to get to know one another

- identifying learning opportunities in home environments

- identifying techniques that can be generalized to other children in the family

- focusing individualized attention on family strengths, interests, and goals (*Head Start Program Performance Standards and Other Regulations,* 1993, p. 144)

Head Start regulations offer alternatives to families who prefer not to have a home visit. Visits may take place at the Head Start site or another place that is deemed to be both safe and private. When safety concerns arise for staff who are required to make home visits, Head Start regulations provide some precautions. Staff who make home visits are highly trained, well-supervised, and have access to support services such as monitoring systems or having another staff member make the home visit with the teacher.

These Head Start guidelines are useful for other early childhood programs implementing a home visit component. It is important that early childhood professionals be polite and respectful when arranging for the visit as well as during the visit. Selecting a mutually acceptable time for the appointment is very important. Teachers must arrive on time and use effective interpersonal skills. It is often helpful to state the ending time of the visit when making the appointment. The role of the teacher changes in interactions in the family's home. In home settings, the teacher is the guest and must take the lead from the family. Typically, teachers are in the comfort of their own classroom when they meet with family members. This changes the balance of power somewhat. While it is true that home visits take a huge time and energy commitment from early childhood teachers, the outcome of increased level of partnerships can be an excellent reward. Such visits often make the family feel very valued and cared about.

Effective Interpersonal Communication

When any two people attempt to communicate, sometimes they misunderstand one another. Clarity may be lacking. Emotion may be heated. Vocabulary may differ. Effective strategies for clear communication can be learned. Practicing these strategies makes them seem more natural for both speaker and listener.

Active Listening. **Active listening** is a process whereby the listener communicates to the speaker that he values what the speaker is saying. An important criteria for active listening is that the listener is not evaluating the content or the speaker but is really open to the speaker's point of view (Gordon, 1970). It is important for teachers to listen to parents to understand their perspective and to be aware of the issues they believe are important. Some teachers find that truly listening to others poses a challenge because the role of a teacher is often to give instruction to others without entering into an extensive dialogue. Another challenge for teachers involves hearing parents' concerns—or complaints—without becoming defensive. Parents may be emotionally charged about an issue. Try to listen for the emotion and understand that as real concern about their children.

Active listening is more easily accomplished when teachers believe in partnerships with parents and have the belief that parents have knowledge about their own family system that can be helpful information to teachers. This ability of a teacher to actively listen to family members is an extremely important application of the bioecological model of human development.

Following are some behaviors associated with active listening (Hanna, 1991):

- Attentive body position
  —comfortable distance between the communicators
  —being on the same level, e.g., both sitting or both standing
  —facing the other person as each of you speaks
  —relaxed body posture, slightly leaning toward the other
  —hands at sides or in lap
- Eye contact
  —maintain eye contact by looking at other's face
  —eye contact is recommended for 50%–75% of time in interaction
- Facial expression
  —facial reaction to what is being said include a smile, frown, or look of surprise at appropriate times
  —change of expression with content of conversation
- Head and body movements
  —nodding the head for feedback to speaker
  —other body movements used as feedback to speaker

- Touching
  —arm is a neutral area generally okay to touch
  —consider appropriateness of touch
- Verbal responses
  —short comments such as "oh" or "I see" offer encouragement
  —open-ended questions to support the speaker
  —paraphrasing to be sure you understand the point the speaker is making
  —expressing your interpretation of the speaker's feelings

These active listening behaviors should be modified to meet the needs of different families and settings.

As teachers attempt to incorporate these skills into their communication with families and other community members, they will soon understand why Hanna states that "good listening is not for the lazy" (p. 186). Helping professionals in many fields often find it helpful to practice behaviors related to listening. Working with a partner, use the list of listening skills as practice. After you have practiced for about 10 minutes, evaluate yourself on each of the skills. Which skills have you already mastered? With which listening behaviors will you need more practice?

Often, early childhood teachers have limited amounts of time for conferencing and other interpersonal communications with parents or other family members. Due to these time constraints, teachers may be tempted to bypass the importance of listening to parents and to move too quickly to offering solutions or telling parents that their concerns are unfounded. In these situations, it is often true that actively listening to parents' comments may be more satisfying to the parent and thus may provide for ongoing positive communication. An example of this was shared by a child care center director. Parents of a three-year-old who was slightly injured on a balance beam requested a conference with the director. The classroom teacher had already "warned" the director that these parents were upset and wanted to have that piece of equipment removed from the classroom. Because this was the only recorded accident with the balance beam in more than 10 years of that teacher's career, the teacher believed strongly that it should not be removed. The director met with the parents, listened to their concern, and said he was sorry that their son had gotten hurt. After having a chance to be heard and noting that there was concern from school personnel about their child's injury, they withdrew their request to have the balance beam taken from the classroom. Further, they increased their involvement with the parent organization and advocated for the center with prospective parents (Figure 8–8).

> **Parent:** Emily's mother and I have separated. Emily and her brother are living with me. I just wanted you to know so that if something unusual happens at school, you may be better able to help Emily. She is sometimes very sad at home.
>
> **Teacher:** You're concerned about how your separation is affecting Emily.
>
> **Parent:** Yes. We hear so much about the effects of divorce on young children. She has been such a joyful child, and now it's hard to see her be so sad.
>
> **Teacher:** I know that this has been a difficult time for both you and Emily.
>
> **Parent:** Thank you for understanding my concerns.
>
> **Teacher:** Let's stay in close communication about Emily during this difficult time. You can call me at school or at my home phone.

Figure 8–8 Examples of active listening in conversation.

Reflecting. Reflecting families' concerns, issues, feelings, suggestions, and complaints allows the teacher to repeat what he has heard. This method gives parents an opportunity to correct or modify the teacher's understanding of the conversation. Reflecting also gives the teacher an opportunity to fully comprehend the meaning of the message being communicated by the parent. Frequently, reflection becomes an excellent problem-solving tool because it increases clarity in interpersonal communication (Figure 8–9).

> "Let me restate what I heard you say."
>
> "To help me remember clearly, may I rephrase your concerns?"
>
> "To help me work on these problems, may I write out some of your complaints?"
>
> "Thank you for sharing your suggestions. I will summarize them to our director. This is the list I have made."

Figure 8–9 Teacher phrases that help in reflective dialogue.

I-Messages and We-Messages. Using I-messages permits teachers to speak from their own perspectives without offending parents. An I-message clearly places the responsibility and the viewpoint of the message on the speaker. In this way, it does not communicate guilt or accusation by using statements that begin with "You should. . . ." Many professionals find that although I-messages are effective in practice, they have not learned to speak that way in their interpersonal conversations. Some even believe it feels "unnatural." Because this strategy is so effective, especially in the heat of emotion, it is advantageous for early childhood teachers in preparation to practice or role-play using I-messages. Gordon (1970) describes three components of an I-message.

1. State concern about other's behavior from your perspective.

2. Pin down the concrete effect the behavior has on the teacher.

3. State feelings teacher has as a result of the effect.

I-messages are effective, not only in working with families but also in all interpersonal contexts, including work with children (Figure 8–10).

Whereas I-messages are useful in that they reduce threat from a powerful figure, there may be times when we-messages are more effective. Rather than focusing on an individual's problem and another individual's behavior, we-messages are used to identify a problem in a group or in a relationship. Examples of we-statements include, "We don't have

Situation—Parent stops teacher in hallway to discuss a concern about his child's progress.

Teacher—"I must be in the classroom now. I'll be glad to phone you after school to arrange for a time for us to talk. Where should I call you?"

Situation—Parents walk into director's office and begin to yell.

Director—"I can tell you're upset about something. Let me get some information from you so that I can figure out what I can do to help."

Situation—Grandmother complains to teacher about her daughter's lack of attention to her child.

Teacher—"I'm sorry you feel so bad about this. I believe that if someone were to read to Jess every day, it would help her a great deal. Is there any chance we could work on this together?"

Figure 8–10 Examples of effective I-messages.

enough affection" or "We ought to have more flexibility" (Burr, 1990).

We-messages are used to emphasize the closeness in relationships; thus, such communication should not be used for casual relationships between educators and family members (Burr, 1990). In early childhood education, however, some caregiver and family member relationships span several years with a great deal of close contact occurring. Often, the topics discussed in these relationships are of a somewhat personal nature: children's difficulties, parents' feelings, a variety of family transitions. In such cases, when teachers want to emphasize the partnership in working for children, use of we-messages may be helpful.

There may be times when it makes sense to combine we-messages with I-messages. This is especially true when the speaker wishes to emphasize the connectedness but also believes adding some uncertainty to the comment may lead to more openness in communication. An early childhood teacher who has had an ongoing relationship with Calvin's parents stated, "I don't think we want Calvin to forget his work anymore." The parents readily agreed, and together—teacher, parents, and Calvin—they set out to solve the problem.

An Example of Building Communication between Teachers and Families

My first experience with realizing the importance of communication between myself and my teacher was when my daughter was in first grade. We were fortunate to be placed in the classroom of Mr. M. months after moving to one state from another. Mr. M. had a total open door policy and stressed the fact that his policy meant we were welcome any time and without notice.

Mr. M. had a monthly "Family Night" where the students invited the entire family, even grandparents, to come into the classroom and share their daily activities. Several times during the year he also had "Game Board Night" where the family brought and shared playing games with the class. Not only did "Family Night" and "Game Board Night" help my husband and me support and encourage our daughter's education, but also prepared her younger brother for what it would be like when he started school. He did not have any of the typical first day jitters because he was so familiar with the school.

The class also witnessed the importance of socialization skills between families and friends. Throughout the year, we had parties and activities out of the school setting as well. We actually made some of our closest friends during this period of our lives and they are still involved in our lives today, five years later.

—L. B., mother of two

An Example of Ineffective Communication between a Teacher and a Parent

When my son was in Kindergarten, I was not prepared for what was to come. We had had a wonderful experience with our daughter from kindergarten all the way to the third grade, and did not realize how a bad situation could avalanche.

Our son was very prepared and excited to start school, and up to this point, we had felt he was very bright. After only two weeks of school, the teacher escorted my son out of the school at the end of the day to have a discussion with his mom about his behavior. This discussion took place in front of all the students and parents that were walking out of the building at the end of the day. Needless to say, my son was devastated, and I was shocked and appalled. I suggested that we go somewhere and discuss this in private, but the teacher did not have tome for that so the conversation continued on the front lawn about how my son yells out answers to questions without raising his hand, can't stay in his seat, and wastes time doodling after assignments are done. I listened to what she had to say but did not make many comments because I felt I needed time to process the information.

After discussing the situation with my husband, I decided to ask her to cooperate with me and keep a behavior journal that I would read each day and, surprisingly, she agreed to do so. My son gave the journal to his teacher for two or three weeks, and she never made an entry so we assumed things were okay until conference time when we heard the same complaints as before. When asked about the journal, she simply said she did not think it would help. Needless to say, this was a long battle that totally turned my son against school and reading.

My son is now in the first grade with a wonderful teacher and is eager to learn. On the first day of school, we were getting dressed and he said, "Mommy, do you remember last year when I kept saying I was dumb and you said I was smart?" I said "Yes" and he said, "Well, I finally figured out what happened. I got yelled at so much last year until my brain just shut down."

As the saying goes, out of the mouths of babes!

—**L. B. mother of two**

Nonverbal Communication.   In addition to the use of language for effective **interpersonal communication**, it is also helpful to examine communication practices that are nonverbal. Following are some behaviors that are components of nonverbal communication:

- personal space
- gestures and posture
- touching
- facial expression
- eye contact
- vocal cues (Knapp & Hall, 1992)

The concept of personal space includes physical distance between people who are engaged in conversation. Clearly, individual differences in personality lead to differences in comfort level of personal space. Cultural backgrounds and the nature of the relationship of those in conversation (Knapp & Hall, 1992) are also factors related to preferences in personal space. Early childhood teachers who are observant and sensitive to family member's preferences for physical space will be able to demonstrate respect in their interactions.

"Gestures are movements of the body . . . used to communicate an idea, intention or feeling" (Knapp & Hall, 1992, p. 187). Consider the many gestures that are used to communicate nonverbally throughout the course of a day. How do you gesture for "hello" and "good-by?" When giving someone directions, gesturing is often as helpful as the words you use. How do teachers use gestures meaningfully in the classroom? Touching when communicating

Observe at least two people who are conversing. Note the kinds of nonverbal communication strategies that they use. How did nonverbal communication contribute to the meaning and understanding among those you observed? Did you observe individual differences? How might you increase your sensitivity to nonverbal modes of communication in your work with young children and their families?

can have many meanings? Knapp and Hall (1992) list the following ways in which touch is used:

- positive affect
- negative affect
- play
- influence
- interaction management
- interpersonal responsiveness
- accidental
- task-related
- healing

Individual differences have been observed in both gesturing and touch. Culture and gender play a role in these differences.

Facial expressions can communicate a lot of information or just a little. Because of individual differences and complexity involved in interpretation of facial expression, sensitivity is needed when interacting with others. Some people are very expressive, others demonstrate little affect. There are times when a facial expression alone does not reveal an individual's honest feelings. For example, nervousness can lead one to smile or even giggle at an inappropriate time. Variations are also observable in the nature and amount of eye contact. How do you use eye contact? What is your belief system about those who look others "right in the eye?"

Vocal cues such as hesitating and pausing may be used to emphasize a point or to demonstrate reflective listening. Practices such as saying one word more loudly or softly than others in the sentence and consistent or inconsistent rhythm in a person's speech contribute to the meaning of communication (Knapp & Hall, 1992).

Guidelines for Giving and Receiving Criticism

Teachers often find it difficult to deliver criticism to family members, or at least they find it difficult to do so in an acceptable manner. Is it possible to give negative information in a positive manner? The challenge is to do so clearly and honestly. It is often very

helpful to rehearse what you want to share and how you want to say it. Choosing a suitable time and place is also worth considering. The use of I-messages is recommended. Be sure to criticize the specific behavior or situation, not the whole person. Offering a compliment before giving the criticism may help to make the situation less uncomfortable for the parent or other person with whom you are talking (Hanna, 1991). In other words, attempt to make the criticism as constructive as possible. This permits the other person to work toward a solution.

Consider the following examples of criticism. Using the preceding guidelines, note what is constructive and what may be destructive about each example. How would you change each one to make it more constructive?

1. During a scheduled conference with parents of a kindergartner, the teacher says, "I have some concern about the way you discipline Kate. She says that you hit her when she misbehaves. You should know better than that!"

2. In a note to the family of a preschooler, the teacher writes: "Nicole has been dropped off at school at 7:30 this week. School begins at 8:00. You may not bring her to school before 7:45. Thank you. Ms. Farver"

3. In a newsletter, a first-grade teacher includes the following in her letter to families: "Some parents have questioned our rule about not bringing special playthings from home. After some discussion, the school staff has decided to keep this rule. Please do not permit your child to bring toys to school."

Teachers must be prepared to receive criticism as well as to deliver it. In some instances, teachers are prepared for the possibility of criticism and other times it may take them by surprise. To maintain positive communication, it is helpful for early childhood professionals to have skills in accepting or responding to criticism. If you agree with the criticism, admitting your mistake, although not easy or comfortable, is a good choice. Let the person who has voiced the criticism know that you agree and briefly state the reason for your behavior. Finally, note what you will do to change the situation or to prevent it in the future (Hanna, 1991). Using these guidelines, assuming you agree with the following criticisms from family members, write down an appropriate response.

1. "I thought you only served healthy snacks at this child care center. Jason told me that he had a chocolate cupcake for afternoon snack yesterday."

2. "I got a notice about the parent meeting tonight just two days ago. That's not enough time for me to make all the arrangements that are necessary to come to the meeting."

It may be even more difficult to respond to criticism with which you do not agree because there is greater likelihood of negative emotions arising. You may feel that a criticism is inaccurate or unfair. These feelings often lead to an emotional or out-of-control response. Taking a deep breath or silently counting to three is useful for some people when they are aware of such emotion. Responding in a calm manner gives a better chance of allowing communication to continue. When you disagree with a criticism, a comment such as "I guess I see this differently from you" or "I have another point of view about what may be the wisest course of action." Give some reasons for your perspective and suggest the possibility of another discussion in the future.

Assertiveness versus Aggression

In efforts to be polite and professional, early childhood teachers often overlook the importance of assertiveness in interpersonal communication. Assertiveness does not rule out flexibility or partnerships; instead, it allows teachers to have a voice about their preferences and feelings. Assertiveness is not the same as aggressiveness. A primary difference is that assertiveness enhances interpersonal communication, and aggressiveness discourages or inhibits communication. Assertiveness is self-focused, not other-focused (Lerner, 1989). Thus, an assertive response will typically use an I-message and not blame or attack others. Such blaming or attacking is often aggressive and counterproductive in forming partnerships. For example, "I have some concerns I

would like to discuss with you about Kelly being sleepy at school" is more effective than "You need to make sure that Kelly gets enough sleep every night."

Boutte, Keepler, Tyler, & Terry (1992) discuss techniques for involving "difficult" parents (Figure 8–11).

Conflict Resolution

When authentic relationships are developed with families, it is inevitable that some conflict will occur. Avoiding conflict is not the best solution to dealing with it. Instead, efforts at resolving conflict peacefully and effectively must be learned and implemented. One difficulty is that people bring previous ideas and feelings about conflict with them. Some believe it is impolite to share a difference of opinion, some are shy, and others may be hostile in the way they present a different point of view.

Essentially, **conflict resolution** often takes the form of problem-solving. Problem-solving typically is a process, taking several steps, which are outlined below. Problems with, between, and about families are common in the life of a teacher. The following strategies are designed to reduce conflict and increase the chances for healthy resolution of a problem.

1. Clearly define the problem at hand. If there is more than one problem, define each one.

2. Let all participants share their viewpoints.

3. As the teacher, reflect each participant's concern.

4. Review any relevant school policy or procedure.

5. Assure the parents that they have been heard and that their issue will be addressed in one of the following ways:

   a. changes will be made and specify the changes.

   b. additional participants will be invited into the discussion such as the principal, director, counselor, or social worker.

   c. another child or family will be contacted if necessary to resolve the problem.

Many early childhood programs find it useful to specify guidelines for conflict resolution.

	The parent who exhibits antagonistic behavior	The parent who frequently complains or is negative.	The parent who exhibits shy/ unresponsive behavior	The parent who is illiterate or is not skilled in Reading or speaking English.
Encourage attendance at all parent—teacher conferences	X	X	X	X
State and restate purpose(s) of the conference	X	X		
Show or tell concrete and specific examples of child's work or behavior	X	X	X	
Do not argue with a parent or become defensive	X	X		
Seek the assistance of other staff when needed	X			X
Elicit parents' ideas and incorporate them into a plan		X		
Frequently state positive strategies or work accomplished		X	X	
Ask open-ended questions and allow for plenty of discussion time	X			X

Figure 8–11   Selected Techniques for Involving Difficult Parents. (Adapted from: Boutte, G. S., Keepler, D. L., Tyler, V. S., & Terry, B. Z. (1992). Effective techniques for involving "difficult" parents. *Young Children 47*(3), 19–22.)

Including these procedures in a parent handbook or newsletter indicates to families that their opinions and views are respected and taken seriously. Such guidelines include the following:

1. First, take your concern to the person directly involved.

2. If the conflict cannot be resolved between the two parties, the guidelines specify who is the next person to be contacted. Typically, this is someone in an administrative or supervisory role.

3. The third person acts as mediator, listening to both perspectives and suggesting a resolution.

4. Some programs will have a process that continues with an appeal or taking the situation to an executive director or board.

Some Ineffective and Inappropriate Practices to Avoid in Interpersonal Communication

In addition to understanding the skills related to effective communication, it is also important to acknowledge that certain types of behaviors are often detrimental to building relationships. Teachers are advised to avoid the following practices:

1. Becoming defensive, argumentative, or combative closes communication.

2. Accusing the child or family is not productive

3. Name-calling is never appropriate.

4. Gossiping about families is unprofessional.

5. Belittling or berating a child because of a conflict with his family is unethical.

6. Reacting so emotionally or irrationally that there is no opportunity for reconciliation is detrimental to all concerned.

Helpful Attitudes for Effective Interpersonal Communication

Behaviors and practices are not the only things that affect positive communication. Attitudes are also important. For some teachers, the following attitudes

It is important for early childhood education teachers to develop mutually respectful working relationships with families.

may be more "natural," and some teachers may find that they need to work to develop these perspectives. Such work, though, will be well worth it when good communication with family members is achieved. Hanna (1991) lists the following attitudes as helpful:

- valuing mutual respect
- honesty
- open to lifelong learning and growing
- willing to share your experiences and ideas
- able to express feelings in appropriate ways
- knowing appropriate content for discussing in professional contexts
- flexibility
- a sense of humor
- ability to think critically and to problem-solve

With a partner, discuss the preceding list of attitudes. Think of a real-life example for each attitude. Think of one or two additional attributes that you might add to this list of helpful attitudes for effective communication.

Examples of successful programs in building family-staff relationships can be found at: http://

pfie.ed.gov/. Other ideas for supporting parents can be found at www.npin.org/. These two sites can help both teachers and parents in finding ideas for building family-school partnerships.

Summary and Conclusions

While most teachers receive some preparation in classroom management of children, very few receive extensive instruction in communicating effectively with parents and other family members, especially in conflict situations. Conflicts or confrontations with parents are very difficult and may not be easily or quickly resolved. They often require great amounts of time, effort, energy, and knowledge. The importance of building and maintaining relationships with families cannot be overstated. Relationships built on trust and understanding go a long way in helping both parties in their efforts to resolve conflict.

Understanding the family is a great resource for teachers to use if a conflict arises. Having an established, mutually respectful working relationship with families prior to a conflict can be very helpful in proceeding to a resolution. Professional ethics and professional practice give school personnel the guidance to sustain their compassion and conduct as they work with families in sensitive and difficult situations, as well as in routine interactions.

Key Terms

co-dependency
empathy
self-disclosure
two-way
   communication

active listening
interpersonal communication
conflict resolution

Chapter Eight Applications

1. Plan a conference with parents about each of the following situations.
   a. A two-year-old has been biting other children. You meet with the parents of the child who is biting.
   b. A preschooler has become increasingly aggressive during outdoor time.
   c. A second-grader is not making expected progress in reading.

2. At the end of the school day, family members come to you with the following situations. What do you say or do?
   a. A father of a kindergarten child is angry and shouts at you that his daughter was not permitted to check out a library book yesterday at the regularly scheduled library time.
   b. The grandmother of a two-year-old tells you that her grandson has been bitten two days in a row and that she expects you to "throw the biter out of the program."
   c. A mother is late picking up her infant for the third day in a row. She is nearly in tears, saying that she is not able to leave work on time to pick up her baby by closing.

3. Create a newsletter article that explains to families the importance of each of the following early childhood education practices:
   a. free play
   b. developmentally appropriate practice
   c. authentic assessment
   d. family involvement
   e. celebrating diversity

Questions for Reflection and Discussion

1. List situations that might occur in the early childhood classroom for which two-way communication strategies between home and school would be preferred over one-way communication strategies.

2. Getting some parents to come to regularly scheduled conferences can be difficult. What are some strategies you could try for getting such hard-to-reach parents to have a conference with you about their child's progress?

3. What is your typical response to a conflictual situation? Do you avoid it, respond emotionally,

or use effective strategies for resolving conflict? Which strategies will you work on for future use in the early childhood profession?

Field Assignments

1. Interview several parents who have their children enrolled in early childhood programs. Ask them about the kinds of communication they have with their child's teachers or the program's administrator. Ask whether they are satisfied or whether they would prefer more communication. If they would prefer more communication, ask about kinds of communication they would like.

2. Contact a number of early childhood education teachers. Request copies of newsletters to place in your file.

3. Contact an administrator of an early childhood program. Ask whether there are policies regarding conflict resolution between home and school. If so, are the policies printed in a parent handbook? If possible, get a copy of the policy.

References

Boutte, G. S., Keepler, D. L., Tyler, V. S., & Terry, B. Z. (1992). Effective techniques for involving "difficult" parents. *Young Children, 47*(3), 19–22.

Burr, W. R. (1990, July). Beyond I-statements in family communication. *Family Relations, 39*(3), 266–272.

Diffily, D., & Morrison, K. (Eds.). (1996). *Family-friendly communication for early childhood programs.* Washington, DC: National Association for the Education of Young Children.

Gordon, T. (1970). *P.E.T.: Parent effectiveness training.* New York: Peter H. Wyden.

Hanna, S. L. (1991). *Person to person: Positive relationships don't just happen.* Englewood Cliffs, NJ: Prentice-Hall.

Head Start program performance standards and other regulations. (1993). Washington, DC: U.S. Department of Health and Human Services.

Hohmann, M., Banet, B., & Weikart, D. P. (1979). *Young children in action* (pp. 328–329). Ypsilanti, MI: High/Scope Press.

Kagan, S. L., & Cohen, N. E. (1997). Not by chance: *Creating an early care and education system for America's children.* New Haven, CT: The Quality 2000 Initiative.

Knapp, M. L., & Hall, J. A. (1992). *Nonverbal communication in human interaction.* New York: Holt Rinehart and Winston.

Krech, B. (1995). Improve parent communication with a newsletter. *Instructor, 105*(2), 67–73.

Lerner, H. G. (1989). *The dance of intimacy: A woman's guide to courageous acts of change in key relationships.* New York: Harper & Row.

Swick, K. (1991). *Teacher-parent partnerships to enhance school success in early childhood education.* Washington, DC: National Education Association.

OUTLINE

CHAPTER 9

Parent Education and
Family Life Education

OBJECTIVES

After reading and reflecting on this chapter, you should be able to:

■ Understand the theoretical foundation for parent education and family life education.

■ Discuss a number of strategies for parent and family life education.

■ Relate the role of early childhood teachers in providing parent and family life education.

Bioecological Theory

Bronfenbrenner's bioecological model supports the premise of parent education in that there is a need for parents to have access to strategies that support all areas of their children's development—intellectual, social, and moral (Bronfenbrenner & Neville, 1994). As children develop, they require "progressively more complex activity," and it is especially important that these interactions exist between the child and parents or parental figures. Central to this model of human development is the special importance of appropriate interactions between children and adults who are committed to the child's well-being over their entire lifetime. This theory stresses the crucial concept of enduring emotional attachment for optimal child development.

Further, this model stipulates the importance of a third party who "assists, encourages, spells, gives sta-tus to, and expresses admiration and affection for the person caring for . . . the child" (Bronfenbrenner & Neville, 1994, p. 14). Parents should also be aware or educated about the importance of having someone support them as a parent. Bronfenbrenner notes that ideally this third person would be a spouse and that the context of marriage ideally supports this concept. However, if the marriage is not providing such support for each parent, other mechanisms will be needed to do so. Children's development will be enhanced when their parents have support for their caregiving. Often, grandparents carry out this family responsibility.

Bronfenbrenner also notes the relevance of mutual respect and communication "between the principal settings in which children and their parents live their lives" (p. 17). So it is necessary for parents and teachers or caregivers to communicate on a regular basis, and to be able to believe in each other. When parents' workplaces provide flexible schedules, part-time jobs with benefits, and other programs that support families, a child's development is likely to be enhanced.

Programs of **parent education** and **family life education** should include application of the theoretical premises from bioecological theory. This means that such programs will always respect the primacy of the family, and the understanding that the basic purpose of parent education and family life education is to support parents in the important task of child-rearing, not to undermine or judge their efforts.

Philosophy about Programs of Parent Education

An undergraduate student in an early childhood teacher preparation program reported to her instructor that she would not be permitted to hold a parent meeting at the center to which she was assigned for her practicum. The director at the center told the student that parents of children at the center told her that they "do not want to be told how to raise their children." Before one jumps to conclusions about the parents' lack of interest, let us hypothesize about what led to such comments. Consider the following list:

- experts on discipline being paid to speak to large audiences in school districts or other early childhood programs, indicating a one-method-fits-all approach
- family values (a need to customize information)
- lack of support given parents in our society
- lack of understanding about the need for communication between home and school for child's optimal development
- relative newness of very young children being in care outside the home
- few programs adopting a family support model

Reflect on each of these possibilities. Can you think of others?

While the center director in the story might have concluded that parents in that center did not want or need parent meetings, other conclusions might better reflect best practices in early education. If it seems to be a widespread concern of parents that parent meetings are to indoctrinate them, then attention probably needs to be given to the source of that perspective.

It is also important for early childhood professionals to note differences in parenting that may be related to ethnicity. (Some of these differences are noted in Chapter 2.)

Parent education programs however, have been less successful among ethnic minority groups, possibly because they are based on and reflect Anglo-American middle-class values. Service providers have demonstrated that parents from ethnic minority groups and from low socio-economic groups will attend and complete parent education programs if the setting and the content are compatible with their values and their lifestyles (McDade, 1995, p. 286).

Thus, it becomes the responsibility of early childhood teachers to understand parenting differences and to find appropriate ways to share information with their particular clientele.

Assessing Needs and Effects

Programs of parent education should not be provided as a unilateral attempt to tell parents how to

> "*It is usually assumed in our society that people have to be trained for difficult roles: most business firms would not consider turning a sales clerk loose on the customers without some formal training; the armed forces would scarcely send a raw recruit into combat without extensive and intensive training; most states now require a course in driver's education before high school students can acquire a driver's license. Even dog owners often go to school to learn how to treat their pets properly. This is not true of American parents.*"
>
> **—LeMasters & DeFrain, 1983, pp. 75–76**

rear their children. Instead, the philosophy, the driving goals, behind such a program should be to offer support for families. One way to initiate such a program is to do a needs assessment with families. Figures 9–1 and 9–2 show two different formats of needs assessments.

It is typical that information sessions have been held for large groups of parents without any evaluation of what happened in homes after the session. Too often, even immediate feedback from parents regarding the program is not solicited. Professionals in early education cannot overlook the need to assess effects of their family involvement activities. Figures 9–3, 9–4, and 9–5 show examples of evaluation forms to be completed by family members after they have participated in planned school activities.

As we plan for the parent/family involvement component of our program, your responses to the following questions will help us to determine some program content. We would appreciate your responses to the following questions by September 15. Please place your completed form in the box outside the Director's Office.

1. Age(s) of children in family _____
2. Who lives in your home? _____
3. What are your three biggest parenting challenges?
   a.
   b.
   c.
4. What questions do you have about how children learn and develop?
   a.
   b.
   c.
5. Do you have questions regarding our school curriculum?
   a.
   b.
   c.
6. What television programs does your child watch? About how much time each day does your child watch TV?
7. What kinds of play or activities does your child like?

Figure 9–2   Needs Assessment B.

Format of Programs

Powell (1989, 1994) discusses emerging directions for parent education that is sponsored by early childhood education programs. Following are some recent changes in both content and format for effective parent education.

1. Matching designs for parent education to the particular population being served is important. Matching is based on the "expressed

At the Campus Early Learning Center, we offer monthly group meetings for parents and other interested family members. Each school term, we ask parents to rank their top three (3) choices of topics for which we might plan. Please rank your first choice as #1, second choice as #2, and third choice as #3, and return this form to the Director's Office by September 10. Thanks for your feedback.

_____ Appropriate and effective discipline

_____ How children learn

_____ New information from brain research

_____ Family involvement in children's education

_____ Preparing your child for kindergarten

_____ Healthy nutrition

_____ The importance of play for children's development

_____ Sibling rivalry

_____ Other:_____

_____ Other:_____

Figure 9–1   Needs Assessment A.

Time and date of meeting: _____
Location: _____
Topic: _____

1. What was the best thing that happened at the meeting?
2. What changes should be made for future meetings?
3. Other comments?

Figure 9–3   Sample assessment for a group parent meeting.

Time and date of meeting: _____
Location: _____
Topic: _____

1. The information presented is useful to me.
   Very   Somewhat   A little   Not at all
2. The information was presented in an interesting manner.
   Very   Somewhat   A little   Not at all
3. The date and time were convenient for me.
   Very   Somewhat   A little   Not at all
4. Based on this meeting, how likely are you to attend another meeting?
   Very   Somewhat   A little   Not at all
5. I felt comfortable asking questions or responding to the presenter's questions/comments.
   Very   Somewhat   A little   Not at all
6. I believe that group parent meetings generally are important.
   Very   Somewhat   A little   Not at all
7. Comments:

Figure 9–4   Sample assessment for a group parent meeting.

Time and date of meeting: _____
Location: _____
Topic: _____

1. The thing I learned that will be most beneficial to me is _____.
2. I wish there had been more information shared about _____.
3. My time and day preferences for future meetings are _____.
4. At a future meeting, I would like to have information shared about _____.
5. Services the school could provide to ensure that I could attend more parent meetings are
   _____.
6. My suggestions for future parent meetings include _____.

Figure 9–5   Sample assessment for a group parent meeting.

need" of the parents rather than on the perceived needs by those planning the programs. Further, models that individualize programs based on parents' needs are believed to be more effective than planning group programs to meet each need.

2. Defining the role of the education professional in a way that encourages empowerment of parents is another recent change. The professional who acts as facilitator rather than all-knowing dispenser of knowledge is typically more effective. Understanding of adult learning supports the notion that when parents have a more active role in their education, they are more likely to change their behavior and use strategies that may be more beneficial to their children.

3. Finally, programs of parent education are responding to the notion in bioecological theory that parenting is enhanced when parents have social support and other buffers against stress in their lives. When parents have the support they need, their functioning as parents is strength-

ened. This idea broadens the notion of parent education for early childhood teachers. Consider not only information about child development, effective guidance strategies, healthy nutrition, and other content traditional in parent education programs but also services that support parents such as parent night out, support groups for single parents, or coordinating the sharing of services such as car pools or children's clothing exchanges.

There is little research to support specific types of parent involvement or parent education practices. Until recently, a belief existed that any kind of parent involvement in early childhood programs, or any content and format for parent education was certainly preferable to none. This view must be questioned in light of the theoretical basis for the family support movement. Concern about the effects of parent education on both children and families must be emphasized.

Current expectations for high-quality early childhood programs universally include the importance of family involvement, but often little detail is given about specific attitudes and strategies that are effective. Based on existing knowledge and theory, Powell (1989) delineates four dimensions that should be incorporated by early childhood teachers into their family involvement plan.

1. Be careful to respond to parents' needs in planning and implementing programs for them. A mismatch, even when the professional believes she is acting in the best interest of children, will not be effective and is likely to subvert the intention.

2. The programs must be managed collaboratively. Using a deficit model of the professional directly telling the clients how to change their parenting is not an effective means of education. Conversations that are respectful and formats that are collaborative are far more effective strategies than one in which there is an "expert" and an amateur.

3. The focus of parent education programs must be balanced on the needs of both children and parents. Using parent education as a way to directly affect child outcomes is risky. Concern for parent needs as well as child needs better serves the entire family. At the same time, sharing details about children's developmental needs should not be overlooked. This balance can be difficult to achieve, and for that reason, must be emphasized in planning, implementing, and evaluating the educational program.

4. One aspect of parent education that is frequently sacrificed to time limitations is that of open-ended discussion. Parents' experiences are most often shared and affirmed or disputed with this approach. Open-ended discussion is a strategy that is favored by many participating in adult education; child caregivers who attended training and then participated in focus groups for data collection by a researcher noted that they especially liked the focus groups, even though that strategy was only accidental to the training (Chrisman, 1996). The temptation to cut the open-ended discussion in parent meetings is one that leaders should not give into because participants frequently rate this time of the session as one of the most valuable.

Methods of Parent Education

When early childhood education staff decide to plan for parenting education for their particular population, they may consider several existing programs. Most of these programs have stated objectives so that staff and parent representatives might review several programs and then make decisions.

Parent Education Packages

Two popular parent education packages are based on the theoretical works of Adler (1923) and Dreikurs and Soltz (1964). Both the Systematic Training for Effective Parenting (STEP), created by Dinkmeyer, McKay, and Dinkmeyer (1980), and Active Parenting, created by Popkin (1983), focus on the goal of teaching children responsibility. Strategies for teaching responsibility include use of natural and logical consequences, reflective listening and I-messages, and democratic family meetings (Figures 9–6, 9–7, and 9–8).

Reasons parents need training are (1) rapid social change; and (2) increasing social equality for all people. The "democratic revolution" means adult-centered systems of rewards and punishments no longer fit the needs that humans have to be successful in society. The STEP system, a democratic child-rearing approach, is based on mutual respect between parent and child, and equality in terms of human worth and dignity. That is, children have as much right to be treated with respect as do adults. Two critical components of STEP are communication and encouragement. This system encourages parents to provide opportunities for children to make some decisions and to be responsible for their decisions. The use of natural and logical consequences replaces rewards and punishments.

There are topics for nine group sessions:

1. Understanding Child Behavior and Misbehavior
2. Understanding How Children Use Emotions to Involve Parents and the "Good" Parent
3. Encouragement
4. Communication—Listening
5. Communication—Exploring Alternatives and Expressing Your Ideas and Feelings to Children
6. Developing Responsibility
7. Decision-making for Parents
8. The Family Meeting
9. Developing Confidence and Using Your Potential

Materials in the package include a leader's manual; a parent handbook with problem situations, charts, points to remember, and a personal plan for improving relationships; two videocassettes; a script booklet for videos; a discussion guidelines poster; charts summarizing major concepts and principles; certificates for participants; and publicity aids.

Figure 9–6   Summary of STEP. (Dinkmeyer, McKay, & Dinkmeyer, 1980)

Goal—to develop innovative methods of presenting existing effective parenting practices to the millions of parents who can benefit from them.

Based on the work of—Alfred Adler, Rudolf Dreikurs, Carl Rogers, Robert Carkhuff, and Thomas Gordon.

Two beliefs about parenting—1. Parenting well is extremely important. 2. Parenting well is extremely difficult.

Three assumptions—1. Most parents have sufficient love and commitment to parent well. 2. Most parents have not been given sufficient information, skills, or support. 3. This can be disastrous in modern society in which children openly reject traditional parenting methods. "Courage is the greatest gift a parent can give a child." (Alfred Adler)

The following topics are included in six sessions:

1. The Active Parent: concept of equality, styles of parenting, fallacy of reward and punishment, courage, responsibility, cooperation, winning positive relationships
2. Understanding Your Child: how children develop, building blocks of personality, family constellation, understanding behavior, four goals of children's behavior, four mistaken goals of misbehavior, parenting and anger, and helping children use their anger
3. Instilling Courage: what is encouragement?, how parents discipline their own children, turning negatives into positives, how to show confidence, building on strengths, valuing the child as she is, stimulating independence
4. Developing Responsibility: responsibility, freedom and the limits to freedom, the problem-handling method for parents, who owns the problem?, I-messages, natural and logical consequences, mutual respect
5. Winning Cooperation: communication: road to cooperation, avoiding communication blocks, listen actively, listen for feelings, connect feelings to content, expressing love
6. Democratic Families in Action: family council meeting, six good reasons for regular meetings, how to get started, a word about the agenda, ground rules, emphasizing the family unit.

Materials in the package include a leader's manual, a parent handbook, two videocassettes, an action guide (parent workbook), and promotional materials.

Figure 9–7   Summary of Active Parenting. (Popkin, 1983)

These approaches are very similar and so have similar strengths and areas of concern. Based largely on the work of Alfred Adler, both methods provide excellent information about effectively communicating with children. Family meetings and democratic methods are very good ways to interact respectfully with children. The notion that children learn responsibility through mutual respect holds up well in existing research. Active Parenting has a broader base and includes ideas from Carl Rogers and others.

A weakness in both packages is that not enough attention is paid to developmental or individual differences in children. Neither do they mention much about cultural differences in families. The strategies seem best for children six or older and are likely to be viewed more positively by middle class or affluent families. Even with these limitations, these packages may be useful to share with parents in your early childhood program. Be sure they understand that this is just one set of useful strategies and not the only method acceptable.

Figure 9–8   Critique of STEP and Active Parenting.

Parent Education Books

How to Talk So Kids Will Listen and Listen So Kids Will Talk, created by Faber and Mazlish (1980), is a program of parent education that is intended for parents to use individually. This plan for parents is based on the theoretical work of Haim Ginott (1969) (Figures 9–9 and 9–10).

Based largely on the work of Haim Ginott. Methods of communication affect relationships and children's behavior. Goals of authors include finding a way to live with each other so that we can feel good about ourselves and help the people we love feel good about themselves, finding a way to live without blame and recrimination, finding a way to be more sensitive to one another's feelings, finding a way to express our irritation or anger without doing damage, finding a way to be respectful of our children's needs and to be just as respectful of our own needs, finding a way that makes it possible for our children to be caring and responsible, and breaking the cycle of unhelpful talk that has been handed down from generations.

Topics in the book are:

1. **Helping Children Deal with Their Feelings**—connections between how kids feel and how they behave; when kids feel right, they behave right; adults often deny children's feelings; suggestions provided to help with acknowledging feelings

2. **Engaging Cooperation**—describe what you see, give information, say it with one word, talk about your feelings, write a note

3. **Alternatives to Punishment**—point out a way to be helpful, express strong disapproval of inappropriate behavior, state your expectations, show the child how to make amends, give a choice, take action, allow child to experience consequences of misbehavior, problem-solve by talking about child's feelings and needs, brainstorm together, write down all ideas, decide on one and follow through

4. **Encouraging Autonomy**—let child make choices, show respect for child's struggles, don't ask too many questions, don't rush to answer child's questions, encourage child to use sources outside the home, don't take away hope

5. **Praise**—praise and self-esteem, describe instead of evaluating, describe what you see and feel, sum up the child's praiseworthy behavior with one word

6. **Freeing Children from Playing Roles**—look for opportunities to show the child a new picture of herself, put child in situations where she can see herself differently, let child overhear you say something positive about her, model the behavior you want to see, be a storehouse for your child's special moments, state feelings and expectations about child's old behavior

Figure 9–9   Highlights of *How to Talk So Kids Will Listen and Listen So Kids Will Talk.* (Faber, & Mazlish, 1980)

This approach offers parents many useful strategies for keeping open communication with their children. These strategies ultimately are likely to help to build positive relationships. And positive relationships are an excellent basis for children's developing skill at self-control. The authors of this method are concerned for both parents and children and increasing the quality of family life for each member. Some parents find the strategies a little artificial sounding when they first begin, but that may be because in general, we lack effective interpersonal capabilities in our society. With practice, many adults feel that the strategies become more natural to them.

Adults place expectations on children, not just for blind compliance to their wishes but also for responsibility in the family. This approach is useful not specifically just for disciplining children, but for all interaction with them. Thus, parents are offered suggestions for their entire relationships with children, not only for disciplining them. This approach is generally viewed as a useful one and is highly recommended.

Figure 9–10 Critique of *How to Talk So Kids Will Listen and Listen So Kids Will Talk.*

Raising Good Children from Birth through the Teenage Years is a parenting resource written by Thomas Lickona (1983). This plan is based on the theoretical work of Kohlberg (1964), emphasizing the importance of child development and how children come to understand the difference between right and wrong (Chrisman & Couchenour, 1997) (Figure 9–11).

Two approaches that are currently being marketed for parents are Assertive Discipline (Canter & Canter, 1985) and 1–2–3 Magic (Phelan, 1995). Concern about the use of these programs with young children is widespread. Research is not available concerning the effects of either approach; however, best practices in early education generally are in opposition to these plans (Figures 9–12 and 9–13).

Parents as Teachers (PAT)

Some parent education models for parenting young children are centered on home visitation. The Parents as Teachers (PAT) program, which originated in Missouri (Burkhart, 1991), is one such approach. Trained parent educators visit homes soon after the birth of a child. They provide practical details and support to parents concerning the child's needs for optimal development.

Parents as Teachers is built on two premises.
1. All families have strengths.
2. Parents are the experts on their child.

Home visitors are specially trained and certified through the Parents as Teachers National Center in St. Louis, Missouri. The original program included training for working with families of children from birth to three years. Additional training is now available for families with three- to five-year-old children. The program is comprised of four components.

1. *Home visits.* Visits by certified home visitors to homes of new parents are individualized. The task of home visitors is to provide child development knowledge and child-rearing information, and to support parents in using this material within their family.

2. *Group meetings.* Group meetings are scheduled for times that parents who work outside the home are available such as Saturdays or evenings. Often, the emphasis in a group meeting is on parent-child activities to emphasize the importance of family interaction on the child's development. At meetings, families have opportunities to share successes and concerns about their children and to receive feedback from staff members or outside experts.

3. *Developmental screening.* Parents and parent educators are encouraged to observe and monitor the child's development; these ongoing informal assessments often provide useful

This approach uses developmental theory and research as a basis for parenting strategies. The underlying theme is noted in this quote, "A child is the only known substance from which a responsible adult can be made." Lickona assumes that a primary goal for parenting is to foster moral development. He states ten big ideas from the moral development approach to parenting:

1. Morality is respect.
2. Kids develop morality slowly and in stages.
3. Respect kids and require respect in return.
4. Teach by example.
5. Teach by telling.
6. Help kids learn to think.
7. Help kids take on real responsibilities.
8. Balance independence and control.
9. Love kids and help them develop a positive self-concept.
10. Foster moral development and a happier family at the same time.

Lickona also offers specific parenting strategies that are supported by child development research for various age groups:

Infancy—love your baby; provide consistent care; smile and talk to baby often.

Toddlerhood—set reasonable limits; provide space for safe exploration; give choices; only say no when you mean it; ignore undesirable behaviors; use distraction; use logical consequences if necessary.

Threes—teach manners; provide habit of helping; read stories with labels such as "naughty" or "nice," but avoid saying "bad girl."

Fours—Offer choices to give child decisions to make; take time to have fun together; reaffirm old limits and set new ones; require kids to give good reasons; assign chores that give a role in the family.

Fives—Be the authority figure children need; fives believe they should obey, so use opportunities to remind them of this belief; reinforce manners and other desirable behavior; begin to teach values about why some things are wrong.

Sixes to eights—Offer explanations and reminders, but be firm; appeal to reciprocity or equal exchange; negotiate and compromise in a spirit of fairness; talk about feelings; help them to know what your expectations are; nurture a loving relationship.

Critique—This approach is concerned both with the parent and the outcome to the child. The goal is child-centered, in that the short-term and long-term effects of parenting strategies on children are geared toward fostering morality. These approaches are supported by a large body of research literature. Variations by ages of children are helpful to parents. Parents can read short segments of the book related to the particular age of their child. It may be helpful to have a professional who is knowledgeable in child development provide support for parents beginning this approach. This book is highly recommended as an approach to parenting.

Figure 9–11 Summary and critique of *Raising Good Children.* (Lickona, 1983)

information about the child's progress or developmental delays. Formal screenings are conducted annually beginning at one year of age. When problems are identified in children's development, parents are helped with resources for appropriate forms of intervention.

4. *Connections with community resources.* Parent educators assist parents in making connections with resources in their particular communities. Examples of possible resources include li-

braries, health clinics, and programs for children with identified special needs (http://www.patnc.org/, November 17, 1998).

Evaluation research completed on Parents as Teachers over the past fifteen years confirms the following:

• At age three, children enrolled in this program were significantly more advanced in language, problem-solving, and social development than comparison children.

Goal—"to help parents take charge before the problems with their children get out of hand" (p. 6).

The authors state, "Assertive Discipline should be used when your everyday approaches to handling children's behavior haven't worked. If talking with your children, reasoning with them or understanding their feelings doesn't help improve their behavior, then it's time for Assertive Discipline" (p. 2). "Through Assertive Discipline, we will teach you how to take charge in problem situations and let your children know you must be the 'boss'" (p. 3).

The step-by-step plan for this approach is:

1. Communicate assertively. Avoid arguments and praise children when they behave. This approach attempts to teach parents how to speak assertively, how to use nonverbal messages, how to handle arguing, and how to catch children being good. The authors emphasize the use of praise and "super praise" for desired behavior.

2. Back up your words with actions. Plan how you will respond if they do or do not listen to you. The authors discuss how to use consequences for inappropriate behavior, how to handle "testing," and how to provide positive support.

3. Lay down the law. Set up a systematic Assertive Discipline plan. Use "parent-saver" techniques; conduct a "lay down the law" session with your children.

Suggested disciplinary actions for minor behavioral problems:

separation
taking away privileges
physical action to remove child or object
"Do what I want" before you do anything else
grounding

Suggested actions for serious behavior problems:

"I am watching you:" close monitoring of all behavior, even violating privacy
Tape recording child with sitter or at school
Unannounced visits
Room grounding: no TV, stereo, phone, games or toys; leaving only for school, bathroom, and eating
Out-of-home grounding with a neighbor or relative

Positive consequences for desirable behavior

choosing dessert, extra TV time, a jelly bean, choose a treat, stickers, later curfew, reading a story together, point system, fishing trip with dad

Critique—The field testing aspect considers only the effects of the approach on parents and children's compliance with parents. No effects on children have been studied. The approach is authoritarian in nature. Some strategies may be useful for parents, but the Assertive Discipline concept is not recommended by experts in child development. This punishment and reward system does not provide a foundation for children to develop responsibility or respect.

Figure 9–12   Summary and critique of Assertive Discipline. (Canter & Canter, 1985)

- Children who participated for at least one year scored higher on the Kindergarten Inventory of Developmental Skills than others.

- At the end of first grade, PAT children scored higher on standardized reading and math tests than others.

- In fourth grade, PAT "graduates" scored higher than the control group on the Stanford Achievement Test.

- By age three, more than half of PAT children with observed developmental delays were on target for expected typical development.

- Even when PAT children and families have many characteristics associated with high risk for educational failure, the children are placing above national norms (http://www.patnc.org/, November 18, 1998).

Recently, the Parents as Teachers National Center has undertaken a new initiative in the form of a revised version of the curriculum with a neuroscience base. This use of new research available on brain development is an exemplary model of an existing program adding new scientific advances. The revised design has been named The Born to Learn

Goal: "When you finish with this book, you will know exactly what to do, what not to do, what to say, and what not to say in just about every one of the common everyday problem situations you will run into with your kids" (p. iii).

Phelan states his viewpoint about the role of parents early in the book, "When your kids are little, your house should be a dictatorship where you are the judge and jury" (p. 13). His view of children is stated with a quote from another writer, " 'Childhood is a period of transitory psychosis.'" Phelan goes on to explain, "She meant that kids, when they are little, are sort of nuts! They are born unreasonable and selfish, and it is our job—and a teacher's job—to help them become the opposite" (p. 12).

Guidelines for this method:

1. Methods must be used exactly as described in the book.
2. Both parents should use the techniques.
3. Single parents can use the methods effectively by themselves.
4. Grandparents, baby-sitters, and other caregivers have found the methods helpful.
5. The kids should be in good physical health.

Premises of this approach:

1. To stop behavior, use the 1-2-3 "counting" procedure.

"That's 1."
"That's 2."
"That's 3—take 5."

2. To start behavior, choose from six tactics:
Sloppy positive verbal feedback (PVF): Praise or reinforcement should be given often.
Kitchen timers: Set timer as deadline for starting desired behavior.
Docking system: If you don't do the work, money is docked each time.
Natural consequences.
Charting: Give stickers or marks for completing tasks.

Information about active listening, self-esteem, and reflecting feelings is added to chapters near the end of the book. In this section, the author warns parents about the dangers of overusing the 1-2-3 counting approach and suggests the importance of listening to their children. However, when the listening turns into an attack by the child, parents are urged to count.

Critique—In this approach to parenting, adults have all of the responsibility to control children, with children being given very little opportunity to develop self-control. A great deal of research shows that children who are parented primarily through a punishment and reward system do not develop a sense of responsibility or conscience.

Figure 9–13 Summary and critique of *1–2–3 Magic.* (Phelan, 1995)

For more information:
Parents as Teachers National Center
St. Louis, Missouri
(314) 432-4330
E-mail: patnc@patnc.org
http://www.patnc.org/

Curriculum. Currently, assessments are being conducted to measure results of this approach to Parents as Teachers (http://www.patnc.org/, November 18, 1998).

Home Instruction Program for Preschool Youngsters (HIPPY)

HIPPY was developed by the National Council of Jewish Women in Jerusalem in 1969. HIPPY USA was started in 1984 in Tulsa, Oklahoma. This national network provides training and assists local communities with start-up materials. Funding for HIPPY USA comes mostly from three sources: training service fees, royalties from the sale of curriculum materials, and grants from foundations and corporations (http://www.hippyusa.org/, April 26, 2003).

In this parent education program, paraprofessionals are trained to provide services to families in their homes. The emphasis is on helping parents prepare their three-, four-, and five-year-old children to succeed in school. Storybooks, creative games, and activity packets are shared by paraprofessionals in home visits and at group meetings. Parents practice the activities with paraprofessionals before using them with their children (http://www.hippyusa. org/, April 26, 2003).

To start a HIPPY program in a local community, there are seven steps to follow.

1. Review HIPPY program requirements.
2. Conduct need assessment in local community.
3. Hold a preliminary meeting with community leaders and other interested parties.
4. Secure funding from local and state sources.
5. Submit application to HIPPY USA.
6. Hire or assign a training coordinator.
7. Sign an agreement with HIPPY USA.

HIPPY USA claims the following benefits for children, parents, and the paraprofessionals involved in the program.

For children:
- skill development
- confidence
- better adapted to the classroom when they begin school

For parents:
- increased sense of their own abilities
- satisfaction of teaching their children
- excitement of seeing children's development
- a time for fun and learning with their children
- a positive relationship with another adult (paraprofessional) who cares about them and their children
- connect with other agencies in the community

For paraprofessionals, many who have been parents in the program previously:
- an opportunity to help others in a leadership capacity

> For more information:
> HIPPY USA
> 220 East 23rd Street
> New York, New York 10010
> (212) 532-7730
> **http://www.hippyusa.org**

- often a first job
- a step to a permanent job elsewhere

Evaluation research on HIPPY programs in the United States confirms the following information:

- In second grade, children who had participated in HIPPY were higher on school performance and in teacher ratings of motivation and adaptation to the classroom.
- HIPPY children had fewer absences.
- HIPPY children were perceived by their teachers as better students.
- Through parent training in specific techniques for book reading, HIPPY children had higher involvement and interest in this activity.

HIPPY emphasizes growth for parents and paraprofessionals at least as much as it does for children. There seems to be even greater evidence for the success of the program with adults than with children. HIPPY USA suggests that future research focus on needed improvements in the program as well as details about variations required by local communities (http://www.hippyusa.org/, April 26, 2003).

Family Life Education

Family life education incorporates a broader view of the needs of families. In addition to parenting, family life education includes topics such as marriage, family relationships, sex education, and work-family issues (Darling, 1987). Family life education is currently driven by ecological theory, emphasizing "wholeness and integration" (p. 819). The family life approach places skills and knowledge about parenting in the context of all of family life, thus making it a broad and diverse approach (Figures 9–14 and 9–15).

Family life education, when incorporated into early childhood teacher education, would lead to discussions and the generation of knowledge about the following areas:

- challenges of families from varying socioeconomic backgrounds and how these situations affect involvement of families in their children's education

- concerns of families from differing ethnic, religious, racial, and sexual orientation backgrounds about their place in the culture of the school

- effects of stressors facing families such as divorce, remarriage, and death in establishing family-school relationships

- strategies for sensitively including various family forms such as foster parents, grandparents, and other extended family members who serve as parents or guardians (Coleman & Churchill, 1997)

The National Council of Family Relations (NCFR) sponsors the only national program to certify

Consider the following:

- accuracy of content
- clear presentation
- nonjudgmental in tone
- logically organized
- interesting and challenging
- material leads to existing goals, objectives, or outcomes
- appealing format
- no sexism, racism, or cultural bias
- appropriate level for intended participants
- active learning required
- reflects various stages of family life cycle
- recognizes variations in family structure
- acknowledges changing roles of family members

Figure 9–15 Griggs' criteria for evaluating family life education material. (*Source:* Griggs, M. B. [1981, October]. Criteria for the evaluation of family life education materials. *Family Relations, 30*(4), 549–555)

family life educators (CFLE). Family life education provides skills and knowledge to enrich individual and family life. For more information about family life education, go to http://www. ncfr.org/.

The Role of Early Childhood Educators in Parent Education and Family Life Education

Early childhood professionals must not presume to know the needs of their particular families in terms of parent and family life education. Rather, possibilities may be brought to families in the form of an assessment. Families should always have a voice in the particular content and format of educational opportunities made available to them.

Family Life Education

1. Human sexuality
2. Family relationships
3. Communication
4. Economic responsibilities of families
5. Diversity of families
6. Spirituality
7. Gender roles in families
8. Parenting
9. Family values
10. Physical and mental health

Figure 9–14 Some topics included in family life education.

It is the responsibility of early childhood teachers to be aware of the pros and cons of any parent or family life education offered to families. If a packaged program is used, discuss the downside of the program as reviewed by experts in the field. Also, ask parents about what they like and find useful, as well as what is less appealing to them.

Topics for Parent Education

In this section, eight topics for parent education are discussed that are recommended for inclusion in most early childhood education settings. Seven topics deal with play, developmentally appropriate practice, positive guidance, limiting television, homework, early brain development, and family literacy. These seem to be frequently requested from parents and/or staff. The remaining topic, healthy sexuality development, is not one that is often discussed by either parents or staff. However, it is included in this book because recent research (Couchenour & Chrisman, 1996; Couchenour, Chrisman, & Gottshall, 1997; Chrisman, Gottshall, Koons, & Couchenour, 1998) into this topic found that early childhood teachers do not believe they have enough preparation in this area or that family involvement is required when this topic is addressed in early childhood education programs.

For each of the topics, a variety of formats may be used for dissemination. Some strategies for educating parents about these topics with the information provided herein include sections of parent handbooks, orientation sessions, workshops, newsletters, brochures, videotapes prepared so that parents can check them out at their convenience, miniconferences with several speakers around the theme, or panel discussions. Use of several formats or strategies for any one topic is likely to increase the effectiveness of educating parents. Early education staff may also wish to divide any of the topics into smaller segments for any one session or strategy.

Topic One: The Value of Play for Young Children.

Purpose:

To explain to parents of children enrolled in an early childhood program the value of play to all areas of children's development, including physical, cognitive, social, and emotional. (Placing a list of outcomes for children at each learning center is helpful for parents as they volunteer in the classroom or simply learn about child development.)

Goals for Parents:

1. To explain how children learn through play and that play is a child's work.

2. To articulate a definition and list the characteristics of play.

3. To describe what children learn as they play in various learning centers around the classroom and outdoors.

   Examples are:

   dramatic play—vocabulary development, cooperation, role identification, and concept development

   blocks—spatial relationships, problem-solving, patterning, measurement, creativity, cooperation, and vocabulary development

4. To observe and facilitate play in home settings.

Concepts to Highlight:

1. Children learn very effectively through play.

2. Play has the following characteristics:

   a. it is intrinsically motivated

   b. it is the child's choice

   c. it is active

   d. it is child-directed

   e. it is fun

3. Teachers have the following responsibilities regarding play:

   a. it is planned

   b. it meets the needs of children

   c. space is organized for safety and best educational results

   d. ample time is allocated in the daily schedule for effective learning through play

   e. the teacher interacts with children during play in ways that support the child's choices

4. Play fosters physical development. Both large muscles and small muscles are used for increased gross motor and fine motor skills.

5. Play fosters cognitive development. Children, who from two to seven years are master players, are likely to become master workers soon after that, often during third grade.

6. Play fosters social development. Cooperation is required to play well with other children. Sometimes, children lead and sometimes, they follow when they play. Children take on a variety of different roles when they play.

7. Play fosters emotional development. Children gain ability to express themselves in a variety of appropriate ways. Self-esteem is enhanced through play.

8. Stages of play related to social development are solitary, parallel, associative, and cooperative.

9. Stages of play related to intellectual development are sensorimotor or practice, constructive, dramatic (or pretend), and games with rules.

10. Effective practice in early childhood education emphasizes play as a useful method for teaching and learning.

11. The teacher's role for fostering children's play includes setting up the environment and interacting in ways that enhance the play.

Resources:

Dimidjian, V. J. (Ed.) (1992). *Play's place in public education for young children*. Washington, DC: National Education Association.

Jones, E., & Reynolds, G. (1992). *The play's the thing: Teachers' roles in children's play*. New York: Teachers College Press.

Rogers, C. S., & Sawyers, J. K. (1988). *Play in the lives of children*. Washington, DC: National Association for the Education of Young Children.

Sawyers, J. K., & Rogers, C. S. (1988). *Helping young children develop through play: A practical guide for parents, caregivers, and teachers*. Washington, DC: National Association for the Education of Young Children.

Wasserman, S. (1990). *Serious players in the primary classroom: Empowering children through active learning experiences*. New York: Teachers College Press.

Children learn effectively through play.

Topic Two: What Is Developmentally Appropriate Practice?

Purpose:

To provide for parents of children enrolled in an early education program the meaning of the term "developmentally appropriate practice."

Goals for Parents:

1. To define and explain the term "developmentally appropriate practice."

2. To understand the role of professionals in planning, implementing, and assessing developmentally appropriate educational practice.

3. To discuss the importance of school, family, and community partnerships in fostering high-quality programs for young children.

Concepts to Highlight:

1. Definition of developmentally appropriate practice in early childhood education is three-pronged:

   a. understanding of child development and learning

   b. attention to individual differences in children's strengths, interests, and needs

   c. knowledge of each child's social and cultural contexts

2. The role of early childhood professionals is expansive:

   a. to create a caring community of learners

   b. to enhance children's development and learning

   c. to construct appropriate curriculum for the group and for individual children

   d. to authentically assess each child's development and learning

   e. to establish reciprocal relationships with families

3. Developmentally appropriate practices consider all areas of children's development: physical, cognitive and language, social, and emotional.

4. It is necessary to understand the inaccuracy of common myths about the meaning of developmentally appropriate practice, including:

   a. there is only one way to implement developmentally appropriate programs

   b. developmentally appropriate classrooms are unstructured, chaotic

   c. teachers do not plan or teach anything in a developmentally appropriate classroom

   d. developmentally appropriate practice requires that existing curricula be "watered down" and that children fall behind academically

   e. academics have no place in developmentally appropriate programs

   f. developmental appropriateness is just a fad, soon to be replaced by another fad.

5. A variety of teaching and learning strategies are used in developmentally appropriate practices, including play, small groups, large groups, cooperative learning, and direct instruction. No one method is relied on exclusively; methods are based on how children learn.

Resources:

Bredekamp, S., & Copple, C. (1997). *Developmentally appropriate practice in early childhood programs* (rev. ed.). Washington, DC: National Association for the Education of Young Children.

The role of the early childhood professional is to enhance children's development and learning.

Clemens, S. G. (1983). *The sun's not broken, a cloud's just in the way: On child-centered teaching.* Mt. Ranier, MD: Gryphon House.

Dodge, D. T., & Bickart, T. S. (1998). *Preschool for parents: What every parent needs to know about preschool.* Naperville, IL: Sourcebooks.

Kostelnik, M. J. (1992, May). Myths associated with developmentally appropriate programs. *Young Children, 47*(4), 17–23.

Mr. Rogers talks with parents [Videotape, 43 minutes]. Washington, DC: National Association for the Education of Young Children.

Whole language learning. [Videotape, 20 minutes]. Washington, DC: National Association for the Education of Young Children.

Topic Three: Positive Guidance.

Purpose:

To explain to parents that discipline is a tool for children's learning and not only about submitting to adult expectations.

Goals for Parents:

1. To understand that when they guide or discipline children, they affect the whole child.

2. To explain that children learn appropriate behaviors through adult modeling and teaching.

3. To describe the effects of various types of discipline on children's development.

4. To foster strategies of positive guidance in their own parenting.

Concepts to Highlight:

1. Positive guidance approaches teach children appropriate behaviors.

2. Positive guidance demonstrates respect to children and models respectful interactions.

3. Positive guidance teaches children to appreciate themselves and others as worthwhile individuals.

4. Positive guidance helps children to use conflict resolution strategies as they interact with other children.

5. Positive guidance considers reasons for children's misbehavior or mistaken behaviors.

6. Positive guidance uses a proactive approach, including creating an environment conducive to learning and less likely to cause children's misbehaviors.

7. Positive guidance creates positive relationships between children and adults as adults model respectful behaviors.

8. Strategies for positive guidance help to build partnerships between parents and teachers.

9. Positive guidance nurtures peacemaking and justice.

10. Positive guidance provides opportunities to resolve conflicts in nonviolent ways.

11. Punishment produces harmful consequences to young children.

12. Punishment does not teach children appropriate behaviors.

Resources:

Condon, C., & McGinnis, J. (1988). *Helping kids care.* Oak Park, IL: Meyer-Stone Books and the Institute for Peace and Justice.

Gartrell, D. (2003.) *A guidance approach for the encouraging classroom* (3rd ed.). Clifton Park, NY: Delmar Learning.

Honig, A. S. (1996). *Behavior guidance for infants and toddlers.* Little Rock, AR: Southern Early Childhood Association.

McGinnis, K., & Oehlberg, B. (1988). *Starting out right: Nurturing young children as peacemakers.* Oak Park, IL: Meyer-Stone Books and the Institute for Peace and Justice.

Nunnelley, J. C. (1995). *Behavior guidance for three- and four-year-old children.* Little Rock, AR: Southern Early Childhood Association.

Topic Four: Limiting Television.

Purpose:

To help parents understand that young children are particularly vulnerable to potentially harmful effects of too much television viewing.

Goals for Parents:

1. To be aware of what the potentially harmful effects of watching too much television are.

2. To be sensitized to the effects of television violence on young children.

3. To identify high-quality children's programming and videos.

4. To create alternatives to television/video viewing.

5. To plan for family viewing time.

Concepts to Highlight:

1. Television has a lot of power to influence children's thinking and behavior.

2. Children may become less caring and more fearful when they view too much television violence.

3. Adults have responsibility to protect children from possible harmful effects of television. Set clear limits and rules about television watching.

4. Parents should monitor all of children's television viewing. It's okay to ban programs that are unacceptable.

5. There is more violence in programming now than when parents were children.

6. When children watch television, they are missing out on play and social experiences that are important to their development.

7. Schools and families can work together to decrease television viewing and to increase better alternative activities for children.

8. Letter-writing campaigns to stations and companies that advertise can be organized by school, family, and community partnerships.

Resources:

Horton, J., & Zimmer, J. (1994). *Media violence and children: A guide for parents.* [Brochure]. Washington, DC: National Association for the Education of Young Children.

Levin, D. E. (1998). *Remote control childhood? Combating the hazards of media culture.* Washington, DC: National Association for the Education of Young Children.

Ten tips for parents to stop the media violence. (n.d.). Minnesota Medical Association. Media Awareness Network at http://www.schoolnet.ca/medianet

Topic Five: Homework.

Purpose:

To help parents understand reasons and expectations for homework in the primary grades.

Goals for Parents:

1. To explain the purpose of homework for primary children.

2. To understand parents' role in helping with homework.

3. To implement effective strategies for assisting children with homework.

Concepts to Highlight:

1. Two common reasons for homework in primary grades:

   a. to practice skills

   b. to collect information, or observe something at home or out of the school setting

2. Homework teaches responsibility and good work habits.

3. Reasonable amount of homework time for first through third grades is fifteen to thirty minutes.

4. Strategies for helping children with homework include:

   a. reminders

   b. setting up a quiet place to work

   c. scheduling time to do homework before other activities

   d. communicating with teachers about expectations and how homework is used at school

Resources:

Bickart, T. S., Dodge, D. T., & Jablon, J. R. (1997). *What every parent needs to know about 1st, 2nd, & 3rd grades: An essential guide to your child's education.* Naperville, IL: Sourcebooks.

Homework: Ways parents can help. Olney, MD: Association for Childhood Education International. http://www.udel.edu/bateman/acei

National PTA National Standards for Parent/Family Involvement Programs. (1998). http://www.pta.org/programs/. November 25, 1998.

Topic Six: Healthy Sexuality Development.

Purpose:

To help parents understand that early sexuality development is related to all areas of children's development: physical, cognitive, social, and emotional.

Goals for Parents:

1. To have an awareness of typical behaviors or questions young children have related to sexuality.

2. To relate their own discomfort with discussions of sexuality.

3. To use appropriate responses to foster healthy sexuality in their children.

Concepts to Highlight:

1. Sexuality is about who we are, not just a set of behaviors.

2. Children are curious about sexuality, just as they are about most everything else that they encounter.

3. Some aspects of sexuality relate to physical development:

   a. body functions

   b. male/female differences

   c. body parts

   d. pleasant sensations

4. Some aspects of sexuality relate to social development:

   a. gender roles

   b. identification of gender

   c. social relationships with those of same and opposite gender

5. Some aspects of sexuality relate to emotional development:

   a. high self-esteem is related to feeling good about who you are

   b. affection is learned in early family relationships

   c. empathy and respect are required for successful relationships

6. Some aspects of sexuality relate to cognitive development:

   a. understanding of facts about reproduction

   b. understanding of family and cultural values about sexuality

   c. understanding why one is labeled as a boy or a girl

7. Teachers and parents must work together to create appropriate responses for fostering healthy sexuality development in young children.

8. Fostering healthy sexuality can be a barrier to sexual abuse.

Resources:

Chrisman, K., & Couchenour, D. (2002). *Healthy sexuality development: A guide for early childhood educators and families.* Washington, DC: National Association for the Education of Young Children.

Couchenour, D., & Chrisman, K. (1996). Healthy sexuality development in young children. *Dimensions of Early Childhood, 24*(4), 30–36.

Lively, V., & Lively, E. (1991). *Sexual development of young children.* Clifton Park, NY: Delmar Learning.

Wilson, P. M. (1991). *When sex is the subject: Attitudes and answers for young children.* Santa Cruz, CA: Network Publications.

Topic Seven: Early Brain Development.

Purpose:

To help parents understand the importance of brain development in the early years of a child's life.

Goals for Parents:

1. To have an awareness of typical brain development.

2. To know some implications of brain development theory for families.

Concepts to Highlight:

1. The importance of multisensory play in brain development.

2. The importance of conversation, singing, and language.

3. The negative effects of unmonitored television viewing.

4. The relationship between emotional development and healthy brain development.

Resources:

Healy, J. M. (1994). *Your child's growing mind: A practical guide to brain development and learning from birth to adolescence.* New York: Doubleday.

National PTA. Ten tips for fueling your child's brain power. http://www.pta.org/.

National Parent Information Network. (1997). Early years are learning years: Brain development research—What it means for young children and families. National Association for the Education of Young Children. http://www.npin.org/

Topic Eight: Family Literacy.

Purpose:

To help parents understand ways to support literacy development at home.

Goals for Parents:

1. To have an awareness of the importance of reading to, with, and being a role model for children.

2. To understand the importance of providing books, writing materials, and other literacy supports during early childhood.

3. To be able to discern fads or gimmicks from age-appropriate literacy stories.

Concepts to Highlight:

1. Singing, playing, and reading to and with your children are important literacy strategies.

2. Making time to read together each day is important

3. Talking with your child and responding to their sounds, words, and questions is important for language development.

Resources:

National Association for Education of Young Children and the International Reading Association. (1998). Raising a reader, raising a writer. Washington, DC: National Association for the Education of Young Children.

Summary and Conclusions

Early childhood teachers can provide much needed support for parents and their caregiving responsibilities. However, it is important that professional personnel provide information that is perceived as being needed by family members. Further, information should be shared in sensitive ways. When parents feel as though they are being criticized or degraded, they are not likely to participate in parent education sessions. It is essential that teachers respect family strengths and cultural differences in parenting values.

In addition to being sensitive to families, early childhood educators must use their knowledge base in child development and parenting styles to critically analyze appropriate topics and strategies for parent and family life education. Some popular par-

ent education packages are analyzed in this chapter. However, new programs are likely to take hold, and it is the responsibility of early childhood professionals to promote those that will foster healthy practices for families. Programs that do not consider current understanding of child development and the importance of the early years should be screened and not recommended for use by parents or teaching staff.

Key Terms

parent education
family life education

Chapter Nine Applications

1. Assess one parent or family life education program using the concepts from bioecological theory as discussed in this chapter.

2. Discuss the concerns held by many early childhood educators about Assertive Discipline and 1–2–3 Magic. Why do you believe these programs have so much popularity?

3. What is the difference between parent education and family life education?

Questions for Discussion and Reflection

1. How would you design a parenting education or family life education program based on the guidelines from this chapter?

2. How would children benefit from use of the guidelines presented in this chapter? How would families benefit? How would early childhood teachers benefit?

3. Discuss the pros and cons of the following strategies for parent education: meetings, newsletters, the Internet, and the resource room.

Field Assignments

1. Attend a parent meeting held by an early childhood program. Discuss the content and format of the meeting you attended in relation to information from this chapter. What were the

best points about the meeting? What suggestions do you have for change?

2. Interview three parents who have their children enrolled in an early childhood education program about their thoughts related to parent education. Ask questions about content they would be interested in and format they would prefer.

3. Interview an early childhood teacher about her perspective on parent or family life education. Does this teacher feel prepared to provide these kinds of programs? Are they needed? Do families want them?

References

Adler, A. (1923). *Practice and theory of individual psychology.* New York: Harcourt, Brace and Company.

Bronfenbrenner, U., & Neville, P. R. (1994.) America's children and families: An international perspective. In S. L. Kagan & B. Weissbourd (Eds.), *Putting families first: America's family support movement and the challenge of change.* San Francisco: Jossey-Bass.

Burkhart, A. D. (1991). *Parents are important teachers.* Kansas City, MO: Westport.

Canter, L., & Canter, M. (1985). *Assertive discipline for parents: A proven, step-by-step approach to solving everyday behavior problems.* New York: Harper & Row.

Chrisman, J. K. (1996). *The effects of training on child care providers' attitudes and practices.* Unpublished doctoral dissertation, University of Louisville.

Chrisman, K., & Couchenour, D. (1997). Comparing faith-based parenting guides: An on-going task for the faith community. *Church and Society, 88*(1), 99–104.

Chrisman, K., Gottshall, A., Koons, T., & Couchenour, D. (1998, November). Incorporating early sexuality development into early childhood teacher preparation programs: A qualitative study. Paper presented at the meeting of the National Association for the Education of Young Children, Toronto, Ontario, Canada.

Coleman, M., & Churchill, S. (1997, Spring). Challenges to family involvement. *Childhood Education,* 144–148.

Couchenour, D., & Chrisman, K. (1996). Healthy sexuality development in young children. *Dimensions of Early Childhood, 24*(4), 30–36.

Couchenour, D., Chrisman, K., & Gottshall, A. (1997, November). Teaching about healthy sexuality development in young children. Paper presented at the meeting of the National Association for the Education of Young Children, Anaheim, CA.

Darling, C. (1987). Family life education. In M. B. Sussman & S. K. Steinmetz (Eds.), *Handbook of marriage and the family.* New York: Plenum Press.

Dinkmeyer, D., McKay, G., & Dinkmeyer, D. (1980). *STEP.* Circle Pines, MN: American Guidance Service.

Dreikurs, R., & Soltz, V. (1964). *Children: The challenge.* New York: Hawthorn Books.

Faber, A., & Mazlish, E. (1980). *How to talk so kids will listen and listen so kids will talk.* New York: Avon Books.

Ginott, H. G. (1969). *Between parent and child.* New York: Avon Books.

Griggs, M. B. (October, 1981). Criteria for the evaluation of family life education materials. *Family Relations, 30*(4), 549–555.

Kohlberg, L. (1964). Development of moral character and moral ideology. In M. L. Hoffman & L. W. Hoffman (Eds.), *Review of child development research,* (vol. 1). New York: Russell Sage Foundation.

LeMasters, E., & DeFrain, J. (1983). *Parents in contemporary America.* Homewood, IL: Dorsey.

Lickona, T. (1983). *Raising good children from birth through the teenage years.* New York: Bantam Books.

McDade, K. (1995). How we parent: Race and ethnic differences. In C. K. Jacobson (Ed.), *American families: Issues in race and ethnicity.* New York: Garland.

Phelan, T. W. (1995). *1–2–3 Magic: Effective discipline for children 2–12.* Glen Ellyn, IL: Child Management.

Popkin, M. (1983). Active parenting. Atlanta, GA: Active Parenting.

Powell, D. (1989). *Families and early childhood programs.* Washington, DC: National Association for the Education of Young Children.

Powell, D. (1994). Evaluating family support programs: Are we making progress? In S. L. Kagan & B. Weissbourd (Eds.), *Putting families first: America's family support movement and the challenge of change.* San Francisco: Jossey-Bass.

OUTLINE

Early Childhood Educators in the Community

After reading and reflecting on this chapter, you should be able to:

- Understand the reasons for and effectiveness of collaborative efforts for children and families.

- Acquire information about appropriate strategies for discussing referrals for special services with families.

- Appreciate the importance of community resources to best meet the needs of all children and families.

Bioecological Theory

The community for the early childhood teacher is not just a theme for a unit, as in community helpers, but is an ongoing reality each day. Understanding how the community affects the children, families, school, and the early childhood teacher will help in planning, reflecting, and organizing the curriculum as well as other aspects of a developmentally appropriate program.

Awareness of both the **community resources** and lack of resources provides important information. Knowing what is available, as well as what is not immediately available, gives teachers an understanding for action and alternatives for decision-making. When communities support families and young children, everyone benefits. As community members, early childhood professionals can find many incidental ways of advocating for young children and their families (Figure 10–1).

Currently, the public education, health, and child welfare systems are working to combine their efforts "especially in addressing the needs of poor children and families. This is occurring in large part because program staffs recognize that the interactive effects of inadequate academic mastery, ill health, poverty, and family dysfunction are toxic for families and neighborhoods" (Massinga, 1994, p. 103). One strategy that will increase effectiveness and reduce stress for families is to provide services "all at once in one place" (p. 103).

In the book, *Grassroots Success!* (Washington, Johnson, & McCracen, 1995), the authors suggest asking the following questions to be sure that schools and families are prepared for and continue to support each other:

- How well does the primary curriculum reflect current research about developmentally appropriate practice?

Many communities have these resources for families. Check your local telephone directory or chamber of commerce.

Hot lines for crisis intervention

Child care (may be listed as day care)

Preschool education programs

Head Start

Literacy Council

Early intervention services

Resource and referral agencies

Library

Individual and family counseling agencies

Employment counseling/training

Red Cross

Food banks

Women, Infants, & Children (WIC)

Human services or welfare offices

Health care services

Hospital

Mental health/mental retardation services

Planned parenthood

Parenting support groups

Parents without Partners

United Way

Figure 10–1   Typical community resources.

- What information do parents of newborns seek?
- Are kindergarten entry requirements fair and appropriate?
- Can all young children receive their immunizations?
- How could neighborhood stability be increased?
- What instills a love of reading in young children?
- How could community awareness about the importance of children's early experiences be raised?

Community Involvement in Early Childhood Education

Public education in the United States has a history and tradition of local control through elected boards of education. Many private or nonprofit institutions also have voluntary boards, either as policy-making or advisory bodies.

Local School Boards

Local elected boards of education have a wide variety of responsibilities to educational issues within communities. Following are some of the common responsibilities of school boards:

- ensuring efficient operation of all schools in jurisdiction
- establishing local tax rates
- ensuring that school policies and practices agree with state statutes
- reviewing and securing contracts for services
- approving the budget and all purchases
- appointing superintendent and other personnel
- reviewing the educational program and student progress
- approving instructional programs to meet needs of all students (www.jefferson.k12.ky.us/boeotherinfo.html, November 27, 1998.)

School board meetings are public events, and times and dates of meetings are provided in newspapers and other community communications. Parts of school board meetings may be closed to the public when members go into "executive session" for various items of business.

Because education is the business of the entire community, involvement of concerned citizens is necessary. Typically, local boards of education have specific procedures for citizens who wish to make public comments. Phoning the local school district office is a good way to find out these procedures. To be effective in a presentation, the following guidelines are recommended.

Have you ever attended a school board meeting? If so, what was your experience? If not, plan to attend to learn about how local communities affect educational practice.

- When called to speak, go to location specified, speak clearly, and state your name and any group you are representing.
- Make your statement, including supporting evidence or examples. Also, suggest a course of action you are requesting of the board.
- Consider making copies of your comments for board members and school district leaders.
- Limit your comments to one issue.
- Always be polite. (www.jefferson.k12.ky.us/boeotherinfo.html, November 27, 1998.)

One current trend is that some school districts have moved to site-based management and planning. In this approach, family members often play a crucial role in decision-making. Parental authority varies across districts.

Reasons to Encourage Family Involvement in Local School Boards.

- To learn about current local issues related to education such as curriculum topics, special education, plans for new or innovative facilities, transportation, and district-wide policies.
- To demonstrate support for teachers and programs at school board meetings.
- To voice parent and family perspectives during the open discussion segment of a school board meeting (Figure 10–2).

Contact an administrator of a private or nonprofit early childhood program in your community. Ask about the existence and responsibilities of board members. How has the program benefited from the existence of a board?

The Kentucky Department of Education is using technology in an innovative manner in its creation of virtual academic villages. This approach certainly lends a new meaning to "village" or community, and demonstrates that the world is, in a sense, getting smaller.

Academic Villages are the Kentucky Department of Education's metaphor for Web sites that provide access to information, resources, and professional interactions in support of specific aspects of the Kentucky Education System. The concept of the Elementary Academic Village is still evolving, but is likely to include features such as:

- important KDE documents . . . sample course outlines, and content guidelines.
- curriculum resources, . . . instructional units or activities from other sources.
- current information about Kentucky's Education System.
- discussion forums for sharing ideas with other educators.
- announcements of professional development opportunities or available positions.
- on-line professional development courses.
- links to other Web sites.

Academic Villages are envisioned to be rich sites in which all resources have been reviewed as being of high quality. Kentucky educators visiting the village will know that what they find there will enhance their effectiveness.

(www.wolfe.k12.ky.us/eav/tc.htm, February 20, 2003)

Figure 10–2 Kentucky's Virtual Academic Villages.

Local school boards may choose to support the Family-School Partnership Promise sponsored by the Partnership for Family Involvement in Education. (Figure 10–3).

Join the Partnership for Family Involvement in Education

Family-School Partnership Promise

PARTNERSHIP
for Family
Involvement
in Education

Families and schools across America increasingly are accepting mutual responsibility for children's learning. When families are involved in children's learning, at school and at home, schools work better and students learn more. Schools and families are working with employers and community organizations to develop local partnerships that support a safe school environment where students learn to challenging standards. By working together, exchanging information, sharing decision-making, and collaborating for children's learning, everyone can contribute to the education process.

Coming together as families, local school board governance, administration, teachers and school staff, we form this partnership and affirm the importance of family involvement in children's learning. We pledge to:

- **Share responsibility** at school and at home to give students a better education and a good start in life.
- **Help schools** to welcome families; to reach out to families before problems arise; to offer challenging courses; to create safe and drug-free learning environments; to organize tutoring and other opportunities that improve student learning; and to support the inclusion of families in the school decision-making process.
- **Help families** to monitor student attendance, homework completion and television watching; to take the time to talk with and listen to their children; to become acquainted with teachers, administrators and school staff; to read with younger children and share a good book with a teen; to volunteer in school when possible; and to participate in the school decision-making process.
- **Promote effective, two-way communication** between families and schools by schools reducing educational jargon and breaking down cultural and language barriers and by families staying in touch with the school.
- **Provide opportunities for families** to learn how to help their children succeed in school and opportunities for school staff to work with families.
- **Support family-school efforts to improve student learning** by reviewing progress regularly and strengthening cooperative actions.

We would like to become a member of the Partnership for Family Involvement in Education. We commit to family-friendly practices and will work with others to form partnerships that support children's learning. (Please type or print the following information.)

School Name _____

School Address _____

City _____ State _____ Zip _____

Phone _____ Fax _____ E-mail _____

Principal _____ Signature _____

Contact person _____ Title _____ Phone _____

 Send to: Partnership for Family Involvement in Education, 600 Independence Avenue, SW, Washington, DC 20202-8173 or fax to 202-205-9133 to receive your **Family-School Partnership Promise certificate**.

Figure 10–3   Family-school partnership promise.

Boards of Trustees and Advisory Boards

Early childhood programs that have related policy-making or advisory bodies often find such boards to be useful in their planning and fund-raising efforts. Having a variety of community members serve on these boards from various professions including education, health, legal, and business, creates wide-ranging support for the program. Responsibilities allocated to these boards will differ greatly depending on whether they have policy-making or advisory capacities.

Caring Communities

Recently, it has become clear that not only will community resources be tapped as they are needed for intervention but also that families need communities to be involved in nurturing all children. The 1991 Report of the National Task Force on School Readiness expounds on the need for comprehensive support for all young children and families in the United States. Included in this call for comprehensive support are the following:

- health care
- security in family life
- high-quality early education
- linkages among services

According to this report, quality early education should not stand alone, but rather should be integrated with other services in the community. Schools and programs should be visible in communities.

In *Ready Schools* (1998), the National Education Goals Panel lists important steps that can be taken by communities that care about preparing all children for kindergarten.

- Encourage parents to read to their children.
- Help parents connect with parent education programs such as Parents as Teachers and family literacy programs.
- Urge parents to take children for regular health examinations and immunizations.

Policy-making or advisory bodies are useful in supporting and planning for early childhood programs.

"One of the first things we learned when we all went to education school twenty years ago—to work with the whole child. I don't know how we got away from that. But we have. Once we start meeting the needs of the whole child again, we'll begin to see real academic improvement. . . . We need to attach more social workers to the school who can go into the home and provide more services directly to children and families, taking care of bad teeth and nutrition and abuse. We've got to do this now, in the preschools and elementary schools—and in fact, before the child is born, with good prenatal care for mothers. We can't do it later. There's no way."

—Sheila Mae Bender,
early childhood teacher ,
Louv, 1990, p. 343 as cited in
**The Report of the National Task
Force on School Readiness**

- Urge pediatricians to share with parents the importance of reading to their children as well as effective parenting strategies.

- Help parents know how to find quality early education programs.

- Support national accreditation of local child care centers.

- Encourage parents to utilize early intervention services when necessary.

- Support programs that help teen parents to complete their education and learn effective, appropriate parenting skills.

The Search Institute has identified a framework of 40 developmental assets for children and adolescents based on research regarding healthy child development. Developmental assets for infants, toddlers, preschoolers, and elementary age children can be found at www.search-institute.org. These assets include the child, the family, and the community. More information is detailed in Chapter One.

Referring Children for Additional or Varying Services

Sometimes, it becomes evident to an early childhood teacher that a child needs some additional support to succeed academically or socially. When teachers are aware of services in the community, they are better equipped to refer children to agencies, services, and programs to best meet the needs of each child. This becomes critical when the teacher is working in a program or school in which there are few support services (such as guidance counselors, social workers, or child psychologists). Without specialists in other disciplines, the early childhood teacher becomes the only qualified advocate for young children in the education system. When children have special needs, early childhood teachers and families alone cannot meet them. Additional professional advice and services are frequently necessary.

Referral is often required when children have difficulty in the classroom. Such difficulty may be academic, behavioral, or developmental. After ef-

forts to individualize have been attempted and when the teacher believes that more information is needed to best help the child, with family agreement, other appropriate professionals are called in to assist the child. Many referrals are related to the child's physical health including vision, hearing, or level of activity or inactivity. Other referrals may be related to immediate crises such as family financial difficulty, a death, illness, or other family transitions.

Referrals by the early childhood teacher most often need to be made in coordination with the program administrator. Effective administrators give support to teachers as they proceed through the referral process. Examples of early childhood programs in which services are integrated include Head Start, Comer Schools, the Kentucky Educational Reform Act (KERA), and most early intervention designs.

To recommend special services for a child, it is important that early childhood teachers follow appropriate procedures before, during, and after a conference with parents. Abbott and Gold (1991) note the following procedures.

1. Collect a great deal of objective data about the child's behavior and development. Keeping a file of the child's work can be very useful.

2. Arrange for a conference with the appropriate family members. Be sure to indicate the purpose for the conference. It is likely that this will not be the first conference you will have had with this family.

3. Be well prepared for your conference. Collect all work and notes you want to share. Think through what you will say and how you will say it. Discuss the changes that have been made to help the child in your classroom. Have information at the meeting about possible referral sources.

4. During the conference:
   - be sure the space is comfortable and private.
   - check with family members about their perceptions of the child's behavior or development that is of concern to you.
   - note that you will assist in exploring sources when all information leads to a logical conclusion that additional help would benefit

the child. Share resources available to your program or from your community.

- avoid the term "special education" because it is premature, and do not, under any circumstances, guess at a diagnosis.
- strive for agreement to have a specialist assess the child based on the data collected by you and the family.
- expect some emotion from the family. Keep your anxiety about this difficult topic in check. Use effective interpersonal communication skills.

5. Arrange for the assessment.

6. After the assessment, plan to meet with the family members to discuss the recommendations from the specialist and how you can best facilitate that implementation. In the case of a need for special education services, be sure to review and follow the procedures that have been mandated (Figure 10–4).

Program Models

Head Start

Started in 1965 with federal funding, Head Start remains a model comprehensive early childhood program. As its name indicates, this preschool program was originated because many children from economically distressed families were not doing well in school. The goal was to counter the effects of poverty for both young children and their families. Head Start emphasizes the whole child, including educational, medical, dental, nutritional, mental health, and family support services (Feeney, Christensen, & Moravcik, 1996) (Figure 10–5).

Head Start hires staff to coordinate all aspects of the program. It is common to see all Head Start staff, including food service workers and bus drivers, at professional development workshops that focus on child development. Head Start programs not only serve the children and families enrolled in the programs, but also are increasing local human resources in the broader community by offering training for

Problem	Appropriate Referral Agency/Person
Child behavior concerns	Child psychologist
Child nutrition concerns	Nutritionist, WIC, food stamp program
Child abuse	Human services agency, family therapist
Speech/language concerns	Speech therapist, speech clinic, health department hearing screening
Concern about vision	Health department vision screening, ophthalmologist
Chemical dependency	Health department, hospital
Domestic violence	Domestic violence shelter hot line, legal aid, family counseling, police
Creditor problems	Credit counselor
Utility payment difficulties	Community Action, United Way
Childhood illness	Health department, pediatrician, support group for specific illness
Developmental delays	Special education office, school district office, early intervention programs
Childhood poisonings	Health department lead screening clinic, poison control center
Family loss	Grief counselor

Figure 10–4 Problems and appropriate referral agency/person. (*Source:* Stephens, K. [1994, September/October]. Aiding families with referrals. *First Teacher*, 34–35)

Education—Head Start provides early childhood education through high-quality classroom experiences and regularly scheduled home visits to families.

Health—Head Start programs ensure timely immunizations; health screenings including vision, hearing, dental, and speech and language development; nutritious meals; and nutrition education for families.

Parent Involvement—Head Start empowers parents to be their child's first teacher, achieve leadership skills, join committees, and volunteer in the classroom. Employment possibilities with Head Start and training and financial support for continued education are additional options for family members.

Social Services—Head Start staff provides services and makes referrals to families that are undergoing crises that may be related to violence, substance abuse, physical or mental health needs, unemployment, and others.

Disabilities—Children with disabilities are included in the early education component. Therapies and services that are needed are coordinated through Head Start.

Family Literacy—Information is shared about general equivalency diplomas, adult basic education, and literacy programs. Parents are encouraged to read daily with their children.

Figure 10–5   Components of Head Start programs. (*Source: All About Head Start* produced by National Head Start Association)

job skills and by reducing the need for remedial programs and placement in correctional facilities (Lazar & Darlington, 1983; Schweinhart & Weikart, 1980).

Comer Schools

The Comer Schools were instituted in 1968 and led by James Comer in New Haven, Connecticut. Dr. Comer believes that for children to learn and succeed, all of their needs must be addressed. Using this emphasis on the whole child as his basis, he put in place successful public school reform (Weissbourd, 1996).

Weissbourd (1996) describes the two components that have made the Comer Schools successful as (1) school-based management teams comprised of an administrator, parents, and teachers and (2) a mental health team consisting of a social worker, a psychologist, a special education teacher, and a school counselor.

Active involvement on the part of families is another hallmark of the Comer model. This activity on the part of parents seems to have a positive effect on the children in the schools. With the excitement of both children and families, teachers and administra-

tors feel a sense of accomplishment. Essentially, the Comer Schools operate as communities that have been created to support children and their families.

Early Intervention

Programs of **early intervention** are those that are designated for children with special needs from birth to three years of age (Figure 10–6). Public law 99–457 requires that comprehensive services be provided for all eligible children. In addition to education for young children with disabilities, a variety of therapies and support services are included for them and their families.

"Times have changed. We have realized that our old views were too simple and our focus on the child needed to be expanded to include the family and its complex support network. The child-focused recipes have been supplemented or even supplanted by family-centered approaches to service."

—**McWilliam & Bailey, 1993**

The Program
Developmental Delays

Many children risk developmental delays due to premature births, abnormal muscle tone, seizure disorders, hydrocephalus, or other unidentified factors. Early intervention programs have proven to be highly effective with children who have virtually any type of developmental delays.

Benefits of Early Intervention

- Enhances the development of infants and toddlers with special needs.
- Provides a support network for families of children with developmental disabilities.
- Reduces the effect of developmental disabilities among infants and preschoolers.
- Lowers cost to society through the reduced need for special education programs in schools.

Space Coast early Intervention Center (SCEIC) Program

The focus of this unique program is an interdisciplinary approach which includes normally developing children in the classroom learning alongside their peers. This interaction allows for role-modeling from peers and prepares the children for the eventual mainstream experience. The team spirit nurtured at SCEIC encourages teachers and therapists to cross boundaries in a cooperative manner using the newest and most develop-mentally appropriate techniques employed in the field.

Infant Program—Birth to approximately 18 months. (Holmes Regional Medical Center provides this component of care.) The infant program concentrates on family involvement. The parents receive home programming suggestions from the therapists. These activities are designed to be implemented by the parents during the child's regular daily routine such as feeding, diapering, or bathing. An occupational therapist and speech/language pathologist provide one to two hours of therapy per week for each child and parent on an individual basis. This training is designed to be continued on a daily basis by the family, striving to influence de-velopmental gains through the home environment.

The families in the infant program receive an Individualized Family Support Plan (IFSP). This plan focuses on the needs and goals of the child and the family. The plan is reviewed and updated on a six-month cycle. Referrals for the infant program come from neonatologists and local area pediatricians.

Therapy is much more effective when parents and other care-givers follow through at home.

Transition Class—18 months to two years (provided by SCEIC). The transition class meets five mornings a week. The class focuses on motor developments, self-feeding skills, and ways to cope with the physical environment. The teachers, in conjunction with the therapists, aid the children in making choices, developing self-assurance and independence, and improving their language and cognitive skills.

Each family also receives an IFSP. Families, teachers, and therapists review and update each IFSP biannually and redevelop it every year.

Toddler Program—Two years to three years (provided by SCEIC). The toddlers come to the Center three mornings a week. The program focuses on age-appropriate and developmentally-appropriate activities for children to develop cognitive and social skills. This includes gross and fine motor, socialization, communication, cognitive, perceptual and feeding skills. An IFSP is also designed and updated for each child.

Preschool Program—Three years to six years (provided by SCEIC). The preschoolers attend five days a week. The preschool program focuses on pre-reading, pre-writing, and pre-math skills. The staff provides a whole realm of real-life and hands-on experiences that offer the environment to develop pre-readiness skills.

To accurately assess each child's progress, an Individualized Education Plan (IEP) is designed. Here, too, families, teachers, and therapists review and update this plan biannually.

Mainstreaming—A major difference between SCEIC and other programs is the concentration on mainstreaming and/or inclusion. The Center believes that the more children with special needs are involved

continues

Figure 10–6 Early intervention series—sample program. (With permission from Space Coast Early Intervention Center)

with their normally developing peers, the more it enhances their opportunities for learning the social skills necessary to help them be truly accepted.

SCEIC's children are fully integrated and share in activities such as story time, art projects, songs, finger play, snack time, and playground fun. All children are learning to share, take turns, and make friends in a cooperative environment. This approach helps children learn their own teaching skills and gain more self-confidence, which allows them to build a symbiotic relationship in the process. This is an important point, considering many of our children will be mainstreamed into the public schools. Our "typically developing" children learn that being different is acceptable and not something to be afraid of or shamed by.

Interacting with children with special needs and learning to accept them is a valuable experience for all children.

Socialization—Our Center gives the children opportunities for social interaction with members of the community. The children attend shows and concerts, and go to pet stores, restaurants, supermarkets, farms, and other real-life destinations. Regular field trips are essential to the growth and development of our children.

Our children have been invited to attend chamber of commerce events and other civic group meetings. Public awareness is crucial in order for all children to be accepted and valued. If the community has an awareness of what the Center does, and if children with special needs are able to participate in daily life activities, then people at large will be much more accepting.

Family Education & Support—Parent education and support is critical to the families involved at SCEIC. Mothers, fathers, foster parents, grandparents, and other family support members are viewed as vital to their child's development, as are the teachers and therapists on staff. Parents work with the staff to evaluate their child, set goals and objectives, implement the program to reach these goals, and reassess their child's progress. SCEIC provides the setting for parental involvement and education through class participation, consultations with staff members, and monthly support meetings where ideas can be shared. Support meetings offer a time for parents to interact with each other as well as with outside presenters and staff members. This networking provides an outlet for discussion of parental concerns specific to the family's needs.

Children deserve a chance to succeed in our society. We Need Your Help

SCEIC's efforts are made possible through funds received from individuals, organizations, foundations and corporations, as well as tuition and annual fund-raising. More than 80 percent of our budget directly benefits the children and less than 10 percent of our budget comes from state funding. Investments from our community are what allow us to continue our programs. For more information call (407) 729-6858.

Space Coast Early Intervention Center
3661 S. Babcock Street, Suite D
Melbourne, FL 32901
(407) 729-6858
http://www.sceic.com

Figure 10–6   continued.

Current recommended practice in early intervention typically concentrates on four areas.

1. *Family-centered practices.*   recognizes the family as central to each child's development.

2. *Practices with children.*   Considers each child's individual needs and strengths, engages children in developmentally appropriate experiences, and uses play as well as incidental experiences in teaching and learning.

3. *Inclusive practices.*   provides opportunities for young children with disabilities to interact and learn with typically developing young children.

4. *Collaboration in delivering services.*   coordinates an appropriate team of professionals to meet the needs of children and families such as special educators; early childhood educators; pediatricians; social workers; physical, speech, and occupational therapists; psychologists; and others (McWilliam & Bailey, 1993).

In order to emphasize a family-centered approach to early intervention services, a family strengths model has been advocated. The family strengths approach in early intervention is viewed as a very different way of working with families than has been typical in the recent past. Using this perspective, all professionals involved in providing services to children and families in early intervention programs would acknowledge the strengths existing in individual families, and they would attempt to build on those existing strengths. Professionals build trusting relationships with families so that they can be viewed as partners in the intervention process. The goal with the family strengths approach shifts from merely providing services to families to supporting and empowering families as they pursue solutions (Dunst, Trivette, & Mott, 1994).

Additionally, when assessing children for early intervention services, it is important to attend to various aspects of functioning that might be related to cultural, ethnic, religious, or language diversity. The diverse population in the United States makes it incumbent on professionals to consider the importance of cultural competence for both children and families. The role of families in early intervention may vary, based on diverse views and values of families. Professionals, as they work to build trusting relationships with families, will make note of differences. Respect must be given to both differences in families and the need that children and families have to be culturally competent (Guralnick, 2000).

Preschool Inclusion

Revisions in the Individuals with Disabilities Education Act (PL 105-17, IDEA) mandate that inclusive programs have highest priority for placement of children with special needs. **Preschool inclusion** programs are those classroom settings that enroll children with and without disabilities. Individual programs may describe additional requirements for their philosophies of inclusion so not all inclusive programs look alike. Some of these programs are found in public school systems, but many districts still do not offer preschool classes for typically developing children. Thus, more common places to find instances of preschool inclusion are in Head Start and community-based programs (Odom, 2002).

Successful preschool inclusion programs consider needs of children and families at all levels of Bronfenbrenner's systems (Odom, 2002). Research with families of children in inclusive programs has shown that the most common concern is that individual children's educational needs are met. As with all high-quality early childhood programs, partnerships between teachers (and other staff) and families is of great importance. Families of young children with disabilities face many decisions in terms of provision of services for their children. When preschool staff share information through frequent clear communication, families are able to make the best decisions for their children (Beckman, Hanson, & Horn, 2002).

Other Models

Other models exist in which teams of professionals from a variety of disciplines collaborate to make joint decisions with families about young children's education and care. Such teams have the advantage of regular meetings to share information and plan incrementally, depending on the needs of the child and family.

Instructional Support Teams. One example of an interdisciplinary model is the Pennsylvania model of team planning in public schools. In this model, the Instructional Support Team (IST) members are typically composed of the child's teacher, the building administrator, parents, counselor, and a certified teacher employed as an IST specialist from the school district. Usually, one of the team members expresses a concern about a child's development in some area and a meeting is called. At the meeting, all team members may express their concern or perspective. The team then arrives at a consensus or plan, which is implemented for a 30-day period. At the end of the 30-day period, the team is reconvened to assess and consider further options as needed.

United Way's Focus on Our Future. In York County, Pennsylvania, a successful child care initiative has been in place for several years. In 1995, three primary purposes were identified.

1. To focus attention on quality, affordable, available child care as integral to York County's human and economic infrastructure.

2. To assess community needs and develop an action agenda to improve early care and education for children and families.

3. To facilitate linkages among business, government, education, families, and others to move forward with a community action agenda.

After a great deal of study, the United Way's Focus on Our Future created three goals based on the national "trilemma" regarding child care and strategies for achieving the goals.

Goal 1:   Advance high-quality child care programs

- Adopt and implement quality standards for York County child care services

- Assist child care programs in achieving national accreditation

- Provide training to providers for achieving necessary competencies for national accreditation

- Develop a model to improve compensation for child care providers

- Provide parent education about quality child care

- Provide community education about the importance of quality child care

Goal 2:   Address the needs of unserved and underserved families seeking child care

- Increase the number of affordable quality child care spaces

- Provide support for providers to increase the number of spaces for infants and children with developmental disabilities

- Study the need for child care beyond traditional workdays

Goal 3:   Develop and support public and private efforts to make quality child care affordable

- Forge partnerships with public and private entities including churches and businesses

- Promote employer participation in family-supportive benefits

- Provide funding for tuition assistance for training child care providers

- Assist child care providers with cost-effective strategies

- Advocate for state and federal policies for expanding subsidized child care and support for early education

In its latest brochure, Focus on Our Future creatively used data from current brain research to compare Pennsylvania's spending on children at various stages. In an effort to get state policy makers to understand the importance of providing funding to early care and education programs, the brochure notes that 85 percent of brain development occurs by age three. View the following graph (Figure 10–7) and note the percentage of state spending on

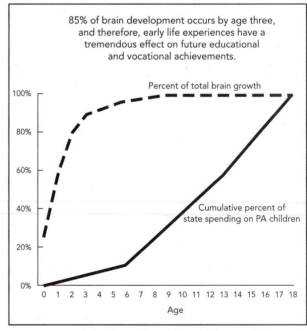

Figure 10–7   Graph viewing percent of total brain growth with cumulative percent of Pennsylvania state spending on children. (Estimates produced by Pennsylvania Partnerships for Children as part of the National Association of Child Advocates Children's Budget Watch project and reprinted with permission of the Pennsylvania Partnership for Children)

young children compared to later years. What's wrong with this picture?

Project Even Start. Even Start is a federally funded program with the following components:

- adult literacy (adult basic education or instruction for English language learners)
- parenting education
- early childhood education
- interactive parent and child literacy activities

Even Start supports family literacy services for parents and children, primarily from birth through age seven, and has three related goals:

1. To help parents improve their literacy or basic educational skills
2. To help parents become full partners in educating their children
3. To assist children in reaching their full potential as learners

Interdisciplinary Collaboration

Benefits

The benefits of **interdisciplinary collaboration** as described in the previous sections of this chapter are as follows:

- utilization of specialists to best help children and families
- a consensus-building method in which the team recommends a course of action as well as ways to implement it
- resource availability from a variety of sources

Challenges

While the benefits are extremely worthwhile, those who have worked at interdisciplinary collaboration have also met with challenges, some of which follow:

- coordination of a number of people for scheduling
- explanation of procedures and language pertinent to each discipline represented

- conflicting views about goals of education or understanding of how children learn
- a lack of or difficulty reaching a consensus about the best course of action to follow

Family-Centered Interprofessional Collaboration

A human services approach to create partnerships among families and professionals from diverse disciplines such as health, education, and social work is known as family-centered interprofessional collaboration. "Central to the family-centered interprofessional curriculum and practicum experience is the understanding that family empowerment and professional collaboration serve as building blocks to help families . . . beliefs will lead to effective, skilled, and caring family/professional interactions which will change the plight of children and families in the 21st century" (Davidson, Taba, Yamashita, & Ambrose, 1998, p. 3). Work in this interprofessional collaboration actually calls for a new paradigm for preparing human service workers, including early childhood teachers. "It is the teamwork and care that professionals and families offer to one another that enables all to identify, understand, and reach goals that ultimately benefit children and families" (p. 4). Collaborative efforts are quite complex, and it seems that when such a model is used in professional preparation, it is more likely that teachers, health providers, and social workers will implement interprofessional collaboration into their practice. It is likely that the wave of the future will be to include interprofessional collaboration models in early childhood teacher preparation programs.

The following principles are central to family-centered interdisciplinary collaboration (Davidson et al., 1998).

1. Family members and professionals work together to ensure interagency coordination to provide improved services for children and families.
2. Collaborators recognize and respect the knowledge, skills, and experiences that families and all professionals bring to the effort.

3. The development of trust is integral to the collaboration.

4. Open communication is expected so that all feel free to express themselves.

5. All cultural traditions, values, and family diversity are honored.

6. Negotiation is essential to collaboration.

7. The mutual commitment and shared vision of families, professionals, and communities serve children and families.

Collaboration is a drastically different way of providing services to families than what currently exists. It will take time before such a revolution vastly changes work with families. But the effort must begin somewhere. Early childhood professionals will be more prepared to meet the future if they can begin early in their preparation to understand and respect diversity, and to keep in perspective that families are children's first teachers and primary nurturers. Understanding families will be necessary for early childhood professionals in the new millennium.

> *"We in business, along with all segments of society, are increasingly aware of the vital significance the earliest years have on childhood development. High quality child care is a key component of a positive experience in those formative years. By supporting high quality child care for children of our employees, York County businesses gain in employee loyalty and help ensure that their children will grow to be constructive members of society."*
>
> —Louis J. Appell, Jr., President of Susquehanna Pfaltzgraff Co.

The Business Community

Some businesses have made a commitment to supporting family involvement in children's education. "'Family-friendly' businesses have at least one of the following policies: allowing time for employees to get involved with schools; initiating, implementing, and funding specific programs that promote family involvement in education; and providing resources to employees on how to become more involved in their own children's education" (Strong Families, Strong Schools, 1994, p. 31).

One way that some employers contribute to family involvement in education is through flextime. Several models for flextime exist. There may be core hours that are required, usually in the middle of the day such as 10:00 A.M. to 2:00 P.M. Employees can then choose to go to work early or to stay late. Some businesses allow for flextime at lunch, either by extending or shortening lunch and employees make up the difference in an agreed-upon manner. Following are other ways that employers support families:

- part-time positions
- job sharing
- alternative work schedules for full- or part-time employees
- flexible policies that allow for employee absences on the first day of school, school holidays, or to attend special events at school
- offering seminars and resources related to parenting and parent involvement in education
- child care options such as on-site care or vouchers for discounts at the center parents choose (Strong Families, 1994)

Another way that businesses link to education is through direct contributions of money or equipment to schools. Some businesses organize volunteer programs and encourage employees to volunteer in various ways for the schools in their communities. When business, education, and families link their efforts in these and many other ways, communities become more caring and everyone benefits.

Professionalism in Early Childhood Education

Knowledge Base

The basis for professionalism stems from a variety of sources. One major source for professional information in early childhood education can be found in the study of child development. Early childhood educators rely on their understanding of children's development when planning educational programs, building or furnishing environments, and in making recommendations to families.

In addition to this child development foundation, early childhood teachers also depend on pedagogical information from the field of early childhood education. Together, the National Association for the Education of Young Children (NAEYC) and the Division of Early Childhood (DEC) of the Council for Exceptional Children (CEC) have created a professional development document for their members (NAEYC, 1994). NAEYC has also developed a statement of professional ethics for those in the early childhood field (Feeney & Kipnis, 1989). These can be found in the appendices.

Continuing Professional Development

Professional standards and **professional ethics** are necessary in early childhood education because of the potential for abuse, neglect, or mistreatment of the very young children who are given by their families into the care of others. Without such standards, programs and teachers would be left to their own authority as the source of appropriate behavior. Professional conduct must ultimately be embodied in the teacher, caregiver, or administrator, but that does not mean that each early childhood staff member is to create his own standards with each incident or situation.

By using professional standards and ethics, early childhood teachers are able to engage in the best known practices. It is through such a professional community that highest standards can be con-

> *"It is everyone's responsibility to be committed to education. And it shouldn't be limited to parents—anyone in the community should be encouraged to think of the local school as 'their' school and should seek active participation in what goes on there."*
>
> —Lois Jean White, 1998
> **National PTA president**

tinuously defined and revised in the best interest of children and their families. Such a professional community is a source of support and guidance for practicing early childhood teachers. According to the systems approach, teachers of young children benefit from such support. In turn, children and families benefit from the work of the early childhood professional community.

Community Update

The United States Department of Education has created a newsletter initiative, *Community Update*. Published by the Office of Intergovernmental and Interagency Affairs, this newsletter highlights projects and programs that intend to connect families and communities with schools. For example, one program that receives annual attention is America Goes Back to School, sponsored by the Partnership for Family Involvement in Education. Ideas for activities as well as resources are made available. A primary objective for the America Goes Back to School movement is to mobilize communities to support quality education.

Community Update also highlighted the America Reads Challenge. This project, which challenges all citizens to help all children learn to read, is intended to improve literacy by focusing on three primary areas.

1. *Before kindergarten*—It is never too early to read to a child. Pediatricians and family practitioners should recommend books and how to use them with very young children. Communities should hold book drives for child care centers, and volunteers are needed to read to children in a variety of early childhood settings, including child care, Head Start, preschool, and library programs.

2. *K–3 students*—Tutors and reading partners are needed for children to help them practice reading on a weekly basis. Communities and schools can sponsor summer programs to help children catch up or build on skills.

3. *Family literacy*—Communities must provide programs for parents and other adults to learn to read well so that they, in turn, can help their

Parents should read daily with their children.

children do well in school. Parents who are literate can also be better role models for their children.

An additional program highlighted in *Community Update* is Making After-School Count. How and where children spend their time before and after school makes a difference in their attitude and sometimes in their aptitude for school. Communities are urged to provide safe, healthy, high-quality programs for children on both ends of the school day. Teachers, administrators, and business and community leaders are encouraged to work together to accomplish the following goals:

- to build community partnerships to support quality before- and after-school programs

- to identify sources of funding for this endeavor

- to increase access to these programs for families in middle- and low-income neighborhoods

- to keep school buildings open longer to provide quality extended learning programs

The presence of quality before- and after-school programs can be a major source of support for young children's parents whose work schedules make it difficult to coordinate with the typical school day. When these programs are held in the school building, children have fewer transitions and greater continuity through their days. Caregivers in programs must be well-trained in early childhood education and should link with children's teachers to optimize the academic help they give. Further, before- and after-school care providers in high-quality programs will communicate with parents of children in the program, both in formal and informal ways. In other words, these programs cannot just be tacked onto both ends of the school day and stand alone. There must be school and family involvement.

The Movement to Leave No Child Behind

Under the leadership of Marian Wright Edelman, the Children's Defense Fund has initiated a public awareness campaign. leave No Child Behind attempts to create a climate that will encourage action by policy makers on children's agenda. Included in the agenda are the following issues:

- child care and Head Start

- education

- family education

- nutrition

- housing

- child welfare

- gun safety

For more information about the status of this initiative, go to www.childrensdefense.org/.

Summary and Conclusions

Early childhood educators must form partnerships, not only with families but also with members of the larger community. Connections among early childhood program professionals, agency personnel, and the business community will serve to increase support and services to young children and their families. The support of the entire community for high-quality early childhood education will encourage excellence. Moving beyond home and school partnerships, relationships with the community are needed to provide a caring society for children and families. Knowledge about community resources is essential as early childhood educators attempt to meet the needs of all children and families in their care. Since its inception, early intervention for young children with identified disabilities has used a collaborative model.

Collaborative efforts between education and business have shown to be extremely beneficial to children, families, education, and the community. Although often seen as challenging work, collaboration often leads to positive results for all entities. Educational programs often become more effective with the deep knowledge that is gained when teachers work with other community members. Families, schools, and communities, working together for young children, can support and nurture each other.

Key Terms

community resources interdisciplinary collaboration
referral professional standards
early intervention professional ethics
preschool inclusion

Chapter Ten Applications

1. Role-play a conference with family members whose children have demonstrated the following behavior in the early childhood education program:
   a. nearly always choosing to play alone
   b. increasingly aggressive behaviors with peers
   c. frequent negative moods
2. List and describe all of the components of the comprehensive early childhood education program Head Start. What do you see as the benefits to children and families enrolled in this type of program?
3. Explain why early childhood teachers should not label children or guess at a diagnosis.

Questions for Reflection and Discussion

1. What concerns would you have about meeting with family members to discuss referring their child for special services? What are the benefits of such referrals?
2. What are the characteristics of a professional in early childhood education?
3. List and discuss benefits and potential conflicts in collaborative efforts.

Field Assignments

1. Visit a Head Start or early intervention program. If possible, ask about the role community members and community agencies play in the program. What agency sponsors the program? Are any volunteers involved?
2. Collect information about resources available in your community (or the one in which you plan to teach) that would be helpful to families of young children.
3. Interview an early childhood teacher about his involvement in any interdisciplinary collaboration. Ask about the challenges and the benefits of such work.

References

Abbott, C. F., & Gold, S. (1991). Conferring with parents when you're concerned that their child needs special services. *Young Children, 46*(4), 10–14.

Beckman, P. J., Hanson, M. J., & Horn, E. (2002). Family perceptions of inclusion. In S. L. Odom (Ed.), *Widening the circle: Including children with disabilities in preschool programs.* New York: Teachers College Press.

Davidson, D., Taba, S., Yamashita, L., & Ambrose, A. (1998). *Bridging out: Lessons learned in family-centered interprofessional collaboration.* Honolulu: Health and Education Collaboration Project, Hawaii Medical Association.

Dunst, C. J., Trivette, C. M., & Mott, D. W. (1994). Strengths-based family-centered intervention practices. In C. J. Dunst, C. M. Trivette, & A. G. Deal

(Eds.), *Supporting and strengthening families, volume 1: Methods, strategies and practices.* Cambridge, MA: Brookline.

Feeney, S., Christensen, D., & Moravcik, E. (1996). *Who am I in the lives of children?* Englewood Cliffs, NJ: Prentice-Hall.

Feeney, S., & Kipnis, K. (1989). Code of ethical conduct and statement of commitment. *Young Children, 45*(1), 24–29.

Guidelines for preparation of early childhood professionals. (1996). Washington, DC: National Association for the Education of Young Children.

Guralnick, M. J. (2000). Interdisciplinary team assessment for young children: Purposes and processes. In M. J. Guralnick (Ed.), *Interdisciplinary clinical assessment of young children with developmental disabilities.* Baltimore: Paul H. Brookes Publishing Co.

Lazar, I., & Darlington, R. (1983). *As the twig is bent: Lasting effects of preschool programs.* Hillsdale, NJ: Lawrence Erlbaum Associates.

Massinga, R. (1994). Transforming social services: Family-supportive strategies. In S. L. Kagan & B. Weissbourd (Eds.), *Putting families first: America's family support movement and the challenge of change.* San Francisco: Jossey-Bass.

McWilliam, P. J., & Bailey, D. B., Jr. (1993). *Working together with children & families: Case studies in early intervention.* Baltimore: Paul H. Brookes Publishing Co.

National Association for the Education of Young Children (1994). *Personnel standards for early education and early intervention: A position statement of the Association of Teacher Educators, the Division for Early Childhood and the National Association of the Education of Young Children.* Washington, DC: author.

Odom, S. L. (2002). Learning about the barriers to and facilitators of inclusion for young children with disabilities. In S. L. Odom (Ed.), *Widening the Circle: Including children with disabilities in preschool programs.* New York: Teachers College Press.

Ready schools. (1998, February). Washington, DC: National Education Goals Panel.

Schweinhart, L. J., & Weikart, D. P. (1980). *Young children grow up: The effects of the Perry Preschool on youth through age 15.* Ypsilanti, MI: High/Scope Foundation.

Search Institute. (2000). www.search-institute.org

Stephens, K. (1994, September/October). Aiding families with referrals. *First Teacher,* 34–35.

Strong Families, Strong Schools. (1994). Washington, DC: U.S. Department of Education.

Washington, V., Johnson, V., & McCracken, J. B. (1995). *Grassroots success! Preparing schools and families for each other.* Washington, DC: National Association for the Education of Young Children.

Weissbourd, R. (1996). *The vulnerable child.* New York: Addison-Wesley.

CASE STUDIES

The following five case studies are intended to be used in a variety of ways by the instructor and students using this textbook. The authors believe that they provide some situational dilemmas commonly experienced by many early childhood teachers. They can be used for a one-time discussion or repeated as greater knowledge, skills, and experience lead to greater depth of understanding by students.

CASE 1

The Teacher

Tricia Clooney graduated two years ago with a bachelor's degree in elementary and early childhood education. She is certified in her state to teach pre-kindergarten through the eighth grade. In her senior year of college, Tricia was assigned to an infant center for her pre-primary field experience. This practicum was a turning point for Tricia, in that now she knew just the age group with which she wanted to work. Being outgoing and independent, Tricia enjoyed the flexible child care environment with some routine and new challenges everyday. She not only enjoyed the infants but also found that she was very competent at working with families.

The Early Childhood Program and the Community

Soon after graduation, Tricia was hired as one of three infant teachers at Grasshopper Hill Child Care Center. She was thrilled. The director, who received her degree in elementary education eight years prior, oversees 60 children and 12 staff members, some of them part time. She has been directing this center for five years; before that, she worked for two years as a kindergarten teacher in another center. Although some of the other teachers in the center have professional preparation as early childhood teachers, Tricia's two colleagues in the infant room, Lil and Roxie, have high school diplomas and regularly attend required training sessions. Roxie is the veteran teacher in this group, with five years' experience with infants at this center. Lil started working in this room just three months before Tricia was hired.

Grasshopper Hill Child Care Center is located in a rural area of southern Indiana. Most of the families who enroll their children at this center are employed in the nearby town of Summitsville. Major employers in Summitsville include a hospital, mall stores, public schools, a textile factory, and several restaurants.

Tricia's Dilemma

Tricia began her work at the center with very high hopes. She carefully studied about developmentally appropriate practices during her early childhood teacher preparation. Under-standing the importance of an infant's environment and the necessity of interacting with babies as they are cared for, Tricia approached her work very seriously and enthusiastically. Some of the staff who had been there for a while expected that as Tricia "got her feet wet," her enthusiasm would decline and she would treat her work as a job, not as a calling. Two years later, Tricia is still enthusiastic and serious about caring for infants. At times, Lil has been known to roll her eyes as Tricia shares the latest information about brain development during a child's first three years. Roxie, though, listens and asks questions. Together, Tricia and Roxie work to implement best practices; Lil does her job caring for babies, completing necessary paperwork and interacting with parents as necessary. Having just completed a graduate course that included information about the family support movement, Tricia was eager to add to the center's existing family involvement plan. She had many ideas and lots of energy to work on them.

Tricia discussed with the director the possibility of creating a family resource room in a small storage area that was no longer used by staff. Additionally, she wanted to incorporate both family social events and programs for parent education at Grasshopper Hill. Lil finally spoke up, "How can we give the best care to babies and do all that work required for your family involvement ideas? I think that we'll begin to forget that the babies need us. Some of our babies' families don't even have time for them as it is. We need to pay attention to these babies, not to their parents. That's not our job." Even though Roxie found Tricia's ideas to be interesting, she had to admit that she wasn't sure when they would find the time in their very busy days to do even more. And she had to admit that she liked this job because of the babies; she wasn't sure that she enjoyed working with adult members of their families.

Tricia's Reaction

Although not completely surprised by Lil's and Roxie's concerns, Tricia was disappointed that they did not seem to want to try to provide more support for families at Grasshopper Hill. Tricia empathized with the moms, dads, and grandparents who sometimes seemed to feel guilty as they dropped off their infants, and most often seemed exhausted when they picked them up after the day's work. Tricia sometimes helped her sister, who is a young professional and the single parent of a toddler; she knew firsthand the challenges that working parents face because they want to provide the best care possible for their young children.

Tricia responded to Lil's comments from her own life experiences. She noted that life is difficult for parents as they try to balance their work and family obligations. Lil also responded from her life experiences: "Parents today want it all. They aren't willing to do without new homes, new cars, and vacations. They let us raise their children because they can't be bothered." These comments did surprise Tricia. She had not realized how different her viewpoint about families was from Lil's.

Tricia had permission from the director to set up a parent resource room and to begin to plan for family events at the center. She intended to conduct a needs assessment of families who had children enrolled in the infant and toddler rooms at Grasshopper Hill. Lil informed Tricia that she was not willing to work on her own time to help with any of these events. Roxie was torn; she did not feel as though she could use her personal time to work on family involvement, but she might be able to help during work hours. Lil warned both Tricia and Roxie that caring for the babies was what they were hired to do.

1. Explain the perspective of each of the three teachers: Tricia, Lil, and Roxie. With which do you most identify?

2. Discuss your life experiences that may affect the perspective you take in this situation.

3. Using information from this textbook, explain how incorporating family support programs with early childhood education may benefit families, schools, and communities.

CASE 2

The Teacher

Amy Gottleib completed her bachelor's degree in early childhood education. She was an honor student all through high school, and she received some criticism from the guidance counselor as well as some of her teachers when she shared her dream of teaching young children. "You're too smart for that," they commented. Her parents and siblings all had graduate degrees and worked as professionals in a variety of fields including engineering and business. However, they supported her desire to teach. During her student teaching experiences, Amy was all the more encouraged to teach in one of the primary grades. She loved being in the classroom with first and second graders. Her cooperating teachers and university supervisors were impressed with Amy's seemingly natural rapport with these young children.

In Amy's teacher preparation program, an emphasis was placed on the importance of family involvement. Many strategies were included for ways to involve families in their children's education. Research was shared that pointed to the importance of family involvement for children's academic success.

The Early Childhood Program and the Community

After graduation in December, Amy was a popular substitute teacher in her home school district. She was called nearly every day before the winter break. At the end of the month, a principal called to ask her to serve as a long-term substitute for a second-grade teacher. She immediately agreed to take this position, even though this school served mostly children from upper middle-class families. Amy's preference had always been teaching children from less privileged backgrounds because she felt they needed her more than others did.

The South Shore School District is made up of a large area, some of it rural and some of it suburban. Since children attend neighborhood schools in this district, school populations tend to be economically homogeneous. The elementary schools have kindergarten through fifth grades. The school in which Amy is employed, Golden Oaks, has three classrooms of each grade and a fairly traditional approach to education. Many teachers have been employed at this school for 20 or more years. They have a reputation for high expectations and no nonsense. The principal, Mr. Brooks, is in his first year as principal after teaching seventh grade in a neighboring district for five years. Amy, now called Ms. Gottleib, is stepping into a second-grade class that had been taught by Ms. Nan Notting. Ms. Notting had taught 30 years; she was known as an effective teacher who was firm with children and held high standards.

Family Involvement Traditions at Golden Oaks

Golden Oaks Elementary School has a history of a very strong Parent Teacher Association group. The primary function of this group has been fund-raising. The money this group has raised has been used to purchase computers and other technology, as well as to provide for more field trips than the district can financially support. In addition to fund-raising, parents have assisted with holiday parties and other events when teachers felt a need for more adult supervision. Essentially, family involvement at Golden Oaks has centered on parents, especially mothers, supporting teachers and curriculum. Most often, parents initiated the carrying out of this function, not school personnel.

Ms. Gottlieb's Approach

Amy spent a great deal of time planning for and reflecting about her new position before her actual beginning day, January 4. Amy had carefully written lesson plans for the entire first week of school. She had spent time in the classroom arranging the environment and getting acquainted with curriculum materials that were available to her. Amy implemented a hands-on program with several learning centers. She interacted frequently with the large group, as well as small groups and individual children. She greeted the children in the morning and said good-by to them at dismissal. Her rapport was excellent. The children liked her and were eager to do their work. Ms. Gottleib challenged her students with projects and supported their interests.

Additionally, Amy drafted a letter to family members, introducing herself and inviting them to participate in the classroom in several different ways. She enclosed an interest survey for parents to complete and sent the letter and survey home with the children on her first day.

By the end of the week, Amy had received only four of the twenty-two interest surveys she sent to parents. She was surprised and concerned about this, but she was also very busy with other teaching responsibilities. Over the weekend, she decided that she would send a reminder home to the parents on Monday.

Some Reactions to Amy's Ideas

On Tuesday morning, Amy received three completed family interest surveys and a note from an unhappy mother regarding the survey. The note read, "Ms. Gottleib, I don't understand the reason for this survey. You are the teacher. Ms. Notting did all of the teaching without parental assistance. I hope that you are capable of teaching our children at Golden Oaks. Sincerely,

Gloria Noteworthy." At the end of the day, Mr. Brooks called Amy into his office. After some polite conversation, he asked her how things were going. Although she was feeling a little disconcerted about Gloria Noteworthy's comments, she shared her enthusiasm for teaching the second graders. Mr. Brooks gave some positive feedback he had heard from some other teachers about Ms. Gottleib's attitude. Then he shared with her that Ms. Noteworthy had complained to him about the parent interest survey. She also told him that she had phoned three mothers who had children in the same class and that they all resented receiving this survey from the "new teacher."

Amy's Reaction

Now, Amy was really stunned. It had not occurred to her that inviting parents to participate in their children's education could be seen in any negative way. She absolutely believed that children had more success when teachers formed partnerships with family members. She sent the interest survey for the sole purpose of being the best teacher she could be. It was a surprise to her that a parent would interpret this letter and survey as her inability to teach their children. She was hurt, confused, and a little less confident in herself after this situation.

1. Explain the perspectives of Ms. Gottlieb, Ms. Notting, Ms. Noteworthy, and Mr. Brooks. With which do you most identify?

2. Discuss your life experiences that may have influenced the way you think about this scenario.

3. Using information from your textbook, discuss why inviting family involvement and collecting information about the interests of family members are often useful strategies for early childhood teachers.

CASE 3

The Teacher

Rick Ramirez completed requirements for a state teaching certificate in early childhood education. He had returned to college after working for three years in accounting. Rick received a bachelor's degree in business, and after some experience, decided that he really wanted to teach. He had always appreciated the special characteristics of young children but never really considered a career in education. He and his wife have a four-year-old daughter and a six-month-old son. Spending time with his own children influenced his decision to become certified in early childhood education.

Rick excelled in and enjoyed his student teaching experiences. He was placed with a kindergarten teacher, Sally Aysse, who loved her job. Together, they planned and implemented a full-day program based on developmentally appropriate practices. The children learned as they played. The classroom had many print materials and appropriate software for use by the children. Children made choices regarding learning centers and projects. Rick was aware of how effective this active learning environment was for young children.

Ms. Aysse and Mr. Ramirez collected work samples and provided portfolios to share children's progress with their family members. Parents frequently volunteered in the classroom and the teachers had frequent interaction with nearly every family. Having this experience as well as other field experiences associated with his early childhood education coursework, Rick was confident and believed that he was very prepared to teach young children.

The Early Childhood Program and the Community

Rick interviewed for a kindergarten position with a private school, Harmony Academy, in the city of Harmony. The school was well established in this urban setting, providing education for children from kindergarten through 12th grade for nearly 50 years. Rick felt that he had interviewed well with the principal. Members of the board, including parents and community professionals, also interviewed all prospective teachers for Harmony Academy. Although that proved to be a challenge, Rick thought that he had demonstrated what he knew about teaching young children as best he could.

Three weeks passed before the principal phoned Rick to offer him a job teaching kindergarten at Harmony. Although the salary was somewhat less than that of the suburban public schools in the area, Rick rationalized that the school was close to his urban home and he would save money by using public transportation. Besides, at this time, there were no other kindergarten positions in the area; Rick realized he especially wanted to teach children this age.

Rick's New Job

Two weeks before the start of school, Harmony Academy scheduled professional development for all teachers. In the morning, teachers met in interest groups, and in the afternoon, they worked to prepare their classrooms. Rick decided to join interest groups so that he could get to know the other early childhood teachers at Harmony. It turned out that neither the other kindergarten teacher nor the first- and second-grade teachers had early childhood certification. Both first-grade teachers were elementary certified, the kindergarten teacher had a degree in social work, one second grade teacher was certified to teach English at the secondary level, and the other second grade teacher had a business degree and was currently enrolled in a teacher intern program at a nearby college. Rick soon found that his early childhood education vocabulary did not mean much to his colleagues. He became more reticent and listened carefully to the words of his colleagues.

Rick began to really look forward to the afternoons and setting up his kindergarten room. He clustered desks and chairs to make some group arrangements, and he set up six learning centers around the room. On the third afternoon, Sandy Yates came by the classroom and introduced herself as a classroom aide for kindergarten and first grades. She had been assigned to work in Mr. Ramirez's kindergarten every Wednesday. After introducing herself, Sandy volunteered to place the desks and chairs in rows and to make name tags for the back of each child's chair, noting that that is what she typically did to help the kindergarten teachers. Rick was aghast that a classroom aide would suggest changing his room arrangement but responded that he would like to have name tags for each child to wear on the first day of school. After Rick and Sandy decided how to construct the name tags, Sandy worked on them and Rick went back to his desk.

Education at Harmony Academy

By the first day of school for the children, Rick had come to realize that the philosophy of his teacher education preparation and his beliefs about how young children learn best were not common among the teachers at Harmony. The other primary teachers had not been exposed to current best practices in early childhood education; some of them used the same teaching methods their own elementary teachers had used many years ago. Harmony Academy had such a reputation for excellence that Rick could hardly believe these teachers' viewpoints. The principal of the school had experience at the secondary level and concerned herself much more with the curriculum and teachers for 10th, 11th, and 12th grades. She was not readily available to any of the primary teachers, so Rick had had little contact with her, even during the two weeks of professional development.

Kindergarten children came to school on buses with the older children. Because many families were dual-career, the board had decided several years ago to establish full-day kindergarten programs at Harmony. Because Rick realized that he would not have a ready opportunity to meet his children's parents, he phoned each family before the start of school. He had many short, pleasant conversations with parents, but he also left messages for four families that had not been returned.

The first day of kindergarten brought 18 five-year-olds into Rick's classroom. He greeted them and met with them on the circle rug to inform them about the day's schedule. Each child had a turn to tell about how he or she got ready and came to kindergarten that day. For most of the day, children were actively engaged in learning centers. They spent some time outdoors and had two large group story times. Rick had renewed confidence about his ability to teach by the time the children left for the day.

Rick's First Official Feedback

On Wednesday of the first week of school, Sandy Yates was in Mr. Ramirez's kindergarten to assist him. He had a plan for her to work with individual children at two different learning centers and then to be stationed near the large climbing apparatus during outdoor time. He also asked her to copy some letters he was sending home to parents and to place the letters in the children's cubbies.

Friday morning before the children arrived at school, the principal had left a message for Rick to come by her office at 3:45, the end of the school day. Surprised by the message, Rick got through the school day with a little anxiety. At 3:45, he met Mrs. Rivers in her office. She apologized for seeing so little of him his first days on the job and then asked how he was doing. Mrs. Rivers was surprised by Rick's enthusiasm for teaching the kindergartners. She was expecting him to state concerns about how best to teach these young children. After she recovered from her surprise, she informed him that Sandy Yates had come to her with some concerns that she and two of the children's parents had about too much playtime in Rick's kindergarten day. It seemed that several people had a lot of concern that children in this kindergarten class would not be learning what they were expected to know as students at Harmony Academy.

Rick's Reaction

Initially, Rick was confused. He had had almost no contact with Mrs. Rivers since he had been hired. Other than some workbooks in the classroom, few curriculum materials existed. Rick had expected that since he had specialized preparation in early childhood education that he might serve as a model for the other teachers, even though they had more experience than he did. Now, he was being criticized because he was applying a model in his classroom consistent with current best practices.

Sometime during the evening, it occurred to Rick that he had plenty of information to share with the principal, the classroom aide, his colleagues, and parents of the kindergarten children. He devised a plan for writing and sending a letter to parents each week that would explain the importance of play and active learning for children in this stage of devel-

opment. Rick also shared similar information with the others who expressed concern about his methods.

Rick learned from the other kindergarten teacher that they each had a small allowance to purchase books and materials. He decided to purchase information for parents—books and brochures—to help them understand how children think and reasons for their behavior.

Reaction of Others

Principal Rivers' belief was that kindergarten was not really very important and she did not want to invest a lot of her time with the issue of play in kindergarten. She was rarely seen and very remote regarding this issue. Sandy Yates remained skeptical about the value of play; however, she did as she was asked in Mr. Ramirez's classroom because she wanted to keep her job. Some parents found the information on play to be not only interesting, but relevant to what they observed in their children. Several of these parents began to actively support Mr. Ramirez's approach to teaching. Other parents continued to question him and state concerns throughout the year. Slowly, a few more parents came to believe that just maybe, Mr. Ramirez knew what he was doing.

1. Explain the perspectives of Mrs. Rivers, Ms. Yates, Mr. Ramirez, and the kindergarten parents. With which view do you most easily identify?

2. Discuss your life experiences that may have influenced your perspective on this issue.

3. Using information from the textbook, discuss ways in which teachers might effectively share information regarding children's development and how they learn.

CASE 4

The Teacher

Jenny Kim was just completing an associate degree in early childhood education from her county community college. During her two years of teacher preparation, Jenny had many hours of experience at the campus child care center. She completed the required practicum there and had also been employed as a student assistant to help staff the center in late afternoons. Jenny often had opportunities to interact with parents and other family members when they came to pick up their children. She began to feel quite comfortable chatting with parents, informing them about how their child's day had gone, and taking messages for the morning child care staff.

Jenny had been required to visit other early childhood settings. She spent at least two hours in an early intervention program, a Montessori preschool, Head Start, and a United Way-funded child care center. With the information she gained from her coursework and from these visits, Jenny knew that her goal was to be a lead teacher in a Head Start program in the nearest city, New Rock.

After her graduation in May, she accepted a position with a YWCA summer camp program, leading the pre-kindergarten group. Later in the summer, she interviewed for a position with Head Start. Jenny was offered a position as assistant teacher. Even though she wanted a lead teacher position, she accepted the offer and began her Head Start work in the middle of August.

The Early Childhood Program and the Community

New Rock has a large Head Start program. Twenty preschool classrooms exist in various parts of the city. Home-based programs are also a part of the New Rock Head Start. With a population of about 100,000, New Rock has a variety of communities, some of them more economically prosperous than others. Also, some neighborhoods are more culturally diverse than others. All of the Head Start preschools are held in churches and agency buildings in the downtown area. Transportation is provided for all of the children enrolled in the program.

Jenny was assigned to be an assistant teacher in Alice Jones' room. Ms. Alice has been a lead teacher for four years. She accepted this position after she worked for two years as an assistant teacher and completed her bachelor's degree in child development. Ms. Alice greeted Jenny at the beginning of their week of professional development meetings before the start of school. Jenny was pleased to hear that the classroom she would be working in was based on developmentally appropriate practices. The campus child care center from which she gained most of her experience had been accredited by the National Academy of Early Childhood Programs, so Jenny had developed many skills that would be useful in her new job.

Jenny in Head Start

The night before the first day for children to come to school, Jenny could hardly sleep. She was very excited that she would be working in Head Start. Alice and Jenny worked together to plan for all aspects of the first day. Jenny believed that Alice valued her contribution and that she could make a difference in the lives of the children.

The first week of school was everything that Jenny had hoped it would be. She loved the children, she felt capable, and Alice was an excellent role model. At the end of the week, when Jenny and Alice had their daily planning meeting, Alice mentioned that next week parents would be volunteering in the classroom. One of their tasks was to assign parents to specific days and times, as well as to think through in advance what the parents could do to contribute in the classroom. Alice had already collected information from them about their interests and available times.

Jenny remembered reading about the importance of family involvement to the Head Start program. There had even been a guest speaker from New Rock College during professional development week who had provided innovative strategies for involving families in their children's education. Although she had experience interacting with family members, it was rare at the campus child care center that parents came to the classroom to volunteer. There seemed little need for more adults when staff and students provided very good ratios of adults to children. The child care center did have some meetings and events for family members, but since they were often at the same time as Jenny had a class, she had not attended them.

During the second week of the Head Start year, many parents and other family members volunteered in the classrooms. Each day, there were at least three adult volunteers in the classroom. Alice had organized a chart in advance and directed each volunteer throughout the course of the day. Everything seemed to be well organized and to flow; Alice was as adept at working with the adults as she was with the children. At the beginning of the next week, Alice was ill; the director asked Jenny if she could take over as lead teacher for the few days Alice expected to be out and to have the volunteers as assistants. Jenny agreed to this plan; she was actually pleased to have the opportunity to "be in charge" for a few days.

As children and parents entered the classroom on Jenny's first day of lead teacher duty, she greeted them all. Most of the children and all of the adults seemed happy to be there. Jenny had carefully planned a group time that would have the children actively involved and then easily tran-

sition the children into learning center activities. The parents who were volunteering that day included one mother, Lois LeGrange; one father, Pete Stovall; and one grandmother, Felicia Sanchez. Lois was assigned to the blocks center, Pete to the art center, and Felicia to the dramatic play center. Lois and Pete sat on chairs at the periphery of each of their centers and next to each other. Soon after the children were busy at play, the two parents started talking with one another. This continued, even when children were asking them questions and in need of some direction or redirection. Although Jenny could not be sure, it seemed that they were talking about Felicia. They looked in her direction on occasion and then talked some more. Jenny did not think that she should intervene in this situation in front of the children, so she chose to ignore it. A few minutes later, Felicia raised her voice and threatened to "send you to time out if you don't stop that." Again, although Jenny was uncomfortable with this approach to disciplining children in the classroom, she did not want to correct the adult in the presence of children. She began to feel very nervous and stressed. By the end of the day, Jenny was questioning whether having family volunteers in the classroom was such a good idea. It seemed to work for Alice, but she'd rather have just the teachers in the classroom.

---

1. Explain the perspectives of Alice, Jenny, Lois, Pete, and Felicia. With which of these viewpoints do you most easily identify?

2. Discuss your life experiences that might relate to the perspective you have taken for this scenario.

3. Referring to the textbook, what knowledge and skills might help Jenny feel more prepared to work with family volunteers in the classroom?

The Teacher

Olivia Ali married right out of high school. She and her husband had three children in eight years. When her youngest child entered first grade, Olivia enrolled in college. In a neighboring town, just 12 miles away, a state university offered a degree in early childhood special education. Olivia knew she wanted to teach; she researched the job market for education majors and found that teachers in this area were likely to be in demand for quite some time. In just six years, Olivia would complete her degree. This meant that she could be employed in a teaching position before their oldest child began college.

During her teacher preparation program, Olivia learned a great deal about children's development, various disabilities and their effects on children and families, and the importance of an interdisciplinary, family-focused philosophy for programs of early intervention. She had opportunities for observation and participatory field experiences in a variety of early childhood settings, some of them inclusive, and others that enrolled only typically developing children or children with identified disabilities. She observed a variety of teaching strategies and teachers with varied kinds of preparation and levels of experience.

Olivia's research paid off. As soon as she graduated, she interviewed for two positions and had offers to teach in both of them. She chose the position that was closest to her home. She would be a member of an interdisciplinary team for an inclusive early intervention program with primary responsibilities for the education component. Most of her work would be planning, implementing, and assessing an educational program for three small groups of children ages one to three years. She was very excited about teaching and

evaluating the children's progress. Olivia also was responsible for a home-based program for infants identified as having a disability and their families. Many hours were also to be spent with an interdisciplinary team, planning and evaluating services for every child and every family.

The Early Childhood Program and the Community

The inclusive early intervention program that hired Olivia is supported by state and federal funds. The local school district is the contact point for the program, with the district's director of special education having a supervisory role over the early intervention coordinator. Twenty children are being served by the center-based program and 12 children are enrolled in the home-based program. Of the 20 center-based children, four are typically developing and 16 have identified disabilities such as pervasive developmental disorder, Asperger's Disorder, Down Syndrome, and cerebral palsy. All of the home-based children have identified disabilities.

Briarville is a small town with a population of about 22,000 and sparsely populated rural areas nearby. Families do not often migrate from the area, so many families have lived there for several generations. Education is not always as high a priority as most of the local educators would like, but there has been a lot of support for the early intervention program. Concern about children with disabilities and their families is evident in Briarville. Fund-raisers have been successful, and the local newspapers and radio station have provided publicity.

Olivia's Doubt

Before long, Olivia's pleasure about getting the position she wanted turned to concern. She did not enjoy or feel confident in the team meetings. The physical therapist, occupational therapist, speech therapist, psychologist, and family services coordinator all seemed to know exactly what each child needed. Sometimes, one or more of them seemed to dominate the session. When she explained the play-based curriculum that she had been prepared to implement, the others passed it off as fluff. They questioned her about what she was teaching, both in her small group sessions and in her home-based plans. At times, one of the therapists would come to her classroom and pull a child out for therapy that was missed earlier in the week for some reason or other. This would occur without advance planning or notice.

Further, nearly all of the parents (or another family member) stayed with their children during the two-hour preschool sessions that were held twice each week. So, instead of Olivia teaching four or five children in her classroom, she was coordinating family members and providing assignments for them to complete with their children during the remainder of the week. Often, there would be five or six adults in the classroom and just four children. This role of teacher was very different from the one Olivia had envisioned for herself. She wanted to teach children, not be a family services coordinator. In her frustration, she began to question why families of these young children could not just let them come to preschool for four hours a week. She would be glad to compose newsletters, call families as necessary, and have conferences with them. But she began to resent their presence. Just when she organized the children for a short group time, invariably one or more of the children would go to their parents or look at a parent and cry.

Even though she studied about the importance of interdisciplinary, family-focused models for early intervention, she questioned how this program was being operated. She wished that she had another educator in her workplace to talk with about her doubts and concerns. All she wanted to do was teach; how had she missed what early childhood special educators really do?

Viewpoints of the Others

Parents noted that Olivia was very warm when interacting with their children. She prepared a bright, cheery, appropriately stimulating environment for the children. Olivia planned interesting activities for the babies whose homes she visited. However, several family members commented to the coordinator that Olivia seemed remote to them. They often did not feel welcome during preschool groups.

Other professionals at Briarville's early intervention program either paid little attention to the new teacher or began to feel irritated that she did not seem to come to team meetings with a cooperative attitude. The coordinator overheard two of the others discussing their frustration regarding Olivia's presence at team meetings.

The coordinator decided to move up a meeting that had been planned with Olivia. The meeting was intended to be the regularly scheduled conference after 30 days of employment. However, it seemed that something needed to be done sooner. Olivia was worried when she received a message from the coordinator asking whether they could meet after her afternoon preschool group the next day.

1. Explain the perspectives of Olivia, family members, other early intervention professionals, and the coordinator. With which do you most identify?

2. Discuss your life experiences that may affect the perspective you take in this situation.

3. From the textbook, what information might help Olivia see the need for such a family-intensive approach to early intervention? Which skills might help to increase her confidence in this situation?

CASE 6

The Teacher

Vera Wozniak was a second-grade teacher in a rural school district. She was asked to serve on a district-wide assessment committee. During the third meeting of the committee, the district psychologist recommended that a standardized test be administered to all second-grade students. Vera stated that the test was not age-appropriate and that reading level could be better assessed in other ways. After several discussions, the majority of the committee voted to approve the use of the test in the second grade.

The Early Childhood Program and the Community

As news of the decision was shared at faculty meetings in the district, Vera began to hear from kindergarten, first- and second-grade teachers. Many of them stated that they did not think it was appropriate to give a standardized test in a primary grade. Some parents of first graders also began to ask questions about the test and asked Vera if they should send their child to a summer school or buy a reading program to "get ready" for the test.

Viewpoints of Others

After hearing these discussions, Vera decided to go to the principal, Mrs. Vellines. During their discussion, Mrs. Vellines revealed that the superintendent was very pleased that the committee had recommended the test since the district's reading scores were not at the state recommended levels.

Vera left the meeting feeling very frustrated. She knew that second graders were too young for a standardized test. She decided that she would make copies of articles she had read from NAEYC and International Reading Association (IRA) and share those with other teachers and parents. After sharing this information, a group of parents asked to be on the agenda for the next school board meeting. These parents spoke at the meeting and expressed their frustration that children were being pressured simply to get the test scores up. The superintendent agreed to review the plan.

The next day, Vera was asked to meet with the principal and the superintendent.

---

1. Explain the perspectives of Mrs. Vellines, the parents, Vera, and the superintendent.
2. Describe which resources Vera should take to the meeting.
3. How would Vera explain her reasoning in involving parent in this issue?

WEB SITES FOR PROFESSIONAL DEVELOPMENT

Family Involvement in Early Childhood Education

(Please note that because Internet resources are of a time-sensitive nature and URL addresses may change or be deleted, searches should be conducted by association and/or topic.)

Adjustment Tasks for Stepfamilies
www.stepfamiliesinfo.org/09/sf-task1.htm

African American Internet Links
http://clnet.ucr.edu/Afro.links.html

A Guide to Children's Literature and Disability
www.kidsource.com/NICHCY/literature.html

Alliance for Full Acceptance
www.affa-sc.org/

Alliance for Parental Involvement
www.croton.com/allpie

Anchor School Project
www.anchorschool.org/

Asian American Resources
www.ai.mit.edu/people/irie/aar

Association for Childhood Education International (ACEI)
www.udel.edu/bateman/acei

Association for Supervision and Curriculum Development (ASCD)
www.ascd.org

Birth Order Affects Career Interests
www.acs.ohio-state.edu/researchnews/archive/birthwrk.htm

Birth Order and Its Effects on Self-Esteem
www.citadel.edu/citadel/otherserv/psyc/scholar2.html

Birth Order & Personality Differences
www.encouragingleadership.com/Birth_Order.htm

Building Family Strengths
http://fyd.clemson.edu/building.htm

Bureau of Indian Affairs
http://doi.gov/bureau-indian-affairs.html

Bureau of Labor Statistics
www.bls.gov/cps

Caring for Babies with AIDS
www.caring4babieswithAIDS.org/

Center for Interventions, Treatment and Addiction Research
www.med.wright.edu/citar

Center for Substance Abuse Treatment
www.samhsa.gov/centers/csat2002/csat_frame.html

Center for the Child Care Workforce
www.ccw.org/home/

Center on Addiction and Substance Abuse
www.casacolumbia.org/

Center on the Family
http://uhfamily.hawaii.edu/index.asp

Character Education Partnership
www.character.org

Child Care Aware
www.childcareaware.org

Child Support Enforcement Office
www.acf.hhs.gov/programs/cse

Child Welfare League of America Center for Children of Prisoners
www.cwla.org/programs/incarcerated

Children Now
www.childrennow.org

Children's Defense Fund
www.childrensdefense.org

Children's Memorial Hospital (Chicago)—Neonatology
www.childrensmemorial.org/depts/neonatology

Children with Disabilities
www.childrenwithdisabilities.ncjrs.org/

Children with Disabilities: Understanding Sibling Issues
www.kidsource.com/NICHCY/sibling.issues.
dis.all.3.1.html

Children, Youth & Family Consortium
www.cyfc.umn.edu/

Chronically Ill Children: How Families Adjust
www.nurseweek.com/ce/ce565a.html

Council for Exceptional Children
www.cec.sped.org/

Creating a Strong Family
www.ianr.unl.edu/pubs/family/nf498.htm

Dads and Daughters
www.dadsanddaughters.org/Research/Fathering/
NFIFacts.htm

Department of Health and Human Services Administration on Children and Families
www.acf.hhs.gov

Divorce Education and Meditation Program
www.hamiltontn.gov/Courts/CircuitClerk/
education.htm

Early Childhood Development
www.worldbank.org/children/

Eastern Orthodox Church in America
www.oca.org/pages/orth-chri/calendar.index.htm

Education of Homeless Children and Youth
http://nch.ari.net/edchild.html

Education of Immigrant Children in New York City
www.ed.gov/databases/ERIC_Digests/ed402399.
html

Erase the Hate
www.usanetwork.com/functions/nhday/
nohateday.html

ERIC Clearinghouse on Disabilities and Gifted Education
www.ericcec.org/

ERIC Clearinghouse on Elementary and Early Childhood Education
www.ericeece.org/

Exceptional Parent Magazine
www.eparent.com/

Facing History and Ourselves
www.facinghistory.org/facing/fha02.nsf

Families and Work Institute
www.familiesandwork.org

Families in Crisis
www.Familiesincrisis.org

Family Education Network
http://familyeducation.com/home/

Family Focus
www.collaboratory.nunet.net/itrc/ff/

Family Literacy
www.pabook.libraries.psu.ed/famlit.html

Family Preservation and Child Welfare Network
www.familypreservation.com

Family Resilience
http://outreach.missouri.edu/extensioninfoline/
youth&family/family_resilience.htm

Family Support America
www.famillysupportamerica.org/

Family Support and Children's Mental Health
www.rtc.pdx.edu/

Family Support and Father Involvement
http://npin.org/library/pre1998/n00288.html

Family Village
www.familyvillage.wisc.edu

Family Violence Prevention Fund
http://endabuse.org/

Family Works, Inc.
www.familyworksinc.com/

Federal Resource Center for Special Education
www.dssc.org/frc/index.htm

Federal Resources for Educational Excellence (FREE)
www.ed.gov/free/

Federation for Children with Special Needs
www.fcsn.org

FERPA
www.ed.gov/offices/Om/ferpa.html

Forum on Child and Family Statistics
www.ChildStats.gov/

Free Appropriate Public Education Site
www.fapeonline.org/

From Family Stress to Family Strengths
www.cdc.gov/niosh/nasd/docs4/sc98015.html

Futures for Children
www.futuresforchildren.com/

Gender Development
www.psy.pdx.edu/PsiCafe/Areas/Developmental/GenderDev/

Health Coverage for Legal Immigrant Children
www.cbpp.org/10-4-00health.htm

Helping Children Adapt to a New Sibling
www.nncc.org/Guidance/cc45_new.sibling.html

Helping Children to Understand Divorce
www.muextension.missouri.edu/xplor/hesguide/humanrel/gh6600.htm

Historical Changes
www.happinessonline.org/MoralDrift/p.6htm

Home Instruction Program for Preschool Youngsters (HIPPY)
www.hippyusa.org/

Homeless Children's Network
www.hcnkids.org/

Homes for the Homeless
www.homesforthehomeless.com/

How Foster Children Impact Sibling Relationships
www.fostercare.net/reportack.htm

I Am Your Child
www.iamyourchild.org

Identifying and Serving Immigrant Children Who Are Gifted
http://ericae.net/edo/ED358676.htm

Immigrant Children Exceed Expectations
www.ilw.com/lawyers/column_article/articles/2001,0627-AILF.SHTM

Index of Native American Resources on the Internet
www.hanksville.org/Naresources/

Individualizing Inclusion in Child Care
www.fpg.unc.edu/~inclusion/

Institute for Child and Family Policy
www.childpolicy.org/

Institute for Responsible Education
www.resp-ed.org/

Jewish Holidays
www.bnaibrith.org/caln.html

Kidsource Online
www.kidsource.com/

Kwanzaa Information Center
www.melantet.com/kwanzaa

Latino Resources
www.latinoweb.com
http://latino.sscnet.ucla.edu/

Lev Vygotsky's Theory
www.psy.pdx.edu/PsiCafe/KeyTheorists/Vygotsky.
htm

**Megaskills from the Home and School
Institute**
www.megaskillshsi.org

Migrant Education Program
www.ed.gov/offices/OESE/MEP/

Migrant Head Start
www.acf.hhs.gov/programs/opu/facts/headst.htm

Multicultural Books Every Child Should Know
www.soemadison.wisc.edu/ccbc/50mult.
htm#repro

Multicultural Pavilion
http://curry.edschool.Virginia.EDU/go/
multicultural

Museum of Tolerance
www.wiesenthal.com/mot/

National Association for Family Child Care
www.nafcc.org

National Association for Gifted Children
www.nagc.org

**National Association for the Education of
Young Children (NAEYC)**
www.naeyc.org

**National Association of Child Care Resource
and Referral Agencies**
www.childcarerr.org/

National Black Child Development Institute
www.nbcdi.org

National Center for Children in Poverty
http://cpmcnet.edu/dept.nccp/

National Center for Education Statistics
http://nces.ed.gov/

National Center for Policy Analysis: Welfare
www.ncpa.org/iss/wel/

National Child Care Information Center
http://nccic.org

**National Clearinghouse on Child Abuse and
Neglect Information**
www.calib.com/nccanch/index.cfm

National Coalition Against Domestic Violence
www.ncadv.org/

**National Coalition for Parent Involvement in
Education**
www.ncpie.org/

**National Council on Child Abuse and Family
Violence**
www.nccafv.org/

National Council on Family Relations
www.ncfr.org

National Domestic Violence Hotline
www.ndvh.org/

National Education Goals Panel
www.negp.gov/

National Head Start Association
www.nhsa.org/

**National Information Center for Children and
Youth with Disabilities**
www.nichcy.org

National Network for Child Care
www.nncc.org/

National Parent Information Network
www.npin.org/

National Parent teacher Association (PTA)
www.pta.org/

New American Studies Web
http://cfdev.georgetown.edu/cndls/asw/
aswsub.cfm?
head1=race%2C%20Ethnicity%2C%20and
%20Identity

Parent Soup
www.parentsoup.com

Parents Anonymous
www.parentsanonymous.org/

Parents as Teachers (PAT) National Center
www.patnc.org

Partnership for Family Involvement in Education
http://pfie.ed.gov/

Primary Project
www.childrensinstitute.net/programs/primary/
htm

Project Resilience
www.projectresilience.com/

Religiosity
www.wikipedia.com/wiki/religion

Research Matters
www.researchmatters.harvard.edu/story.php?
article_id=233

Research with the Circumplex Model
www.lifeinnovation.com/fip.html

Rocking the Cradle—and the Marriage
http://seattletimes.nwsource.com/news/lifestyles/
html98/tran_19991024.html

Search Institute
www.search-institute.org/assets/

Sexual Orientation and Gender Identity
www.aclu.org/issues/gay/GLSEN.html

Sibling Relationships
http://npin.org/pnews/1999/pnew599b.html

Siblings in Adoption—Expanded Families
www.pactadopt.org/press/articles/
sib-attach.html

Special Child
www.specialchild.com/index.html

Stages of Adaptation for Immigrant Children
http://members.aol.com/lacillo/immigrant.html

Stand for Children
www.stand.org

STARBRIGHT Foundation
www.starbright.org

State Departments of Education Listing
http://ericeece.org/statlink.html

Teaching Strategies
www.TeachingStrategies.com

Teaching Tolerance
www.Tolerance.org

The Effect of Birth Order on Intelligence
www.mwsc.edu/psychology/research/psy302/fall
95/lowery.htm

The Reading Connection
www.thereadingconnection.org/

Tufts University Child and Family Web Guide
www.cfw.tufts.edu

University Research on Families
www.childwelfare.com/kids/university_
research.htm

Urie Bronfenbrenner's Theory
www.psy.pdx.edu/PsiCafe/KeyTheorists/
Bronfenbrenner.htm

U.S. Census Bureau—Poverty
www.census.gov/hhes/www/poverty.html

U.S. Government Publications for Parents
www.ed.gov/pubs/parents/

Various Faiths and Practices
http://dir.yahoo.com/Society_and_Culture/
Religion_and_Spirituality/Faiths_and_
Practices/

Wheelock College Institute for Leadership and Career Initiatives
http://institute.wheelock.edu

What Is Culture?
www.wsu.edu:8001/vcwsu/commons/topics/
culture/culture-index.html

Zero to Three
www.zerotothree.org/

THE NAEYC CODE OF ETHICAL CONDUCT

Preamble

NAEYC recognizes that many daily decisions required of those who work with young children are of a moral and ethical nature. The NAEYC Code of Ethical Conduct offers guidelines for responsible behavior and sets forth a common basis for resolving the principal ethical dilemmas encountered in early childhood education. The primary focus is on daily practice with children and their families in programs for children from birth to eight years of age: preschools, child care centers, family day care homes, kindergartens, and primary classrooms. Many of the provisions also apply to specialists who do not work directly with children, including program administrators, parent educators, college professors, and child care licensing specialists.

Standards of ethical behavior in early childhood education are based on commitment to core values that are deeply rooted in the history of our field. We have committed ourselves to:

- Appreciating childhood as a unique and valuable stage of the human life cycle;

- Basing our work with children on knowledge of child development;

- Appreciating and supporting the close ties between the child and family;

- Recognizing that children are best understood in the context of family, culture and society;

- Respecting the dignity, worth and uniqueness of each individual (child, family member and colleague);

- Helping children and adults achieve their full potential in the context of relationships that are based on trust, respect and positive regard.

The Code sets forth a conception of our professional responsibilities in four sections, each addressing an arena of professional relationships: 1) children, 2) families, 3) colleagues, and 4) community and society. Each section includes an introduction to the primary responsibilities of the early childhood practitioner in that arena, a set of ideals pointing in the direction of exemplary professional practice, and a set of principles defining practices that are required, prohibited and permitted.

The ideals reflect the aspirations of practitioners. The principles are intended to guide conduct and assist practitioners in resolving ethical dilemmas encountered in the field. There is not necessarily a corresponding principle for each ideal. Both ideals and principles are intended to direct practitioners to those questions which, when responsibly answered, will provide the basis for conscientious decision-making. While the Code provides specific direction for addressing some ethical dilemmas, many others will require the practitioner to combine the guidance of the Code with sound professional judgment.

The ideals and principles in this Code present a shared conception of professional responsibility that affirms our commitment to the core values of our field. They publicly acknowledge the responsibilities that we in the field have assumed and in so doing they support ethical behavior in our work. Practitioners who face ethical dilemmas are urged to seek guidance in the applicable parts of this Code and in the spirit that informs the whole.

Section I: Ethical Responsibilities to Children

Childhood is a unique and valuable stage in the life cycle. Our paramount responsibility is to

Feeney, S., & Kipnis, K. (1989). Code of ethical conduct and statement of commitment. *Young Children 45*(1), 24–29.

provide safe, healthy, nurturing and responsive settings for children. We are committed to supporting children's development by cherishing individual differences by helping them learn to live and work cooperatively, and by promoting their self-esteem.

Ideals:

I-1.1 To be familiar with the knowledge-base of early childhood education and to keep current through continuing education and in-service training.

I-1.2 To base program practices upon current knowledge in the field of child development and related disciplines and upon particular knowledge of each child.

I-1.3 To recognize and respect the uniqueness and the potential of each child.

I-1.4 To appreciate the special vulnerability of children.

I-1.5 To create and maintain safe and healthy settings that foster children's social, emotional, intellectual, and physical development and that respect their dignity and their contributions.

I-1.6 To support the right of children with special needs to participate, consistent with their ability, in regular early childhood programs.

Principles:

P-1.1 Above all, we shall not harm children. We shall not participate in practices that are disrespectful, degrading, dangerous, exploitative, intimidating, psychologically damaging or physically harmful to children. This principle has precedence over all others in this Code.

P-1.2 We shall not participate in practices that discriminate against children by denying benefits, giving special advantages or excluding them from programs or activities on the basis of their race, religion, sex, national origin, or the status, behavior or beliefs of their parents. (This principle does not apply to programs that have a lawful mandate to provide services to a particular population of children.)

P-1.3 We shall involve all of those with relevant knowledge (including staff and parents) in decisions concerning a child.

P-1.4 When, after appropriate efforts have been made with a child and the family, a child still does not appear to be benefiting from a program, we shall communicate our concern to the family in a positive way and offer them assistance in finding a more suitable setting.

P-1.5 We shall be familiar with the symptoms of child abuse and neglect and know community procedures for addressing them.

P-1.6 When we have evidence of child abuse or neglect we shall report the evidence to the appropriate community agency and follow up to insure, that appropriate action has been taken. When possible, parents will be informed that the referral has been made.

P-1.7 When another person tells us of their suspicion that a child is being abused or neglected but we lack evidence, we shall assist that person in taking appropriate action to protect the child.

P-1.8 When a child protective agency fails to provide adequate protection for abused or neglected children, we acknowledge a collective ethical responsibility to work toward improvement of these services.

Section II: Ethical Responsibilities to Families

Families are of primary importance in children's development. (The term family may include others, besides parents, who are responsibly involved with the child.) Because the family and the early childhood educator have an interest in the child's welfare, we acknowledge a primary responsibility to bring about collaboration between the home and school in ways that enhance the child's development.

Ideals:

I-2.1 To develop relationships of mutual trust with the families we serve.

I-2.2 To acknowledge and build upon strengths and competencies as we support families in their task of nurturing children.

I-2.3 To respect the dignity of each family and its culture, customs and beliefs.

I-2.4 To respect families' child-rearing values and their right to make decision for their children.

I-2.5 To interpret each child's progress to parents within the framework of a developmental perspective and to help families understand and appreciate the value of developmentally appropriate early childhood programs.

I-2.6 To help famliy members improve their understanding of their children and to enhance their skills as parents.

I-2.7 To participate in buiding support networks for families by providing them with opportunities to interact with program staff and families.

Principles:

P-2.1 We shall not deny family members access to their child's classroom or program setting.

P-2.2 We shall inform families of program philosophy, policies, personnel qualifications, and explain why we teach as we do.

P-2.3 We shall inform and, when appropriate, involve families in policy decisions.

P-2.4 We shall inform and, when appropriate, involve families in significant decisions affecting their child.

P-2.5 We shall inform the family of accidents involving their child, or risks such as exposure to contagious disease that may result in infection and of events that might result in psychological damage.

P-2.6 We shall not permit or participate in research which could in any way hinder the education or development of the children in our programs. Families shall be fully informed of any proposed research projects involving their children and shall have their opportunity to give or withhold consent.

P-2.7 We shall not engage in or support exploitation of families. We shall not use our relationship with a family for private advantage or personal gain, or enter into relationships with family members that might impair our effectiveness in working with chidren.

P-2.8 We shall develop written policies for the protection of confidentiality and the disclosure of children's records. The policy documents shall be made available to all program personnel and families. Disclosure of children's records beyond family members, program personnel and consultants having an obligation of confidentiality shall require familial consent (except in cases of abuse or neglect).

P-2.9 We shall maintain confidentiality and shall respect the family's right to privacy, refraining from disclosure of confidential information and intrusion into family life. However, when we are concerned about a child's welfare, it is permissible to reveal confidential information to agencies and individuals who may be able to act in the child's interest.

P-2.10 In cases where family members are in conflict we shall work openly, sharing our observation of the child, to help all parties involved make informed decisions. We shall refrain from becoming an advocate for one party.

P-2.11 We shall be familiar with and appropriately use community resources and professional services that support families. After a referral has been made, we shall follow up to ensure that services have been adequately provided.

Section III: Ethical Responsibilities to Colleagues

In a caring, cooperative workplace human dignity is respected, professional satisfaction is promoted and positive relationships are modeled. Our primary responsibility in this arena is to establish and maintain settings and relationships which support productive work and meet professional needs.

A. Responsibilities to Co-Workers

Ideals:

I-3A.1 To establish and maintain relationships of trust and cooperation with co-workers.

I-3A.2 To share resources and information with co-workers.

I-3A.3 To support co-workers in meeting their professional needs and in their professional development.

I-3A.4 To accord co-workers due recognition for professional achievement.

Principles:

P-3A.1 When we have concern about the professional behavior of a co-worker, we shall first let that person know of our concern and attempt to resolve the matter collegially.

P-3A.2 We shall exercise care in expressing views regarding the personal attributes or professional conduct of co-workers. Statements should be based on firsthand knowledge and relevant to, the interests of children and programs.

B. Responsibilities to Employers

Ideals:

I-3B.1 To assist the program in providing the highest quality of service.

I-3B.2 To maintain loyalty to the program and uphold its reputation.

Principles:

P-3B.1 When we do not agree with program policies, we shall first attempt to effect change through constructive action within the organization.

P-3B.2 We shall speak or act on behalf of an organization only when authorized. We shall take care to note when we are speaking for the organization and when we are expressing a personal judgment.

C. Responsibilities to Employees

Ideals:

I-3C.1 To promote policies and working conditions that foster competence, well-being and self-esteem in staff members.

I-3C.2 To create a climate of trust and candor that will enable staff to speak and act in the best interests of children, families, and the field of early childhood education.

I-3C.3 To strive to secure an adequate livelihood for those who work with or on behalf of young children.

Principles:

P-3C.1 In decisions concerning children and programs, we shall appropriately utilize the training, experience and expertise of staff members.

P-3C.2 We shall provide staff members with working conditions that permit them to carry out their responsibilities, timely and non-threatening evaluation procedures, written grievance procedures, constructive feedback, and opportunities for continuing professional development.

P-3C.3 We shall develop and maintain comprehensive written personnel policies that define program standards and, when applicable, that specify the extent to which employees are accountable for their conduct outside of the workplace. These policies shall be given to new staff members and shall be available for review by all staff members.

P-3C.4 Employees who do not meet program standards shall be informed of areas of concern and, when possible, assisted in improving their performance.

P-3C.5 Employees who are dismissed shall be informed of the reasons for their termination. When a dismissal is for cause, justification must be based on evidence of inadequate or inappropriate behavior which is accurately documented, current, and available for the employee to review.

P-3C.6 In making evaluation and recommendations, judgments shall be based on fact and relevant to the interests of children and programs.

P-3C.7 Hiring and promotion shall be based solely on a person's record of accomplishment and ability to carry out the responsibilities of the position.

P-3C8 In hiring, promotion and provision of training, we shall not participate in any form of discrimination based on race, religion, sex, national origin, handicap, age, or sexual preference. We shall be familiar with laws and regulations that pertain to employment discrimination.

Section IV: Ethical Responsibilities to Community and Society

Early childhood programs operate within a context of an immediate community made up of families and other institutions concerned with children's welfare. Our responsibilities to the community are to provide programs that meet its needs and to cooperate with agencies and professions that share responsibility for children. Because the larger society has a measure of responsibility for the welfare and protection of children, and because of our specialized expertise in child development, we acknowledge an obligation to serve as a voice for children everywhere.

Ideals:

I-4.1 To provide the community with high quality, culturally sensitive programs and services.

I-4.2 To promote cooperation among agencies and professions concerned with the welfare of young children, their families and their teachers.

I-4.3 To work, through education, research and advocacy, toward an environmentally safe world in which all children are adequately fed, sheltered, and nurtured.

I-4.4 To work, through education, research and advocacy, toward a society in which all young children have access to quality programs.

I-4.5 To promote knowledge and understanding of young children and their needs. To work toward greater social acknowledgment of children's rights and greater social acceptance of responsibility for their well-being.

I-4.6 To support policies and laws that promote the well-being of children and families. To oppose those that impair their well-being. To cooperate with other individuals and groups in these efforts.

I-4.7 To further the professional development of the field of early childhood education and to strengthen its commitment to realizing its core values as reflected in this Code.

Principles:

P-4.1 We shall communicate openly and truthfully about the nature and extent of services that we provide.

P-4.2 We shall not accept or continue to work in positions for which we are personally unsuited or professionally unqualified. We shall not offer services that we, do not have the competence, qualifications, or resources to provide.

P-4.3 We shall be objective and accurate in reporting the knowledge upon which we base our program practices.

P-4.4 We shall cooperate with other professionals who work with children and their families.

P-4.5 We shall not hire or recommend for employment any person who is unsuited for a position with respect to competence, qualifications or character.

P-4.6 We shall report the unethical or incompetent behavior of a colleague to a supervisor when informal resolution is not effective.

P-4.7 We shall be familiar with laws and regulations that serve to protect the children in our programs.

P-4.8 We shall not participate in practices which are in violation of laws and regulations that protect the children in our programs.

P-4.9 When we have evidence that an early childhood program is violating laws or regulations protecting children, we shall report it to persons responsible for the program. If compliance is not accomplished within a reasonable time we will report the violation to appropriate authorities who can be expected to remedy the situation.

P-4.10 When we have evidence that an agency or a professional charged with providing services to children, families or teachers is failing to meet its obligations, we acknowledge a collective ethical responsibility to report the problem to appropriate authorities or to the public.

P-4.11 When a program violates or requires its employees to violate this Code, it is permissible, after fair assessment of the evidence, to disclose the identity of that program.

The NAEYC Statement of Commitment

As an individual who works with young children, I commit myself to furthering the values of early childhood education as they are reflected in the NAEYC Code of Ethical Conduct.

To the best of my ability I will:

- Ensure that programs for young children are based on current knowledge of child development and early childhood education.

- Respect and support families in their task of nurturing children.

- Respect colleagues in early childhood education and support them in maintaining the NAEYC Code of Ethical Conduct.

- Serve as an advocate for children, their families and their teachers in community and society.

- Maintain high standards of professional conduct.

- Recognize how personal values, opinions and biases can affect professional judgment.

- Be open to new ideas and be willing to learn from the suggestions of others.

- Continue to learn, grow and contribute as a professional.

- Honor the ideals and principles of the NAEYC Code of Ethical Conduct.

The Statement of Commitment expresses those basic personal commitments that individuals must make in order to align themselves with the profession's responsibilities as set forth in the NAEYC Code of Ethical Conduct. (Courtesy of the National Association for the Education of Young Children)

NATIONAL ACADEMY OF EARLY CHILDHOOD PROGRAMS ACCREDITATION CRITERIA

A. Interactions among Teachers and Children

Goal: Interactions between children and adults provide opportunities for children to develop an understanding of self and others and are characterized by warmth, personal respect, individuality, positive support, and responsiveness. Teachers facilitate interactions among children to provide opportunities for development of self-esteem, social competence, and intellectual growth.

B. Curriculum

Goal: The curriculum engages children actively in the learning process, provides a variety of developmentally appropriate learning experiences, and encourages children to pursue their own interests in the context of life in the community and the world.

C. Relationships among Teachers and Families

Goal: Teachers and families work closely in partnership to ensure high-quality care and education for children, and parents feel supported and welcomed as observers and contributors to the program.

D. Staff Qualifications and Professional Development

Goal: The program is staffed by adults who understand child and family development and who recognize and meet the developmental and learning needs of children and families.

E. Administration

Goal: The program is efficiently and effectively administered with attention to the needs and desires of children, families, and staff.

F. Staffing

Goal: The program is sufficiently staffed to meet the needs of and promote the physical, social, emotional, and cognitive development of children.

G. Physical Environment

Goal: The indoor and outdoor physical environment fosters optimal growth and development through opportunities for exploration and learning.

H. Health and Safety

Goal: The health and safety of children and adults are protected and enhanced.

I. Nutrition and Food Service

Goal: The nutritional needs of children and adults are met in a manner that promotes physical, social, emotional, and cognitive development.

J. Evaluation

Goal: Systematic assessment of the effectiveness of the program in meeting its goals for children, families, and staff is conducted to ensure that good quality care and education are provided and maintained, and that the program continually strives for improvement and innovation.

From: *Accreditation criteria & procedures of the National Association for the Education of Young Children.* (1998). Washington, DC: National Association for the Education of Young Children.

NATIONAL
EDUCATION GOALS

Goal 1: Ready to Learn

By the year 2000, all children in America will start school ready to learn.

Goal 2: School Completion

By the year 2000, the high school graduation rate will increase to at least 90 percent.

Goal 3: Student Achievement and Citizenship

By the year 2000, all students will leave grades 4, 8, and 12 having demonstrated competency over challenging subject matter including English, mathematics, science, foreign languages, civics and government, economics, arts, history, and geography, and every school in America will ensure that all students learn to use their minds well, so they may be prepared for responsible citizenship, further learning, and productive employment in our Nation's modern economy.

Goal 4: Teacher Education and Professional Development

By the year 2000, the nation's teaching force will have access to programs for the continued improvement of their professional skills and the opportunity to acquire the knowledge and skills needed to instruct and prepare all American students for the next century.

Goal 5: Mathematics and Science

By the year 2000, United States students will be first in the world in mathematics and science achievement.

Goal 6: Adult Literacy and Lifelong Learning

By the year 2000, every adult American will be literate and will possess the knowledge and skills necessary to compete in a global economy and exercise the rights and responsibilities of citizenship.

Goal 7: Safe, Disciplined, and Alcohol- and Drug-free Schools

By the year 2000, every school in the United States will be free of drugs, violence, and the unauthorized presence of firearms and alcohol and will offer a disciplined environment conducive to learning.

Goal 8: Parental Participation

By the year 2000, every school will promote partnerships that will increase parental involvement and participation in promoting the social, emotional, and academic growth of children.

(*Source:* National Education Goals Panel, 1255 22nd Street, NW, Suite 502, Washington, DC 20037)

Early Childhood Teacher Certification

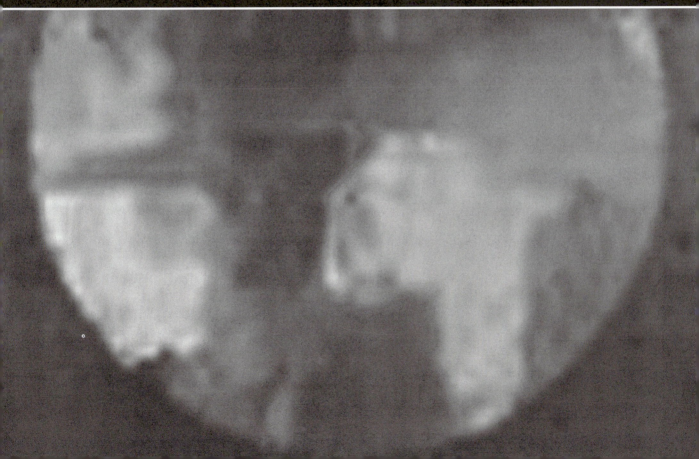

A Position Statement of the Association of Teacher Educators and the National Association for the Education of Young Children

Adopted July/August 1991

Background Information

The Association of Teacher Educators (ATE), through its Commission on Early Childhood Teacher Education (ECTE), and the National Association for the Education of Young Children (NAEYC) jointly developed these guidelines to inform decision-makers about certification standards for teachers in programs serving children from birth through eight years of age. The purpose of this document is to ensure that all young children and their families have access to qualified early childhood teachers by guiding teacher educators and policymakers to (1) make informed decisions about early childhood teacher certification, (2) evaluate existing teacher certification standards, and (3) advocate for more appropriate early childhood teacher certification standards.

Development of the Guidelines

Several hundred early childhood and teacher education professionals participated in developing these guidelines. The following individuals constituted the ATE Commission on Early Childhood Teacher Education and contributed to and guided the development of these guidelines: John M. Johnston, Chairperson; Doris Bergen; Sue Bredekamp; Jim Campbell; Michael D. Davis; Anne Dorsey; Stacie G. Goffin; Marcy Guddemi; Beverly Gulley; Mary Jensen; Michael Kalinowski; Joyce Munro; Steven Silvern; and Bill Dixon, ATE Executive Board Liaison. The ATE/ECTE Commission drew initial drafts of the position statement and certification standards from a survey of related policy documents, early childhood teacher certification standards (Illinois State Board of Education, 1988; Tennessee State Board of Education, 1990), teacher education standards (NAEYC, 1991), and working papers prepared by members of the ATE/ECTE Commission. An initial draft of the position statement and certification standards was reviewed at an open hearing by participants at the NAEYC Annual Conference. A revised draft was then sent to a selected national sample of over 900 early childhood teacher educators, state department certification specialists, and the NAEYC Teacher Education Guidelines Panel. Two separate mailings requesting feedback were sent to selected ATE members. Feedback was also sought from 27 related professional organizations. The *Early Childhood Teacher Certification Guidelines* position statement, presented here in its entirety, was adopted by the Executive Boards of the Association of Teacher Educators and the National Association for the Education of Young Children in July/August 1991.

Next Steps

The September 1991 *Young Children* announced NAEYC's new initiative, the National Institute for Early Childhood Professional Development. One of the goals of the Institute is to influence the quality and content of early childhood teacher preparation programs and to advocate for policies that promote an articulated career

---

*For the purposes of this document, certification refers to the mandatory, state-level process whereby an individual who meets certain minimum standards gains a permit/license to practice and/or an institution is approved by the state to grant teaching certificates.

development system for the field. The certification position will be an important tool for the Institute and NAEYC leaders to use to influence state policies. Our goal is to achieve specialized early childhood certification in every state, which in turn will influence the content and delivery of preparation programs throughout the nation.

NAEYC continues to work with the ATE Commission on Early Childhood Teacher Education. Work is proceeding on a companion position statement on certification for early childhood special education.

If you have suggestions or requests for using the certification position statement or other initiatives relevant to early childhood professional preparation and development, please contact Sue Bredekamp, Director of Professional Development, or call or write to the Institute at NAEYC Headquarters.

Position

In recognition of the need for qualified teachers throughout a child's early education (birth through age eight), the Association of Teacher Educators and the National Association for the Education of Young Children recommend the establishment of specialized early childhood teacher certification standards for teachers working with children from birth through age eight. This certification* should be developed exclusively for early-childhood education and be distinctive from, and independent of, existing elementary and secondary certifications.

We recognize that recommending a free-standing teacher certification standard developed exclusively for teachers working with children from birth through age eight will require many states to reconsider their current practices (McCarthy, 1988). Current teacher certification standards, however, were devel-

oped prior to the extensive availability of, and demand for, early childhood education programs. Furthermore, many current state standards do not reflect the existing knowledge base about the education of children nor do they appreciate the significance of the distinctive developmental and educational characteristics of programs for children from birth through age eight.

In addition, to a large extent, existing certification patterns (K–6/K–3; K–8, 7–12) are artifacts of school building organizational structures that are rapidly becoming obsolete. Many school districts are now experimenting with early childhood units (for example, see NASBE, 1988) and middle school configurations that do not match the existing certification structure. In addition, enormous variety exists in school organization that often depends more on enrollments than on other considerations. For example, the state of Alabama reports 32 different school configurations (Ward, 1990).

State departments of education, state certification boards, and other responsible state agencies exert critical leadership in setting standards for teacher preparation. They define educational expectations for public and private early childhood preparation programs. They are, therefore, in a pivotal position to influence teacher preparation programs and help ensure the qualification of those in daily interaction with young children. It is imperative that state departments of education and other state certification offices review their program standards in light of essential characteristics of early childhood education and the professional requirements of early childhood teachers.

The absence of consistent standards for specialized early childhood certification in approximately half the states has led to the lack of adequate preparation programs in early childhood education at the baccalaureate level in these states. Because institutions typically plan programs to meet state certification standards, it is impossible in some states to major in early childhood education. Other states may only provide an endorsement program that consists of two courses and a kindergarten student teaching placement (Bredekamp, 1990). As a result, there is a shortage of well-qualified early childhood teachers to meet current needs, much less anticipate future demand as programs expand.

The last decade has witnessed a dramatic growth in early childhood programs for children from birth through age eight. By 1995, 70% of children younger than age eight will be in school settings (Children's Defense Fund, 1987). This growth is evident in every sector of early childhood education: early intervention programs such as Head Start, programs for children with special needs, child care centers, private nursery schools, kindergarten education and primary programs in all 50 states, and increasingly available programs for 3- and 4-year-olds in the public schools.

In addition, there is increasing recognition and acceptance of the early primary years (grades 1 through 3) as part of the continuum of early childhood and therefore as being most appropriate when conceptualized within the framework of early childhood education (National Association of Elementary School Principals, 1990; National Association of State Boards of Education, 1988). Therefore, children in early childhood programs from birth through third grade need quality early childhood education (Association for Childhood Education International, 1983; Bredekamp, 1987; National Association for Elementary School Principals, 1990; National Association of State Boards of Education, 1988).

The developmental characteristics of children from birth through age eight help inform decision-makers about the characteristics of appropriate education for this age group (Bredekamp, 1987; Elkind, 1986). Our recommendations encompass birth through age eight to help ensure that early childhood teachers, regardless of which age group they work with, are adequately prepared. They also recognize that all early childhood teachers need to be aware of the continuum of development from birth through age eight.

Consequently, early childhood teachers must be adequately informed about the unique developmental characteristics of young children and the implications for curriculum and instruction. Furthermore, this knowledge must embody an understanding of variations due to cultural differences and/or the presence of a handicapping condition. These are not separate aspects of a young child's life and therefore should be merged in teacher education programs.

This specialized knowledge must be reflected in standards for early childhood teacher certification established by state boards of education and other certifying agencies. This conclusion is supported by recent recommendations delivered by the National Association for the Education of Young Children (1991), the Association for Childhood Education International (1983), the National Association of Elementary School Principals (1990), the National Education Association (1990), the National Association of State Boards of Education (1988). the Association for Supervision and Curriculum Development (Wagner, 1988), and the National Board for Professional Teaching Standards (1990).

The significance of specialized knowledge in early childhood education is also confirmed by research findings that early childhood teachers with a strong background in early childhood development and education interact with children in ways that are more growth promoting (Ruopp, Travers, Coelen, & Glantz, 1979; Weikart, 1989). This conclusion is further supported by the research on teaching that showed that decision making and other thinking skills are enhanced by a well-developed and integrated knowledge base specific to the discipline being contemplated (Brand, 1990, Gardner, 1990, Shulman, 1987).

This document does not promote any single route to the acquisition of early childhood certification, but it does call for all teachers of young children from birth through age eight to be adequately prepared with the knowledge, skills, and understandings specific to their teaching specialization, regardless of where they are employed.

Essential Characteristics of Early Childhood Education

At least five characteristics are essential for an early childhood teacher preparation program:

1. Teachers must be educated in the liberal arts and knowledgeable about a variety of disciplines in order to recognize the learning embedded in children's activity. Early childhood teachers must be knowledgeable in various subject matter pedagogies to be skillful in interactive teaching strategies that advance children's developing understandings.

Early childhood curriculums are organized as an integrated whole and are informed by children's (versus adults) interests (National Association for the Education of Young Children and National Association of Early Childhood Specialists in State Departments of Education, 1991). Subject matter content and skill development are therefore woven into children's daily interactions with materials, peers, and adults.

2. Early childhood teachers must be well informed about developmental theories and their implications for practice.

Concern for all aspects of a child's growth and development is emphasized. Especially during the years of early childhood, sociomoral, emotional, and personality development are inseparable from cognitive/intellectual growth (Biber, 1984; DeVries & Kohlberg, 1987). Concern for the whole child, in addition to the physical needs of very young children, significantly extends the scope of the early childhood teacher's role (Johnston, 1984).

3. Early childhood teachers must understand the significance of play to children's educational development and develop skills in facilitating enriching play in early childhood classrooms.

Play is a critical component of the early childhood classroom. It is respected as a powerful integrator and generator of knowledge. Through play, children develop sociomoral judgments, advance their social and language skills, elaborate upon their intellectual understandings, and assume personal responsibility for learning (Fein, Rubin, & Vandenberg, 1983).

4. Early childhood teachers must understand families as the primary context for children's learning and development, respect diversity in family structure and values, and develop skills in interacting with parents in ways that enhance children's educational success.

Parents are valued as educational partners. Early childhood teachers recognize that their educational objectives cannot be fully achieved without collaboration with families. Early childhood education also recognizes itself as an important component of a family's support system (Galinsky & Hooks, 1977; Goffin, 1988; Kagan & Holdeman, 1989). The ability to collaborate with families and be a support to their child-rearing efforts demands an understanding and respect for cultural and familial diversity.

5. Early childhood teachers need to acquire the ability to supervise and coordinate their teaching with other adults. With the expansion of shared decisionmaking in these settings, early childhood teachers also should be able to reflect on their own professional development.

Early childhood teachers often function as members of a professional team. As team members, they model adult interactions and cooperative decision making for children. In such circumstances, their coordinated efforts are also needed for the smooth functioning of their classrooms.

Policy Considerations

The intent of this position statement is to ensure that all young children and their families have access to qualified early childhood teachers. This goal will not be achieved unless policies that influence the practice of early childhood education are also addressed. Because issues within the field of early childhood education relate to the delivery of early childhood programs, early childhood teachers must also be informed about issues of policy and strategies for influencing change (Almy, 1985; Katz & Goffin, 1990).

Specifically, the Association of Teacher Educators and the National Association for the Education of Young Children recommend that state departments of education and other certifying agencies develop policies that ensure . . .

- that the unique learning styles of children from birth through age eight be acknowledged as an essential knowledge base of early childhood education that requires free-standing certification distinctive from existing certifications for elementary and secondary education;

- that certification standards are age- and content-congruent across the 50 states in order for states to have truly reciprocal agreements and to ensure that all children are cared for and educated by teachers appropriately prepared as early childhood educators;

- that all early childhood preparation programs meet the standards set forth in this document;

- that all early childhood teacher preparation programs, especially in the configuration and coordination of their individual programs, recognize the inseparability of the care *and* education of children;

- that states initiate articulation agreements between two-year and four-year institutions within a state in order to provide a continuum of teacher preparation opportunities, promote professional development, and facilitate professional growth; and

- that states create ways to coordinate the efforts of those departments that credential teachers who teach children in child care settings and those who teach children in public and private school settings.

Certification Standards for Teachers of Children From Birth Through Age Eight

The Association of Teacher Educators and the National Association for the Education of Young Children believe that every state should adopt certification standards for teachers of children from birth through age eight. In order for professionals to act, it is impossible to separate knowledge, abilities, dispositions, values, and attitudes, one from the other. Therefore, statements of understanding and ability necessarily incorporate dispositions, values, and attitudes. The certified early childhood teacher will demonstrate professional knowledge, abilities, dispositions, values, and attitudes regarding growth, development, and learning; family and community relations; curriculum development, content, and implementation; health, safety, and nutrition; field experiences and professional internship; and professionalism.

I. Growth, development, and learning

This group of standards includes understanding of the various domains of development of infants, toddlers, and preprimary and primary-age children, and the processes by which these domains are integrated. It also includes understanding of how learning and developmental processes interact and the influences of sociocultural and other ecological factors on learning and development. It further includes the ability to appropriately assess the development of children from birth through age eight who come from a range of sociocultural backgrounds and who may be at risk for developmental delay. Specifically, it addresses the teacher's understanding and ability regarding the following:

A. physical development of young children, including variable growth and behavioral patterns during prenatal, perinatal, infant, toddler, preprimary, and early primary years

B. cognitive development and the relation of children's early experiences to their individual differences in cognitive development

C. receptive and expressive communication, speech, and language development in the young child

D. emotional, social, and moral development, including emergence of identity and development of self-esteem in the young child

E. integration of various developmental domains and ways in which individual differences affect development in all areas

F. the importance of play and of active involvement in sensory and motor development and

their influence on later cognitive, perceptual, and language skills

G. biological and environmental factors that promote wellness and sound nutrition and that influence development of and exceptionalities in children's motor, sensory, cognitive, and psychosocial development

H. recognition of signs of emotional distress, child abuse, and neglect in young children and knowledge of responsibility and procedures for reporting known or suspected abuse or neglect to appropriate authorities

I. observation and recording of young children's behavior and conducting of accurate and meaningful assessments in order to be aware of individual differences that occur among young children

J. utility and limitations of developmental screening tests administered to young children

II. Family and community relations

This group of standards encompasses understanding the vital role of the family and the community in the care and education of infants, toddlers, preprimary children, and primary-age children. It stresses the teacher's ability to cooperate with family and community systems in an effort to build upon the child's sociocultural background and, with support staff, to work with families and children who have special needs. Specifically, it addresses the teacher's understanding of and ability regarding the following:

A. explaining to parents the fundamentals of child growth, development, and learning; articulating the rationale for developmentally appropriate education programs for young children and the need for community support for such programs

B. articulating the concept of developmental delay and the rationale for early intervention services for children who are developmentally delayed or at risk of developmental delay

C. services that provide information and support for families and children and the role of related disciplines in supporting young children and their families

D. roles of parents as primary caregivers and informal teachers of young children, understanding the importance of parents' expectations for their children, and acknowledging the collaborative role of parents and teachers in early childhood programs

E. how young children affect and are affected by parents, siblings, extended family, and community

F. working cooperatively and supportively with families, especially those that have special educational needs, including those in which English is not the dominant language

G. including families in assessing a child's development, reporting assessment results in a clear and supportive manner to family members and other appropriate professionals, and identifying strengths and needs when setting goals

H. special education community services for the young child, including prevention, early intervention, integration into mainstreamed environments, and referral to specialized programs

III. Curriculum development, content, and implementation

This group of standards includes understanding of planning for and facilitating learning by infants, toddlers, preprimary children, and primary-age children in the content areas of language, literacy, mathematics, science, social studies, the arts and health and safety. It also includes understanding of planning for and facilitating interactions in appropriate environments. Finally, these standards emphasize the importance of as-

sessing children's abilities and the importance of sociocultural background for the planning of environments and experiences that meet the needs of all children, regardless of cultural background or special needs. Specifically, it addresses the teacher's understanding and ability regarding the following:

A. observing, recording, and assessing young children's behavior for the purpose of planning appropriate programs, environments, and interactions

B. using theories of development, learning, and assessment in planning appropriate programs, environments, and interactions

C. planning and implementing learning environments including the physical and psychosocial environments; management of time, space, and materials; and adjusting for children's age, cultural background, and special needs

D. physical growth and development and implementing developmental approaches to large and small motor skills

E. developing and implementing an integrated curriculum that focuses on children's developmental needs and interests; incorporating culturally valued contents and children's home experiences

F. using play, themes, and projects in planning experiences that integrate all developmental domains (emotional, physical, social, and cognitive)

G. creating and managing a learning environment that emphasizes direct experience, active manipulation of concrete materials, child choice and decision making, exploration of the environment, and interaction with others

H. using developmentally appropriate methods that may include play, open-ended questioning, group discussion, problem solving, cooperative planning, and inquiry experiences to help young children in developing intellectual curiosity, solving problems, making decisions, and becoming independent learners

I. using group and individual guidance and problem-solving techniques to assist the construction of knowledge and nurture prosocial interactions among children, to encourage interpersonal problem solving, and to develop self-control and positive self-esteem

J. supporting children's actions that increase the likelihood that children will be mentally alert, curious, confident, and honest in expressing their views; encouraging them to take initiative in generating ideas, problems, questions, and relationships

K. assisting young children in developing decision-making and interpersonal skills necessary to promote good health and personal safety

L. integrating multicultural/antibias themes, literature, and experiences in all curricular areas

M. participating and assisting other professionals in family-centered assessments and in developing and implementing individualized service and educational plans for young children with handicaps

N. adapting curriculum content to meet the needs of all young children, including those who may be gifted, handicapped, developmentally delayed, or at risk for developmental delay

IV. Health, safety, and nutrition

This group of standards addresses understanding of managing an environment that provides for the health, safety, and nutritional well-being of infants, toddlers, preprimary children, and primary-age children. Teachers should be able to apply this knowledge regardless of children's sociocultural background and should be aware of the special needs of children who may have

disabilities that put them at risk. Specifically, it addresses the teacher's understanding and ability regarding the following.

A. basic health, nutrition, and safety management procedures for infants, toddlers, and young children; also, basic health and safety management procedures regarding childhood illness and communicable diseases

B. using appropriate health appraisal procedures and recommending referral to appropriate community health and social services when necessary

C. identifying hazards, assessing risks and taking appropriate corrective steps in early childhood settings

V. Field experience and professional internship

This group of standards includes understandings needed for implementation of a quality program for infants, toddlers, preprimary children, and primary-age children, and an appreciation for differences in sociocultural backgrounds and special needs. It includes 300 clock hours of experience serving children in two of these age groups in various early childhood settings, including supervised interactions with families and children from a variety of cultural and socioeconomic backgrounds and varying degrees of special needs, and experience working with interdisciplinary teams of professionals, where appropriate. Specifically, it addresses the teacher's understanding and ability regarding the following:

A. integrating theory and practice through field work in conjunction with coursework and professional consultation

B. assuming the full range of teaching duties in exemplary early childhood settings

C. accepting and reflecting upon supervision from on-site as well as other clinical personnel

D. analyzing, evaluating, and discussing field experiences in seminar meetings with supervisors and colleagues

VI. Professionalism

This group of standards includes understanding of the importance of continued professional growth and of working with others in the profession and in the greater community to advocate for infants, toddlers, preprimary children, and primary-age children. It further includes an appreciation and advocacy for children and families with diverse sociocultural backgrounds and special needs. Specifically, it addresses the teacher's understanding and ability regarding the following:

A. articulating a personal philosophy of early childhood teaching and demonstrating interest and commitment to young children's development, learning, and well-being

B. how historical, philosophical, and social foundations of early childhood education affect current practices and future trends.

C. current issues, trends, legislation, and other public policy affecting children, families, and programs for young children and the early childhood profession

D. value issues and the need for incorporating codes of ethics in professional practice

E. working cooperatively with colleagues to organize, supervise, and lead staff and volunteers in planning and maintaining a safe, appropriate group environment for young children's development and learning

F. participating in advocacy activities on behalf of sound programs and services for young children and their families and enhanced professional status and working conditions for early childhood educators.

G. the importance of career-long growth and development activities for professional early childhood educators, e.g., active membership and participation in early childhood professional organizations and activities

References

Almy, M. (1985). New challenges for teacher education: Facing political and economic realities. *Young Children 40*(6), 10–11.

Association for Childhood Education International. (1983). *Preparation of early childhood teachers.* Wheaton, MD: Author

Biber, B. (1984). *Early education and psychological development.* New Haven, CT: Yale University Press.

Brandt, R. (1990). On knowledge and cognitive skills: A conversation with David Perkins. *Educational Leadership, 47*(5), 50–53.

Bredekamp, S. (1987). *Developmentally appropriate practice in early childhood programs serving children from birth through age 8* (exp. ed.). Washington, DC: National Association for the Education of Young Children.

Bredekamp, S. (1990). Setting and maintaining professional standards. In B. Spodek & O. N. Saracho (Eds.), Early childhood teacher preparation: *Yearbook in early childhood education* (vol. 1, pp. 138–152). New York: Teachers College Press.

Children's Defense Fund. (1987). *A children's defense budget.* Washington, DC: Author.

DeVries, R., & Kohlberg, L. (1987). *Constructivist early education: Overview and comparison with other programs.* Washington, DC: National Association for the Education of Young Children.

Elkind, D. (1986). Formal education and early childhood education: An essential difference. *Phi Delta Kappan, 67,* 631–636.

Fein, G., Rubin. K., & Vandenberg, B. (1983). Play. In P. Mussen (Ed.), *Manual of child psychology* (4th ed) (vol. 4. pp. 693–675). New York: Wiley & Sons.

Galinsky, E., & Hooks, W. (1977). *The new extended family.* Day care that works. Boston: Houghton Mifflin.

Gardner, H. (1990). The difficulties of school: Probable causes, possible cures. *Daedalus, 19,* 85–113.

Goffin, S. G. (1988). Putting our advocacy effort into a new context. *Young Children, 43*(3), 52–56.

Illinois State Board of Education. (1988). *Early childhood certificate (birth–grade three).* Springfield, IL: Author.

Johnston, J. M. (1984). Problems of prekindergarten teachers: A basis for reexamining teacher education practices. *Journal of Teacher Education, 35,* 33–37.

Kagan, S. L., & Haldeman, A. L. (1989). Family support and the schools. *Family Resource Coalition Report 8*(2), 1–2.

Katz, L. G., & Goffin, S. G. (1990). Issues in the preparation of teachers of young children. In B. Spodek & O. N. Saracho (Eds.), *Early childhood teacher preparation: Yearbook in early childhood education* (vol. 1, pp. 192–208). New York: Teachers College Press.

McCarthy, J. (1988). *State certification of early childhood teachers: An analysis of the 50 states and the District of Columbia.* Washington, DC: The National Association for the Education of Young Children.

National Association for the Education of Young Children. (1991). *Early childhood teacher education guidelines: Basic and advanced.* Washington, DC: Author.

National Association for the Education of Young Children and the National Association of Early Childhood Specialists in State Departments of Education. (1991). Guidelines for appropriate curriculum content and assessment in programs serving children ages 3 through 8. Young Children 46(3), 31–38.

National Association of Elementary School Principals. (1990). *Early childhood education and the elementary school principal: Standards for quality programs for young children.* Alexandria, VA: Author.

National Association of State Boards of Education. (1988). Right from the start. Alexandria, VA: Author.

National Board for Professional Teaching Standards. (1989). *Initial policies and perspectives of the National Board of Professional Teaching Standards.* Detroit: Author.

National Education Association. (1990). *Early childhood education and the public schools.* Washington, DC: Author.

Ruopp, R., Travers, J., Coelen, C., & Glantz, F. (1979). *Children at the center: Final report of the National Day Care Study* (vol. 1). Cambridge, MA: Abt Books.

Shulman, L. S. (1987). Knowledge and teaching: Foundations of the new reform. *Harvard Educational Review, 57*(1), 1–22.

Tennessee State Board of Education. (1990). *Early childhood education teacher licensure standards (PreK–3).* Nashville, TN: Author.

Wagner, C. (Ed.). (1988). *A resource guide to public school early childhood programs.* Alexandria, VA: Association for Supervision and Curriculum Development.

Ward, B. (1990). Coordinator Basic Skills & Early Childhood Section, State Department of Education, Montgomery, Alabama. Personal communication.

Weikart, D. (1989). *Quality preschool programs: A long-term social investment.* Occasional paper No. 5, Ford Foundation Project of Social Welfare and the American Future. New York: Ford Foundation.

NAEYC POSITION STATEMENT ON THE PREVENTION OF CHILD ABUSE IN EARLY CHILDHOOD PROGRAMS AND THE RESPONSIBILITIES OF EARLY CHILDHOOD PROFESSIONALS TO PREVENT CHILD ABUSE

Adopted September 1996

Child abuse is any nonaccidental injury or pattern of injuries to a child for which there is no "reasonable" explanation (National Committee to Prevent Child Abuse 1995). It includes physical, emotional, and sexual abuse. As the nation's largest organization of early childhood professionals and others dedicated to improving the quality of early childhood programs in centers, schools, and homes, the National Association for the Education of Young children (NAEYC) is committed to safeguarding the well-being of children. Child abuse violates children's health and safety and betrays their trust.

Most child abuse is perpetrated by family members; 1994 figures indicate that in 90% of reported cases of abuse, perpetrators were parents or other relatives (U.S. Department of Health and Human Services, 1996). Early childhood programs in centers, homes, and schools can help minimize the potential for this type of abuse by working to support families and providing referrals to appropriate helping services as needed. Although much less frequent than abuse by family members, child abuse also occurs in out-of-home settings such as schools, child care, foster care, and organized youth activities. Child abuse by those working with children violates the fundamental principle in NAEYC's *Code of Ethical Conduct* for working with young children: "Above all, we shall not harm children" (Feeney & Kipnis 1992).

Estimates of the proportion of child abuse in out-of-home settings vary, ranging from 1% to 7% of reported rates of abuse (Wells et al. 1995). Fortunately, the majority of employees and volunteers working with young children are caring individuals committed to promoting children's safety, healthy development, and learning. However, because previous and potential abusers may seek opportunities with access to children, those organizing and operating any type of out-of-home setting for children and youth must take proper precautions to minimize the potential for harm to children.

NAEYC deplores child abuse in any form in any setting and believes that all early childhood professionals, families, and communities must be vigilant in protecting children from all forms of abuse. NAEYC offers the following recommendations as strategies to prevent child abuse, including physical, emotional, and sexual abuse, in early childhood programs to the greatest extent possible. These recommendations outline specific roles for early childhood professionals, early childhood programs, family members, and public regulation. Particular attention is given to the role of early childhood programs, focusing on the importance of carefully planned and implemented policies with regard to practices with children, staff screening and recruitment, and partnerships with families. In addition, this statement outlines responsibilities of early childhood professionals to prevent child abuse in other settings. These recommendations focus on children from birth through age eight attending any type of group program, including child care centers and preschools, kindergarten and the primary grades, and family child care homes.

Role of Early Childhood Programs

NAEYC recommends that early childhood programs in centers, homes, and schools adopt policies consistent with the guidelines that follow. In some cases these policies will be set by a larger organizational structure, such as a school district, religious group, corporation, or community agency.

Program policies

1. Early childhood programs should employ an adequate number of qualified staff to work with children and to provide adequate supervision of program staff and volunteers.

Limiting the number of children for which each adult is responsible and the overall group size helps staff to better meet the individual needs of each child. Teachers are better able to provide supervision of all children and to recognize signs or changes in behavior that may indicate the possibility of abuse. NAEYC's accreditation criteria for centers (NAEYC 1991) recommend group sizes of no more than 6 to 8 infants, 8 to 12 toddlers, 14 to 20 preschoolers, 16 to 20 kindergartners, and 20 to 24 primary grade children, always with at least 2 adults per group. Smaller numbers may be necessary for children with certain emotional or behavioral problems who require more intensive and direct supervision.

2. The program environment (including both indoor and outdoor areas) should be designed to reduce the possibility of private, hidden locations in which abuse may occur.

Young children need opportunities for solitude and quiet play in small groups throughout the day, but all early childhood program spaces should be regarded as public. Both indoor and outdoor areas can be designed and set up in ways that provide opportunities for solitude while also allowing for unobtrusive adult supervision. Likewise, the program environment should be designed to reduce the likelihood that staff members, volunteers, or others have opportunities for hidden interactions with children.

3. All program staff, substitutes, and volunteers should receive preservice orientation and refresher training at regular intervals that include but are not limited to (a) an understanding of what constitutes child abuse, (b) the program's discipline policy and appropriate guidance of children, (c) means of preventing potential abuse situations in group settings, (d) identification of signs of potential abuse, and (e) indi-vidual obligations and procedures for reporting suspected cases of abuse.**

Individuals who work with young children and their families are obligated to report any suspicions of child abuse to the appropriate authorities. Ensuring that staff members and program volunteers understand and keep abreast of (a) strategies to reduce abuse, (b) ways to recognize potential signs of abuse, and (c) appropriate actions for reporting abuse helps reduce risks and meets legal obligations while minimizing the potential for false reports.

4. Centers, schools, and homes should have clear policies and procedures for maintaining a safe, secure environment.

Access to the facility should be controlled, for example, by requiring all visitors to sign in and sign out of the program area or to check in and check out with the administrative office. In the case of family child care homes, parents should be informed prior to the use of a substitute, and children should never be left in the care of an individual without their parents' knowledge.

5. Teachers and caregivers should be supervised by qualified personnel on an ongoing basis, and parents should be encouraged to spend time in the program.

In instances when a teacher or caregiver works primarily alone, periodic, drop-in visits by supervising personnel, parents, or others should be encouraged; such visits can reduce the isolation sometimes experienced by individual providers, thus minimizing the potential for abuse.

6. Programs should not institute "no-touch" policies to reduce the risk of abuse.

In the wake of well-publicized allegations of child abuse in out-of-home settings and increased concerns regarding liability, some programs have instituted such policies, either explicitly or implicitly. No-touch policies are misguided efforts that fail to recognize the importance of touch to children's healthy development. Touch is especially important for infants and toddlers. Warm, responsive touches convey regard and concern for children of any age. Adults should be sensitive to ensuring that their touches (such as pats on the back, hugs, or ruffling a child's hair) are welcomed by the children and appropriate to their individual characteristics and cultural experience. Careful, open communication between the program and families about the value of touch in children's development can help achieve consensus on acceptable ways for adults to show their respect and support for children in the program.

Staff Screening, Recruitment, and Retention Policies

Programs should employ careful screening and recruitment practices to increase the likelihood of selecting appropriate candidates as staff, substitutes, or volunteers to work with children. NAEYC's recommendations reflect the screening decisionmaking model developed by the American Bar Association's Center for Children and the Law (Wells et al. 1995) that identifies a variety of potential screening mechanisms, including personal interviews, verification of personal and professional references and education qualifications, criminal record checks, and affidavits attesting to history of conviction for abuse or other violent crimes. NAEYC recommends that all early childhood programs in centers, homes, and schools have a comprehensive screening policy in place and that this policy be publicized to existing and potential staff and volunteers, families and other interested policies.

NAEYC recommends the following guidelines be used in developing a screening policy.

1. At a minimum, basic screening should be conducted on all staff members, substitutes, volunteers, and other individuals who may have access to young children but do not have direct responsibility for their care and education.

For example, bus drivers, janitors, cooks, and administrative assistants should be screened in the cases of centers and schools, and all older children and adults present in a family child care provider's home (family members, friends, or employees) should be screened. The basic screening should include a signed, written application, careful review of employment record, checks of personal and professional references, and a personal interview. Additional screening, such as verification of educational status and checks of motor vehicle record, criminal record, and other registries may be appropriate depending upon the duration, frequency, and type of contact between the adult and children and the degree of supervision. In the case of self-employed family child care providers, public agencies should provide for screening and make the results of the screening available to parents on request.

2. All potential employees, substitutes, and volunteers should be required to attest to any previous convictions, in particular, whether they have ever been convicted of any crime against children or other violent crime.

Factors such as the relevance and recency of any conviction and demonstration of rehabilitation should be weighed in making hiring and placement decisions for individuals who admit to previous convictions. A volunteer's or employee's failure to fully disclose previous convictions should be viewed as automatic grounds for dismissal.

3. All potential employees and volunteers should be required to provide at least three personal references from previous employers, parents of children served, or educators.

Programs should check these references carefully.

4. All new employees and volunteers should be required to complete a mandatory probationary period.

Although new staff members or volunteers should have no unsupervised access to children during the probationary period, they should have supervised interactions with children so that their competencies in working with young children can be assessed.

5. In addition to screening policies designed to ensure that appropriate individuals are engaged in work in the program, early childhood programs should have policies designed to retain competent staff and remove others if necessary.

Programs that provide competitive salaries, good benefits and working conditions, and regular opportunities for advancement are more likely to recruit and retain competent staff who provide better quality care to children. In addition, the provision of employee assistance programs can provide support to staff facing stressful circumstances, thus minimizing the potential for abuse.

Policies also should provide for the removal of individuals whose performance on the job is deemed unacceptable or whose behavior outside the job could affect their performance (such as a bus driver being convicted for driving under the influence).

6. Clear procedures should be in place for responding to an accusation of abuse in the program.

These procedures should address steps to protect children and provide due process for the accused, and they should be publicized in advance to staff as well as parents.

Policies to Promote Close Partnerships with Families

Ongoing program policies that strengthen partnerships with families also can help minimize the likelihood of abuse in the program. Examples of such policies follow.

1. Programs should strongly encourage and provide ample opportunity for family participation.

2. Family members should have access to any part of the center, school, or family child care home to which children have access while their children are in care.

3. Field trips should include parents when possible, be approved by the program administrator, be supervised by regular program personnel, and be conducted with written parental permission.

4. Programs should require that children be released only to parents or legal guardians or to those persons authorized in writing by their parents or guardians. Staff should check identification of authorized individuals who are unfamiliar to them.

5. Programs should inform parents about the characteristics of good quality programs and the signs of potential abuse. Parents should be informed also about the child protection practices implemented by the program through (a) written policies shared with parents and family members, (b) access to public records documenting regulatory compliance (when applicable), and (c) publicized mechanisms for registering complaints and the procedures to be followed in response to a complaint.

Close partnerships with families also can help reduce the potential for child abuse by family members. Early childhood programs can provide information to parents and families regarding child development and effective strategies for responding to children's behavior. Teachers and caregivers should be knowledgeable about and alert to signs of family stress and provide support to families. Early childhood professionals can collaborate with state agencies, such as protective services, to promote understanding of child development, support and empower families, and advocate for children. Working with families in this way may help break cycles of family violence and prevent children from becoming abusers themselves.

Role of Family Members

Parents and other family members can assist in the prevention of child abuse in early childhood programs by

- increasing their sensitivity to children's communications,
- participating in and observing their children's programs,
- talking regularly with other families who use the program, and
- understanding and using child abuse reporting procedures when appropriate.

Children have minimal responsibility in the prevention of child abuse. Indeed, many of the child-oriented abuse prevention materials and techniques that have been developed in the wake of highly publicized allegations of abuse do not reflect an understanding of children's development and learning. They can be confusing to children and promote anxiety and fear. Rather than placing the responsibility on children to prevent abuse, NAEYC believes it is the responsibility of parents, early childhood professionals, and other adults to ensure to the greatest degree possible that abuse does not occur by providing safe, well-planned, and well-supervised environments.

Role of Public Regulation

An effective regulation system is an essential component in public efforts to reduce the potential for abuse in early childhood programs. The nature of public regulatory systems governing early childhood programs varies by program auspice. States license or employ other means of regulation for the majority of programs in centers and schools. Nearly all states also have regulatory processes in place for family child care homes, although it is estimated that only a small fraction of family child care providers in the nation is indeed regulated (Willer et al. 1991).

Public regulatory processes help reduce the potential for abuse when

- all settings providing education and care to children of two or more families are subject to regulation;
- waivers that erode the intent of the regulatory standards are not allowed;
- funding is sufficient to provide adequate regulatory staff for inspection on at least an annual basis;
- regulatory personnel are knowledgeable about complaint and law enforcement procedures so that implementation of all regulatory requirements is ensured;
- regulatory standards require policies regarding parental access to programs, authorization of children's release, and parental notification and approval of children's participation on field trips; and
- parents and the public are provided information about what defines good quality care, regulatory standards and monitoring procedures, and complaint procedures.

Some child care settings, such as in-home care in which families employ someone to care for the child in their home or other private arrangements in which an individual provides care for only one family, are not subject to public regulation. Therefore, public mechanisms to prevent child abuse in out-of-home settings must extend beyond traditional licensing and regulatory processes.

Most states require individuals working in schools, centers, and family child care homes to successfully complete a criminal background check prior to full employment. NAEYC supports the use of such background checks but warns that they are only one of many necessary strategies to reduce risk. Even the most sophisticated system of criminal background checks is limited by the fact that many instances of abuse go unreported and therefore never result in a conviction. Also, no system for such checks can detect first-time or potential abusers. Because many problems exist with the current system of background checks, parents and the community should not be lulled into a false sense of complacency regarding children's safety when such a system is in place. Given this caveat, NAEYC offers these recommendations for the effective use of criminal record checks.

1. The costs of completing a criminal record background check should be kept as low as possible, and the check should be completed in a timely manner.

2. The scope of the check should be clear. State regulations vary as to which records are searched: local, state, and/or federal criminal convictions; child abuse registries; or sex offender registries. With regard to child abuse registries, states employ different standards as to the type of information recorded, resulting in serious shortcomings of these data. For example, some registries include unsubstantiated allegations, and some registries record instances of abuse by the name of the victim rather than the perpetrator, making it difficult to track abusers (Cohen 1985).

3. If convictions are uncovered, clear procedures for action should be in place. Some states require individuals to undergo a background check before they can be hired to work with children but have no clear procedures for action when substantiated convictions are found.

4. Results of background checks should be readily available to families, especially those families using in-home child care, family child care, or other settings exempt from public regulation. Some states have used technology to make information on background checks readily available to families and providers. Colorado has instituted a system that allows access to information at public libraries and child care resource-and-referral programs. California was the first state to institute a Child Care Trustline. This database includes current and potential child care providers who have successfully undergone a criminal record background check. Parents and programs can check potential employees against the database to ensure that their names appear (as opposed to a criminal background check in which being listed is a negative).

Role of Early Childhood Professionals

Monitoring by public agencies helps to ensure basic acceptable levels of quality in early childhood programs. However, it is the responsibility of early childhood professionals to

1. Promote standards of excellence toward which programs may strive. NAEYC encourages centers and eligible schools to pursue NAEYC accreditation. This process requires programs to undertake a rigorous self-study process and provides for an independent external assessment to determine whether high standards are met. Other accreditation systems are available for family child care homes and schools not eligible for NAEYC accreditation.

2. Assist in informing the public about the need for and the ingredients of high-quality early childhood programs.

3. Encourage the continued professional development of all early childhood professionals.

4. Advocate for well-designed, sufficiently funded, and effectively implemented public regulations and programs that reduce the incidence of abuse against children.

5. Understand their ethical obligations to recognize and report suspicions of abuse (see Feeney & Kipnis 1992).

Early childhood professionals can also play an important role in helping to prevent the incidence of child abuse in other settings beyond early childhood programs. The vast majority of child abuse is committed by family members or others who are close to the family. By establishing supporting relationships with families, early childhood professionals may help reduce the likelihood of child abuse by family members. Programs should make readily available to families under stress appropriate information and referrals to community services and provide information and support for families regarding appropriate discipline and guidance of young children. In addition, early childhood professionals should advocate for effective community support services, including child protective services, social services, and mental health services that include sufficient numbers of qualified staff sensitive to meeting the individual needs of children and families.

Conclusion

The National Association for the Education of Young Children is strongly committed to promoting high quality in early childhood programs. Practices that lead to high-quality programs help reduce the likelihood of abuse of children in out-of-home settings, and high-quality programs can provide support to families to reduce instances of abuse in the home. Thus, the members of NAEYC pledge their commitment and expertise to work with other concerned individuals and groups to provide a safe and wholesome environment for all of America's children.

References

Cohen, A. 1985. Use of statewide central child abuse registries for purposes of screening child care workers: *False promises and troubling concerns.* San Francisco: Child Care Law Center.

Feeney, S., & Kipnis, K. 1992. *Code of ethical conduct & statement of professional commitment.* Washington, DC: NAEYC.

NAEYC. 1991. *Accreditation criteria and procedures of the National Academy of Early Childhood Programs* (rev. ed.). Washington, DC: Author.

National Committee to Prevent Child Abuse. 1995. *Annual survey of incidence of child abuse.* Chicago: Author.

U.S. Department of Health and Human Services. National Center on Child Abuse and Neglect. 1996. *Child maltreatment 1994: Reports from the states to the National Center on Child Abuse and Neglect.* Washington, DC: GPO.

Wells, S., Davis, N., Dennis, K., Chipman, R., Sandt, C., & Liss, M. 1995. *Effective screening of child care and youth service workers.* Washington, DC: American Bar Association Center on Children and the Law.

Willer, B., Hofferth, S. L., Ksiker, E. E., Divine-Hawkins, P.,Farquhar, E., & Glantz, F. B.. 1991. *The demand and supply of child care in 1990.* Washington, DC: NAEYC.

Additional Resources

Code of Ethical Conduct and Statement of Commitment. 1992. S. Feeney & K. Kipnis. [Brochure available in English and Spanish editions.] NAEYC.

Healthy Young Children: A Manual for Programs. 1995 ed. A. S. Kendrick, R. Kaufmann, & K. P. Messenger, eds. Washington, DC: NAEYC.

NAEYC Position Statement on Violence in the Lives of Children. 1993. [Brochure.] Washington, DC: NAEYC.

National Committee to Prevent Child Abuse. 332 S. Michigan Ave., Chicago, IL 60604.

The Role of Educators in the Prevention and Treatment of Child Abuse and Neglect: The User Manual Series. 1992. C. C. Tower. U.S. Department of Health and Human Services, National Center on Child Abuse, and Neglect. DHHS publication No. (ACF) 92-30172.

GLOSSARY

accreditation: A voluntary process with a goal of increasing and maintaining high quality in early childhood programs

active listening: An interpersonal communication strategy that promotes clear and honest exchanges of information

adoption: A legal process of taking a child into one's family and raising that child as one's own

advocacy: activities that support and call for support for children and families

artificial insemination: The introduction of semen into the female reproductive organs without sexual contact

at-risk children: Children at risk for developmental delays or disabilities due to family situations including poverty, psychopathology, loss of members, or inability to nurture

authoritarian parenting: An approach to child-rearing that emphasizes adult control of children's behavior

authoritative parenting: An approach to child-rearing that includes stating expectations for children and communicating with them in respectful ways

balanced families: According to the circumplex model, families that demonstrate a balance in both cohesion and flexibility

bioecological theory: Theory proposed by Urie Bronfenbrenner that relates ecological systems to human development

birth order: The sequence in which children are born or adopted into families

blended families: Families in which one or both partners bring children from another relationship

child abuse and neglect: Maltreatment of a child and the failure of parents or other responsible adults to provide necessary care and supervision

child care trilemma: The concern for quality, affordability, and accessibility of child care

chronosystem: According to bioecological theory, the sociohistorical context of an individual

circumplex model: A family systems model intended to demonstrate how all family members are interconnected

codependency: When a person sacrifices his or her own needs to serve another person to an unhealthy extreme

cohesion: According to the circumplex model, family togetherness

community resources: Support available to children and families in a particular community

conflict resolution: Strategies for constructively processing differences between individuals or groups

congruence: The degree of similarity between home and school

contextualist theories: Approaches that demonstrate the importance of relationships among children, families, and communities that are crucial to effective family involvement in early childhood education

continuity: Efforts made to support children as they move from home to school or from one school setting to another

culture: Socially transmitted behavior patterns typical of a population or of a community at a given time

developmental assets: Critical factors necessary for children's healthy development

developmental contextualism: A theoretical approach to understanding human development that considers both a strong biological foundation and family as the central social institution

developmentally appropriate practices (DAP): Those practices in early childhood education that are derived from deep knowledge of individual children and the context in which they develop and learn

dialectical theory: A theory of human development with the premise that for each action (thesis), there is an opposite reaction (antithesis), and that together these cause a new action (synthesis)

disabilities: Physical, learning, or emotional factors that call for adaptations

diversity: The understanding that family structures, functions, characteristics, and interests are varied

downsizing: A phenomenon of corporations reducing number of employees

early childhood education: Any program of care and education for children from birth through eight years of age

early intervention: Comprehensive educational programs for young children who are at risk or who have been identified as having a disability

empathy: Understanding another's feelings, situation, values, and goals

empowering: The establishment of a model whereby all families can assert an active role in the education of their children

ethnicity: Identification with or belonging to a religious, racial, national, or cultural group

exosystem: According to bioecological theory, a system that has indirect effects on an individual

expressive role: Traditionally, the role that mothers have in providing the primary care and love for their children

extended family: Family members beyond parents and children, especially grandparents, aunts, uncles, and cousins

extended family relationships: The nature of the connection between an individual and extended family members

extreme families: According to the circumplex model, classification of families that are extreme in both cohesion and flexibility

family accord: Relates to a family's impression of competency in dealing with conflict

family coping: Strategies of families for dealing with stress

family-friendly work policies: Employer policies that consider the primacy of the family

family functions: Primary reasons for existence of the family unit

family life cycle: An approach to understanding families that considers how families typically change over time

family life education: A broad understanding of the influences in a child's life including quality of relationships with family members

family of origin: The family into which one is born

family of procreation: The family that one creates by having children

family pride: Characteristics such as mutual respect, trust, loyalty, optimism, and shared values in a family

family size: The number of family members residing together

family strengths: An approach to understanding families that emphasizes characteristics of healthy family relationships

family structure: The unique ways that families organize

family support movement: A perspective that recognizes that families are responsible for their children's development and that no family can function alone

family systems theory: A framework that emphasizes the notion that everything that happens to any family member affects all other family members

family violence: Abuse or injury within families

FERPA: Family Education Rights and Privacy Act is a federal law designed to protect the privacy of students' academic records

flexibility: According to the circumplex model, a family's ability to deal with change

gender inequality: The phenomenon of males having greater power than females in society

gender role: Expected social behavior relating to being male or female

high-quality, affordable child care: Child care that local families can pay for and meets these criteria: child-centered curriculum, well-trained teachers, and planned family involvement

homeless: Having no home or refuge

horizontal stressors: According to family systems theory, stress-producing events that occur over time

immigrant families: Families that leave one country to settle in another

incarcerated: Jailed or imprisoned; denied freedom

inclusion: An educational practice whereby programs enroll both typically developing children and children with identified disabilities

inclusiveness: An educational approach that is welcoming to all children and families

instrumental role: Traditionally, the role of fathers with their children that has a minimal role in caring for children

interdisciplinary collaboration: A consensus-building model that uses a variety of perspectives to determine a plan for family involvement in a child's education

interpersonal communication: Effective strategies of human interaction between or among people

linkages: The level, type, and frequency of communication between families and schools

macrosystem: According to bioecological theory, the culture in which one lives

marital transition: Process involved in moving into or out of marriage

maternal employment: The number of hours mothers of young children are employed outside the home

mesosystem: According to bioecological theory, relationships between contexts in the microsystem

microsystem: According to bioecological theory, the setting in which one lives or the near environment

midrange families: According to the circumplex model, families that are extreme with either cohesion or flexibility and balanced with either cohesion or flexibility

migrant families: Families who travel from place to place in order to gain employment

nuclear unit: Self-contained family unit consisting of parents and children

nurturance: Caring for and providing for children

overlapping spheres of influence: The understanding that families, schools, and communities are intermingled and not discrete

parent education: Providing a variety of sources of support for the parents' role in caring for their children

parental attachment: The strong emotional bond that exists between parents and their children

parental rights: An educational philosophy based on the understanding that parents have the primary role in their children's lives

parenting: Care, love, and guidance provided by parents to their children

permissive parenting: An approach to child-rearing that exercises little control over children and exerts few demands on children's behavior

permissive-indifferent parenting: A permissive approach to parenting that is disconnected in nature

permissive-indulgent parenting: A permissive approach to parenting that allows children to control their own behavior without much limit-setting

primacy of parental rights: A view that upholds the strict limits of the U.S. Constitution to interfere with family life

professional standards and ethics: Guidelines used by early childhood educators for appropriate professional behavior and best educational practices

public policy: Federal, state, and local laws

quality indicators: Standards used by the National Parent Teacher Association to assess family involvement in schools

race: A group of people distinguished by more or less distinct genetically transmitted physical characteristics

religiosity: The degree to which a family values or practices religious beliefs

resilient children: Children who exhibit good developmental outcomes despite high-risk family situations

right of family integrity: The legal basis for parents to bear and rear children according to their own beliefs

self-disclosure: Sharing information from one's own life situation

serious illness: Health conditions that are chronic or life-threatening

sibling relationships: Connections and interactions between or among children in the same family (sisters and brothers)

socialization: A parental responsibility to teach and support children in how to get along with others

spirituality: The quality of being concerned with the soul, God, and/or a religious institution

substance abuse: Illegal or overuse of drugs or alcohol

Temporary Assistance for Needy Families (TANF): Federal legislation that provides support to families in poverty

transition to parenthood: Adjustment of an individual to new roles as a parent

vertical stressors: According to family systems theory, stress-producing events that are embedded in particular families' patterns of relating

zone of proximal development (ZPD): According to Vygotsky, the mechanism by which human development occurs

INDEX

Page numbers followed by f indicate figures